The Levinas Dictionary

BLOOMSBURY PHILOSOPHY DICTIONARIES

The Bloomsbury Philosophy Dictionaries offer clear and accessible guides to the work of some of the more challenging thinkers in the history of philosophy. A-Z entries provide clear definitions of key terminology, synopses of key works, and details of each thinker's major themes, ideas, and philosophical influences. The Dictionaries are the ideal resource for anyone reading or studying these key philosophers.

The Derrida Dictionary, Simon Morgan Wortham
The Gadamer Dictionary, Chris Lawn and Niall Keane
The Hegel Dictionary, Glenn Alexander Magee
The Husserl Dictionary, Dermot Moran and Joseph Cohen
The Marx Dictionary, Ian Fraser and Lawrence Wilde
The Merleau-Ponty Dictionary, Donald A. Landes
The Sartre Dictionary, Gary Cox
The Deleuze and Guattari Dictionary, Eugene B. Young
The Heidegger Dictionary, Daniel O. Dahlstrom

The Levinas Dictionary

JOSEPH COHEN AND DONNA ORANGE

BLOOMSBURY ACADEMIC
LONDON • NEW YORK • OXFORD • NEW DELHI • SYDNEY

BLOOMSBURY ACADEMIC
Bloomsbury Publishing Plc, 50 Bedford Square, London, WC1B 3DP, UK
Bloomsbury Publishing Inc, 1359 Broadway, New York, NY 10018, USA
Bloomsbury Publishing Ireland, 29 Earlsfort Terrace, Dublin 2, D02 AY28, Ireland

First published in Great Britain 2026

A catalogue record for this book is available from the British Library.

A catalog record for this book is available from the Library of Congress.

ISBN: HB: 978-1-3502-7501-0
PB: 978-1-3502-7502-7
ePDF: 978-1-3502-7503-4
eBook: 978-1-3502-7504-1

Series: Bloomsbury Philosophy Dictionaries

Typeset by Deanta Global Publishing Services, Chennai, India
Printed and bound in Great Britain

For product safety related questions contact productsafety@bloomsbury.com.

To find out more about our authors and books visit www.bloomsbury.com and sign up for our newsletters.

For Donna . . . in memoriam

No words can capture the encounter of the Other. And yet, it was always through the extraordinary generosity of words that Donna Orange sought to give, and give others, the responsibility of engaging with the Other and all Others...

The idea of *The Levinas Dictionary* was hers and, as she countlessly told me, she dreamed of seeing it published for all those desiring to approach, as she said, the "extraordinary ethics of Emmanuel Levinas." We can only imagine the joy she would have had in its realization and now publication. Notwithstanding the critiques she would have certainly leveled on our own work, I believe she would feel we had engaged without reserve in presenting Levinas' words with as much accuracy, fidelity, and commitment as compassion. Yes, compassion—for Donna believed above all that philosophy spoke primordially of compassion. That is, Donna believed in a philosophy speaking beyond comprehension, and understanding, beyond its traditional and classical intention—a philosophy reaching the exceptional and each time singular possibility of responding in compassion to the Other.

Brutally taken in the winter of 2024, Donna believed wholeheartedly in *The Levinas Dictionary*. And while I painfully inherited the nearly impossible task of bringing it to its completion alone, she accompanies it throughout and speaks through its every word. Which is why, and although the *Levinas Dictionary* for me is marked by mourning, and the mourning of Donna, I know and trust she would have commanded it, above all, to be a book of life.

Contents

Acknowledgments

We wish to thank wholeheartedly for their support and patience in the writing and composition of *The Levinas Dictionary*, Liza Thompson and Miraya McCoy from Bloomsbury.

For their invaluable comments, suggestions, the rich discussions over so many years, and thus for their friendship and generosity in thinking *with* Levinas, we express our utmost gratitude to Nicolas de Warren, Orietta Ombrosi, Robert Bernasconi, Gérard Bensussan, Jeffrey Bloechl, Dermot Moran, Dragos Calma, Carla Canullo, Giuseppe Pintus, Carmelo Meazza, Ethan Kleinberg, Andrea Bellantone, Claire Katz, and Joseph Eidelheit.

And finally, as no philosophical gesture ever occurs without the undenying support and love of those most close, we also thank, from the bottom of our hearts, Reverend Donald A. Braue who shared Donna's life, Lorraine and Marc Cohen who accompany me always, Gabriela Zapponi whose life I am blessed to share . . . and, of course, *Milky* . . .

Chronology

30 December 1905 Born in Kovno (Lithuania, Russian Empire) to a traditional Jewish family. Levinas was the eldest of three brothers. Both his younger siblings, Boris (born in 1909) and Aminidab (born in 1913), were murdered by the Nazis in the Second World War.

1915–16 The Levinas family is forced to flee Kovno and emigrate to Kharkov (Ukraine) due to the approaching German army during the First World War. In Kharkov, as one of five Jews under the *numerus clausus,* Levinas was admitted to a Russian *Gymnasium.*

1920 The Levinas family returns to Kovno. Levinas is then enrolled in a Jewish *Gymnasium* where, under the directorship of a German Jewish Professor, he receives a full secondary school education in German language.

1923 Levinas begins studies in philosophy at the University of Strasbourg (France) where his professors include Henri Carteron, Maurice Pradines, Maurice Halbwachs, and Charles Blondel.

He also meets, at the University of Strasbourg, Maurice Blanchot, who will remain a lifelong close friend.

1928–9 Attends Husserl's last seminar and Heidegger's first lectures at the University of Freiburg (Germany). Levinas will later claim: "I went to Freiburg because of Husserl, but I discovered Heidegger."

1929 From 17th March to 6th April, Levinas attends the second *Davos Hochschulkurs* (Switzerland), commonly known as the "Cassirer–Heidegger debate". Also in attendance were Rudolf Carnap and Joseph B. Soloveitchik.

The theme chosen for the encounter was the fourth Kantian question "What is Man?" and therefore was concentrated on the significance of the Kantian notions of freedom, reason, finitude, and humanity.

1930 Levinas publishes his doctoral dissertation, *La Théorie de l'intuition dans la phénoménologie de Husserl* (*The Theory of Intuition in Husserl's Phenomenology*). This publication introduced Jean-Paul Sartre to phenomenology[1] and is considered to be the first presentation of phenomenology in the French philosophical context.

1930 Levinas moves to Paris and marries Raïssa Levi, whom he had known since childhood. Begins teaching at the *École Normale Israélite Orientale* in Paris.

1931 Translates into French language, with the collaboration of Gabrielle Pfeiffer, and publishes Husserl's Paris Lectures (delivered at the University of Paris—Sorbonne on 23rd and 25th February 1929), the *Cartesian Meditations* (Paris, Vrin).

1931–2 Attends the philosophical meetings and readings coordinated by Gabriel Marcel in Paris. In these, Levinas also meets Jean-Paul Sartre, Simone de Beauvoir, Jeanne Hirsch, and Alphonse de Waelhens.

1932 Publication: "Martin Heidegger et l'ontologie," in *Revue Philosophique de la France et de l'étranger* (vol. CXIII, 5/6, pp. 395–431) and republished in *En découvrant l'existence avec Husserl et Heidegger*, Paris, Vrin, 1949. ("Martin Heidegger and Ontology," trsl. The Committee of Public Safety, in *Diacritics*, vol. 26, no. 1, Baltimore, John Hopkins University Press, Spring 1996, pp. 11–32).

1934 Publication: "Quelques réflexions sur la philosophie de l'hitlérisme," in *Esprit*, (Vol. 26, Nov. 1934, pp. 199–208). ("Reflections on the Philosophy of Hitlerism," trsl. S. Hand, in *Critical Inquiry*, Vol. 17, no. 1, Chicago, Chicago University Press, Autumn 1990, pp. 62–71.)

1935 Publication: *De l'évasion* in *Recherches Philosophiques* (vol V, pp. 373–92) and republished in 1982, Montpellier, Fata Morgana. (*On Escape*, trsl. B. Bergo, Stanford, Stanford University Press, 2003.)

1939 Levinas is naturalized French citizen and is enlisted in the French office corps as a French–German translator.

1940 Publication: "L'Oeuvre d'E. Husserl" in *Revue Philosophique de la France et de l'étranger* (vol. CXXIX, 1/2, pp. 38–85) and republished in *En découvrant l'existence avec Husserl et Heidegger*, Paris, Vrin, 1949.

Made prisoner and sent to the Prisoner of War Labor Camp in Fallingbostel (Germany). Levinas is spared from being sent to an extermination camp because of his status as military prisoner of war and thereby is protected by the 1929 Geneva Convention.

Raïssa, by that time Levinas' spouse, and Simone Levinas, their daughter, are hidden first by Maurice Blanchot in Paris and then, for the last two years of the Second World War, in a convent near Orléans (France). Levinas' entire Lithuanian family, evoked in the Hebrew epitaph of *Otherwise than Being or Beyond Essence*, are assassinated in Nazi extermination camps.

Levinas returns to Paris after the end of the war.

During his captivity, Levinas wrote numerous notes and short texts now published in the *Carnets de captivité, Oeuvres Complètes, Vol. I* (Paris, Grasset, 2009).

1946–7 Levinas is invited by Jean Wahl to deliver a series of four lectures, *Le temps et l'autre* at the newly founded *Collège Philosophique* in Paris.

These were published in 1948 in the first volume, entitled *Le Choix, le Monde, l'Existence*, of the philosophical journal published by the *Collège Philosophique*.

Le temps et l'autre lectures were then republished first in 1979 at Fata Morgana (Montpellier) and then in 1983 at the *Presses Universitaires de France*.

Levinas becomes director and school master of the *Ecole Normale Israélite Orientale* in Paris.

1947 Publication: *De l'existence à l'existant*, Paris, Editions de la Revue Fontaine; republished in 1993, Paris, Vrin (*Existence and Existents*, trsl. A. Lingis, Pittsburg, Duquesne University Press, 2001).

1947–50 Begins studying extensively with Chouchani, an unconventional and itinerant Talmudist who also taught and greatly influenced among others, Elie Wiesel.

1949 Publication: *En découvrant l'existence avec Husserl et Heidegger*, Paris, Vrin (translated as *Discovering Existence with Husserl*, trsl. R. Cohen and M. B Smith, Evanston, Northwestern University Press, 1998).

1957 Levinas is invited to deliver his first *Talmudic Reading* at the *Colloque des Intellectuel Juifs de Langue Française*. He will give these *Readings* at every edition of the *Colloque* until 1991.

1961 Receives the *Doctorat ès Lettres* from the University of Paris–Sorbonne for *Totalité et infini. Essai sur l'extéritorité* which is, in the same year, published by the prestigious phenomenology and philosophy press, Martinus Nijhoff (The Hague). (*Totality and Infinity. An Essay on Exteriority*, trsl. A. Lingis, Pittsburgh, Duquesne University Press, 1969.)

1963 Publication: *Difficile liberté*, Paris, Albin Michel (*Difficult Freedom*, trsl. S. Hand, Baltimore, Johns Hopkins University Press, 1997).

1964 Professorship at the University of Poitiers.

1964 Jacques Derrida's "Violence and Metaphysics. An Essay on the Thought of Emmanuel Levinas" is published in two parts in the *Revue de Métaphysique et de Morale* (Part 1, Year 69, vol. no. 3, July-September 1964, pp. 322–54; Part 2, Year 69, vol. no. 4, Octobre–décembre 1964, pp. 425–73, Paris, Presses Universitaires de France) and republished in *Ecriture et différence*, Paris, Seuil, 1967 (*Writing and Difference*, trsl. A. Bass, Chicago, Chicago University Press, 1978, pp. 79–153).

This article is the first philosophical and scholarly study of Levinas' thought and considered by numerous interpreters to have greatly influenced Levinas' own thinking, most noticeably in the passage from *Totality and Infinity* (1961) to *Otherwise than Being, or Beyond Essence* (1974).

1967 Professorship at the University of Paris–Nanterre.
Publication: Second edition of En découvrant l'existence avec Husserl et Heidegger, augmented by Essais nouveaux, Paris, Vrin.

1968 Publication: *Quatres lectures talmudiques*, Paris, Editions de Minuit (English translation of this volume is included in *Beyond the Verse. Talmudic Readings and Lectures*, trsl. G. Mole, Bloomington, Indiana University Press, 1994).

1970 First honorary doctorate from Loyola University of Chicago (USA).
Others subsequently followed: University of Leiden (Netherlands) in 1975; Catholic University Leuven (Belgium) in 1976; University of Fribourg (Switzerland) in 1980; University of Bar-Ilan (Israel) in 1981.

1971 Levinas receives the *Albert Schweitzer Prize* for philosophy.

1972 Publication: *Humanisme de l'autre homme*, Montpellier, Fata Morgana (*Humanism of the Other*, trsl. N. Poller, Urbana-Champaign, University of Illinois Press, 2003).

1973 Professorship at the University of Paris–Sorbonne.

1974 Publication: *Autrement qu'être, ou au-delà de l'essence*, The Hague, Martinus Nijhoff (*Otherwise than Being, or Beyond Essence*, trsl. A. Lingis, Pittsburg, Duquesne University Press, 1998).

1975 Publication: *Sur Maurice Blanchot*, Montpellier, Fata Morgana.

1976 Levinas retires from the University of Paris–Sorbonne.
Last seminars, entitled *La mort et le temps* and *Dieu et la philosophie*, delivered in 1975–6 are published under the title *Dieu, la mort et le temps* (Paris, Grasset, 1993); this publication is composed and edited by J. Rolland and was entirely reviewed by Levinas (*God, Death, and Time*, trsl. B. Bergo, Stanford, Stanford University Press, 2000).
Despite retirement, Levinas continues to lecture and give specialized postgraduate seminars at the University of Fribourg (Switzerland), at the *Institut Catholique de Paris* (France), and at the Hebrew University of Jerusalem (Israel).

	Publication: *Noms propres*, Montpellier, Fata Morgana (Proper Names, trsl. M. B. Smith, Stanford, Stanford University Press, 1997).
1977	Publication: *Du sacré au saint*, Paris, Editions de Minuit.
1980	Participates in the *Castel Gandolfo Conferences* led by Pope John-Paul II.
1982	Publication: *De Dieu qui vient à l'idée*, Paris, Vrin (*Of God Who Comes to Mind*, trsl. B. Bergo, Stanford, Stanford University Press, 1988) and *L'au-delà du verset*, Paris, Editions de Minuit (*Beyond the Verse. Talmudic Readings and Lectures*, trsl. G. Mole, Bloomington, Indiana University Press, 1994). Also published are the 1981 *France Culture* radio dialogues with Philippe Nemo entitled *Ethique et infini*, Paris, Fayard (*Ethics and Infinity. Conversations with P. Nemo*, trsl. R. A. Cohen, Pittsburg, Duquesne University Press, 1985).
1984	Publication: *Ethique comme Philosophie première*, Paris, Rivages; and *Transcendance et intelligibilité*, Montpellier, Fata Morgana.
1987	Publication: *Hors sujet*, Montpellier, Fata Morgana (*Outside the Subject*, trsl. M. B. Smith, Stanford, Stanford University Press, 1993).
1988	Publication: *A l'heure des nations*, Paris, Editions de Minuit (*In the Time of Nations*, trsl. M. B. Smith, London, Athlone Press, 2000).
1989	Levinas receives the Swiss *Prix Balzan*.
1991	Publication: *Entre Nous. Essais sur le penser-à-l'autre*, Paris, Grasset (*Entre Nous: On Thinking-of-the-Other*, trsl. M. B. Smith and B. Harshav, New York, Columbia University Press, 2000).
1994	Death of Raïssa Levinas on 11th September. Publication: *Les imprévus de l'histoire*, Montpellier, Fata Morgana (Unforeseen History, trsl. N. Poller, Urbana-Champaign, University of Illinois Press, 2004).
25 December 1995	Death of Emmanuel Levinas. His lifelong friend, philosopher Jacques Derrida, gives the funeral oration, subsequently published in *Adieu—à Emmanuel Levinas* (*Adieu—To Emmanuel Levinas*, trsl. P.-A. Brault and M. Naas, Stanford, Stanford University Press, 1999).

Chronological Bibliography

Emmanuel Levinas' philosophical writings, all originally published in the French language, can be divided into the following chronological periods:

The Pre-Second World War Years (1929–39)

1930: *La théorie de l'intuition dans la phénoménologie de Husserl*, Paris, Alcan. Republished in 1963, Paris, Vrin.
1931: French translation of E. Husserl's *Cartesian Mediations* with G. Pfeiffer, Paris, Vrin.
1934: "Quelques réflexions sur la philosophie de l'hitlérisme," in *Esprit*, vol. 26, Nov. 1934, pp. 199–208. Republished in 1990, Paris, Payot.
1935: *De l'évasion*, Montpellier, Fata Morgana.

The Post-Second World War Years (1945–60)

1947: *De l'existence à l'existant*, Paris, La Fontaine. Republished in 1993, Paris, Vrin.
1948: *Le temps et l'autre*, in *Les Cahiers du Collège Philosophique*, Paris, Artaud. Republished in 1979, Montpellier, Fata Morgana. Republished in 1985, Paris, Presses Universitaires de France.
1949: *En découvrant l'existence avec Husserl et Heidegger*, Paris, Vrin. 2nd augmented edition in 1967, Paris, Vrin.

Doctorate and University Professorship Years: Poitiers, Nanterre, Sorbonne (1960–76)

1961: *Totalité et Infini. Essai sur l'extériorité*, La Haye, M. Nijhoff.
1963: *Difficile Liberté. Essais sur le judaïsme*, Paris, Albin Michel.
1972: *Humanisme de l'autre homme*, Montpellier, Fata Morgana.
1974: *Autrement qu'être ou au-delà de l'essence*, La Haye, M. Nijhoff.
1975: *Sur Maurice Blanchot*, Montpellier, Fata Morgana.

The Post-University Years (1976–95)

1976: *Noms propres*, Montpellier, Fata Morgana.
1982: *De Dieu qui vient à l'idée*, Paris, Vrin.
1984: *Ethique et infini*, Paris, Fayard.
1987: *Hors sujet*, Montpellier, Fata Morgana.
1991: *Entre nous. Ecrits sur le penser-à-l'autre*, Paris, Grasset.
1993: *Dieu, la mort et le temps*, Paris, Grasset. This publication is composed of the notes of two university seminars professed by Levinas in 1975 and 1976 at the University of Paris-Sorbonne, entitled respectively (1) *La mort et le temps* and (2) *Dieu et la philosophie*. Both seminars were compiled and edited by J. Rolland before being entirely reviewed by E. Levinas before publication.
1994: *Les Imprévus de l'histoire*, Montpellier, Fata Mogana. This publication is a collection of previously unpublished texts dating from 1929 to 1992.

1994: *Liberté et commandement*, Montpellier, Fata Morgana. This publication is composed of two texts: *Liberté et commandement* (1953) and *Transcendance et hauteur* (1962).
1995: *Altérité et transcendance*, Montpellier, Fata Mogana. This publication is a collection of previously unpublished texts dating from 1967 to 1989.
1998: *Ethique comme philosophie première*, Paris, Rivages. Publication of the 1984 lecture, and edited by J. Rolland.

Alongside his philosophical writings, Levinas also published Talmudic readings and lectures, interpretations, and commentaries which were presented at the *Colloque des Intellectuel Juifs de Langue Française*. Levinas was indeed one of the major actors and coordinators of this *Colloque*, founded in 1957. Levinas customely delivered the *Talmudic Lesson*, whereas V. Jankélévitch delivered the *Philosophical Lesson*. Naturally, we are to pose the question of the relation between Levinas' philosophical writings and his Talmudic readings. In which manner do these two orientations in Levinas' work interact? How are we to think their dialogue and in which way does each inspire the other? Considerable scholarship has been devoted to this question as well as to understanding and interpreting the reception of Levinas' Talmudic lectures in and for Jewish studies in particular and theology in general.

Levinas' Talmudic readings and lectures were all published at the Editions de Minuit, Paris.

The Talmudic Readings and Lectures

1968: *Quatre lectures talmudiques.*
1975: *Du sacré au saint. Cinq nouvelles lectures talmudiques.*
1982: *L'au-delà du verset. Lectures et discours talmudiques.*
1988: *A l'heure des nations.*
1996: *Nouvelles lectures talmudiques.*

Choices

Throughout *The Levinas Dictionary*, we have had to make two kinds of choices: first, of audience or audiences, and second, of terms and concepts to present, explicate, and interpret. Along side these choices, we wished our work to address all, in whichever discipline, who want to read and think *with* Levinas but who find that, in order to do so, they are in need of a certain support in understanding and comprehending the *revolution* this thinker has inscribed in our Western tradition of philosophical questioning. This is why *The Levinas Dictionary* seeks to define and propose a reading both of the major terms employed by Levinas and of those concepts more discrete which also inhabit his thinking and writing.

Why?

For what occurs in Levinas' thinking and writing is both a radical break and rupture of our philosophical tradition, its foundational and essential concepts and notions, while, *and at the same time*, an oblique intrusion in this very history where our very philosophical *logos* is oriented *otherwise* and elected to express itself differently and toward a wholly other source of significance: the significance of the Other. Indeed, as in any philosophical gesture and creative endeavor, Levinas experiments with conceptuality, confronts traditional concepts with novel redefinitions of these same inherited conceptual frameworks, and introduces unheard and unthought significations in our tradition which incessantly awaken it toward other headings than its own: the transcendence of the Other as heterogeneous ethical commandment; the election of the Self in and as *infinitization* of responsibility to the point of substitution and expiation for the Other; the immemoriality of the ethical *before* and *beyond* the truth and the totality of Being and the gathered meaning of essence; the Infinite otherness of the Other as overwhelming and interrupting, exceeding, and suspending the order of manifestation and phenomenality; the Other's commandment as face-to-face relation awakening and electing the Self in responsibility *before* its autonomy and sovereignty and *beyond* all judgment or fulfillment of its response; the absolute transcendence of the Other as separation and as that which arrives *before* and *beyond* presence and absence, *before* and *beyond* the binarism of identity and difference, and thus commands, demands, pleads, and addresses *before* and *beyond* intersubjectivity, community, recognition, relation, or relatedness.

Levinas insistently deploys, throughout his writing, an overwhelming re-orientation of philosophical thinking as well as a discrete displacement, dislocation, and disruption of the very intent of the Western philosophical tradition. Indeed, the Levinasian philosophical gesture calls onto wholly other signifiers which also find their expression, their translation and transliteration through Western philosophy by re-orienting it otherwise and elsewhere: toward the Other. Levinas' *revolution* in philosophy purports nothing less than a call to other signifiers at once *beyond* and yet inspiring *otherwise* the order of our philosophical *logos*. As if the *other* of philosophy, the other heterogeneous to the Greek event of philosophy, always also animated, awakened, spurred on this event to rethink itself *otherwise* and thereby *exceed* itself *beyond* itself and toward a wholly other source of meaning than its own: a justice anterior to truth, a responsibility anterior to the question and thus preempting the ontological economy of *givenness* and *donation*. Levinas formulates this alteration and displacement in the philosophical and yet *beyond* and *before* the philosophical in *Totality and Infinity* where the philosopher marks how and why, and marking thereby a singular exception in our philosophical tradition: "truth presupposes justice."[1]

What could this *presupposition* entail or mean? In which sense can the universality of truth presuppose an irreducible and unique justice toward singularity? How are we to think the precedence of justice *before* truth and thus the irreducibility, heterogeneity, and inspiration of a justice commanding and awakening truth to incessantly exceed itself *beyond* itself?

And Levinas pursues the *ambiguity* of this "logic" of alteration throughout *Otherwise than Being, or Beyond Essence*. Indeed, throughout this text, Levinas radicalizes this exigency of the Good *before* and *beyond* Being, truth, meaning, reconciliation, identity, and community. When marking the Self's election as responsibility for the responsibility of the Other, when insisting on how and where the Self, as creature, responds always *before* and *beyond* autonomy and morality, freedom and universality, Levinas inscribes in the ethical Self the demand of a *diachrony* without reserve, without beginning or end, without *logos* or *telos*: anarchy of the Good *before* and *beyond* Being. Indeed, the Other commands the Self to an infinite responsibility for the Other where this commandment also occurs *before* the autonomy, sovereignty, or self-consciousness of the subject and thus orients the Self to its election, its "being elected" *beyond* all the determinations of its reappropriable subjectivity. This *diachrony* at work in Levinas' philosophical exigency provokes an incessant and unending unquietness of the ethical and thereby an infinite *alteration* of the Self *before* the subject and always oriented *beyond* the determinations or categorizations of subjectivity *for* the Other, *for* the responsibility to the Other to the point of substitution and expiation in the name of the Other.

In this sense, it was necessary for our choices of terms to remain as faithful to the complex array and network of significations at work when Levinas engages in rethinking and reformulating the ethical *before* and *beyond* our philosophical history of conceptualization and comprehension.

Deciding which terms from the Levinas lexicon to include in this *Levinas Dictionary* has thus been a complex task. For when one enters into Levinas' rethinking of the entire philosophical tradition through the renewal and reinvention of the ethical as "First Philosophy," one cannot not understand and comprehend the revolution this thinker engaged within the very terms which constitute our philosophical heritage. In this sense, our task was to translate and express the radicality of Levinas' philosophical revolution of philosophy and show, demonstrate, and explicate how and where the terms he had inherited from the philosophical canon are also reoriented toward a certain creation of wholly other performatives—which implies a rupture where each notion inherited is brought to the point of its estrangement, to its breaking-point, breach, split, and is thereby commanded to its transmutation toward *another Saying*: which speaks to the absolute transcendence by responding to the irreducible alterity of a *wholly Other*.

Introduction

Every philosopher invents a singular language, develops specific contexts for each signifier proposed, and meticulously weaves words and concepts to offer novel meanings while each time engaging other performatives to orient thinking, through a specific discourse, toward *wholly other headings* than those it has inherited. And indeed, Emmanuel Levinas commands *our* thinking toward such philosophical innovations and inventions, which—as Derrida so eloquently and judiciously phrased it in the 1967 "Violence and Metaphysics" essay[1]—engages us in nothing less than a "community of the question" always testifying to an "immeasurable teaching": that of an infinite responsibility *for* the Other.

Levinas' singular language however contains an inherent discipline, rigor, and precision. Without system or systematicity, outside the dialectical hegemony of the Same and thus always suspicious of conciliatory or reconciliatory tropes which ultimately reduce and annul the alterity of the Other to identity, meaning and recognition, concept and comprehension, categorization, indifference, and anonymity, Levinas' language intends the extravagant and messianic *promise* of awakening the Greek by and through the Hebraic and, at the same time, of translating, without relegating, the Hebraic into the Greek. That is, of expressing the Other *beyond* the Same and yet *before* the Same, thereby *opening* and *awakening* the Same toward the wholly Other alterity of the Other.

How are we to *define* this *extravagant hypothesis* as well as its effects in and for philosophical discourse and its history? How are we to identify, and thus typify, this messianic *promise* for philosophy *without* reducing its heading in totalization, systematicity, teleology?

Our task here was to provide, in view of responding to these questions, more than a simple dictionary of terms and concepts. Indeed, our desire was to give a *philosophical explication* of Levinas' words, writing, discourse, and thereby offer an *interpretation* of Levinas' singular philosophical language which engages thinking toward a responsibility for the infinite transcendence of the Other. Furthermore, we also sought to present a comprehensive lexicon where one can discover indications and engage, from these, further hypotheses and propositions of reading in the hope of incessantly expanding our general understanding of Levinas' extraordinary philosophical gestures. Such was the greatest challenge for us: write a *Levinas Dictionary* which, while proposing interpretative definitions, also remained resolutely open to that which may come in and to the philosophy of Emmanuel Levinas.

Writing a dictionary focused on a unique author of our philosophical tradition is always a daunting and difficult enterprise. Indeed, this *Series* is a testament to this complex and demanding exercise. Not only are we engaged in presenting succinctly and methodically the terms, and their contexts, at work in a philosophical gesture, develop the inherent significations of ideas and concepts as well as the modalities by which these are related and intertwined within the general economy of a philosophical oeuvre but also, and at the same time, actively *translate* the multiple sources and diverse languages which are always and already speaking through a singular philosophy. By definition, translators think *in more than one language*, and in at least two. Usually, their work concerns two languages at a time and involves a transfer from one language to another and thus from an *other's* to *one's own* or from *one's own* to an *other's*. But, and however true this first appreciation is, anyone who has ever experienced or exercised the work of translation or even reflected on its practice will recognize that it always engages *more than two languages*, and thereby always effectuates *more* than the one passage from one language to another language. Indeed, to translate is also to incessantly render the concealed *other* multiple languages speaking through the supposedly "original" language. The translator, in this sense, must also give a voice to those languages unwritten and yet speaking through the "original" language. That is, give the unspoken languages in the "original" language a *further* voice. We ought even risk the following: the task of the translator is to show how a supposedly "original" language is always inhabited by countless *other* languages, alterities, and histories.

This situation is exemplary and paradigmatic in the philosophy of Emmanuel Levinas.

Indeed, Levinas' singular philosophical language is traversed, inhabited and informed, transformed, and altered by a multiplicity of *other* languages. In other words, Levinas' philosophy is not one of *one* language, source or resource, origin or *arche*—it is always *multilingual* and supposes at least and always *more than one language in its own language*.

What then of Levinas' *languages*?

From his earliest childhood in Kovno (Lithuania), Levinas read, wrote, and spoke Hebrew. He was also, in the midst of the German invasion of Lithuania during the First World War and after his family was forced into exile to Kharkov (Ukraine), schooled in Russian, a language which he spoke at home until the end of his life. This linguistic duality undoubtedly shaped Levinas' early education and formative years where, lulled in Russian literature (and especially Pushkin, Dostoyevsky, Tolstoy, and Lermontov) as well as Biblical commentary, the desire for philosophy fomented silently within him.

Following the end of the First World War and his family's return to Lithuania, the young Levinas studied the German language throughout his secondary school education. However, it was not before he moved to Strasbourg in 1923, where he began studying philosophy at the University, that Levinas began to learn a fourth language, French.

These languages, German and French, saved Levinas' life. As an interpreter and translator enrolled in the French military, Levinas endured his 5-year captivity during the Second World War in the *Fallingbostel* camp, protected from deportation to the Nazi extermination camps by the 1929 Geneva Convention on Prisoners of War. Levinas was, in this sense, protected by, as he later termed it, the "French uniform."

Before the Second World War, at the University of Strasbourg, and later at the University of Freiburg in Germany, and as part of the classical university education in philosophy, Levinas was also fully trained in Ancient Greek and Latin.

This multiplicity of languages tempts us to suggest that, for Levinas, language itself is never simply reducible to the mark of an identity. Going to the limit of this proposition, we could add that, for Levinas, each language is already traversed by *other languages* and thus is *always in search of other languages* in its own expression. In a certain sense, for Levinas, as for ethical responsibility, language incessantly *exceeds* its expression and thereby expresses itself always and already *otherwise*, that is from other sources than its own, always calling for, within its own expression, alterities, the other, and others. In this sense, Levinas' extraordinary "ethical" hypothesis is that of the Other's language, always and already speaking through the Self and indeed commanding and demanding the Self to express, in its own language, the otherness of the Other, the absolute alterity of the Other as already inhabiting the Self, engaging thus a response of infinite responsibility *for* the Other, *beyond* and *before* the order of norms or intersubjective recognition. This is why, for Levinas, the ethical response and infinite responsibility *for* the Other must *exceed* all possible contract between the Self and the Other, and thus surpass all reciprocal forms of recognition or intersubjectivity. As if to speak and write in one language would also engage speech and writing in opening toward a multitude of other languages. As if one language, for Levinas, always and already speaks of, testifies to, and remains inhabited by the Other, the Other's language, contaminated and traversed by alterity to the point where multiple linguistic contexts inform and re-play thinking, speech, and writing.

The incompressible languages, *always more than two*, inhabiting the language of Levinas' philosophical thinking and writing are stratified in multiple layers of meaning and discourses: (1) the literary/poetic/philosophical classics of Russian literature, including, as he often quoted, Pushkin, Lermontov, Gogol, and above all, Dostoevsky; (2) the Biblical text and its Hebraic hermeneutic heritage (*Tanakh*, *Talmud*, and *Midrash*) and (3) the

Western philosophical and theological traditions, from Plato, through German Idealism, to Phenomenology and Hermeneutics. This multiplicity of languages is also manifest in Levinas' incessant retrievals of French, German, Russian, and Hebraic literatures. Indeed, when bringing a specific ethical orientation in his philosophical writing, Levinas calls onto the writings of Pushkin and Dostoevsky, Maupassant, Blanchot, Proust, Grossman, Agnon, Celan, Goethe, to name here but a few which considerably influence and even shape his readings and interpretations of the Western philosophical tradition. Many examples of such influences could be put forward, but certainly the most important and obvious one, which also reappears frequently in his later work, is unquestionably Dostoevsky's *The Brothers Karamazov*, of which Levinas quotes "We are all guilty/responsible above all and before all, and I more than all the others." This recourse to the literary ought also to be understood as a manner of decentering philosophical thinking and most particularly as injecting an ethical supplement into the canon of Western rationality, sovereignty, universality, conceptuality. Levinas retrieves the literary word to perpetually offset philosophical *logos* and engage it to say *otherwise than Being* the infinite responsibility for the Other electing the Self inescapably and irrefutably. In this sense, Levinas, through literature, seeks to re-orient toward the unthought possibilities of the philosophical narrative and through these possibilities toward the force of singularity *beyond* and *before* the unitary concretion of essence, reason, teleology, and ontology.

Levinas also performs the same de-structuring by calling onto another source than the Greek from which to inform and exceed philosophy itself. Indeed, the Hebraic—including *Tanakh, Talmud, Midrash*—undoubtedly shaped Levinas' creative and critical readings of the Western philosophical tradition. As early as 1934, and along with "Reflections on the Philosophy of Hitlerism" and "On Escape," Levinas also published a series of articles on or around Jewish thinking, such as "The Contemporary Relevance of Maimonides." And of course, throughout his life, Levinas lectured and published on the role and the task, the challenges and the demands contemporary Jewish thought needed to confront and embody after the destruction of European Jewry. Most known are the Talmudic readings and lectures Levinas gave at the *Colloque des Intellectuels Juifs de Langue Française* but we must also underline and highlight the numerous and deeply seeded references in his philosophical oeuvre to Jewish philosophers and thinkers—Maimonides, Chaïm of Volozhin, Buber, Rosenzweig, Heschel, Fackenheim, to name here the most salient. The references to *Tanakh* and Jewish philosophy, as well as his Talmudic readings, make Levinas' philosophy impossible to simply categorize or fixate in any simple manner. Indeed, Levinas' writing is multiple and engages philosophical thinking to venture *beyond* identity, unity, unification, or appropriation. Always searching for novel resources and other callings, that is, always influenced and informed by the

Other, Levinas marks an undeniable point in contemporary philosophy: to philosophize is to revive the Other and awaken the Others in the Self *before* and *beyond* the Same. And thus, a philosophical tradition can only deploy itself by the incessant confrontations to otherness awakening it always *beyond* and *before* its ownmost meaning and comprehension. And in this sense, Levinas revives a certain Judaic calling in philosophy—one entirely orchestrated around the ideas of election, address, creation, revelation, redemption, messianicity, prophetism, responsibility, interruption and separation, suspension of the reconciliatory logic of sacrifice, Sainthood, or Sanctity, the sharp distinction between the *Saying* and the *Said*, the predominance of Justice *before* and *beyond* Being as truth, and so on—precisely in order to incessantly revive, animate, awaken philosophical rationality, universality, the ontological determination of meaning and history, truth, and essence to that which escapes it irreducibly: the absolute alterity of the Other. Which also entails that Levinas engages the Greek and the Hebraic not in a hierarchy of primacy, but rather in the unresolved *interplay* whereby each calls onto the other thereby provoking a *futurity* yet unthought *in* and *beyond* both the Greek and the Hebraic and toward a wholly other demand and responsibility.

It is in this manner that philosophy, for Levinas, requires its incessant creative translation between the Greek and the Hebraic and thus demands at once a hermeneutical project which, while explicating the meaning of Being as identity, presence, unity and unification, as intersubjectivity, morality, recognition of the Other, *always provokes this philosophical history of conceptualization to step beyond itself, search outside its ownmost horizon of signification, engage it otherwise than in and within its own meaning, identity, presence, unity, unification, projecting it always beyond its own Being* toward *wholly other sources of signification*: that of irreducible *alterities* inhabiting the philosophical and orienting it toward another calling always inspired by the irreducible transcendence of the Other.

In this sense, if the entirety of Levinas' thinking rests on a certain ethical suspicion toward ontology, it nonetheless always calls for and demands, commands for philosophical *logos* to be inspired by the irreducible alterity of the Other and thus incessantly search for other formulations of itself as ethically awoken by the transcendence of the Other. Certainly, Levinas understands all too well how, where, why, and in which manner ontology and the history of Western philosophy possess and produce, engage and instill, from Antiquity to Modernity and Contemporaneity, an ethics and a morality. Certainly, Levinas understands how and why the question of the Other, of the recognition of the Other in and as difference, has always been a theme in the history of Western metaphysics from Plato to Heidegger.

However, and throughout this history, Levinas' question remains and is perpetually reiterated in the wake of our philosophical tradition: from which commandment, according to which Law, in which engagement or assignation are we to think toward an *irreducible* ethical responsibility? From which and according to which responsibility are we to respond to the irreducibility of the Other? How are we to express and enact a justice for the irreducible singularity of the Other and, at the same time, for all Others in the Other?

Reading Levinas is to experience and question the philosophical, its meaning and signification, its tradition and orientation, from an irreducible, hyperbolical, absolutely infinite alterity engaging the Self toward a *wholly other* heading than the one set forth in the classical determinations of onto-theology for the subject. Which also entails how *thinking with Levinas* is to engage an *otherwise* than the philosophical, an *otherwise* than the totality of meaning by which the subject can define and determine its ownmost meaning as well as the sense or signification of its intersubjective community. *Beyond* totality and intersubjectivity, Levinas' ethics as "First Philosophy" claims, from an irreducible alterity, the philosophical to exceed and succeed itself, to surpass itself without return or reserve. Ethics as "First Philosophy" thereby means the ethical incessantly exceeding and succeeding the ontological by invoking the Self to always and already respond *before* itself and *beyond* what it can determine *for* the Other. Which means: each notion and concept, terms and ideas Levinas inherits from the philosophical tradition are always subjected to a certain redefinition, and thereby each is oriented differently as each is seen to reveal singular significations which always resist their appropriation or reappropriation in a fixed ontological or logical determination or comprehension.

Levinas incessantly engages philosophical concepts in a movement where they singularly exceed their ownmost signification to the point where each is never as such delimited, delineated, or circumscribed. Each philosophical notion is projected in a movement where each passes into another without fixed or determined hierarchical order. This is why Levinas' thinking and writing is never static or fixed: it incessantly calls onto a further formulation of itself and opens to a hyperbolical expression, a *Saying* interrupting and suspending, rupturing and shattering the context, the contextualization and the totalization of the Same, of Sameness, of identity, of the *Said*, that is, interrupting and suspending, rupturing and shattering the order of presentation and representation, the predominance of presence and of manifestation and where is revealed a piercing of the essential horizon of meaning and the enveloping signification of Being toward irretrievable and irrecuperable transmutations and alterations of itself in the name of the singularity of the Other.

In this sense, for Levinas, the philosophical signifies a certain *polysemy* which engages thinking into an incessant transfiguration of its notions and concepts, terms and ideas, all oriented toward an infinite transcending of their very significations toward *other expressions yet unthought*—perhaps *unthinkable*—by their traditional definitions and which, in their novel expressions, incessantly awaken, reawaken, repropose these in an unforeseen *otherwise than self-determination*. Which means: this a-dialectical *polysemy* of concepts, far from forming a system or unifying themselves in a systematicity, produces irreducible *singularities* within our philosophical tradition, each engaging unique trajectories of sense *as if* responsibility for the philosophical expected an incessant re-invention and re-creation of its concepts *beyond* their originary meanings to the point where they always *say* an *otherwise* than what they have *said*.

The Levinas Dictionary A–Z

Absolute (*Absolu*)

The Latin word *absolutus* contains a double meaning, that of an accomplished, perfect term which indicates an ultimate principle *and* that of "being separated from," untied, untangled, unconditioned, marking, in this second sense, a separation, a distinction, and by extension a "being freed from . . ." and, thus, of severance, division, and disjointing.

In all senses, however, the absolute is strictly opposed to the relative and remains irreducible to relationality. In the history of Western philosophy, the idea of the absolute belongs primordially to the theological, metaphysical, ontological and gnoseological lexicons. However, the term also appears in aesthetics, linguistics ("nominative absolute," "absolute clause," "absolute construction"), and mathematics ("absolute value").

Ontologically, the absolute designates a First or Primary Being, both as Being *qua* Being and denotes a foundational or fundamental ground. Consequently, the absolute is interpreted *either* as a permanent and intelligible substance from which ensues all other reality *or* as an initial act or activity from which is engaged the development and becoming of all that exists.

From the gnoseological point of view, the absolute means both the first term conceived in and from itself and the ultimate principle from which all existents can be conceived, grasped, and known. Furthermore, and as the absolute poses itself by and from itself, the term determines the beginning point of knowledge as well as ensures the validity of its methodology as end-point of the investigation which, retrospectively or retroactively, grounds the entire process of cognition.

For Levinas, the term is found in expressions such as "absolute alterity" or "Other absolutely Other" which each mark a *radical separation*, and thereby, an irreducibility of the Other as wholly heterogeneous, heteronomous, and transcendent to the Same, to identity, and which thus remains always *wholly other* to Being, *wholly other* than essence, comprehension, appropriation, intuition, cognition, presentation, representation, or recognition.

The sense of absolute as separation is thus privileged in Levinas' thinking and writing. It signifies the Other *as* Other, as that which remains uncategorizable and consequently ungraspable within a unified *logos*—the absolute, for Levinas, is *wholly other* than the possibility to encompass it or envelop it in a gathered meaning or totality of meaningfulness. The Other as "absolute alterity" is *absolutely other* than Being, meaning, truth, universality, and thereby commands from *beyond* essence, signification, and intentionality.

Which entails: this "absoluteness" of the Other never means *non-being* or *absence*. Rather, it signifies the *irreducibility to Being* and *heterogeneity to essence—irreducibility* and *heterogeneity* from which is engaged an incessant interruption and suspension of presence, representation, appropriation—a break and rupture thus of the synchronized temporal horizon in which the Other is comprehended and ultimately reduced and negated, annulled and annihilated. In this sense, for Levinas, the interruption and suspension of the perseverance, indifference, and anonymity of Being, this break and rupture of the "there is" (*il y a*) of presence and Sameness reveals the Other as absolute transcendence and thus as radically irreducible to an identified moment within the comprehension of a generalized and generalizing context of meaning and totality of similitude, resemblance, and identicalness.

This is why Levinas understands in the word "absolute" the *absolution* as *separatedness* of the Other—an *absolution* which is always and already presupposed by the infinite transcendence as separation of the Other. Contrary to the Western tradition of metaphysics, which has always sought to reduce and ultimately annul the transcendent separation of the Other, Levinas urges to think the absolute otherness of the Other *as* separation, thereby extracting the Other from all forms of reduction, or modalities of comprehension. All to the contrary, the absolute otherness of the Other *as* separation opens toward the Infinite transcendence of the Other *as* Other and thus toward a *wholly other* signification, that of the Good *beyond* and *before* Being—*beyond* and *before* meaning and truth, community and intersubjectivity. That is: as "Other-*in-the*-Same," engaging the possibility to think a novel "structure" of signification as "One-*for-the*-Other," wherein the ethical Self is always and already engaged and elected toward the Other *as infinitizing* responsibility *for* the Other.

The absolute alterity of the Other opens toward an idea of justice irreducible to truth or meaning, irreducible also to forgiveness or clemency, reconciliation, or conciliation. That which Levinas also calls Good, the ethical responsibility for the Other. As Levinas indeed writes in *Totality and Infinity*:

> It is necessary to cease interpreting separation as pure and simple diminution of the Infinite, a degradation. Seperation with regard to the Infinite, compatible with the Infinite, is not a simple "fall" of the Infinite. [. . .] In reality what is a issue is an order where the very notion of the Good first takes on meaning: what is at issue is society. Here the relation connects

> not terms that complete one another and consequently are reciprocally lacking to one another [. . .]. Infinity thought concretely, that is, starting with the seperated being turned toward it, surpasses itself. In other words, it opens to itself the order of the Good.[1]

Accusation (*Accusation*)

The Self, for Levinas, is always already assigned to the accusative commandment of the Other as ethical demand for the Other. What does this accusative carry and engage, mean and signify? Nothing less than an infinite *excess* of responsibility for the Other. The accusative ethical demand binds the Self *before* any wrongdoing or fault engaging the Self *before* its autonomy or decision to respond for the Other *beyond* what it can or will—a response of responsibility incessantly exceeding itself *beyond* its possible fulfillment and which thus can never subsume or satisfy itself. For Levinas, ethical responsibility always responds more and overwhelms its own response for the Other.

The idea of accusation in Levinas marks thus the Self as always and already responding ethically for the Other *before* any contract or intersubjective relation with the Other. The extreme radicality of this ethical reformulation opens to a responsibility never determinable and always responding *before* the call of the Other as already *beyond* what the autonomy or the sovereignty of the Self can fulfil.

In this sense, and as *face* (*visage*), the Other's heteronomous commandment is *accusative* in that it also *elects* the Self to respond *before* any self-identity to the point of incessantly exceeding its response and by always furthering its responsibility for the Other *beyond* its possible fulfillment. The ethical Self responds always *before* the Other's commandment, *before* the commandment is heard or the accusation is recognized as such, and already *beyond* its own capacity or capability, autonomy or decision, judgment or evaluation.

Levinas indeed remarks:

> Responsibility for the other, going against intentionality and the will, which intentionality does not succeed in dissimulating, signifies not the disclosure of a given and its reception, but the exposure of me to the other, prior to every decision. There is a claim laid on the same by the other in the core of myself, the extreme tension of the command exercised by the other in me over me, a traumatic hold of the other on the same, which does not give the same time to await the other. Through this alteration the soul animates

> the object; it is the very pneuma of the psyche. The *psyche* signifies the claiming of the same by the other, or inspiration, *beyond* the logic of the same and the other, of their insurmountable adversity. It is an undoing of the substantial nucleus of the ego that is formed in the same, a fission of the mysterious nucleus of inwardness of the subject by this assignation to respond, which does not leave any place of refuge, any chance to slip away, and is thus despite the ego, or, more exactly, despite me. Quite the contrary of nonsense, it is an alteration without alienation or election. The subject in responsibility is alienated in the depths of its identity with an alienation that does not empty the same of its identity, but constrains it to it, with an unimpeachable assignation, constrains it to it as no one else, where no one could replace it. The *psyche*, a uniqueness outside of concepts, is a seed of folly, already a psychosis. It is not an Ego, but me under assignation. There is an assignation to an identity for the response of responsibility, where one cannot have oneself be replaced without fault. To this command continually put forth only a "*Here I am*" can answer, where the pronoun "I" is in the accusative, declined before any declension, possessed by the other, sick, identical. Here I am—is saying with inspiration, which is not a gift for fine words or songs.[2]

Always responsible for the Other, the ethical Self is already subjected to the Other, accused by the Other, and thus instituted as Self by and through its infinite response of responsibility for the Other, response of responsibility *beyond* the normative order of autonomy and *before* any decision or engagement. Levinas insists, in this manner, on the radical passivity of the Self, a passivity more passive than all passivity and in which the ethical Self is incapable of remaining indifferent to the Other's commandment—accused *before* any accusation, exposed *before* any constitution or institution to a responsibility *beyond* measure or judgment. Which means: the ethical Self responds *before* and *beyond* its own identity as infinite excess of responsibility, responsibility *for* responsibility *for* the Other.

This temporal *diachrony*—responding *before* and *beyond*, responding always *too late* on the Other's commandment and already *before* hearing, recognizing, or comprehending the Other's accusation—engages the Self in a responsibility to the point of *substitution* and *expiation* for the Other. Always and already *for* the Other, responsible *before* the Other's plea, and *beyond* any determination or norm, the ethical Self cannot remain indifferent or abandon the Other—the ethical Self always subjected to the commandment of the Other, inhabited by the Other *before* and *beyond* comprehending itself as autonomous subject, is elected by and through its infinite response, incessantly responding as inescapable and unsubstitutable responsibility for the Other.

À-Dieu

Literally: "To God." The word is engaged by Levinas in reference to that which, in the infinite ethical response, orients toward the immemorial *trace* of the absolutely transcendent Other: irrepresentable, unrecognizable, unconditional, and unnamable alterity of the Other.

Without typifying or defining God as a purveyor, immanent presence or *causa sui*, Levinas inscribes the ethical response for the Other in the *trace* of a non-plenitude and infinite transcendence, an *Illeity*, as an inescapable and undeniable orientation toward that which incessantly elects the Self *beyond* the Self *before* the Self thereby commanding the Self to an infinite responsibility for the Other without measure or resolution, unaccomplished and unfulfilled—already *given* as always *to come* for the Other.

"To God" inscribes in responsibility an inherent *un*-accomplishment and *un*-fulfillment, unconditionality and incessantly overwhelming demand and Law toward the irreducible otherness of the Other. That is, the election of a Self in the ethical awakening toward the singularity of the absolute transcendence of the Other.

This is why Levinas never dissociates the idea of God "coming to mind" as *à-dieu*, that is as an incompressible orientation toward the irreducible transcendence of the *wholly Other* and the idea of justice as inescapable and inexorable responsibility for the Other. As Levinas writes:

> Ethics is the spiritual optics. The subject-object relation does not reflect it; in the impersonal relation that leads to it, the invisible but personal God is not approached outside of all human presence. The ideal is not only a being superlatively being, a sublimation of the objective, or, in the solitude of love, a sublimation of a Thou. The work of justice—the uprightness of the face-to-face—is necessary in order that the breach that leads to God be produced—and "vision" here coincides with this work of justice. Hence metaphysics is enacted where the social relation is enacted—in our relations with men. There can be no "knowledge" of God separated from the relationship with men. The Other is the very locus of metaphysical truth, and is indispensable for my relation with God. He does not play the role of a mediator. The Other is not the incarnation of God, but precisely by

his face, in which he is disincarnate, is the manifestation of the height in which God is revealed.[3]

Alterity (*Altérité*)

Irreducible to contradiction, opposition or difference, irreducible to the Kantian *noumena*, to the Fichtean *non-I*, to the Hegelian *other*, to the Husserlian *alter-ego* or to the Heideggerian typification of *other Daseins* always and already co-existing *with* the *Dasein*, alterity, for Levinas, entails a critical reappraisal of the figures of otherness deployed and developed in the history of philosophy. As early as *Time and the Other*, Levinas questions the traditional distinction between the Same and the Other and engages a certain *alteration* of the scope and breadth, the horizon, and the intention always supposed or presupposed within this relationship. Levinas indeed questions the difference between the two *genres* of Being and engages the ethical *beyond* the ontological binarism of the Same and the Other, of identity and difference, and thus projects thinking as ethical toward an alterity absolutely Other, transcendent and heterogeneous, an alterity which is wholly dissociated from ontological categorizations and radically independent from the order and the logic of the Same and Sameness, of unity or unification, and thereby wholly irreducible to the modalities of recognition, reconciliation, and intersubjectivity.

This is why Levinas insists repeatedly on how and why alterity is not graspable within a perceptual, representational, or conceptual determination or intentional horizon. Alterity engages an Otherness always and already Other, heteronomous and, in this sense, entails an anteriority or an antecedence *before* any attribute, quality, qualification, or definition. In this sense, alterity, for Levinas, precedes all determination and any identification, precedes all intuition and any constitution or institution, context, and contextualization.

Alterity, for Levinas, is *absolute exteriority* and as such not appropriable within the unifying order or *logos* of Being, meaning, intentionality, and by the same token, remains irreducible to any formal category and representation within the *logic* of presence and presencing. Alterity awakens *beyond* and *before* Being to and toward the ethical. That is, alterity elects to the ethical Law in preceding, from its irreducible heterogeneity, the order of presence and the ontological context of meaning and truth, comprehension, recognition, and representation.

Which poses the question of the *relation* (this question indeed will be one of the central interrogations of *Totality and Infinity*): How to think or rethink the relation between a Self toward an Other absolutely Other, irreducible, heterogeneous, and heteronomous to the Self? Levinas:

> The absolutely other is the Other. He and I do not form a number. The collectivity in which I say 'you' or "we" is not a plural of the "I." I, you—these are not individuals of a common concept. Neither possession nor the unity of number nor unity of concepts link me to the Stranger [*l'Etranger*], the Stranger who disturbs the being at home with oneself [*le chez-soi*]. But the Stranger also means the free one. Over him I have *no power*. He escapes my grasp by an essential dimension, even if I have him at my disposal. He is not wholly in my site. But I, who have no concept in common with the Stranger, am, like him, without genus. We are the same and the other. The conjunction *and* here designates neither addition nor power of one term over the other. We shall try to show that the *relation* between the same and the other—upon which we seem to impose such extraordinary conditions—is language. For language accomplishes a relation such that the terms are not limitrophe within this relation such that the other, despite the relationship with the same remains transcendent to the same. The relation between the same and the other, metaphysics, is primordially enacted as conversation where the same, gathered up in its ipseity as an "I," as a particular existent unique and autochtonous, leaves itself.[4]

Which means that the relationship between the Same and the Other, and thus between the Self *toward* the Other is in no manner simply negated or voided by and through the absolute transcendence of the Other calling onto the Self. Rather, as Levinas remarks, the absolute transcendence of the Other opens a wholly other relation, that which is awakened by another language: that of the ethical as commandment which elects the Self as singular respondent for the Other. By and through the transcendent heterogeneity and the heteronomy of the Other is engaged an irreducible ethical commandment as language which, incessantly expressing itself through the *face* (*visage*) of the Other, demands an infinite and inexorable responsibility. Indeed, the ethical Self is, *before* autonomy or sovereignty, judgment or decision, elected to respond "*Here I am*" ("*Hineni*"), as infinite responsibility, for the Other.

It is through the expression of the ethical commandment as advent of the face of the Other—irreducible to manifestation or physicality or materiality and thereby irreducible to the erotic relation—that the alterity of the Other demands and elects the Self to an inescapable response and responsibility for the Other. In effect, thus, the ethical Self *cannot not* respond to the call of the Other and is thereby elected, *before* and *beyond* its own autonomy, to an infinite responsibility for the Other. As Levinas remarks:

> A relation whose terms do not form a totality can hence be produced within the general economy of Being only as proceeding from the I to the other, as a *face-to-face*, as delineating a distance in depth—that of conversation,

> of goodness, of Desire—irreducible to the distance the synthetic activity of the understanding establishes between the diverse terms; other with respect to one another, that lend themselves to its synoptic operation. The I is not a contingent formation by which the same and the other, as logical determinations of being, can in addition be reflected *within a thought*. It is in order that alterity be produced *in being* that a "thought" is needed and that an I is needed. The irreversibility of the relation can be produced only if the relation is effected by one of the terms as the very movement of transcendence, as the *traversing* of this distance, and not as a recording of, or the psychological invention of this movement. "Thought" and "interiority" are the very break-up of being and the production not the reflection of transcendence. We know this relation only in the measure that we effect it; this is what is distinctive about it. Alterity is possible only starting from *me*.[5]

For Levinas, alterity is not justifiable logically; it is wholly indiscernible. Alterity marks the absolute transcendence of the Other as uniquely and singularly Other—irreducible, heteronomous, heterogeneous, and incessantly awakening or electing the Self, and no one other than the Self, as infinite responsibility for the Other. The relation between the Self and the Other is here entirely redefined and reoriented toward the Other, *beyond* and *before* a shared normativity, contractual intersubjectivity or community, an "in-between," communal "belonging" or "being-together."

The alterity of the absolute Other precedes the presupposition of a Sameness between the Self and the Other. Neither identity nor reducible to a comprehensible or compressible difference, the Other suspends and interrupts the "*between*" the Self and the Other, suspends and interrupts the identity or the Sameness in relation. In this sense, Levinas re-orients the relation toward the absolute transcendence of the Other from which erupts an unassimilable expression: the ethical commandment.

As Levinas remarks, it is not difference which opens to the absolute alterity of the Other; it is rather the encounter with the infinite transcendence of the Other which awakens difference, opposition, or contradiction. Which means the alterity of the Other, the Otherness of the Other, is more ancient than difference, opposition, or contradiction. The absolute Otherness of the Other commands *immemorially* and remains irretrievable in retention, irreducible to presence and unpredictable to protention; *wholly Other* than the play between protention and retention—*immemorial*:

> The way in which the Other presents himself, exceeding *the idea of the other in me*, we name here face. This *mode* does not consist in figuring as a theme under my gaze, in spreading itself forth as a set of qualities forming

an image. The face of the Other at each moment destroys and overflows the plastic image it leaves me, the idea existing to my own measure and to the measure of its *ideatum*—the adequate idea. It does not manifest itself by these qualities, but *kath auto*. It expresses itself. The face brings a notion of truth which, in contradistinction to contemporary ontology, is not the disclosure of an impersonal Neuter, but *expression*: the existent breaks through all the envelopings and generalities of Being to spread out in its "form" the totality of its "content", finally abolishing the distinction between form and content. This is not achieved by some sort of modification of the knowledge that thematises but precisely by 'thematisation' turning into expression. The condition for theoretical truth and error is the word of the other, his expression, which every lie already presupposes.[6]

Approach (*Approche*)

Approach is always of the Other. Indeed, for Levinas, to approach is to approach the infinite transcendence of the Other. In this sense, to approach occurs *before* any perception, representation, intuition, categorization, or recognition of the Other. That is, to approach is to *encounter* the Other *before* the binarism between the Same and the Other. This entails the following: the approach of the Other engages a relationship *before* the autonomy and sovereignty of the Self. In this sense, to approach the Other is to be elected for the Other by the Other; the ethical Self is thereby engaged *before* itself and subjected *beyond* itself to an infinite responsibility for the Other.

This approach occurs as *face-to-face* encounter, that is, in the exposition and the receptivity, passivity more passive than all passivity, to the incommensurable vulnerability, defenselessness, and nakedness of the Other which expresses itself as commandment and demand to an irrecusable and inexorable ethical responsibility. And thus as infinite "teaching"—the Other expresses its mastery incessantly calling the Self and instructing it to its ineluctable and inescapable response, responsibility, care, and devotion:

> To approach the Other is to welcome his expression, in which at each instant he overflows the idea a thought would carry away from it. It is therefore to *receive* from the Other *beyond* the capacity of the I, which means exactly: to have the idea of infinity. But this also means to be taught. The relation with the Other, or Conversation, is a non-allergic relation, an ethical relation; but inasmuch as it is welcomed this conversation is a teaching [*enseignement*]. Teaching is not reducible to maieutics; it comes from the exterior and brings me more than I contain. In its non-violent

> transitivity the very epiphany of the face is produced. The Aristotelian analysis of the intellect, which discovers the agent intellect coming in by the gates, absolutely exterior, and yet constituting, nowise compromising, the sovereign activity of reason, already substitutes for maieutics a transitive action of the master, since reason, without abdicating, is found to be in a position to a *receive*.[7]

The approach of the Other exposes the Self *before* autonomy or sovereignty and where the Self is already commanded, demanded, and which entails its election to a response *beyond* what it can respond, a response incessantly exceeding the possibility of responding: that is, for Levinas, a response of irrecusable responsibility for the Other. This is why, for Levinas, the approach of the Other puts into question the spontaneity of the subject's freedom and will: the approach of the Other "puts the spontaneous freedom within us into question. It commands and judges it and brings it to its truth."[8]

This is why the approach of the Other as encounter of the *face* of the Other does not consist in a simple altruism where the Self, sure and assured of its own egoism, would leave sufficient room or carve out a reasonable space in which it could place or situate the Other and thereby respond to it in accordance to a predetermined moral norm and measurable ethical disposition. All to the contrary! The approach of the Other implies, for Levinas, a displacement of the Self which, far from abrogating the Self, elects it to an unconditional responsibility for the Other. Indeed, to approach the Other as encountering the *face* of the Other

> brings us to a notion of meaning prior to my *Sinngebung* and thus independent of my initiative and my power. It signifies the philosophical priority of the existent over Being, an exteriority that does not call for power or possession, an exteriority that is not reducible, as with Plato, to the interiority of memory, and yet maintains the I who welcomes it. It finally makes possible the description of the notion of the immediate. [. . .] Such a relationship is metaphysics itself. History would not be the privileged plane where Being disengaged from the particularism of points of view (with which reflection would still be affected) is manifested. If it claims to integrate myself and the other within an impersonal spirit this alleged integration is cruelty and injustice, that is, ignores the Other. History as a relationship between men ignores a position of the I before the other in which the other remains transcendent with respect to me. Though of myself I am not exterior to history, I do find in the Other a point that is absolute in regard to history—not by amalgamating with the Other, but in speaking with him. History is worked over by the ruptures of history in

> which a judgment is borne upon it. When man truly approaches the Other he is uprooted from history.[9]

Which is precisely why Levinas always thinks the approach of the Other as the *opening* of sacrifice. But this *opening* does not mean a self-sacrifice or a sacrifice of the Self. Levinas' ethics as "First Philosophy" is *not* an ethics of sacrifice or of self-sacrifice. Again, all to the contrary! The approach of the Other *opens* in the Self an orientation always and already electing the Self as ethical *infinitization* of responsibility for the Other. That is, for Levinas, the approach of the Other means a certain ethical election *beyond* death which implies an infinite responsibility for the Other. Or otherwise said, to approach the Other means to give, *beyond* death, a response of responsibility irreducible to death for the Other. And thus, irreducible to a simple self-sacrifice of the Self, the approach of the Other implies an incessant iteration and reiteration of responsibility, without *arche* and without *telos*, a responsibility never fulfilled and unfulfillable for the Other:

> The approach, inasmuch as it is a sacrifice, confers a sense on death. In it the absolute singularity of the responsible one encompasses the generality or generalization of death. In it life is no longer measured by being, and death can no longer introduce the absurd into it. Death gives lie to pleasure, in which for the space of an instant the tragi-comedy is forgotten, and which would be defined by this forgetting. But despite all its adversity, it is accorded with the for-the-other of approach. No one is so hypocritical as to claim that he has taken from death its sting, not even the promisers of religions. But we can have responsibilities and attachments through which death takes on a meaning. That is because, from the start, the other affects us despite ourselves.[10]

Autrui

Autrui (Other) means the Other as *absolute Other*, irreducible transcendence commanding as electing the Self, instructing and already inspiring the Self to an infinite responsibility for the Other. The Other absolutely Other is the source and the resource, without fixed origin or emplacement, of the signification of the Self—indeed, the Other absolutely Other in the Other human is the transcendence from which the Self is elected and inspired as Self *for* the Other. In this sense, the Other absolutely Other and the Self do not share the same ontological plane and are thereby always and already heterogeneously related. Their relation is wholly other than a relationship founded on Sameness, identity, unity, accord, or co-belongingness. The Other absolutely Other is absolute singularity from which the Self is singularized as irreplaceable and exceptional, unsubstitutable responsibility for the Other.

It is here that Levinas breaks with the phenomenological accounts of the relation to the Other, as well as with the intersubjective recognition of the Other—always too reductive and ultimately objectifying of the absolute transcendence of the Other. As Levinas marks:

> To renounce the psychology, demagogy, pedagogy rhetoric involves is to face the Other in a veritable conversation. Then this being is nowise an object, is outside of all emprise. This disengagement from all objectivity means, positively, this being's presentation in the face, his expression, his language. *The other qua other is the Other.* To "let him be" the relationship of discourse is required; pure "disclosure" where he is proposed as a theme, does not respect him enough for that. *We call justice face-to-face approach, in conversation.* If truth arises in the absolute *experience* in which being gleams with its own light, then truth is produced only in veritable conversation or in justice.[11]

The absolute Other engages what Levinas names "conversation" which firstly emanates from the expression of the Other's heterogeneous commandment electing the Self irrevocably and unsubstitutably for the Other. In this sense, the "experience" of the Other as incessant dismantling of the autonomy and sovereignty of the Self and electing the Self *before* the Self and *beyond* the Self as unsubstitutable responsibility for the Other engages the ethical where the Self is *always and already exposed* as *always and already responding for the Other.* This is also why Levinas never dissociates the Other as absolute Other from the face of the Other, and thus from the proximity of the Other, from the approach of the Other, from the call and the commandment of the Other which are always expressing the singular Law incessantly electing the ethical Self to an infinite responsibility to the point of substitution and expiation for the Other.

Which entails: the ethical Self is always and already engaged and elected in the hyperbolical movement of responding *before* and *beyond* the Self for Other through the face-to-face encounter with the Other as absolute Other. For it is in this face-to-face encounter that is revealed at once the *deposition* and the *overwhelming* of the egotistic sovereignty of the subject as consciousness and freedom, will and autonomy. Furthermore, it is through this *deposition* and *overwhelming* of the Self's selfhood in the face of the Other's commandment that the ethical is revealed and where the Self is always and already summoned as elected by the Other to an infinite responsibility for the Other.

This absolute exposition to the Other as absolute Other occurs in and through language and discourse which Levinas also sees as engaging a certain traumatism, which is also marked as the anarchy of the Good *before* and *beyond* Being. As early as *Totality and Infinity*, indeed, Levinas indicates:

> The relationship of language implies transcendence, radical separation, the strangeness of the interlocutors, the revelation of the Other to me. In other words, language is spoken where community between the terms of the relationship is wanting, where the common place is wanting or is yet to be constituted. It takes place in this transcendence. Discourse is thus the experience of something absolutely foreign, a *pure* "knowledge" or "experience", a *traumatism of astonishment.*[12]

This traumatism (which will be radicalized in *Otherwise than Being, or Beyond Essence*) awakens the Self to an infinite responsibility for the Other *before* and *beyond* judgment and measure, *before* and *beyond* the self-determination of the Self. The Other absolutely Other commanding and electing the Self as *host* and *hostage* to the point of substitution and expiation for the Other. Unique and singular, never identifiable within the categories of the understanding or the forms of intuition, never reproducible in imagination, never reducible to Sameness or appropriable within a horizon of intentionality, unrecognizable and ultimately unknowable, the Other elects the Self irreplaceably to an irrecusable responsibility—elects the Self to being host as hostage—for the Other.

The Other absolutely Other, for Levinas, is indissociably *foreigner* and *heteronomous* while, and at the same time, *defenseless, orphan, nakedness* commanding and appealing, demanding and pleading: *to give* and thus to a generosity *beyond* measure and *without* reserve—substitution and expiation for the Other. The relation with the Other absolutely Other

> consists in entering into relationship with a nudity disengaged from every form, but having meaning by itself, *kath auto*, signifying before we have projected light upon it, appearing not as a privation on the ground of an ambivalence of values (as good or evil, as beauty or ugliness), but as an *always positive value*. Such a nudity is the face. The nakedness of the face is not what is presented to me because I disclose it, what would therefore be presented to me, to my powers, to my eyes, to my perceptions, in a light exterior to it. The face has turned to me—and this is its very nudity. It *is* by itself and not by reference to a system. [. . .] This gaze is precisely the epiphany of the face as a face. The nakedness of the face is destituteness (*dénûment*). To recognize the Other is to recognize a hunger. To recognise the Other is to give. But it is to give to the master, to the lord, to him whom one approaches as "You" in a dimension of Height.[13]

Always and already electing the Self to respond uniquely and singularly for the Other, the Other absolutely Other engages a *diachrony* which marks, for Levinas, the temporality of the ethical as irreducible to synchrony. Indeed, the commandment of the Other absolutely Other expressing itself from the foreignness and the nakedness of the *face* of the Other in the face-to-face encounter, exteriority and defenselessness, engages and elects a Self which at once responds always *too late* on the call of the Other and yet always *in advance of* hearing the commandment of the Other: *diachrony* of the ethical Self, temporality incessantly "out of joint" in which the responsibility for the Other as substitution and expiation exceeds itself always more than what it can or could settle or fulfill.

An important point: the absolute otherness of the Other, always and already commanding and appealing, cannot not also awaken the desire to murder, the will to annihilate, and the inclination to negate the Other. Indeed, the absolute foreignness and nakedness of the Other can also initiate a will to murder the Other. However, for Levinas, the ethical arises precisely where this will and desire of murder is turned into an ethical election of the Self as infinite responsibility for the Other. Otherwise said, the absolute exposition of the Other can also evoke and kindle, instigate the desire to kill the Other; but it is precisely in this desire that can also occur, through the *face* of the Other in its expression, the awakening and election of an infinite care and responsibility for the Other, a responsibility inseparable from an ethical obsession of and traumatism for the Other. As Levinas remarks, the demand of the Other opens to the persecution of the Self *by the ethical*, that is by responding as unconditional *host* and irrecusable *hostage* of the Other for the Other.

Being (*Être*)

The concept of Being is foundational in the history of Western philosophy. Aristotle's *Metaphysics* is often quoted as the origin of the history of ontology. Indeed, metaphysics, what Aristotle understood as "First Philosophy," is the science which studies *Being qua Being*. In this sense, metaphysics as ontology is distinguished from the study of the specific or particular regions of Being, which are only concentrated on the specialized order in which beings or entities are structured and coordinated, organized and categorized.

Ontology, or the discourse on *Being qua Being*, as Aristotle marks in *Metaphysics* Γ 2, is "said in many ways." That is, the verb "to be" (*einai*) has different senses, as do its cognates "Being" (*on*) and "entities" or "beings" (*onta*). Which, for Aristotle, poses the following question: How are we to explicate and deploy a single science of Being (ontology) when the very term, "Being," is itself ambiguous and multiple?

Aristotle approaches the concept of Being in relation to its verbality and thus from the predicative meaning inherent to "to be." Being contains whatever can be the subjects of propositions containing the word *is*. In this sense, Aristotle distinguishes four significations of Being: (1) *Being as accident*; (2) *Being as truth*; (3) *Being according to the categories*; and (4) *Being as act*. This ambiguity however entails a foundational and substantial idea as base and ground: that of *substance*. Every being is a property or a modification of substance. The centrality of substance in ontology is framed when Aristotle explicates, in *Metaphysics* Z: Being is said in many ways; however, the primary sense of Being is as *substance*. What is substance? In which manner are we to approach and understand that which *stands under* every manifestation, every appearance, every presence? *Metaphysics* Z 3 engages with marking the four categorizations of *substance* for each existent: essence, universal, genus, and subject.

The *question* of Being is retrieved and redefined by Heidegger and most particularly in *Being and Time* where it is famously asserted that the meaning of Being "has today been forgotten."[14] Heidegger engages thus a *repetition* of the question pertaining to the meaning of Being, a "fundamental ontology", by and through a suspension of the classical and traditional approaches to this question: idealist, realist, materialist, spiritualist, dialectical or speculative, and so on. Indeed, Heidegger, by "critically dismantling" the inherited conceptions of Being, and their inherent methods, proposes to question in direction of the meaning of Being through the horizon of temporality approached not as *becoming, duration, flux*, but rather as the unified *extasies* of temporality, that is, as the clearing and openness in which and from which "past," "present," "future," the three determinations of time, can occur and *be*. This is why ontology is always primary and indeed Heidegger marks the ontological priority of the question pertaining to the meaning of Being in the *Introduction* to *Being and Time*:

> The question of Being aims therefore at ascertaining the a priori conditions not only for the possibility of the sciences which examine entities as entities of such and such a type, and, in so doing, already operate with an understanding of Being, but also for the possibility of those ontologies themselves which are prior to the ontical sciences and which provide their foundations. Basically, all ontology, no matter how rich and firmly compacted a system of categories it has at its disposal, remains blind and perverted from its ownmost aim, if it has not first adequately clarified the meaning of Being, and conceived this clarification as its fundamental task.[15]

Levinas retrieves this tradition, from Aristotle to Heidegger, and marks within it the *instances* in which the Other erupts as inassimilable, irreappropriable, and irreducible to an essence or a genesis, irreducible to a foundational deployment and substantial determination by which and from which it could be signified and comprehended. For Levinas, Being comprehends itself by and through *indifference* and *anonymity*. The indifference and anonymity of Being means that, in its "embracing"[16] comprehension of beings, it also entails the *reduction* of the transcendence of the Other to the Sameness, identity, totality and essence of Being. Indeed, from Aristotle's typification of Being as *substance* to Heidegger's as *Ereignis* in which are *appropriated* Being *and* Time, Levinas poses the question: "To be or not to be is not the question where transcendence is concerned. The statement of being's other, of the *otherwise than being*, claims to state a difference over and *beyond* that which separates being from nothingness—the very difference of the *beyond*, the difference of transcendence."[17]

Indeed, remarks Levinas:

> To exist has a meaning in another dimension than that of the perduration of the totality; it can go *beyond* Being. Contrary to the Spinozist tradition, this going *beyond* death is produced not in the universality of thought but in the pluralist relation, in the goodness for the Other in justice. The surpassing of Being starting from being—the relation with exteriority, with the Other—is not measured by duration. Duration itself becomes visible in the relation with the Other where Being is surpassed.[18]

Hence, the ethical as "First Philosophy" implies a certain devalorization or secondarization of the concept and idea of Being as presence, substance, event, or appropriation of Being through time. That is, for Levinas, "First Philosophy" means, contrarily to the Aristotelian and Heideggerian heritage of ontology, the dismantling of the perseverance, the suspension of the perduration, and the interruption of the primacy of the meaning of Being to reveal, *beyond* and *before* ontology, an irreducible ethical commandment and Law expressed singularly by the heterogeneous and transcendence of the Other.

For Levinas, ontology deploys itself as *evil* by incessantly reducing the alterity of the Other, its singular transcendent commandment, plea, demand, to a Sameness, a unified essence, a substantial identity or totality which always entails indifference, anonymity, homogeneity. A foreclosure of the Other in the uniformity of essence, meaning, truth, Being as totality and Sameness and in which the Self and the Other are reduced to a substantial communal identity. This is why Levinas always associates Being with war and furthermore with the destruction of the ethical: the evil effacement of the Other's otherness:

> The essence works as an invincible persistence in essence, filling up every interval of nothingness which would interrupt its exercise. *Esse* is inter*esse*; essence is interest. This being interested does not appear only to the mind surprised by the relativity of its negation, and to the man resigned to the meaninglessness of his death; it is not reducible to just this refutation of negativity. It is confirmed positively to be the *conatus* of beings. And what else can positivity mean but this *conatus*? Being's interest takes dramatic form in egoisms struggling with one another, each against all, in the multiplicity of allergic egoisms which are at war with one another and are thus together. War is the deed or the drama of the essence's interest. No entity can await its hour. They all clash, despite the difference of the regions to which the terms in conflict may belong. Essence thus is the extreme synchronism of war. Determination is formed, and is already undone, by the clash. It takes form and breaks up in a swarming. Here is extreme contemporaneousness, or immanence.[19]

To the foreclosure and the annihilation of the Other in war, in Being's indifference and anonymity, Levinas thinks toward an idea of the Good which, *before* and *beyond* Being, passes over Being and commands an irreducible responsibility for the transcendence of the Other. For Levinas, the Good *before* and *beyond* Being, the *otherwise* than Being as *beyond* essence, marks the passage to the Other, and thereby a denucleation of the Self as responsibility for the Other immemorially electing the Self to an irrecusable exposition as substitution and expiation for the Other:

> Chosen without assuming the choice! If this passivity is not reducible to the passivity of an effect in a causal relation, if it can be conceived to be on the hither side of freedom and non-freedom, it must have the meaning of a "goodness despite itself" a goodness always older than the choice. Its value, that is, its excellence or goodness, the goodness of goodness, is alone able to counterbalance the violence of the choice (and, *beyond* counterbalancing, be for the better!). Goodness is always older than choice; the Good has always already chosen and required the unique one. As chosen without choosing its election, absent from the investiture received, the one is a passivity more passive still than all the passivity of undergoing. The passivity of the one, its responsibility or its pain, do not begin in consciousness—that is, do not begin. On the hither side of consciousness, they consist in this pre-original hold of the Good over it, always older than

> any present, any beginning. This diachrony prevents the one from joining up with itself and identifying itself as a substance, contemporary with itself, like a transcendental ego. Uniqueness is without identity. Not an identity, it is *beyond* consciousness, which is in itself and for itself. For it is already a substitution for the other.[20]

The Good *before* and *beyond* Being, "goodness despite itself and elected," "chosen without assuming the choice" marks the primordiality of the Other and engages a rupture of and from Being, truth and essence, substance and community, toward an ethical responsibility without economy, a *diachronical* responsibility:

> Immemorial, unrepresentable, invisible, the past that bypasses the present, the pluperfect past, falls into a past that is a gratuitous lapse. It cannot be recuperated by reminiscence not because of its remoteness, but because of its incommensurability with the present. The present is essence that begins and ends, beginning and end assembled in a thematizable conjunction; it is the finite in correlation with a freedom. Diachrony is the refusal of conjunction, the non-totalizable, and in this sense, infinite. But in the responsibility for the Other, for another freedom, the negativity of this anarchy, this refusal of the present, of appearing, of the immemorial, commands me and ordains me to the other, to the first one on the scene, and makes me approach him, makes me his neighbor. It thus diverges from nothingness as well as from being. It provokes this responsibility against my will, that is, by substituting me for the other as a hostage. All my inwardness is invested in the form of a despite-me, for-another. Despite-me, for-another, is signification par excellence. And it is the sense of the "oneself", that accusative that derives from no nominative; it is the very fact of finding oneself while losing oneself.[21]

The idea of justice remains precisely the insistent reference for Levinas: a justice which precedes truth and which truth presupposes and yet which remains irreducible and unassimilable to truth. And by consequence, irreducible and unassimilable to Being and essence, meaning and history. As Levinas had already marked in *Totality and Infinity*: "To account for being or to be in truth is not to comprehend or take hold of . . . , but rather to encounter the Other without allergy, that is, in justice."[22]

Justice for Levinas opens to an ethical irreducibility to knowledge, truth, or recognition and yet always instructs and corrects Being from the Good *beyond* Being, re-orienting the essence of truth and the becoming of History elsewhere than in its ownmost exigency for unity, unification, reunification, rationalization, or justification. In this sense, the idea of justice opens to the question, *beyond* and *before* the definition or the determination of Being: *How to justify Being?* That is, in which manner can justice *inspire* Being *beyond* Being?

A question which Levinas engages, in the opening pages of *Otherwise than Being, and Beyond Essence*:

> Being then would not be the construction of a cognitive subject, contrary to what idealism claims. The subject opening to the thought and truth of being, as it incontestably does, opens upon a way quite different from that which lets the subject be seen as an ontology or an understanding of being. Being would not derive from cognition. This not coming from cognition has a quite different meaning than ontology supposes. Being and cognition together signify in the proximity of the other and in a certain modality of my responsibility for the other, this response preceding any question, this saying before the said. Being signifies on the basis of the one-for-the-other, of substitution of the Same for the other. Both being and the vision of being refer to a subject that has risen earlier than being and cognition, earlier than and on this side of them, in an immemorial time which a reminiscence could not recuperate as an a priori. The "birth" of being in the questioning where the cognitive subject stands would thus refer to a before the questioning, to the anarchy of responsibility, as it were on this side of all birth. We will try, with the notion of the *saying* without the *said*, to expose such a modality of the subjective, an otherwise than being. How many conditionals here! What singular eventualities! We will have to answer for the liberties that we are thus taking with the eventual as though there were no risks, forgetting the first pages and the warnings of the *Introduction* to the *Phenomenology of Spirit*. At least the first indications of these eventualities permit us to announce the orientation of this chapter, which does not begin by running up against the finitude of the subject devoted to the relativity of a forever unfinished science. Instead, in this very finitude, taken as an outcome of the-one-for-the-other structure characteristic of proximity, we already catch sight of the excellence, the height and the signification, of responsibility, that is, of sociality, an order to which finite truth—being and consciousness—are subordinate.[23]

Beyond (*Au-delà*)

Transcending Being and essence, the Other always arrives *before* and *beyond* the Self's constitutive power, representational faculty, constitution and institution, horizon of intentionality, and thus from *above* the curvature of the intersubjective relation informing the phenomenological context through which the *alter-ego* is intentionally constituted as other Self and thereby recognized as a same transcendental Ego conforming and reducing it to the Self's presence.

For Levinas, and in sharp contrast with the phenomenological contextualization of intersubjectivity, the Other arrives in the irreducible asymmetry of a *beyond*, of an absolute transcendence from which erupts an ethical commandment which befalls and elects, subjects and awakens the Self *before* its autonomous self-constitution or institution. This ethical commandment *beyond* any measure or prevision, prediction, or community elects the Self to the ethical and to a responsibility *without* finality, a responsibility always exceeding and thus already *beyond* the Self's autonomy and will. Levinas' ethics entails a modality of excess by which the *beyond* of the Other inspires the Self *beyond* itself. This hyperbolical and heteronomous, irreducible, and unconditional ethical commandment arrives always *beyond* Being and manifestation, *beyond* essence and presence, and from this *beyond* engages the Self always *beyond* what it could determine for itself in a rational or universally normative relation with its Other.

Far from simply situating the ethical in the space of the common, in the *between* where the Other is always recognized as another Self, Levinas insists on the radicality of a rupture and separation between the Other and the Self, a rupture and separation from where emerges an *anarchy* of ethical responsibility which, wholly independent of contracts and irreducible to agreements, uniquely awakens the Self to an unsubstitutable subjectivation in an infinite responsibility for the Other. Levinas engages this *beyond* as the Good *beyond* Being, as responsibility *beyond* measure and freedom, as *beyond* the Self for the Other:

> Goodness in the subject is anarchy itself. As a responsibility for the freedom of the other, it is prior to any freedom in me, but it also precedes violence in me, which would be the contrary of freedom. For if no one is good voluntarily, no one is a slave of the Good. The plot of goodness and of the Good, outside of consciousness, outside of essence, is the exceptional plot of substitution, which the said in its dissimulated truths betrays, and conveys, before us. The I approached in responsibility is for-the-other, is a, denuding, an exposure to being affected, a pure susceptiveness. It does not posit itself, possessing itself and recognizing itself; it is consumed and delivered over, dislocates itself, loses its place, is exiled, relegates itself into itself, but as though its very skin were still a way to shelter itself in being, exposed to wounds and outrage, emptying itself in a no-grounds, to the point of substituting itself for the other, holding on to itself only as it were in the trace of its exile. What verbs like "to deliver itself", "consume itself",

"exile itself" (*se livrer, se consumer, s'exiler*), suggest by their pronominal form is not an act of reflection on oneself, of concern for oneself; it is not an act at all, but a modality of passivity which in substitution is *beyond* even passivity. To be oneself as in the trace of one's exile is to be as a pure withdrawal from oneself, and as such, an inwardness. Inwardness is not at all like a way of disposing of private matters. This inwardness without secrets is a pure witness to the inordi-nateness which already commands me, to give to the other taking the bread out of my own mouth, and making a gift of my own skin. It is not commitment that describes signification; it is signification, the-one-for-the-other characteristic of proximity, which justifies all commitment. In the non-indifference to a neighbor, where proximity is never close enough, the difference between me and the other, and the undeclinability of the subject are not effaced, as they are in the situation in which the relationship of the one with the other is understood to be reciprocal. The non-indifference to the other as other and as neighbor in which I exist is something *beyond* any commitment in the voluntary sense of the term, for it extends into my very bearing as an entity, to the point of substitution. It is at the same time prior to commitments, for it disengages in this extreme passivity an undeclinable and unique subject. Responsibility, the signification which is non-indifference, goes one way, from me to the other. In the saying of responsibility, which is an exposure to an obligation for which no one could replace me, I am unique. Peace with the other is first of all my business. The non-indifference, the saying, the responsibility, the approach, is the disengaging of the unique one responsible, me. The way I appear is a summons. I am put in the passivity of an undeclinable assignation, in the accusative, a self. Not as a particular case of the universal, an ego belonging to the concept of ego, but as I, said in the first person-I, unique in my genus. It is indeed true that this I has already become a universal in the present exposition itself. But I am capable of conceiving of a break with this universal, and the apparition of the unique I which always precedes the reflection which comes again (with an alternating which we find in the refutation and rebirth of skepticism) to include me in the concept—which I again evade or am torn up from. The uniqueness of this ego, this I, is not due to a unique trait of its nature or its character; nothing is unique, that is, refractory to concepts, except the I involved in responsibility. In signification I am disengaged as unique. In the saying in responsibility, the one is not concealed in itself, but denudes itself in recurrence, substituting itself for another on the hither side of its own identity for another. This is the only way for it to be not multiplied in this relationship, but for its unity to be brought out in it. The "never enough" of proximity, the restlessness of this peace, is the acute uniqueness of subjectivity. The subject arising in the passivity of unconditionality, in

> the expulsion outside of its being at home with itself, is undeclinable. This undeclinability is not that of transcendental subjectivity, is not an intentionality or openness upon the world, not even a world that overflows me, and in which the alleged ecstatic subjectivity is only dissimulated.[24]

Caress (*Caresse*)

It is in *Totality and Infinity*, and most specifically in the first pages of *The Phenomenology of Eros* that Levinas delivers a phenomenological description of the "sensibility" of the caress as contact which incessantly transcends sensibility itself and thus typifies a desire always searching *beyond* what can be grasped or interiorized, comprehended, intuited, or determined. Dissociating the caress from "need" which always seeks to fulfill and satisfy, by interiorization and appropriation, grasping, and seizing the object or the subject needed, Levinas typifies the caress as *desire*: desire always desiring more than the seizable or the graspable: desire for that which incessantly surpasses intuition, presence, presentation, representation, categorization, or comprehension. Levinas writes indeed:

> The caress, like contact, is sensibility. But the caress transcends the sensible. It is not that it would feel *beyond* the felt, further than the senses, that it would seize upon a sublime food while maintaining, within its relation with this ultimate felt an intention of hunger that goes unto the food promised, and given to, and deepening this hunger, as though the caress would be fed by its own hunger. The caress consists in seizing upon nothing, in soliciting what ceaselessly escapes its form toward a future never future enough, in solliciting what slips away as though *were not yet*. It *searches*, it forages. It is not an intentionality of disclosure, but a search: a movement unto the invisible. In a certain sense it expresses love but suffers from an inability to tell it. It is hungry for this very expression, in an unremitting increase of hunger.[25]

The caress defines a relation of incessant desire and unfulfillable relation toward the absolute transcendence of the infinite, of the Other: it testifies of the experience which surpasses and exceeds incessantly experience itself. Which is why Levinas insists on the non-theoretical quality of the caress: it is *metaphysical* in that it does not contend or settle for the objectifiable, the material, or the physical—it *transcends* precisely the objectifiable, the material, or the physical in searching incessantly for the irreducible otherness to the object, the physical, or the material. For Levinas, the caress opens to a *diachronic* temporality always absolving the ethical from the present: that is, as an event always coming from a futurity which already escapes its comprehension in the unifying order of presence. In this sense, the caress is not anticipation of a future as it never reduces futurity to a present in waiting or in reserve. Rather, "what the caress seeks is not situated in a perspective and in the light of the graspable."[26] In this sense, the caress opens to a futurity *without* present and incessantly abstracts itself from the order of presence. It opens to a temporality of the *not yet* from which is expressed the *immemoriality* of the ethical as infinite responsibility for the Other.

The caress can however be appropriated in the erotic relation which always transforms and converts the caress into profanation, an objectification, and engages a structure of domination and dominion. This is why Levinas insists and marks against this risk of objectification how and why the caress

> does not *act*, does not grasp possibles. The secret it forces does not inform it as an experience; it overwhelms the relation of the I with itself and with the non-I. An amorphous non-I sweeps away the I into an absolute future where it escapes itself and loses its position as a subject. Its 'intention' no longer goes forth unto the *light* unto the meaningful. Wholly passion, it is compassion for the passivity, the suffering, the evanescence of the tender.[27]

Cogito

From "Ego cogito, Ego sum," "I think, I am": the foundational proposition of Descartes' *Meditations on First Philosophy*. The term *cogito* indicates the grounding of all certain knowledge as it constitutes the self-reflexive basis by which the subject ensures a first certainty *beyond* all possible doubt: the existence of the thinking I. Having subjected external reality, perceptions, and representations, mathematical and geometrical truths to the hyperbolical and methodical doubt in the *First Meditation*, and after invoking the hypothesis of an evil genius always set to wrong him, Descartes grounds the certainty of all knowledge on the thinking Ego who cannot, without performing a blatant performative contradiction, be doubted in its thinking activity as self-reflexive validity of its own existence. By means of a hyperbolical and methodical doubt, Descartes therefore sought to establish for philosophy a *fundamentum inconcussum* or an "unshakable foundation" which is constituted and instituted in the "Ego cogito, ego sum," the "I think, I am," from which the subject can develop the theory of clear and distinct ideas which serve, together with the proofs for the existence of a benevolent God, as ground for all true and valid knowledge.

For Levinas, however, the importance of Descartes lies elsewhere than in the rational justification of true and certain, clear and distinct knowledge based on the certainty of the *cogito* and the benevolence of God within the scope of rationalism. For Levinas, the importance of Descartes's *cogito* lies rather in how it relates to the idea of the Infinite which occurs to the Ego as that which precedes and surpasses the possibility of comprehending its source or its origin. Indeed, for Levinas, the occurrence of the Infinite in the Ego far from justifying the existence of a benevolent architect in view of epistemological certainty marks that which exceeds the Self's comprehension, understanding, and rational categorization. The idea of the Infinite opens in the Ego that which always and already surpasses and overwhelms the Ego: the Other. Which entails the Self's exposition and exposedness to that which it cannot contain nor appropriate and for whom it remains always and already allied to. In this sense, the *cogito* means for Levinas an outdoing of subjectivity as autonomous will and thus reveals in the subject that which incessantly lies *beyond* and occurs *before* the subject.

This is why, always for Levinas, the *cogito* also marks a resistance to the indifference and the anonymity of Being. Indeed, the *cogito* signifies a mark of separation as a dimension of psychism and thus a break and rupture of the totality of the Same, of Sameness, of identity, and thereby a suspension and interruption of the reduction of the Self and the Other to their common inter-relationality. Notably in *Totality and Infinity*, Levinas writes:

> The *cogito*, we said, evinces separation. The being infinitely surpassing its own idea in us—God in the Cartesian terminology—subtends the evidence of the *cogito*, according to the Third *Meditation*. But the discovery of this metaphysical relation in the *cogito* constitutes chronologically only the second move of the philosopher. That there could be a chronological order distinct from the "logical" order, that there could be several moments in the progression, that there is a progression—here is separation.[28]

Separation and thus extraction from the indifference of Being and the totality of Sameness in conciliation, reconciliation, recognition, intersubjectivity, or community, the *cogito* for Levinas opens in the subject a thinking which transcends and surpasses, transports, and projects the Self always outside and *beyond* the sovereign affirmation of its own Selfhood and thereby toward an infinitely transcendent Otherness. The *cogito* opens the subject to the Other *beyond* and *before* the certainty, evidence, and assuredness of the *cogito*. As Levinas indeed remarks:

> The evidence of the *cogito*—where knowledge and the known coincide without knowledge having had to be already in operation, where knowledge

> thus involves no commitment prior to its present commitment, is at each instant at the beginning, is not in *situation* (which, moreover, is what is proper to all *evidence*, the pure experience of the present without condition or past)—cannot satisfy the critical exigency, for the commencement of the *cogito* remains antecedent to it. It does indeed mark commencement, because it is the awakening of an existence that takes charge of its own condition. But this awakening comes from the Other. Before the *cogito* existence dreams itself, as though it remained foreign to itself. It is because it suspects that it is reaming itself that it awakens. The doubt makes it seek certainty. But this suspicion, this consciousness of doubt, implies the idea of the Perfect. The knowing of the *cogito* thus refers to a relation with a Master—with the idea of infinity or of the Perfect. The idea of Infinity s neither the immanence of the *I think* nor the transcendence of the object. The *cogito* in Descartes rests on the other who is God and who has put the idea of infinity in the soul, who had taught it, and has not, like the Platonic master, simply aroused the reminiscence of former visions.[29]

The *cogito* reveals in the subject the Infinite otherness of the Other *beyond* the subject and thereby marks in the Self the ineffaceable trace of a precedence, an antecedence, a primacy of the Other incessantly calling the Self to respond to the *face* of the Other *before* knowledge, certainty, assuredness, self-determination. In *Totality and Infinity*, Levinas indeed quotes the last paragraph of the Descartes' *Third Meditation*:

> The last paragraph of the Third *Meditation* brings us to a relation with infinity in thought which overflows thought and becomes a personal relation. Contemplation turns into admiration, adoration, joy. It is a question no longer of an "infinite object" still known and thematized, but of majesty: ". . . it seems to me right to linger for a while one the contemplation of this all-perfect God, to ponder at leisure His marvellous attributes, to intuit, to admire, to adore, the incomparable beauty of this inexhaustible light, so far at least as the powers of my mind may permit, dazzled as they are by what they are endeavoring to see. For just as by faith we believe that the supreme felicity of the life to com consists in the contemplation of the Divine majesty, so do we now experience that a similar meditation, though one so much less than perfect, can enable us to enjoy the highest contentment of which we are capable in this present life . . . ." To us this paragraph appears to be not a stylistic ornament or a prudent homage to religion, but the expression of this transformation of the idea of infinity conveyed by knowledge into Majesty approached as a face.[30]

Commandment (*Commandement*)

Retrieved from the Biblical context, the ethical commandment, for Levinas, is irreducible to a norm, nor is it assimilable to a universal moral Law posed by the exercise of an autonomous rationality. The commandment is, for Levinas, always and already *singular*. It marks a *singularity*: that of an unsubstitutable election, an irrevocable obligation and injunction, that of an ethical responsibility incessantly exceeding itself for the Other. The ethical commandment as absolute transcendence is an orientation expressed in the *face* (*visage*) of the Other—an expression which orders substitution and expiation for the Other. This is why the commandment "is" unmediated *obligation* of responsibility for the Other, ethical injunction which cannot be shifted nor alleviated, claiming the Self to the point of substitution and expiation for the Other. In this sense, the commandment requests the Self *before* decision, *before* autonomy, *before* sovereignty and thus *before* the Self itself by incessantly overwhelming the Self and thus engaging it to respond *beyond* itself in infinite responsibility, substitution and expiation, for the Other.

This is why the commandment is *prior* to deliberation or judgment. The commandment commands an immediate and unmediated obedience to an inescapable, irrecusable, and undeniable responsibility for the Other. In this sense, the ethical commandment means the irreducible *exceedance* of the Infinite overwhelming the Self to its awakening as a Self *for* the Other. The commandment of the Other "shows," without phenomenality or manifestation, the Infinite, the *Illeity*, overwhelming the Self as elected to the ethical. The commandment of the Other remains transcendent and *beyond* all materialization or imagination, phenomenalization or appearance and, as such, exposes the Self to a responsibility always exceeding phenomenality, interrupting and suspending the horizon of intentionality, and which, as trace, awakening the Self to respond—infinite responsibility—*beyond* all intersubjective recognition or social contract.

Commandment *beyond* and *before* the Self to the point of emptying the Self of all sovereignty, autonomy, freedom, will, Levinas marks how and why the Other informs the ethical as irreducible to intentionality and where to respond means to incessantly exceed the response for the Other. The commandment of the Other instills and elects a responsibility as non-indifference toward the vulnerability, the singularity, and unrepresentability of the Other which ruptures and breaks the "being-there" of a subjectivity assured of its autonomy and identity, sovereignty or freedom. The commandment of the Other awakens to a responsibility in the Self *before* its free will, that is *before* any moral universal norm. This is why the commandment calls onto an ethical response which, not emanating from free choice or deliberation, elects a Self as *testimony* of the expression in the *face* of the Other—*Thou shall not kill*—and to which the Self finds itself always and already responding to the point of substitution and expiation for the Other.

The commandment of substitution and expiation for the Other—commandment to take on one's Self the fault of the Other, the fault committed by the Other—erupts from the absolute transcendence of the Other. The commandment of the Other "is" the trace of the Other. For in the wake of this commandment, the Self is emptied from its substance, essence, and identity: however, it also redefines, awakens and elects the Self ethically as that Self which must carry the weight of creation. Hence, where no other can substitute itself for the Self, the Other confers the Self its election as ethical, its unicity and uniqueness for the Other. Such is the idea of the ethical as "First Philosophy": the Self, the singularity of the Self is elected in the emptying out of its ownmost Self toward an incessant excess of response and responsibility for the Other. *Beyond* passivity and *before* activity, the election of the Self as passivity more passive than all passivity, marks the unicity of the Self's unsubstitutable responsibility, substitution, expiation for the Other. The ethical Self is wholly inspired and exceeded, overwhelmed, surpassed by the immemorial commandment of the Other in infinite responsibility for the Other.

Consciousness (*Conscience*)

For Levinas, the term "consciousness" is retrieved from Husserl's phenomenology. Consciousness means *consciousness of* . . . and thus marks the active knowing, constitution, and recognition of the Self by the Self:

> "Despite the great contribution of Husserl's philosophy to the discovery, through the notion of non-theoretical intentionality, of significations other than those of appearing, and of the subjectivity as a source of significations, defined by this upsurge and connection of meanings, a fundamental analogy is constantly affirmed by Husserl between the cognitive *consciousness of* . . . , on the one hand, and axiological or practical intentions, on the other. Between the experience of being, on the one hand, and action and desire, on the other, a rigorous parallelism is maintained. Axiology becomes a "cognition" of values or of what ought to be, and practice becomes the cognition of what is to be done or of usage objects. Sensation, a "primary content" in the *Logical Investigations*, or a *hyle* in the *Ideas*, participates in the meaningful only inasmuch as it is animated by intentionality, or constituted immanent time according to the

schema of theoretical *consciousness of* . . . in retention and protention, in memory and expectation.

And Levinas describes this structure amply:

Of course no one would deny that in the olfactory or the gustatory sensation the *openness upon* . . . , *consciousness of* . . . , or *experience of* . . . is not the dominant, that the enjoying or suffering which these sensations are do not signify like knowings, even if their signification shows itself in knowing. The distinction between a representational content and the content called affective in sensation belongs to the most ordinary psychology. But how does a signification signify, if its presentation in a theme, its shining forth, is not its signifyingness or its intelligibility, but only its manifestation, if its breakthrough into the light is not all there is to its signifyingness? This signifyingness is then conceived in the philosophical tradition of the West as a modality of its manifestation, a light 'of another color' than that which fills the theoretical intentionality, but still a light. The structure of intentionality still remains that of thought or comprehension. The affective remains an information: about oneself, about values (as in Max Scheler), about a disposition in being's essence, and at the same time, through this disposition, an understanding of essence (as in the *Stimmung* of Heidegger), an ontology, whatever be the modalities and structures of existence that overflow all that the intellectualist tradition understood by thought, but which are nonetheless packed into a logos of being. But perhaps this prior cognition and comprehension in intentionality seem to so easily accommodate themselves to significations different from thematization only because Husserl himself imperceptively introduces into his description of intention an element that is different from pure thematization: intuition fills (that is, contents or satisfies) or deceives an aim aiming emptily as its object. From the emptiness that a symbol involves with respect to the image which illustrates the symbolized, one passes to the emptiness of hunger. Here there is a desire outside of the simple *consciousness of* . . . . It is still an intention, but intention in a sense radically different from theoretical aim, and the practice that theory involves. Intention is now taken as desire, such that intention, occurring between deception and *Erfüllung*, already reduces the "objectifying act" to a specification of a tendency, rather than hunger being a particular case of "*consciousness of. . .*" *Consciousness of. . .* , correlative with manifestation, a structure of every intentionality, would, on the other hand, be, in Husserl, founding of everything that shows itself, or even the essence of all that shows itself. Does not Heidegger himself maintain the founding primacy of cognition inasmuch as being's essence which stamps

> every entity, and outside of which one cannot go, a mystery ungraspable in itself, conditions, by its very withdrawal, the entry of light, and manifests its own mystery by the disclosure of entities? The cognition that is stated in predicative judgments is naturally founded on it. Since being's essence makes truth possible, by this very essence, the subject (whatever be the name one gives it) is inseparable from knowing and the showing effected by intentionality. But cannot significations *beyond* essence, which do not signify phosphorescence and appearing, show themselves even if only by betraying themselves in their manifestation by their appearing taking on the appearances of essence, which, however, call for a reduction? Does the fact of showing oneself exhaust the sense of what does indeed show itself, but, being non-theoretical, does not function, does not signify as a monstration? Where are we to situate the residue which is neither what shows itself in the openness, nor the disclosure itself, the openness, idea or truth of what shows itself? Is it certain that manifestation founds all that manifests itself? And must it not itself be justified by what manifests itself?[31]

In this lengthy exposition and explication, Levinas poses the question: from which Law can consciousness be inspired? And furthermore, in the wake of which event can the consciousness of the Self engage itself *beyond* itself and thus respond as elected, awakened, aroused? In this sense, for Levinas, consciousness and self-consciousness, *consciousness of. . .* does not exhaust the idea of the Self. All to the contrary: It is consciousness as *consciousness of. . .* which reduces the Self, voids the Self, empties out the Self as a simple entity of measure, representation, categorization, understanding. *Consciousness of. . .* envelops and consigns the Self to being for itself and in itself. In this sense, consciousness, for Levinas, always founds and grounds a certain identity, identification, determination, and equation or equivalence of the Self to Being where being conscious means grounding and founding the meaning of Being and beings. Consciousness marks thus the place and space in which the subject appropriates Being as presence, being-present, manifestation.

But Levinas will open a *wholly other orientation* in subjectivity, an inspiration and election, one where the Self is always *preceded* by the Other and, *beyond* consciousness and *before* being *conscious of. . .* , the Self is already commanded for the Other. Radical inspiration, the Self is always and already, *before* and *beyond* its *consciousness of. . .* as intentional constitution of phenomenality and presence, inhabited and engaged by the Other for the Other. In this sense, for Levinas, the Self is wholly called to respond to that which precedes it, the Other. By and through this precedence and antecedence, the Self remains always and already irreducible to the subject's consciousness, mastery, presentation, autonomy or representation, institution or constitution.

The Other calls the Self *before* the Self's autonomy and *beyond* what the Self could categorize or identify for itself in its consciousness. What Levinas also calls the *psyche* of the Self. The Self as ethical is always and already preceded by the call and commandment of the Other. Levinas:

> The *psyche* involved in intentionality does not lie in *consciousness of. . .* , its power to thematize, or in the "truth of Being" which is discovered in it through different significations of the said. The *psyche* is the form of a peculiar dephasing, a loosening up or unclamping of identity: the Same prevented from coinciding with itself, at odds, torn up from its rest, between sleep and insomnia, panting, shivering. It is not an abdication of the Same, now alienated and slave to the other, but an abnegation of oneself fully responsible for the other. This identity is brought out by responsibility and is at the service of the other. In the form of responsibility, the psyche in the soul is the other in me, a malady of identity, both accused and self, the Same for the other, the Same by the other. *Qui pro quo*, it is a substitution, extraordinary.[32]

And furthermore:

> The animation, the very pneuma of the psyche, alterity in identity, is the identity of a body exposed to the other, becoming "for the other," the possibility of giving. The non-assemblable duality of the elements of this trope is the diachrony of the One-for-the-Other, the signifyingness of intelligibility which does not arise out of presence or out of the simultaneity of essence, of which it would be the subsiding. Intentionality is not a psyche through the thematizing it operates, whatever role manifestation has in the commencement of philosophy, and whatever necessity light has for the very signification of responsibility. The psyche in intentionality, *beyond* the correlation of the said and the saying, is due to the signifyingness of the saying and the incarnation, the diachrony; for intentionality never makes itself simultaneous with the theme it aims at, except by losing its sense, betraying itself, appearing according to the intelligibility of a system. The signification which animates the affective, the axiological, the active, the sensible, hunger, thirst, desire, admiration, is not due to the thematization one can find in them, nor to a variation or a modality of thematization. The-one-for-the-other which constitutes their signifyingness is not a knowing of being, nor some other access to essence.[33]

And Levinas engages precisely the meaning of this anteriority of consciousness: the ethical Self as "one-for-the-other":

> The one-for-the-other characteristic of the psyche, signification, is not an ordinary formal relation, but the whole gravity of the body extirpated from its conatus. It is a passivity more passive still than any passivity that is antithetical to an act, a nudity more naked than all "academic" nudity, exposed to the point of outpouring, effusion and prayer. It is a passivity that is not reducible to exposure to another's gaze. It is a vulnerability and a paining exhausting themselves like a hemorrhage, denuding even the aspect that its nudity takes on, exposing its very exposedness, expressing itself, speaking, uncovering even the projection that the very form of identity confers upon it. It is the passivity of being-for-another, which is possible only in the form of giving the very bread I eat.[34]

Death (*Mort*)

Levinas develops a sustained analysis of the question of death in *Totality and Infinity* where it is explicated in the horizon of the idea of totality. Critically retrieving Hegel's philosophy of history, most particularly in the *Preface* of the *Phenomenology of Spirit* where death is always "converted"[35] into the process of a dialectic reconciliation and thus informs, both through *negation* and its *Aufhebung*, the totality of truth as "Absolute Knowledge," Levinas also questions and contests Heidegger's existential analytic in *Being and Time*, where the existential disposition of *Being-toward-death* (*Sein-zum-Tode*) marks the resolution of the *Dasein*'s ownmost existentiality and by which is also engaged its *being-with other Daseins*.[36]

Levinas writes:

In the totality of the historiographer the death of the other is an *end*, the point at which the separated being is cast into the totality, and at which, consequently, *dying* can be passed through and past, the point from which the separated being will continue by virtue of the heritage his existence had amassed. But the psychism extracts an existence resistant to a fate that would consist in becoming nothing but the past'; interiority is the refusal to be transformed into a pure loss figuring in an alien accounting system. The death agony is precisely in this impossibility of ceasing, in the ambiguity of a time that has run out and of a mysterious time that yet remains; death is consequently not reducible to the end of a being. What 'still remains' is totally different from the future that one welcomes, that one projects forth and in a certain measure draws from oneself. For a being to whom everything happens in conformity with projects, death is an absolute event, absolutely a posteriori, open to no power, not even negation. Dying is agony because in dying a being does not come to an end while coming to an end. . . .[37]

For Levinas, death is unconvertible in a totality of meaning and knowledge: death is a resisting singularity to the universality and totality of a system in which death would always be reconciled within a narrative capable of interiorizing and ultimately appropriating and reappropriating, comprehending it within a general teleological economy of reason in and as history. Levinas is, in his manner, recalling Rosenzweig's opening pages of the *Star of Redemption* where philosophy is called to confront the undialectical, ungeneralizable, unsubstitutable singularity of death. Rosenzweig indeed had famously written in the opening pages of the *Star of Redemption* and against Hegel's system of philosophy: "If philosophy did not wish to cover its ears before the screams of our anguished humanity, it would be required to take its point of departure—and so in full consciousness—from this fact: the *nothingness* of death is 'some-thing', and each renewed nothingness of death is a further and novel 'some-thing' which, every time anew, terrifies and horrifies, and which remains impossible to quiet or to mute. Instead of the universal nothingness which, before the anguished scream of death, buries its head in the sand and engages only a universal knowledge, philosophy needs to have the courage to lend an ear to this singular scream and not shut its eyes on this ghastly reality. Nothingness is not nothing, it is 'some-thing'. And in the obscure back drop of the world rises up, as its inexhaustible presupposition, thousands of deaths; instead of the one nothingness which would really be nothing rise up thousands of *nothingnesses* which are 'some-thing' as they are multiple. The multiplicity of *nothingnesses* that philosophy presupposes, the reality of death impossible to ban from the world, which announces itself in the scream of its victims and which is impossible to choke, it is this which reveals how and why the fundamental thought of philosophy, the thought of a universal knowledge of totality, is a lie even before it is ever thought."[38]

These words are echoed in Levinas' writing, most particularly in marking the absolute singularity of death which opens to a novel dimension of signification and, without interiorizing or sublimating death in the general economy of a totality still, "flows on in a dimension of its own where it has meaning, and where a triumph over death can have meaning. This triumph is not a new *possibility* offered after the end of every possibility—but a resurrection in the son in whom the rupture of death is embodied. Death—suffocation in the impossibility of the possible—opens a passage towards descent."[39]

For Levinas, death opens not to its interiorization in a general economy of meaning where its singularity would be converted and appropriated into the possibility of fostering and spurring on a signification, a memorialization, and thus its comprehension in which one can *move on* from death, and most specifically from the death of the Other. Death opens to a meaning in itself and from itself: that of *fecundity*, and thus of a certain exigency for the Other, the Other as the "son," exigency of already being called to a responsibility *beyond* mortality for that which erupts and occurs *beyond* the Self. That is fecundity and thus natality marks that possibility to survive the end of death not because the "mortal being would survive the death that strikes at the hour common to men,"[40] but rather because evolves out of death that which it cannot appropriate or contain, that which escapes its grasp: the birth of an Other irreducible to the Self and for which the Self is responsible *beyond* its own death.

Levinas seeks to think death from natality and fecundity. Wholly otherwise than Heidegger's existential analytic, Levinas shifts the question of death away from the fundamental disposition of "*Being-toward-death*" engaging the *Dasein* in *its own and ownmost* projection and resolution, committing it to the eclosion of the meaning of Being. Indeed, Levinas extracts that which in death can instruct and inform the meaning and the signification of the history of the Self and pries open within the Self another possibility, a possibility *beyond* the Self, *beyond* the *Dasein*'s "*Being-toward-death*". This possibility *beyond* death means a responsibility for an Other irreducible to the Self. For Levinas seeks to think here the interiority of the Self as that in which and through its death ruptures and interrupts its inclusion and reappropriation within a system and comprehension of meaning. In this sense, Levinas also dismantles and deconstructs the logics of sacrifice which operate at once, albeit differently, in Hegel and in Heidegger's exposition of the question of death. As Levinas writes: "Interiority is essentially bound to the first person of the I. The separation is radical only if each being has its own time, that is, its interiority, if each time is not absorbed into the universal time. By virtue of the dimension of interiority each being declines the concept and withstands totalisation—a separation by its own force. The psychic life, which makes birth and death possible, is a dimension in being, a dimension of non-essence, *beyond* the possible and the impossible. It does not exhibit itself in history; the discontinuity of the inner life interrupts historical time. The thesis of the primacy of history constitutes an option for the comprehension of being in which interiority is sacrificed. The present work proposes another option. The real must not only be determined in its historical objectivity, but also from the *secrecy* that interrupts the continuity of historical time. Only on the basis of this secrecy is the pluralism of society possible. It attests this secrecy. [. . .] The interval of discretion or of death is a third notion between being and nothingness."[41]

It is however in the section entitled *The Will and Death* (*Totality and Infinity*, III, C, 3, pp. 232-236) that Levinas offers his most succinct and concise interpretation of the question of death. Indeed, in this section of *Totality and*

Infinity, Levinas marks the singularity of his analysis: death marks a *beyond* the duality between Being and nothingness. Death is not reducible to a moment inscribed and inscribable in the meaning of Being, nor simply relegated to nothingness. Death opens to another possible *beyond* the duality between Being and nothing, or between the possible and the impossible: "One might wonder that we contest here the truth of the thought that situates death either in nothingness or in being, as though the alternative of being and nothingness were not ultimate." And Levinas to pose the question: "Shall we deny that *tertium non datur*?"[42] And as Levinas marks, death is always irreducible to this binary alternative. Death "is contained in the refusal of this ultimate alternative."[43] Why? Levinas answers: "The unforeseeable character of death is due to the fact that it does not lie within any horizon. It is not open to grasp. It takes me without leaving me the chance I have in a struggle, for in reciprocal struggle I contend with the invisible. Struggle must not be confounded with the collision of two forces whose issue one can foresee and calculate. Struggle is already, or again, *war*, where between the forces that confront one another gapes open the interval of transcendence across which death comes and strikes without being received."[44]

As suggested, for Levinas, death in its unpredictability and unforeseeability also marks the impossibility of interiorizing it within a general economy of historical meaning and signification. It is however important to also mark how and why Levinas opens here to a radical interpretation of the question of death, namely that death can also be perpetrated by the Other. Radical, indeed, as Levinas here marks how and why his ethics as "First Philosophy" is not a simple and empty moralism. All to the contrary: Levinas marks how the "Other, inseparable from the very event of transcendence, is situated in the region from which death, possibly murder, comes. The unwonted hour of its coming approaches as the hour of fate fixed by someone. Hostile and malevolent powers, more wily, more clever than I, absolutely other and only thereby hostile retains its secret."[45] And Levinas follows through on this analysis: "Death threatens me from *beyond*. This unknown that frightens, the silence of the infinite spaces that terrify, comes from the other, and this alterity, precisely as absolute, strikes me in an evil design or in a judgment of justice."[46]

Which implies, for Levinas, that the Self, even when facing and fearing death, is always engaged by death to the aperture of a *beyond death*. Otherwise said, the Self, always confronting death and without sublimating or passing over death, brackets death by turning toward the Other. Indeed, death opens to a *beyond* the Self, the Other, and thus to an unsubstituable relation to the Other. As Levinas writes: "In the being for death of fear, I am not faced with nothingness, but faced with what *is against me*, as though murder, rather than being one of the occasions of dying, were inseparable from the essence of death, as though the approach of death remained one of the modalities of the relation with the Other."[47] Death opens to a certain relation to the Other—indeed, death can come from the Other as murder, will to murder. The Other can murder the Self. For my "death comes from an instant upon which I can in no way exercise my power. I do not run up against an obstacle which at least I touch in that collision, which, in surmounting or in enduring it, I integrate into my life, suspending its alterity. Death is a menace that approaches me as a mystery; its secrecy determines it—it approaches without being able to be assumed such that the time that separates me from my death dwindles and dwindles without end, involves a sort of last interval which my consciousness cannot traverse, and where a leap will somehow be produced from death to me. The last part of the route will be crossed without me; the time of death flows upstream; the I in its projection toward the future is overturned by a movement of imminence, pure menace which comes to me from absolute alterity."[48]

Death as it opens a relation *beyond* the Self *toward* the Other also shows the Other as a possible murderer, and thus as the murderer of the Self. Levinas sees here the Other as that foreignness and transcendence who can murder and annihilate the Self. Which also reveals another dimension of the same situation: faced with murder, the Self is also in a perpetual "postponement." Faced with murder, the Self reveals a will to postpone the instant of murder and thus to a certain evasion, escape, abstraction from the actuality of the menace of death. By reference to Poe, Levinas pursues his phenomenological analysis of the Other as murderer of the Self: "as the walls that imprison the narrator close in inexorably, he looks upon death with a look which as a look has always an expanse before it, but perceives also the uninterrupted approach of an instant infinitely future for the I who awaits it—*ultima latet*—which, in a countercurrent movement, will efface this infinitesimal—but untraversable—distance. This interference of movements across the distance that separates me from the last moment distinguishes the temporal interval from spatial distance."[49]

Levinas here shows how and why the imminence of death and its menace engages a certain *indetermination* between *menace* and *postponement*. Which engages a radical turn and pivot in this phenomenological description of the question of death. Levinas liberates, in the face of the Other as murderer of the Self, a certain *delay* and *deferment* of death and in this sense reveals an exposition of the Self, not as *ego*, but as "desire" for the Other, that is as responsibility and care for the Other: "I am exposed not merely because of a Pascalian diversion, or a fall into the anonymity of everyday life in the Heideggerian sense of the term. The enemy [the Other as murderer] or the God over whom I can have no power and who does not form a part of my world remains yet in relation with me and permits me to will, but a will that is not egoist, a will that flows into the essence of desire that is for the Other. Murder, at the origin of death, reveals a cruel world but one to the scale of human relations. The will, already betrayal and alienation of itself but postponing this betrayal, on the way to death but a death ever future, exposed to death but not *immediately*, has time to be for the Other, and thus to recover meaning despite death. [. . .] The Desire into which the threatened will dissolves no longer defends the powers of a will, but, as the goodness whose meaning death cannot efface, has its center outside of itself. We shall have to show this in the course of bringing to light the other chance that the will seizes upon in the time left it by its being against death: the founding of institutions in which the will ensures a meaningful world *beyond* death."[50]

Levinas marks thus how and why "postponement" in the face of imminent death, in the face of the Other as the murderer of the Self, *reveals* to the Self a being *against* death and thus the Self's ethical disposition for an infinite responsibility for the for the Other *beyond* death.

It is important to also mark here that this *revelation* does not mean an abdication, abandonment, or renunciation of the Self. Levinas' ethics as "First Philosophy" is not and never claimed to be a complete resignation of the Self to the Other, and certainly not when the Other engages and seeks the murder or the negation of the Self. Levinas' ethics as "First Philosophy" never aborts the Law—and most particularly the Law commanded by the Other in its defenselessness and fragility "Thou shall not kill." This is why Levinas concludes the above quoted passage with the foundation of "institutions in which the will ensures a meaningful world," that is a world which voids out the actuality of war where the Other and the Self are engaged in the murderous cycle of violence and tyranny. Levinas' ethics as "First Philosophy" does not succumb to the Platonic moral ideal which marks how and why it is higher to suffer injustice than to commit evil. For Levinas, and in this sense more Hebraic than Greek, the Self responds to the Other for the Other by incessantly upholding the Law, *Thou shall not kill* and thus in accordance to the Talmudic formulation (*Hillel*) of the Golden Rule (a formulation which, by its double negation, also puts into question the ethics of reciprocity): *Do not treat the Other in the manner in which one would not desire to be treated.*[51]

Desire (*Désir*)

Levinas always distinguishes desire from *need*, and thus differentiates desire from volition, want, and neediness which are always mundane and object-oriented. Indeed, Levinas opposes desire to the subjective pulsion of satisfying a lack or fulfilling an absence. Desire, for Levinas, rises from and is awakened in the relation to transcendence and thus to the absolute exteriority, height, and Infinity of the Other. Desire expresses itself through the relationship to the transcendent Otherness of the Other. Indeed, desire marks a singular experience where the Self is overwhelmed, deranged, besieged by the Other, by the occurrence of the *face* (*visage*) of the Other and thereby where the Self sees itself as always and already subjected to the Infinity of the Other.

The relation to the Infinite is desire where the Self is overcome by the Other—an overwhelming which, *before* the theoretical and the practical, awakens the Self to its singular desire, as responsibility, for the Other. As relation to the infinite otherness and transcendence of the Other, and where the Self is provoked and inspired *beyond* that which it can contain, comprehend, grasp, interiorize, or represent, desire expresses a concrete disposition: one which, overwhelming the Self, purports and transports the Self *beyond* itself, *beyond* what the Self can intentionally constitute and institute for itself.

Indeed, for Levinas, desire typifies an "experience" *beyond* experience, an "experience" of the *overwhelming* of experience and thereby an "experience" incessantly exceeded by what it cannot constitute and surpassed by what it can never appropriate, objectify, intuit, or represent. This "experience" *beyond* experience is also qualified by Levinas as inherently *metaphysical*, that is, as that which projects the Self *beyond* the physical, *beyond* materiality, *beyond* the object, *beyond* the traditional duality between the I and the non-I and thereby toward the transcendent Other without return or reserve: pure ethical responsibility for the infinitely otherness of the Other.

In this sense, desire *as meta*-physical, for Levinas, and thus as that which projects the Self *beyond* itself for the Other indicates an *indetermination* which animates and awakens it, elects it and names it by engaging it in an infinite movement of expropriation where the desired or the beloved, the Infinite, the Other, is never reappropriated as it remains always *beyond* conceptualization or representation, *beyond eros* and *logos*. Levinas writes in *Totality and Infinity*:

> The metaphysical desire has another intention [than satisfaction or voluptuosity]; it desires *beyond* everything that can simply complete it. It is like goodness—the Desired does not fulfill it, but deepens it. It is a generosity nourished by the Desired, and thus a relationship that is not the disappearance of distance, not a bringing together, or—to circumscribe more closely the essence of generosity and of goodness—a relationship whose positivity comes from remoteness, from separation, for it nourishes itself, one might say, with its hunger. This remoteness is radical only if desire is not the possibility of anticipating the desirable, if it does not think it beforehand, if it goes toward it aimlessly, that is, as toward an absolute, unanticipatable alterity, as one goes forth unto death. Desire is absolute if the desiring being is mortal and the Desired invisible. Invisibility does not

> denote an absence of relation; it implies relations with what is not given, of which there is no idea. Vision is an adequation of the idea with the thing, a comprehension that encompasses. Non-adequation does not denote a simple negation or an obscurity of the idea, but—*beyond* the light and the night, *beyond* the knowledge measuring beings—the inordinateness of Desire. Desire is desire for the absolutely other. Besides the hunger one satisfies, the thirst one quenches, and the senses one allays, metaphysics desires the other *beyond* satisfactions, where no gesture by the body to diminish the aspiration is possible, where it is not possible to sketch out any known caress nor invent any new caress. A desire without satisfaction which, precisely, *understands* the remoteness, the alterity, and the exteriority of the Other. For Desire, this alterity, non-adequate to the idea, has a meaning. It is understood as the alterity of the Other and of the Most-High. The very dimension of height is opened up by metaphysical Desire. That this height is no longer the heavens, but the Invisible is the very elevation of height and its nobility.[52]

Desire opens a novel relation to the Infinite. Indeed, it opens to the relation toward the Other as ethical responsibility for that which is ungraspable, unrepresentable, unmeasurable, incomprehensible and incalculable in the Other. And furthermore, as this desire can never tame itself in a satisfaction, a fulfillment or a contentment, it spurs on an exposition *without* reserve as infinite responsibility for the Other, and thus, for Levinas, as response which is always reactivated, incessantly exceeded, reanimated, surpassing itself *beyond* itself for the uniqueness and singularity of the Other. In this sense, the Other always occurs to the Self as electing in the Self an unsatiable desire for a desired (the Other) as infinite compassion for the Other. The desired (the Other) is never appropriated by the desire of the Self—for the Other always escapes the grasp of the Self; the desired (the Other) already infinitely burrowing desire, accentuates and aggravates desire, to the point of an infinite ethical compassion for the Other.

Diachrony (*Diachronie*)

From Aristotle to Heidegger, the horizon in which the question pertaining to the meaning of Being, and thus what the latter typified as the fundamental question of metaphysics has always been thought within the horizon of temporality. Indeed, throughout the history of philosophy, the relationship between Being and meaning is thought within the determination of time and temporality. This classical determination was certainly retrieved by Levinas, however also entirely rethought, requestioned, and radically displaced and shifted toward a *wholly other* formulation and signification. *Otherwise than Being, or Beyond Essence* means to undermine and question again by shifting and deconstructing, splicing and rupturing the identity between Being and meaning which thereby projects a *wholly other* idea of temporality—a temporality of responsibility infinitizing itself, exceeding itself, incessantly transcending itself for the Other—a *diachrony* interrupting and suspending the *synchrony* of Being and meaning as substance and essence in the totality of presence.

In this sense, Levinas supersedes the traditional question of temporality by inscribing within the *synchrony* of Being and meaning a *separation*, a *caesura*, or a *distinction*, thereby opening in temporality a *beyond presence* and thus the possibility of thinking toward *another* meaning than that of Being, an *otherwise than Being* and a radically novel approach to temporality, *wholly other* than presence. Which also entails another thinking of history, historical events, signification, and consciousness. In this sense, far from *negating* the question of temporality, Levinas *rethinks* this question by suspending and interrupting the traditional philosophical unification between Being as meaning and temporality as presence.

Levinas engages thus a radical shift *beyond* the essence of presence and the determination of ontological meaning by opening an *otherwise than* Being and *beyond* essence. This radical shift toward a *beyond* Being as meaning and temporality as presence reveals the *diachrony* of the ethical.

Diachrony, for Levinas, marks firstly a rupture and break of *synchrony* and *synchronization*—rupture and break which engage an irreversible, irreducible, and disinterested relation to that which occurs *beyond* presence: the Other than presence—the absolute and transcendent Other. Which engages the Self to face that which already overwhelms its intentional appropriation of temporality. Levinas marks thus, through diachrony, a *temporality out of joint* by which the *Otherwise than Being* suspends and interrupts the order of Being, and thus breaks the ontological perseverance of essence and substance by undoing, deformalizing, and disrupting the temporal order of presence and phenomenality. Diachrony points toward an irrecuperable past, an *immemorial* past, that is, a pre-original and anarchical past which remains always transcendent to the subject's transcendental grasp of temporality as co-belonging of past, present, future in the essence of presence. The question thus becomes, for Levinas:

> Can it preserve a relationship across the break of the diachrony, without, however, restoring to representation this "deep formerly" as a past that had flowed on, without signifying a "modification" of the present and thus a commencement, a principle that would be thematizable, and therefore

would be the origin of every historical or recallable past? Can it, on the contrary, remain foreign to every present, every representation, and thus signify a past more ancient than every representable origin, a pre-original and anarchical passed! The signalling of this pre-original past in the present would not again be an ontological relation.[53]And a little further:

> But how is the saying, in its primordial enigma, said? How is time temporalized such that the dia-chrony of transcendence, of the other than being, is signalled? How can transcendence withdraw from esse while being signalled in it? In what concrete case is the singular relationship with a past produced, which does not reduce this past to the immanence in which it is signalled and leaves it be past, not returning as a present nor a representation, leaves it be past without reference to some present it would have "modified," leaves it be a past, then, which can not have been an origin, a pre-original past, anarchical past?[54]

The diachrony of temporality means, for Levinas, the subjection of the temporal order of presence to its suspension and interruption. Diachrony undoes the temporal stability, gathering, belonging, or co-belonging of temporal presence. Which means: as diachrony, the *otherwise than Being* affects Being, surges in Being, as suspending and interrupting the essence of Being as presence. And in this opening to an *otherwise than presence*, occurs the *Saying* of the Other *beyond* the ontological *Said* which engages the revelation of an *immemorial past* from which the Self, without place and emplacement, and thus *before* its autonomy and sovereignty, is exposed and, passivity more passive than all passivity, remains oriented toward an unrepresentable and uncategorizable Other—and thus wholly elected to a response and a responsibility toward that which overwhelms presence and exceeds all intuition or intentional fulfillment. As Levinas writes, in *Otherwise than Being, or Beyond Essence*: the

> relationship with a past that is on the hither side of every present and every re-presentable, for not belonging to the order of presence, is included in the extraordinary and everyday event of my responsibility for the faults or the misfortune of others, in my responsibility that answers for the freedom of another, in the astonishing human fraternity in which fraternity, conceived with Cain's sober coldness, would not by itself explain the responsibility between separated beings it calls for. The freedom of another could never begin in my freedom, that is, abide in the same present, be contemporary, be representable to me. The responsibility for the other can not have begun in my commitment, in my decision. The unlimited responsibility in which I find myself comes from the hither side of my freedom, from a 'prior to every memory,' an 'ulterior to every accomplishment,' from the non-present par excellence, the non-original, the anarchical, prior to or *beyond*

> essence. The responsibility for the other is the locus in which is situated the null-site of subjectivity, where the privilege of the question 'Where?' no longer holds. The time of the said and of essence there lets the pre-original saying be heard, answers to transcendence, to a diachrony, to the irreducible divergency that opens here between the non-present and every representable divergency, which in its own way—a way to be clarified—makes a sign to the responsible one.[55]

It is important to note again that diachrony, for Levinas, and precisely in its interruption and suspension of presence, the ontological co-belonging of Being and temporality as meaning and truth, does not negate the ontological *Said*. As Levinas remarks, the diachrony of the ethical *signals* (*clignotement*) as tracing of an *immemorial* and irrecuperable past before and beyond while in the temporality of presence. Levinas here marks the temporal modality of the "Other-in-the-same"—the *immemorial* past *traces* itself from its *immemorial* transcendence in the temporality of presence thereby fracturing and interrupting its ontological perseverance. Which means: the diachronical breaks and ruptures the ontology of presence and reveals the eruption in this ontology of its suspension and interruption, the *trace* of the Other irreducible to Being and meaning.

For Levinas, diachrony marks the *trace* of the Other as the occurrence of the Infinite electing the Self *beyond* and *before* its ownmost identity and egoity. Which means that the diachrony of the Infinite engages thinking *beyond* and *before* the duality and the binarism of the "known and the unknown." As Levinas remarks:

> The plot of the Infinite is not elaborated according to the scenario of being and consciousness. The extraordinary Illeity, in its diachrony of which the present is incapable, is not an extrapolation of the finite, is not the invisible taken to be behind the visible. The refusal that the infinity opposes to assembling by reminiscence does not come to pass in the form of a veiling and does not exhaust its meaning in terms of consciousness: clarity and obscurity, or distinctness and confusion, known and unknown. The not-known and the unknowable would still refer to a present, would form a structure in it, would belong to order. Diachrony is not a difference amounting to relations between the known and the unknown, where the dissimulated and the knowable would already share the thematizable plane of essence. The transcendence of the Infinite is an irreversible divergency from the present, like that of a past that was never present.[56]

Which means: diachrony engages a *wholly other* relation between the Self and the Other—a relation where the transcendence of the Other commands a responsibility *before* the autonomy of the Self and *beyond* its capacities and capabilities—hyperbolical ethical Self which, inspired by the Infinite otherness of the *immemoriality* of the Other, is engaged to respond always *before* the call of the Other while already responding *too late* on the call of the Other.

Which entails how and why the commandment and calling, demand and plea of the Other occur *diachronically*. Indeed, for Levinas, the Other's commandment and calling, demand and plea, vulnerability and defenselessness interrupts the order of presence as it overwhelms the Self's categorial intuition, intellectual comprehension, theoretical understanding, or practical autonomy. The Other breaks the order of presence and instaures, inscribes, reveals another temporality than presence: a temporality of *without* presence which calls onto a diachronical *disjointure* between a futurity *without* finality and an immemoriality *without* origin, that is an ethical responsibility incessantly *infinitizing* itself for the Other.

A temporality of responsibility for the Other *beyond* and *before* the order of presence and which finds no fulfillment in the temporal extasies—past, present, future—as it engages into a responsibility always already irreducible to recollection or rememoration, expectation or anticipation, and presentification or representation.

Clearly differentiating the idea of diachrony from both Bergson's concept of *duration* and/or Heidegger's deployment of the temporal horizon of Being as the gathering presence of donation and the givenness of the truth of Being—where both, Bergson and Heidegger presuppose, albeit differently, a certain logic of unification and recollection—Levinas proposes to think temporality as torn between an *immemorial* antecedence, irrecuperable past, *and* a non-appropriable and irretrievable futurity *without* present, and thereby opens to the excellence of the Good *otherwise* than Being.

Diachrony, in this sense, *disjoins* the temporality of presence and—as the mark of the *otherwise than presence in presence beyond presence, otherwise than being in being beyond being*—severs the constitution of the Self by electing it to an utmost paradoxical and umpteenth *ethical aporia*: that of always responding *before* the call of the Other while also and already responding *too late* on the call of the Other. Such is Levinas' most radical ethical exigency which leads to an ethics *at the limits of the thinkable*: the commandment of the Other occurs *before* the constitution of the Self as autonomous *ego* thereby awakening and electing it to a response both *in advance* of the Other's demand and yet always responding *too late* on the plea of the Other.

Always responding *before* the call of the Other and always responding *too late* on the Other, *diachrony* projects the ethical in an *infinitization* of responsibility incessantly deranging and disordering the order of presence. That is, incessantly liberating the ethical *Saying beyond* the ontological *Said*, the absolute transcendence of the Other *beyond* the anonymity of Being and the indifference of essence. Levinas marks this *ethical aporia* which opens to the *infinitization* of responsibility for the Other in this telling passage from *Otherwise than Being, or Beyond Essence*:

> The Infinite orders to me the neighbor as a face, without being exposed to me, and does so the more imperiously that proximity narrows. The order has not been the cause of my response, nor even a question that would have preceded it in a dialogue. I find the order in my response itself, which, as a sign given to the neighbor, as a "here I am," brings me out of invisibility, out of the shadow in which my responsibility could have been evaded. This saying belongs to the very glory of which it bears witness. This way for the order to come from I know not where, this coming that is not a recalling, is not the return of a present modified or aged into a past, this non-phenomenality of the order which, *beyond* representation affects me unbeknownst to myself, "slipping into me like a thief," we have called *Illeity*. It is the coming of the order to which I am subjected before hearing it, or which I hear in my own saying. It is an august command, but one that does not constrain or dominate and leaves me outside of any correlation with its source. No structure is set up with a correlate. Thus the saying that comes to me is my own word. Authority is not somewhere, where a look could go seek it, like an idol, or assume it like a logos. It is not only outside of all intuition, but outside of all thematization, even that of symbolism. It is the pure trace of a "wandering cause," inscribed in me. An obedience preceding the hearing of the order, the anachronism of inspiration or of prophecy is, for the recuperable time of reminiscence, more paradoxical than the prediction of the future by an oracle. "Before they call, I will answer," (Isaiah, 65, 24) the formula is to be understood literally. In approaching the other I am always late for the meeting. But this singular obedience to the order to go, without understanding the order, this obedience prior to all representation, this allegiance before any oath, this responsibility prior to commitment, is precisely the *other-in-the-same*, inspiration and prophecy, the passing itself of the Infinite.[57]

The deformalization of temporality as diachrony deranges and dis-orders, overwhelms and exceeds the Self by awakening it to a response of infinite responsibility which is incessantly marked by this *ethical aporia*: the ethical Self is subjected to responding *always before* (*before* recognizing, hearing, evaluating, judging) the call of the Other and yet *always too late* on the commandment of the Other. Certainly, Levinas retrieves this incessant deformalization of temporality from a re-reading of the Husserlian notion of the *Ur-impression* which the former interprets as an *originary caesura* and thus as a originary break, gap, or hiatus within sensibility and which intentionality will always and already seek to appropriate, fulfill, and palliate. However, and despite Levinas' active interpretation of Husserl, he engages a radicality *beyond* the *originary impression* as *originary caesura* in the irreappropriable *temporal flux* of the phenomenological ego. Diachrony witnesses an *irreversible* relation toward the absolute and transcendent alterity of an irrecuperable past, a past never present and thus never reducible to a "past-present" which re-orients the ethical Self toward a futurity *without* present, irreducible to a future-present and thus toward an elected Self, elected *before* and *beyond* itself to a responsibility incessantly exceeding itself, *without* measure or limit, for the Other. Which is why Levinas always marks how and why the ethical Self and its unique and unsubstitutable responsibility for the Other is always and already impossible to synchronize: it is always and already *aporetical* and thus incessantly exceeding itself for the Other. Otherwise said, as non-indifference, host as already hostage, passivity *beyond* all passivity responding in sincerity to the glory of the Infinite as testimony or witnessing of the *immemorial* otherness of the Other to which the ethical Self *can only respond as the only one responding in* substitution and expiation for the Other:

> The glory of the Infinite is glorified only by the signification of the-one-for-the-other, as sincerity, that in my sincerity the Infinite passes the finite, that the Infinite comes to pass there, is what makes the plot of ethics primary, and what makes language irreducible to an act among acts. Before putting itself at the service of life as an exchange of information through a linguistic system, saying is witness; it is saying without the said, a sign given to the other. Sign of what? Of complicity? Of a complicity for nothing, a fraternity, a proximity that is possible only as an openness of self, an imprudent exposure to the other, a passivity without reserve, to the point of substitution. It is thus exposing of the exposure, saying, saying that does not say a word, that signifies, that, as responsibility, is signification itself, the-one-for-the-other. It is the subjectivity of the subject that makes itself a sign, which one would be wrong to take as a babbling utterance of a word, for it bears witness to the glory of the Infinite. This witness is not reducible to the relationship that leads from an index to the indicated. That would make it a disclosure and a thematization. It is the bottomless passivity of responsibility, and thus, sincerity. It is the meaning of language, before language scatters into words, into themes equal to the words and dissimulating in the said the openness of the saying exposed like a bleeding wound. But the trace of the witness given, the sincerity or glory, is not effaced even in its said. I can indeed state the meaning borne witness to as a said. It is an extraordinary word, the only one that does not extinguish or absorb its saying, but it cannot remain a simple word. The word God

is an overwhelming semantic event that subdues the subversion worked by Illeity. The glory of the Infinite shuts itself up in a word and becomes a being. But it already undoes its dwelling and unsays itself without vanishing into nothingness. It invests being in the very copula with which it receives attributes. (It is receiving them at this very moment, when this semantic adventure is here being thematized.) A said unique of its kind, it does not narrowly espouse grammatical categories like a noun (neither proper nor common noun), and does not incline exactly to logical rules, like a meaning (being an excluded middle between being and nothingness). This said gets its meaning from the witness borne, which thematization does betray in theology which introduces it into the system of a language, in the order of the said. But this abusive statement is at once forbidden. The limits of the present in which infinity betrays itself break up. Infinity is *beyond* the scope of the unity of transcendental apperception, cannot be assembled into a present, and refuses being recollected. This negation of the present and of representation finds its positive form in proximity, responsibility and substitution. This makes it different from the propositions of negative theology. The refusal of presence is converted into my presence as present, that is, as a hostage delivered over as a gift to the other. In proximity, in signification, in my giving of signs, already the Infinite speaks through the witness I bear of it, in my sincerity, in my saying without said, preoriginary saying which is said in the mouth of the very one that receives the witness. Its signification has let itself be betrayed in the logos only to convey itself before us. It is a word already stated as a kerygma in prayer or blasphemy. It thus retains in its statement the trace of the excession of transcendence, of the *beyond*.[58]

Disinterestedness (*Dés-intéressement*)

Levinas forges the term, "*dés-interessement*," by the Latin *esse*, the French *intérêt*, and the negative prefix *dé-* to mark how and why the response to the Other as Other, the infinite responsibility for the Other, occurs to the ethical Self as a radical dispossession and deprivation of its autonomy and egoity, choice and decision, essence and interest. In this sense, for Levinas, the ethical Self is always and already decentered from itself by the commandment of the Other which always precedes the question pertaining to the meaning of Being and thus already anterior to the Self's consciousness, will, or volition.

For Levinas, the response to the Other for the Other always and already presupposes the irreplaceability of the Other's commandment and the unsubstitutable election of the Self in its singular response of responsibility as giving more than what it can determine, respond more than what it can decide. *Beyond* contract or intersubjective recognition, the ethical Self is elected *before* its own Self to respond *beyond* what it could judge as sufficient or adequate for the Other. This unique form of *individuation* through the election of the Self for the Other never founds a Self as an autonomous identity or entity capable of measuring its response and calculating its engagement toward the Other. All to the contrary, the ethical Self is elected for the Other and in the wake of the Other's commandment as always and already dispossessed from practical autonomy or reflexive judgment. The responsibility for the Other occurs to the ethical Self as election and *without interest* for one's Self or appropriation of the Self.

The ethical is awakened for the Other as *disinterestedness*, that is as an-economy—responsibility given *before* and *beyond* return or expectation of a recognition or a gratitude. In this sense, for Levinas the ethical is always *without* justification, warrantedness, or assuredness. That is, the ethical Self's responsibility for the Other does not express itself as a consequence of the Self's interest nor give itself by and through its being justified or grounded in universal moral norms. Ethical responsibility as *disinterestedness* is always and already *beyond* and *before* the regime or the economy of justification, judgment, and self-interest. Which means, the ethical Self's responsibility is irreducibly and gratuitously limitless for the Other.

Irreplaceable, the Other commands from its absolute transcendence and demands the Self's escape and evasion from its selfishness and self-identity—commands the escape and the evasion from the Self's self-interestedness, escape and evasion from the economy of morality.

Ego (*Moi*)

The Latin term "*ego*" is understood, in Modern philosophy, as the "thinking subject" and thereby as source, foundation, and ground of knowing, feeling, possessing, willing, judgment, and representation. The *ego* marks the "place" of the Self as an autonomous entity always capable of determining its ownmost faculties, of constituting its experience, of appropriating exteriority in the horizon of intentionality, and of instituting the rational normativity to which it conforms and commits itself to theoretically and practically. In this sense, the *ego* implies and presupposes self-consciousness which establishes both theoretical and practical knowledge. Notably employed by Descartes, in the *Meditations on First Philosophy* (but also in the *Discourse on Method*), as the undisputable and undoubtable ground of sure and certain knowledge as foundation in Being ("*Ego cogito, ego sum*"). Also retrieved by Kant, who defines the *ego* as the *subjective a priori* synthetic unity of categorial representation and objective experience. In the phenomenological tradition, reappraising and redefining the foundational tenets of Cartesianism and Kantianism, Husserl defines the *transcendental ego* as a psychical entity *in* the world as the *constituting* entity which furnishes the intentionality of its lived-world, and by extension, the intentionality of the intersubjective sphere by which the *alter-ego* is recognized as an *other transcendental ego* in its own right.

Levinas, retrieving the history of this term, questions and ultimately undermines the classical, Modern and phenomenological definitions of the *ego*. Resuming this history where Levinas marks pointedly how and why the *ego* is not a simple, static, predetermined identity, but a constant modality of appropriation, of identification, of comprehension, Levinas indeed writes:

> The I is, over and *beyond* any individuation that can be derived from a system of references, to have identity as one's content. The I is not a being that always remains the same, but is the being whose existing consists in identifying itself, in recovering its identity throughout all that happens to it. It is the primal identity, the primordial work of identification. The I is identical in its very alterations. It represents them to itself and thinks them. The universal identity in which the heterogeneous can be embraced has the ossature of a subject, of the first person. Universal thought is an "I Think."[59]

Which means, ultimately for Levinas, that the relation between the *ego*, the I, and the Other always and already involves a reduction of the alterity of the Other. First, the *ego* reduces the alterity of the world to a "being at home with one's self"

> The way of the I against the "other" of the world consists in sojourning, in identifying oneself by existing here at home with one's self [*chez soi*]. In a world which is from the first other the I is nonetheless autochthonous. It is the very reversion of this alteration. It finds in the world a site [*lieu*] and a home [*maison*]. [. . .] The site, a medium [*le lieu, milieu*], affords means. Everything is here, everything belongs to me; everything is caught up in advance with the primordial occupying of a site, everything is comprehended. The possibility of possessing, that is, of suspending the very alterity of what is only at first other, and other relative to me, is the *way* of the Same. I am at home with myself in the world because it offers itself to or resists possession.[60]

And Second, the *ego* reduces the alterity of the Other human to its "egoism," the "egoism of ontology," and thus to the "inhumanity" of the impersonal, indifference, anonymity of universality, ontology, thematization and conceptualization, cognition and recognition:

> The existing of an existent is converted into intelligibility as *ego*; its independence is a surrender in radiation. To broach an existent from Being is simultaneously to let it be and to comprehend it. [. . .] To affirm the priority of *Being* over *existents* is to already decide the essence of philosophy; it is to subordinate the relation with someone, who is an existent, (the ethical relation), to a relation with the Being of existents, which impersonal, permits the apprehension, the domination of existents (a relationship of knowing), subordinates justice to the freedom. [. . .] Thematisation and conceptualisation, which moreover are inseparable are not peace with the other but suppression or possession of the other. For possession affirms the other, but within a negation of its independence. "I think" comes down to "I can"—to an appropriaton of what is, to an exploitation of reality.[61]

Indeed, for Levinas, the *ego* is nominative and as such institutes a reduction to itself and, as "egoism"—that is, as "identification of the Same"[62]—deploys an indifference and an anonymity incessantly suppressing the alterity of the Other. The *ego* is always, in this sense, the principle of its ownmost activity and judgment, sovereign, central point of representation, and presence already determining its ground, comprehension, identity, and selfhood for itself and in itself. For Levinas, this ownmost activity proper and appropriated by the *ego* for the *ego* implies and engages nothing less than an allergy of the Other. For Levinas however, the alterity of the Other lies *beyond* the grasp and the comprehension of the *ego*. The absolutely Other engages a relation "whose terms do not form a totality," a relation "face-to-face as delineating a distance in depth—that of conversation, of goodness, of Desire—irreducible to the synthetic activity of the understanding."[63] That is, a relation which is marked by an "irreversibility," that is, a *diachrony*, as the "*traversing* of this distance"[64] incessantly electing and awakening the Self to an ethical responsibility *beyond* the *ego*'s self-identity and in which "the Other has a right over this egoism."[65]

Levinas will mark this shift from the *ego* to the Self in *Otherwise than Being, or Beyond Essence*:

> The conjuncture in which a man is responsible for other men, the ethical relationship, which is habitually considered as belonging to a derivative or founded order, has been throughout this work approached as irreducible. It is structured as the-one-for-the-other. It signifies outside of all finality and every system, where finality is but one of the principles of systematiza-tion possible. This responsibility appears as a plot without a beginning, anarchic. No freedom, no commitment undertaken in a present, a present among

> others, recuperable, is the obverse of which this responsibility would be the reverse; but no slavery is included in the alienation of the same who is "for the other." In responsibility the Same, the *ego*, is Self summoned, provoked, as irreplaceable, and thus accused as unique in the supreme passivity of one that cannot slip away without fault. The models of being and the subject-object correlation, which are justifiable but derivative, do not depict signification, the *one-for-the-other*.[66]

Which also explains why Levinas engages a certain critique of the appropriation and apprehension of the Other as *alter-ego* in and within the horizon of a phenomenology of intersubjectivity.

The term "alter-ego," literally "other-self," is employed by Husserl in the description and explication of the other transcendental subject in the horizon of a phenomenology of intersubjectivity where the Other appears first in its otherness, foreignness, exteriority, and then, second, as identifiable and identified as *another-self* within an intentional reciprocity between the self and the other.

This term is retrieved and put into question by Levinas—who had translated, together with G. Pfeifer, Husserl's *Cartesian Meditations* into French language, published in 1931. Indeed, for Levinas, to categorize the Other as *alter-ego*—and consequently the very impulse of the phenomenology of intersubjectivity—fails to think *toward the Other* in its *absolute alterity*. For Levinas, the phenomenology of intersubjectivity reduces the Other's otherness to an intentional Sameness or identity. The *alter-ego* implies and presupposes a reduction of the absolute alterity of the Other to the identity of an intentional relationality founded and grounded on the possibility of an identification and recognition, appropriation and reappropriation within the horizon of presence where the self and the other are seen as participating in a Sameness and reduced to a commonality, identicalness, anonymity.

Levinas' retrieval of the term "alter-ego" is therefore negative, although he also salutes in which manner the founder of phenomenology, Husserl, posed and confronted the question of the Other through the task of constituting an intentional intersubjectivity, opening thus to a certain recognition of the Other. But Levinas repeatedly refuses the phenomenological reduction of the Other to its determination as *alter-ego* and, in this sense, to its conformation as *an-other-ego, an-other same self as the self*. Levinas in this sense engages toward an *ethical* responsibility always and already animating and electing the Self *beyond* and *before* the symmetry of an intersubjective community or essential Sameness between the Self and the Other. Levinas refuses thus the semblance, the identity, and the equivalence between the Other and the Self by marking the irreducible height and absolute transcendence of the Other commanding and subjecting, electing and awakening the Self *before* the Self and purporting it *beyond* its sovereign autonomy toward an infinite responsibility for the Other.

The irreducibility of the Other elects the Self to an ethical responsibility without limitation and already preceding any subjectively determined intent or autonomy, identity or decision, judgment or evaluation. For Levinas, the Other precedes the Self and, in this antecedence, elects the Self to its uniqueness, to its singularity, to its inescapable and undeniable response of responsibility toward and for the absolute otherness of the Other.

Election (*Élection*)

The approach and the commandment of the Other *elects*, that is, uniquely calls onto a singular irreplaceable Self to an infinite responsibility for the Other. The irrecusable and inescapable commandment erupting from the vulnerable and defenselessness call and plea of the Other, for Levinas, cannot *not* also *elect* a unique Self to an unconditional and unconditioned response—a response where no other can respond for the Self and where the Self takes on, in spite of its own Self, an infinite responsibility for the Other.

The idea of election designates the inauguration and awakening of the Self by the Good, by the ethical *beyond* Being as inescapable responsibility for the Other. The ethical Self is thereby elected to respond and as election engaged to the point of substitution and expiation for the Other. In this sense, the Self is chosen as accused, elected as subjected, awakened as responsibility for the Other *before* any contract or decision, autonomy or free will—anterior to any recognition or intersubjective community. For the Other precedes the structure of "being-with" the Other; and indeed Levinas insists repeatedly on how and why the ethical Self is designated and singled out to respond in responsibility *before* assuming its own selfhood and *beyond* what is to be expected from the autonomy or the sovereignty of a subjectivity.

To illustrate this election to the ethical, to the infinite responsibility incessantly exceeding itself for the Other, Levinas often quotes from Dostoevsky's *The Brothers Karamazov:* "We are responsible for all, before all, and I more than all the others." Indeed, the idea of election in Levinas' writing is by no means a mark of superiority or sovereignty, a form self-privilege over and above the Other or others; rather, it signifies the inauguration of the Self by the ethical, by the Good *beyond* Being, by the immemoriality of the Illeity of the Infinite irreducible to presence and thereby marks the ethical Self's absolute dedication and commitment for the Other in a responsibility infinitizing itself *without* finality or fulfillment and *before* assuring or ensuring its own autonomous selfhood.

The idea of election engages the Self *before* and *beyond* its ownmost identity for the Other. In this sense, the commandment of the Other is always an election which singularly designates the Self to an inescapable and ineluctable response. Which means: the commandment of the Other is not a negation of the Self, a simple effacement of will and freedom as sovereignty and autonomy; it elects the Self *beyond* will and freedom, *before* sovereignty and autonomy, for the Other.

The idea of election in Levinas' ethics as "First Philosophy" retrieves the Biblical, Judaic, and prophetic notion of "chosenness" which is commanded from the Infinite transcendence of God and, through the call of the Other, singles out a Self to an inescapable and irreducible ethical response and responsibility: "Here I am for the Other." Election thereby marks, for Levinas, an individuation where the Self is chosen, elected as already responsible for the Other and where no other but the Self can respond, no other can *substitute* itself for *my* response nor respond in *my* place.

This is why the idea of election marks a responsibility as an irrecusable individuation of the Self which does not emanate from the autonomous freedom of a sovereign transcendental subject, but rather from the transcendent Other *beyond* the Self commanding and demanding it to respond, *before* its ownmost Self and *beyond* what it can, for the Other. Election thus means to already be responding for the Other. Indeed, the Other is always, as a splinter in the skin, unsettling and awakening the Self *before* the ethical thereby carrying the ethical always *beyond* its determination and finality. As Levinas will often mark it in *Otherwise than Being, or Beyond Essence*: the Self is commanded by the Other, and this commandment is *ipso facto* an *election* whose specificity and unicity mark an assigned, inescapable and undeniable responsibility for the Other:

> To be responsible over and *beyond* one's freedom is certainly not to remain a pure result of the world. To support the universe is a crushing charge, but a divine discomfort. It is better than the merits and faults and sanctions proportionate to the freedom of one's choices. If ethical terms arise in our discourse, *before* the terms freedom and non-freedom, it is because *before* the bipolarity of good and evil presented to choice, the subject finds himself committed to the Good in the very passivity of supporting. The distinction between free and non-free would not be the ultimate distinction between humanity and inhumanity, nor the ultimate mark of sense and nonsense. To understand intelligibility does not consist in going back to the beginning. There was a time irreducible to presence, an absolute unrepresentable past. Has not the Good chosen the subject with an election recognizable in the responsibility of being hostage, to which the subject is destined, which he cannot evade without denying himself,

> and by virtue of which he is unique? A philosopher can give to this election only the signification circumscribed by responsibility for the other. This antecedence of responsibility to freedom would signify the Goodness of the Good: the necessity that the Good choose me first before I can be in a position to choose, that is, welcome its choice. That is my pre-originary susceptiveness. It is a passivity prior to all receptivity, it is transcendent. It is an antecedence prior to all representable antecendence: immemorial. The Good is before being.[67]

The idea of election entails the singularization of the ethical for the Other which befalls onto the Self to respond *without* limits, limitations, pacification, or reconciliation. The elected ethical Self responds diachronically to the commandment of the Other *before* hearing the Other's call and thus *without* reserve, calculation, or economy of exchange. The ethical Self responds in spite of itself to the Good always and already anterior to the sovereign capacity of the autonomous and sovereign subject to decide, choose, and judge. The idea of election not for privilege, but for responsibility as that which individuates and singularizes the Self to the Good *beyond* Being, and where the *ego* is transferred to the ethical, as an unsubstitutable Self responding without reserve to the irreducible suffering and defenselessness of the Other.

This idea of election powerfully animating the very heart of Levinas' ethics as "First Philosophy" differentiates it from a morality based on the subject's free will, the self's autonomy or sovereignty, nor on a morality based on a universal normativity. Levinas' ethical exigency marks the *ethical as an election*—an election which, unsurpassable and inescapable, exposes the Self for the Other, disposes and subjects the Self to an infinite responsibility to the point of substitution and expiation for the Other. As Levinas writes, in *Otherwise than Being, or Beyond Essence*:

> The response of the responsible one does not thematize the diachronical as though it were retained, remembered or historically reconstructed. It can not thematize or comprehend. Not out of weakness—to what could not be contained there corresponds no capacity. The non-present is in-comprehendible by reason of its immensity or its "superlative" humility or. for example, its goodness, which is the superlative itself. The non-present here is invisible, separated (or sacred) and thus a non-origin, an-archical. The Good cannot become present or enter into a representation. The present is a beginning in my freedom, whereas the Good is not presented to freedom; it has chosen me before I have chosen it. No one is good voluntarily. We can see the formal structure of non-freedom in a subjectivity which does not have time to choose the Good and thus is penetrated with its rays

unbeknownst to itself. But subjectivity sees this nonfreedom redeemed, exceptionally, by the goodness of the Good.[68]

Which also entails that Levinas opens to an *ethics of singularity*, that is, an ethical engagement informing the Self as infinite responsibility for the irreducible singularity of the Other. This *ethics of singularity* incessantly problematizes, in this sense, the universality of practical or moral rational norms by calling onto, and indeed expecting thus, for a *wholly other reformulation* of the relation between the singular and the universal: a reformulation entirely oriented by an idea of *justice for the singular*, and thereby of *testimony*, which suspends, interrupts and exceeds the horizon of an intersubjective relation where ultimately, for Levinas, the Other is always reduced or reducible to the Same and to that which the Self can contain and comprehend in the order of recognition, intentionality, identity, Sameness.

The idea of election thereby engages the exceptionality of the ethical as each time *singular*. It demands the incessant refusal of the reduction of the singularity of the commandment of the Other by calling on to the unicity of the Self's *infinitizing* responsibility for the Other.

Elemental (*Élémental*)

The word "elemental" typifies, for Levinas, the irremediable pre-objective and pre-subjective exteriority of the world, that which at once *exceeds* and *supersedes* both the forms of intuition and the categories of understanding. In this sense, the elemental constitutes that *in which resides* and *sojourns* the *ego*.

As said, the world *is* elemental. But the being of the world as elemental means not, for Levinas, that which stands before and against the subject's judgment, that which *stands there*, *present*, and *faces* the categorizing transcendental subject. Rather, the elemental designates the anonymous background, backdrop, and context in which resides and sojourns the Self. The elemental is thus not only the ground, but also the environment in which the I, the *ego*, abides. Which means: the elemental is inaccessible by the reflexive capacity of reason. The elemental signifies the contextual plane in which and from which entities come to manifestation, presence, presentation. It marks the ontological situation in which and from which the subject sojourns and embodies its representing and constituting activity. The elemental is the medium which contains and possesses its own density and extent: "the medium from which things come to me lies escheat, a common fund or terrain, essentially non-possessable, 'nobody's': earth, sea, light, etc. Every relation or possession is situated within the non-possessable which envelops or contains without being able to be contained. We shall call it the elemental."[69] Levinas indicates thus, in *Totality and Infinity*, that the elemental is that "ground or common terrain" which essentially is "nobody's," that is, belongs to no one and is irreappropriable by no one. Indeed, Levinas insists in *Totality and Infinity*:

> The elemental has no forms containing it; it is content without form. Or rather it has but a side: the surface of the sea and of the field, the edge of the wind; the medium upon which this side takes form is not composed of things. It unfolds in its own dimension: depth, which is inconvertible into the breadth and length in which the side of the element extends. To be sure, a thing likewise presents itself by but one unique side; but we can circle round it, and the reverse is equivalent to the obverse; all the points of view are equivalent. The depth of the element prolongs it till it is lost in the earth and in the heavens. "Nothing ends, nothing begins."[70]

The Self is *within* the elemental, or as Levinas defines it:

> He is *within* what he possesses such that we shall be able to say that the domicile, condition for all property, renders the inner life possible. The I is thus at home with itself. Through the home our relation with space as distance and extension is resubstituted for the simple "bathing in the element". But the adequate relation with the element is precisely bathing. The interiority of immersion is not convertible into exteriority.[71]

This irrepresentable and irreappropriable *middle*, the elemental, is *directly* and *immediately* accessible to *sensibility* and through *enjoyment* (*jouissance*): "Sensibility establishes a relation with a pure quality without support, with the element. Sensibility is enjoyment. The sensitive being, the body, concretizes this *way of being*, which consists in finding a condition in what, in other respects, can appear as an object of thought, as simply constituted."[72] Sensibility as enjoyment directly accesses the elemental. For sensibility and enjoyment mark a receptivity *before* intuition and understanding, anterior or antecedent to experience and conceptual representation:

> sensibility is therefore to be described not as a moment of representation, but as the instance of enjoyment. Its intention does not go in the direction of representation. It does not suffice to say that sensation lacks clarity and distinctness, as though it were situated on the plane of representation.

> Sensibility is not an inferior theoretical knowledge bound however intimately to affective states: in its very *gnosis*, sensibility is enjoyment; it is satisfied with the given, it is contented. Sensible "knowledge" does not have to surmount infinite regression, that vertigo of the understanding, it does not even experience it. It finds itself immediately at the term; it concludes, it finishes without referring to the infinite.[73]

Finition *without* reference to the infinite, finition *without* limitation, sensibility *as* enjoyment engages an exposition *before* categorial knowledge, intuition, or representation. It is by and through unmediated sensibility as enjoyment (*jouissance*) that the elemental can be reached, and where it is, for Levinas, synonymous of pure materiality. Enjoyment is thus an exposition to the materiality of sensibility itself and thus pure receptivity to the event of sensibility, always and already unseizable and ungraspable by perception, unappropriable through objectified intuition or intentional formalization.

Levinas' description and phenomenological analysis of the elemental contrasts with Heidegger's analyses, in *Being and Time* notably, of the *Dasein*'s "Being-in-the-world." Indeed, Levinas distinguishes the elemental from the "ontico-ontological" ordering of *Vorhandenheit* and *Zuhandenheit*, where entities are organized in a referential system of utilization, practice, or technical finality of utility. The elemental signifies, contrarily to the ontological referential order of *Vorhandenheit* and *Zuhandenheit*, an unmediated and immediate exposition already open to materiality *without* utility, utilization, or manipulation. However, for Levinas, this *without* is not only or simply negative. Sensibility as enjoyment opens to a certain *possibility*: "To enjoy without utility, in pure loss, gratuitously, without referring to anything else, in pure expenditure—this is the human."[74] This is why the elemental, for Levinas, is not a simple reversal of the primacy of form. The elemental is not understood as a simple anti-form or anti-formalization—a materiality replacing formalization. The elemental opens, rather, to the very possibility of rethinking a materiality which remains always active, and thus, engages a sensibility as enjoyment exposed to the Other *before* formalization, *antecedent* to presentation or representation, always and already preceding the possibility of utilization, utility, or manipulation. As Levinas remarks:

> In sensibility itself and independently of all thought there is announced an insecurity which throws back in question this quasi-eternal immemoriality of the element, which will disturb it as the *other* [. . .]. Enjoyment seems to be in touch with an *other* inasmuch as a future is announced within the element and menaces it with insecurity. We will speak further of this insecurity belonging to the order of enjoyment; for the moment what is

> important for us is to show that sensibility is of the order of enjoyment and not of the order of experience. Sensibility thus understood is not to be confused with still vacillating forms of "consciousness of".[75]

It is important here to remark how and why, for Levinas, sensibility as enjoyment exposes alterity to futurity, which is, in regard to the elemental, indissociable from insecurity. Such is, as Levinas indicates it, the mythical format of the elemental. Indeed, as Levinas writes, in stark contrast with Heidegger:

> The sensible world, overflowing the freedom of representation, does not betoken the failure of freedom, but the enjoyment of a world, a world 'for me' which already contends me. The elements do not receive man as a land of exile, humiliating and limiting his freedom. The human being does not find himself in an absurd world in which he would be *geworfen*. And this is true absolutely. The disquietude that manifests itself within the enjoyment of the element, in the overflowing of the instant that escapes the gentle mastery of enjoyment . . . .[76]

Sensibility as enjoyment opens to the alterity of a futurity ungraspable by representation or imagination. As Levinas writes: "This is not yet a representation of the future, in which the threat allows for respite and liberation. By representation the enjoyment that has recourse to labor becomes again absolutely mistress of the world, interiorizing it with respect to its dwelling. The future as insecurity is already in the pure quality which lacks the category of substance, of something."[77] Levinas marks thus how and why sensibility as enjoyment opens to the alterity of a futurity, a *coming forth*, an event. However, this futurity is that of enjoyment itself, and thus that of an alterity which is enveloped and encased in a certain anonymity, namelessness, facelessness—to which Levinas will oppose the "name of the face, where precisely an existent presents itself personally."[78] Which means: enjoyment is riveted to futurity and as such, for Levinas, the elemental enjoyed through sensibility is that of an incessant *surplus* of itself, an "ever new depth of absence, and existence without existent, the impersonal par excellence. As such, thus, the elemental through sensibility as enjoyment reveals the *il y a*, the *there is*, its indifference and "horror, trembling, and vertigo."[79]

Levinas will engage thus a rupture and break of this primary and pure sensibility of enjoyment in and through the elemental to express the pre-primordial character of a unique, singular, and unescapable responsibility for the Other outside enjoyment and sensibility: *before* and *beyond* the elemental.

Enigma (*Énigme*)

The word "enigma" is often employed by Levinas to indicate a certain paradoxality: that of the absolute transcendence—non-phenomenality and irreducibility to presence—of the Other announcing itself in the realm, the space and the order of phenomena. The word "enigma" is thus indicating a certain aporetic movement where the non-phenomenality of the Other arrives, occurs, and penetrates the phenomenal horizon, engaging the dimension of an *other signification*—the *Other-in-the-Same*—which leaves within phenomenality the trace of its absolute alterity by remaining irreducibly heterogeneous to and radically irretrievable by manifestation, presentation, representation, presence. The enigma of the *Other-in-the-Same* signifies a *rupture* of manifestation *in* manifestation—the face of the Other manifesting itself *without* manifesting itself and which fosters and keeps, preserves and reserves an absolute separation of transcendence. For Levinas, the enigma engages a re-orientation of thinking toward the transcendence of the Other as an irreducible heteronomy to presence while at the same time as *trace* appearing *without* appearance in phenomenality.

The enigma, irreducible to a matter of simple faith, irreducible to its comprehension in a determined knowledge, irretrievable to judgment, proposes and engages, fosters and furthers the possibility of an ethical language entirely undetermined, other than will, heterogeneous to the autonomy of the moral subject. It engages the Self to a response in the face of that which breaks and exceeds intuition and understanding, decision, and judgment: a responsibility always surpassing itself in a further responsibility, incessantly exceeding itself, toward the Other and irreducible to the economy of an intersubjective contract, or community. As Levinas indicates:

> "He is looking at me"—everything in him looks at me; nothing is indifferent to me. Nothing is more imperative than this abandon in the emptiness of space, this trace of infinity which passes without being able to enter. In it is hollowed out the face as a trace of an absence, as a skin with wrinkles. In the duplicity of beauty there is the strange trope of a presence which is the shadow of itself, of a being which, anachronously, lurks in its trace. Does this imperative force which is not a necessity come from this very enigma, this ambiguity of being a trace? In this enigma tends and distends the infinite, the nonoriginal and anarchic as well as infinite, which no present, no historiography, could assemble, and whose passing precedes every memorable past. A gaping open of an abyss in proximity, the infinite which blinks, refusing speculative audacities, is distinguishable from pure and

> simple nothingness by the committing of the neighbor to my responsibility. But it is also distinguishable from the *Sollen*, for proximity is not a simply asymptotic approach of its "term." Its term is not an end. The more I answer the more I am responsible; the more I approach the neighbor with which I am encharged the further away I am. This debit which increases is infinity as an infinition of the infinite, as glory.[80]

The enigma is that through which the responsibility for the Other is "seen" *without* manifestation or presentation, and thus as that which awakens and elects the Self to the ethical as responsibility always increasing and burrowing itself for the Other, and, in this sense, as inescapable and ineluctable "mineness" entirely and unequivocally for the Other to the point of substitution and expiation.

The enigma signifies the *trace* of the *otherwise than* Being *in* Being, the wholly Other of phenomenality and manifestation *in* phenomenality and manifestation: incessant ambiguity and equivocity which is not a simple negative determination but, on the contrary, the animation and vibrancy of the transcendence of the *Other than Being in Being*, of the absolute separatedness of the Other *in* the Self.

In this sense, the enigma is interruption, rupture, and *caesura* in Being of Being by the Other than Being. Interruption, rupture, and *caesura* of synchronization, intentional constitution, categorial representation—the enigma breaks and dismantles, suspends, brackets the possibility of contextualization. The enigma opens toward an infinite responsibility *without* context, unconditionally given, substitution and expiation for the Other. This is why, for Levinas, the enigma provokes an engagement in the *diachrony* of the ethical. As proximity, the enigma awakens the Self to its infinitizing responsibility for the Other—substitution and expiation—which also means that it, the enigma, reveals the ethical Saying *beyond* and *before* the ontological Said, reveals the face as

> a trace, trace of itself, trace expelled in a trace, does not signify an indeterminate phenomenon; its ambiguity is not an indetermination of a *noema*, but an invitation to the fine risk of *approach qua approach*, to the exposure of one to the other, to the exposure of this exposedness, the expression of exposure, saying. In the approach of a face the flesh becomes word, the caress a saying. The thematization of a face undoes the face and undoes the approach. The mode in which a face indicates its own absence in my responsibility requires a description that can be formed only in ethical language.[81]

This is why the enigma is not a problem for which we could find, eventually, a sound and acceptable resolution and clarification. Neither is the enigma reducible to a simple irrationality, an absence of meaning or signification. On the contrary, the enigma testifies of a *wholly other source of signification*. The enigma, as *wholly other source of signification*, interrupts the order of phenomenality and manifestation *without* negating it and yet *without* succumbing to it; it disturbs and deranges the structure of presence and the constitution of representation *without* denying it and yet *without* settling for it—in other words, the enigma inhabits presence *without* letting itself be captured and comprehended, compromised and reduced by it. Which means: the enigma opens to another, to the Other *beyond* and *before* the distinction between phenomenality and non-phenomenality, manifestation and non-manifestation, Being and non-Being.

The enigma inhabits the Self as Other *without* being captured or comprehended by the Self and thus animates and elects the ethical Self *beyond* the binarism between Self and Other by engaging it, the Self, to an excess of response, of responsiveness, of responsibility: substitution and expiation for the Other as *approach* of the transcendence of the Other. In this sense, the enigma marks the very movement of the *ethical approach beyond* and *before* the dualism of the theoretical and the practical: the Other inhabiting the Same *without* being reduced to the Same and which incessantly elects the Same to always exceed, come out of itself, express itself *beyond* and *before* itself and thus always and already *beyond* and *before* its ownness, Sameness, sovereignty toward the singularity of the Other.

Enjoyment (*Jouissance*)

The idea of enjoyment is central in *Totality and Infinity* and certainly one of the most capital in Levinas' early writings prior to the 1961 essay. It also appears significatively in *Otherwise than Being, or Beyond Essence*.

Enjoyment signifies being in a state of complete synchrony with one's experience of the world. It means to be entirely absorbed in one's immediate and unmediated relation with the world. Indeed, enjoyment signifies, foremostly for Levinas, participating and experiencing the Self itself in and through its place, its placing, its milieu, and thereby wholly enveloped in its corporeal involvement in and within the world. Enjoyment is the modality by and through which the Self experiences and fulfills its being-in-the-world. As experience of *its* world, as appropriation of the world as *its* world, enjoyment is not simply fulfilling a lack or satiating an absence; it supersedes the satisfaction of a privation. Levinas always intends to show, most particularly in *Totality and Infinity* and the analyses on "nourishment", how and why enjoyment is constitutive of "living-in" the world and thereby marks an experience of life itself as living within its "lived-world." Enjoyment is primarily: to rejoice in that which envelops the Self *before* the Self. In this sense, enjoyment inhabits the Self as a living existent in and within its pre-rational world. Enjoyment means to rejoice in the contents and the elemental materiality of the world wholly enveloping, encasing, enclosing and fulfilling the Self.

As early as *Existence and Exitents* and confirmed in *Totality and Infinity*, Levinas marks, and in sharp contrast with Heidegger's existential analytic, how the Self is not reducible to anxiety from which erupts an "anticipatory resolution," project, and ontological engagement in the meaning and temporality of Being through its unsubstitutable "Being-towards-death."

On the contrary, for Levinas, the life of the Self is "*bonheur d'être*," "joy," and "happiness," "being *in* joy and *in* happiness," and where "nourishment" and *eros* indicate a worldliness of relishing, exaltation, fulfillment, enjoyment *of* enjoyment. This is why, for Levinas, enjoyment institutes a difference between the life of the Self and the *Dasein*'s existential anxiety of and for Being as meaning and temporality. When Levinas marks this distinction, he carefully indicates how and why enjoyment is neither a dependence nor an independence, a pure passivity, or a pure positivity. Enjoyment occurs *before* the dualisms of dependence and independence, passive and positive, negation and affirmation. Enjoyment is an infused reflexivity of life with life and as life. In this sense, Levinas seeks to deploy a phenomenological description of the Self's relation to *its* world in which the Self is wholly engaged in a Desire which reveals within the Self a specific type of individuation:

> Already the I exists in an eminent sense: for one cannot imagine it as first existing and in addition endowed with happiness as an attribute added to this existence. The I exists as separated in its enjoyment, that is, as happy, and it can sacrifice its pure and simple being to happiness. It *exists* in an eminent sense; it exists above being. But in Desire the being of the I appears still higher, since it can sacrifice to its Desire its very happiness. It thus finds itself above, or at the apex, at the apogee of being by enjoying (happiness) and by desiring (truth and justice). Above being. Desire mars a sort of inversion with regard to the classical notion of substance. In it being becomes goodness: at the apogee of its being, expanded into happiness, in egoism, positing itself as *ego* here it is beating its own record, preoccupied with another being! This represents a fundamental inversion not of some one of the functions of being, a function turned from its goal, but an inversion of its very exercise of being, which suspends its spontaneous movement of existing and gives another direction to its unsurpassable apology.[82]

Enjoyment reveals the individuation of the Self which engages a transitiveness and thus a passage, a transfer, a transcending movement where is revealed, through the self-constitution of the Self, of identity, of self-recognition, of self-fulfillment, the alterity of the Other. For Levinas, enjoyment as it envelops the Self to itself through its living-in *its* world, does not simply close the Self on itself but also obliquely opens it to the Other, that is, to that which remains, in enjoyment, ungraspable and irreappropriable: the Other. Enjoyment, and in enjoyment a certain "gentleness," opens to the Desire of the Other as exposition to the revelation of the transcendence of the Other:

> The Other precisely reveals himself in his alterity not in a shock negating the I, but as the primordial phenomenon of gentleness. The whole of this work aims to show a relation with the other not only cutting across the logic of contradiction, where the other of A is the non-A, the negation of A, but also across dialectical logic, where the Same dialectically participates in and is reconciled with the other in the Unity of the system. The welcoming of the face is peaceable from the first, for it answers to the unquenchable Desire for Infinity. War itself is but a possibility and nowise a condition for it. This peaceable welcome is produced primordiality in the gentleness of the feminine face, in which, the separated being can recollect itself, because of which it *inhabits*, and in its dwelling accomplishes separation. Inhabitation and the intimacy of thee dwelling which make the separation of the human being possible thus imply a first revelation of the Other.[83]

Enjoyment occurs *beyond* and *before* binarisms as it presupposes only and uniquely the inspiration of the Other. Which, again, is why Levinas always associates enjoyment to Desire and principally to the encounter and inspiration of the Other animating and awakening, arousing and electing the Self. In effect—and Levinas' analysis already purports and engages the *passage* or the *shift* from enjoyment *to* the infinite ethical engagement for the transcendence of the Other—to savor the world in the experience of enjoyment, to enjoy consumption in itself and for itself, to enjoy enjoyment itself is also to be exposed to the revelation of that which is given and offered to the Self—the otherness of the Other. Indeed, for Levinas, the principle of egoism is the appropriation of the Self through its enjoyment of the world and that which the world offers the Self for its consumption and expenditure—*and yet*: egoism also reveals paradoxically the Other of egoism, of the Self, of the Same.

We alluded to this point above: Levinas follows here a singular phenomenological thread. The enjoyment of the world by the Self, the enjoyment of the Self enjoying itself through *its* appropriation of *its* world, always and already presupposes a transitivity which indicates, within itself, how the Self's enjoyment of itself refers and implies a relation to the Other.

Indeed, for Levinas, the Self's enjoyment of itself, of *its* own appropriation of *its* world for *its* own enjoyment, not only leads it, the Self, to its own selfhood and to a self-enclosed egoistic identity with itself. All to the contrary, for Levinas, the Self is also thrown back toward the Other. Enjoyment does not lead to a self-reflexive identity where the Self is always and already enjoying *its* own immanence; rather, for Levinas, transcendence surges in and within this enjoyment as if the Self sees itself as always and already inhabited by the Other, traversed and overwhelmed by the alterity of the Other. A transcendence which does not awaken a subject of power or individuate an autonomous *ego*, always assured and ensured of its ownmost identity through its own enjoyment. Rather, Levinas proposes a Self whose freedom to enjoy the world in appropriating it for its own consumption is always and already overcome by the Other and by the Other's call, demand, plea, and thus by a certain commandment of justice overseeing and binding the immanent pleasures of enjoyment.

The transitivity of enjoyment, for Levinas, spurs on an entirely novel modality of significance which counters and offsets the parameters of constitution and furthermore suspends and interrupts the *ego*'s transcendental institution and constitution of itself. Where constitution reduces all phenomena to an intentional content for a transcendental consciousness, enjoyment shows and reveals, in and within the constituting *ego* absorbed in its own activity, an overwhelming and overpowering event and occurrence: the antecedence of the Other and, in this precedence, the Other's commandment exceeding all intentional act of constitution.

This antecedence and precedence of the Other opens toward an undetermined ethical response for the Other, a responsibility surging from the Other's antecedence and precedence revealed in and through the experience of enjoyment. Enjoyment in this sense is seen as that experience of being overwhelmed by the Other than the Self, an alterity displacing and supplanting the *ego*'s instituting and constituting power which singularly projects the Self toward another idea of justice than retribution, and furthermore toward a wholly other idea of sociality.

However and although enjoyment, for Levinas, engages an orientation toward the ethical in infinite response to the Other as responsibility for the Other, Levinas will also insist on the ethical as *interruption* and *suspension* of the experience of enjoyment. Otherwise said, the experience of enjoyment, as it can also orient the Self away from its egoism by revealing the Other overwhelming the Self, projects it, the Self, toward a response of responsibility for the Other, and thus implies a suspension and an interruption of *its* enjoyment.

And Levinas insists: the face of the Other always resists and already refuses its appropriation and its assimilation in enjoyment. For the Self *cannot* enjoy without disfiguring. The Other claims and elects, commands and pleads the Self *beyond* and *before* itself, that is, *beyond* and *before* the Self's enjoyment. It orients toward an inescapable response to the Other's suffering, hunger and vulnerability, solitude and mortality. What Levinas also calls *love* and deploys as the *caress* which "transcends the sensible, which feels *beyond* the felt, further than the senses [. . .]. The caress consists in seizing upon nothing, in soliciting what ceaselessly escapes its form toward a future never future enough, in soliciting what slips away as though it *were not yet*. It *searches*, it forages."[84] This caress, opposed to comprehension, Levinas engages it in the realm of the ethical *beyond* and *before* enjoyment: "Transcednence is time and goes unto the Other. But the Other is not a term; he does not stop the movement of Desire. The other that Desire desires is again Desire; transcendence transcends toward him who transcends—this is the true adventure of paternity, of the trans-substantiation which permits going *beyond* the simple renewal of the possible in the inevitable senescence of the subject. Transcendence, the for the Other, the goodness correlative of the face, founds a more profound relation: the goodness of goodness."[85]

Eros (*Eros*)

The term is present most importantly in Levinas' early writings.[86] Levinas defines *eros* not as a fusion or a merging, but as an exemplary non-fusional relation to the Other. *Eros* marks a dissymmetry in the relation to the Other. Levinas clearly breaks with an entire tradition which situates the sovereign individual *ego* at the center of the erotic relationship, thereby defining it—this relationship—as a movement of concupiscent love which ultimately transforms and converts the Other into a graspable object of pleasure. All to the contrary, *eros* is thought and analyzed by Levinas as a *diachronic* relation to the alterity of the transcendent Other from which the Self can emerge as a Self.

Eros is understood by the early Levinas as a movement toward the Other and thus as a thrust, a desire where the Self is moved by an Other toward the Other always ungraspable and unperceivable, hidden and dissimulated, radically and absolutely transcendent.

Levinas thus sees in *eros* the possibility of thinking a relation to the Other which escapes and evades the entrapment and the entanglement of a fusional identity and which repudiates the egoism of a self-controlling and mastering domination of the Other. Exemplary in this analysis of *eros* is how Levinas distinguishes the erotic relation from other intersubjective relationships—camaraderie, friendship, societal, or contractual. Indeed, for Levinas, the erotic relation is exemplary as it embodies a relation to *an* Other *as* singular Other, an Other irreducible to an *alter-ego*: the feminine, the Beloved. Which is precisely why Levinas engages a novel phenomenological lexicon to approach the erotic relation: caress, desire, nudity, intimacy, proximity, virginity—terms which all mark, each specifically, the inviolability of the Other as irreducible otherness of the Other.

Levinas thinks *eros* as a relation where the Self is lov*ed before* lov*ing* the Other, that is where the Self is always and already inhabited, called, and awakened by the absolute and ungraspable alterity of the Other. Otherwise said, *to love* . . . is always, primarily, *to be loved by the Other before loving the Other*. That is: *to be called to love by and for the Other where the Self never dominates or can direct, constitute, institute the meaning, form and content, of loving the Other*. *Eros* transfigures the *ego* who "henceforth owes his identity not to his initiative of power, but to the passivity of the love received. He is passion and trouble, constant initiation into a mystery rather than initiative."[87]

Levinas marks an *eros* as passivity rather than as activity, *being loved* rather than *loving*: To love "is to love the love the Beloved bears me"[88] and in which the *ego* sees itself as always *preceded* by the Other and where the *ego* never initiates the act of loving. Rather, the *ego* is *loved* as elected and awakened to that which "is behind the gates of being."[89] In the erotic relationship is revealed how the Other precedes the Self, the Other awakens and arouses the Self, the Other elects the Self by stripping it of its sovereignty and virility.

Eros means *being loved* by the Other for the Other *before* the determined intention of *loving* the Other, of possessing or grasping, of dominating or ruling over the Other. What Levinas is here engaging in his redefinition of *eros* is nothing less than a *being loved by the Other as being called by the Other, a being summoned and commanded to respond before and beyond the autonomy or the sovereignty, the virility and power of the ego*. For Levinas, *eros* opens to the Other always and already irreducible to the Self and thus irreducible to the satisfaction of the *ego*'s will or wants. In a certain sense, Levinas engages an ethical response erupting from *being loved before the ego's act of loving*: a more original responsibility for the absolutely inviolable Other. Absolutely other than the sovereign Self's act always capable of appropriating the Other, transforming and reducing the Other to a possession, an object of pleasure, and which would mark, according to Levinas, a radical erasure and effacement of the absolute transcendence and singular alterity of the Other.

Escape (*Évasion*)

The word is the title of Levinas' first major essay, *On Escape* (1935). And thus, the idea of escape or evasion emerges at the very outset of Levinas' philosophical thinking. Furthermore, and although this term will progressively disappear from Levinas' lexicon, the inherent significance of this idea of escaping or evading the general climate of ontology, of Being, of escaping or evading the order of indifference and anonymity will remain a persistent thrust throughout the philosopher's writing and thought.

From the very first texts to the very last, Levinas will insist on a certain urgency—in the name of ethics as "First Philosophy," and thus of an ethics as infinite responsibility for the Other to the point of substitution and expiation—to escape and evade the climate of the ontological indifference always and already reducing the transcendence of the Other to the Sameness of Being. The idea of escape or evasion is seen as a radical possibility to break apart from and thereby suspend or interrupt the perseverance and permanence of Being or the fundamental essence of ontology which—by incessantly reducing the Other to the Same, the singular to the general, the exceptional and transcendent alterity of the commandment to the universality of a rational evaluation and communicability—Levinas also calls "evil." To escape or evade the climate of Being *for* the ethical, called and commanded, inspired and elected by the Other *for* the Other marks a primary disposition of the Self as always and already inspired by the Good *beyond* Being.

In *On Escape*, Levinas marks the experience of Being as a suffocating concatenation of the Self to the Self, a closing in of the Self on the Self, and thereby a situation in which the Self suffers the impossibility of extracting itself from the indifference of Being. But, at the same time, Levinas also indicates, *within* and *through* this impossibility, the "experience of its interior antagonism and of the evasion also imposing itself."[90] As with *enjoyment* or *eros*, Levinas inscribes, in his phenomenological analyses, the oblique and extraordinary possibility *beyond* and *before* phenomenality to think toward an *otherwise*, that is: to think toward an irreducible and transcendent alterity which breaks and ruptures the immanence of meaning and identity, fundamental ontology and sameness. In the impossibility of escaping Being, within the impossibility of evading the perseverance and permanence of Being incessantly reducing of the transcendence of the Other to an ontological essence of the Same, also lies the exceptional possibility of a *rupture* and *break*, *suspension* and *interruption* revealing itself from an irreducible antecedence by which occurs the absolute transcendence and heteronomy of the Other. This exceptional possibility of rupture and break, suspension and interruption "is" escape and evasion from Being *toward* the irreducible transcendence of the Other.

This is why Levinas, since *On Escape*, already seeks to transfer and engage, and indeed elect and awaken the Self toward an *otherwise than Being*, and thus toward an *otherwise than its ownmost Selfhood*: an *otherwise* as *ethical* where the autonomy and the sovereignty of the Self is voided out and emptied to be elected by the Other for the Other in infinite responsibility.

To escape, for Levinas, means to evade the climate and the horizon of Being by revealing the break and the rupture of Being *beyond* and *before* Being. That is, for the Self to empty itself out from its ownmost substantiality and essence, identity and ipseity and, without abandoning itself in a pure vacuity or nothingness, remain re-engaged and awakened, elected and subjected to respond to the calling and the commandment of the Other irreducible to the meaning or the truth of Being. At this precise point of rupture of the Sameness of Being and election toward the wholly other than Being that the Self takes on its ethical meaning, that is takes on its entire significance, *before* and *beyond* Being, as responsibility to the point of substitution and expiation for the Other.

It is thus important to note how and why for Levinas the idea of escape or evasion is not a *denegation* of the Self. Rather, for Levinas, it *opens* toward the invention of a novel manner of describing the Self, and thus toward a wholly other and novel *ethical* engagement of the Self as Self wholly elected *for* the Other.

For Levinas, escape and evasion mean to *redefine* the Self by and through a *wholly other* orientation than its own: an orientation for the Other as responsibility *before* and *beyond* the Self's autonomy for the Other. In this sense, Levinas marks how the Self is awakened and elected against its own concatenation to its ownmost Being and thereby wholly elected to responding as a singular responsibility for the Other incessantly breaking, rupturing, interrupting its own confinement in the indifference of Being. To escape Being as evasion of being one's sovereign and autonomous Self opens to a novel thinking of the Self as responsibility, substitution, and expiation, *for the Other*. The idea of escape or evasion of Being from Being, *before* and *beyond* Being toward an *otherwise* than Being, will carry Levinas to rethink the *exceptionality* of the ethical as the singularity and unicity of the Self subjected and elected to the responsibility, substitution, and expiation, for the singularity of the Other. The singularity of the Self through its escape from the indifference and anonymity of Being ultimately marks the impossibility for the Self of alleviating itself from the infinite responsibility for the Other and to the point of being at once *host* and *hostage* of the Other—at once and simultaneously, traumatized, obsessed, subjected by the Other's suffering, vulnerability, and mortality and also always and already responding as responsibility *before* and *beyond* the Other's commandment or demand.

Eschatology (*Eschatologie*)

The term appears in the opening pages of *Totality and Infinity* where Levinas interprets the "extraordinary phenomenon of prophetic eschatology" as that which ruptures the totality of war in which the individuality of the human being is negated, annihilated, sacrificed to the generality and indifference of Being. Eschatology opens to a *beyond* the totality of Being and, in this sense, projects toward an *interruption* of the historical-ontological temporality of indifference, anonymity, and namelessness. Levinas offers here a pointed meaning and reading of the term *eschatology* whose

> real import lies elsewhere. It does not introduce a teleological system into the totality; it does not consist in teaching the orientation of history. Eschatology institutes a relation with being *beyond the totality* or *beyond* history, and not with being *beyond* the past and the present [. . .]. It is a relationship with *a surplus always exterior to the totality*, as though the objective totality did not fill out the true measure of being, as though another concept, the concept of infinity, were needed to express this transcendence with regard to totality, non-encompassable within a totality and as primordial as totality.[91]

Indeed, Levinas proposes a novel formulation of what has traditionally been understood by *eschatology*. Historically, the term literally means the discourse (*logos*) on the last or ultimate (*eschatos*) times or ages, things, or events. A central concept in all monotheistic religions—Judaism, Christianity, and Islam—eschatology always signifies and informs a historical temporality founded on a teleology which, constituted through divine will, opens and engages, orients, and directs human action and deeds into the fulfillment and accomplishment of History in its comprehension with the absolueity of God. This renewed relationship is at once judgment and salvation, rule and deliverance, Law and resurrection, sentence and liberation in the revelation of a transformative redemption for all humankind. In this sense, eschatology is classically allied to peace and reconciliation *beyond* evil and despair in the historical becoming of humanity — peace and reconciliation wholly embodied and founded by and on a reunification and reconsolidation in the *love* of God.

Levinas however proposes a particular and other understanding of eschatology. Certainly, always allied to the idea and the advent of peace, eschatology for Levinas engages toward a *wholly other relation*, one *beyond totality* as *beyond History* which, without befalling into the void or meaninglessness of an-historicity, opens toward what Levinas calls a "signification without context."[92]

Eschatology breaks and ruptures the totality of war in which singularities are sacrificed in the proliferation of its rationalization. The eschatological breaks and ruptures the essence of war and thereby opens, *beyond* the destruction of the Other and Others in the immanence of the Same, toward a signification of the relation between *singular* existents *without* inscribing these in the generality and indifference of Being. Indeed, Levinas dismantles, through the idea of eschatology, the modality of reconciliation, conciliation, identification, mutuality, or commonality which always purports the reduction of concrete singularities to the abstract generality and blind universality of a totality of meaning and signification. Eschatology, for Levinas,

> as the *beyond* of history, draws beings out of the jurisdiction of history and the future; it arouses them in and calls them forth to their full responsibility. Submitting history as a whole to judgment, exterior to the very wars that mark its end, it restores to each instant its full signification in that very instant: all the causes are ready to be heard. It is not the last judgment which is decisive, but the judgment of all the instants in time, when the living are judged. The eschatological notion of judgment (contrary to the judgment of history in which Hegel wrongly saw its rationalisation) implies that beings have an identity 'before' eternity, before the accomplishment of history, before the fullness of time, while there is still time; implies that beings exist in relationship, to be sure, but on the basis of themselves and not on the basis of the totality. [. . .] The eschatological vision breaks the totality of wars and empires in which one does not speak. It does not envisage the end of history within being understood as a totality, but institutes a relation with the infinite which exceeds the totality.[93]

Levinas thinks eschatology as the rupture of the totality of the Sameness of reconciled meaning. And hence, eschatology engages a constant relation to an absolutely heteronomic commandment and transcendent law by which the Self is awakened *beyond* and *before* its autonomy and sovereignty for the Other. In a certain sense, Levinas lets eschatology *inspire* philosophy and thus defines ethics as "First Philosophy":

> Without substituting eschatology for philosophy, without philosophically "demonstrating" eschatological "truths" we can proceed from the experience of totality back to a situation where totality breaks up. Such a situation is the gleam of exteriority or of transcendence in the face of the Other. The rigorously developed concept of this transcendence is expressed by the term infinity. This revelation of infinity does not lead to the acceptance of any dogmatic content, whose philosophical rationality

> cannot be argued for in the name of the transcendental truth of the idea of infinity.[94]

As the opening of the idea of *infinity* which is revealed through the rupture of the totality of Being, eschatology engages the Self in a responsibility *without* finality—a responsibility incessantly exceeding, *infinitizing itself*, for the Other. For Levinas, eschatology is therefore not an end-point or final, ultimate, closing historicity of redemption and emancipation of History through reconciliation or comprehension. Rather, eschatology marks an "*infinition*," that is an *infinitely reiterated* ethical exigency as peace between singularities which calls and commands a responsibility *without* reconciliatory identicalness. To *hope* is thus, for Levinas, to respond in responsibility *for* Other—a responsibility *beyond* the narrative of historical rationalization and thus as responsibility as urgent and unmediated ethical response for the Other, a response never reconciling itself with itself or appeasing itself in its givenness; always supplementing itself as a response for the Other, *without* end or reserve:

> The relation with infinity cannot, to be sure, be stated in terms of experience, for infinity overflows the thought that thinks it. Its very *infinition* is produced precisely in this overflowing. The relation with infinity will have to be stated in terms other than those of objective experience; but if experience precisely means a relation with the absolutely Other, that is, with what always overflows thought, the relation with infinity accomplishes experience in the fullest sense of the word.[95]

In a certain sense, the eschatological for Levinas requires and commands a certain voiding and emptying out of any ultimate finality; it demands the eruption of the idea of the infinite transcendence of the Other as incessantly inspiring an infinitizing responsabilisation of the Self for the Other. And thus, through this idea, an incessant reiteration of responsibility as ethical Law to the point of always responding *more* than what the Self can or could respond for the Other.

Levinas' idea of responsibility as eschatology overwhelms the theological reconciliatory ideal of eschatological dialectic; indeed, Levinas insists on the ethical Good *beyond* History *in* History, *beyond* the present in the immediate urgency of a responding Self responding "Here I am for the Other" implying a responsibility *always* to engage for the Other, and thus always *futural*, always *to come* and irreducible to recognition or economy, reward or return, reconciliation or forgiveness.

The ethical, as eschatology, marks the *urgency* of a response as inextinguishable responsibility *beyond* measure and *before* any autonomous decision or choice for the Other.

Essence (*Essence*)

Essence (*essentia*)—latin translation of the Greek *ousia*—signifies the necessary *being* of a thing, of an entity, of that which "is" and thus is opposed to its *existence* (*existentia*). That is, essence is irreducible to the accidents or contingencies of such and such an existing thing or entity. Irreducible to that which can modify or alter a thing or an entity. The essence of a thing or an entity is its invariability and unchangingness; its *being* as that as which the thing or the entity deploys and gives itself as such, *its* meaning and signification.

The concept of essence is omnipresent in the history of metaphysics since Plato, who understood essence as *idea*, and Aristotle, who referred essence (*deutera ousia*) to *substance* and thereby defined essence as a property of substance: that property which cannot be removed or negated without destroying or annihilating the entity itself. Naturally, the concept of essence will be retrieved throughout Medieval philosophy as well as in the entire history of philosophical Modernity, from Descartes to Hegel. Essence will also be invoked by Husserl who will attribute to this term a central function in the method of phenomenology. Essence is, for Husserl, *eidetical* and thus constitutes the *being* of the thing or the entity; it marks in the thing or the entity that which *cannot not be* for the thing or the entity *to be*. In this sense, for Husserl, the essence is always an *a priori* and expresses that which necessarily belongs to the thing or entity by remaining the very condition by which that thing or entity *is*. This is precisely why essence always indicates that which remains invariable in a thing or entity—that which is identical in the thing itself or entity as such and thereby is not affected by exterior contingencies or accidents imposed on the thing or entity.

Levinas retrieves the concept of essence, its historical development and definition, to question and critically undermine its inherent categorization and totalization of beings in the immanence of Being as presence. Otherwise said, for Levinas, to the concept of essence as Being of beings, presence of present entities, unitary and invariant meaning of that which manifests itself, will succeed a transcendence of a signification irreducible to Being: the Other. This irreducible transcendence, the absolute alterity of the Other, this otherness to Being will open toward a *beyond essence* and thus toward that which occurs and arrives as ethical commandment and plea, demand and law irreducible to the Sameness of ontology.

This occurrence *beyond* essence and irreducible to the Same is singular and immemorial. For Levinas, *beyond* essence means the *ethical*. Which engages nothing less than the following: the ethical breaks the essential deployment and becoming of Being. Irreducible transcendence, the Other interrupts the essential deployment of the immanence of Being by referring incessantly to the irreducible heteronomy and heterogeneity of an each time singular commandment and demand: "*Thou shall not kill*" to which the Self can only respond "*Here I am for the Other*." Levinas always links the singularity of the transcendent commandment to the singularity of a response which need express itself incessantly *as* singular. In this sense, Levinas' ethical exigency is that of and for the singularity of the Other's call, engaging the singularity of the Self's response: an ethical exigency in the name of singularity.

It is here that the *otherwise than being* or *beyond essence* takes on the entirety of its unique signification: in and through the singularity of the Other's commandment and the singularity of the ethical Self's response of responsibility:

> What is positive in responsibility, outside of essence, conveys the infinite. It inverses relationships and principles, reverses the order of interest: in the measure that responsibilities are taken on they multiply. This is not a *Sollen* commanding the infinite pursuit of an ideal. The infinity of the infinite lives in going backwards. The debt increases in the measures that it is paid. This divergency perhaps deserves the name glory. The positivity of the infinite is the conversion of the response to the infinite into responsibility, into approach of the other. The Infinite is non-thematizable, gloriously exceeds every capacity, and manifests, as it were in reverse, its exorbitance in the approach of a neighbor, obedient to its measure. Subjectivity, prior to or *beyond* the free and the non-free, obliged with regard to the neighbor, is the breaking point where essence is exceeded by the infinite.[96]

To the concept of essence succeeds the irreducible and infinite transcendence of the Other commanding the Self to an ethical response of responsibility *without* end and thus infinite for the Other. As the title of *Otherwise than Being, or Beyond Essence* suggests, the heteronomy of the Other in its irreducible transcendence engages the Self not in the search and the research of essences but as elected to the ethical responsibility of responding *without* knowledge, *before* judgment and *beyond* its ownmost capacities, capabilities, will, or freedom. The question of essence is not the primary question questioning the Self: the Other questioning the Self *beyond* essence—there lies that toward which the ethical Self incessantly responds to.

It is in *Otherwise than Being, or Beyond Essence* that Levinas insists repeatedly on how essence distills the truth of the *Said* but reduces the expressive commandment of the *Saying*. The *Saying beyond* essence precedes the *Said* of essence, thereby incessantly awakening and electing the *Said* to the infinity of a response always exceeding its own configuration and inexhaustibly responding more than it can for the Other. The *Saying* elects the *Said*, the *beyond* essence *awakens* essence *beyond* itself and into the infinite accentuation and aggravation of its responsibility to the point where it always and already expresses itself *beyond* its ownmost identity or sameness.

Ethics (*Éthique*)

Levinas, inscribing his thinking within the phenomenological tradition as well as differentiating the ethical from this very filiation, repeatedly indicates how and why philosophy depends on a pre-philosophical experience which is not that of *thaumazein*, wonderment, but rather "address," "demand," and "commandment." The Other, *before* the autonomy of the Self, addresses, demands, and commands, and thus elects the Self to an infinite responsibility. This address, demand or plea, commandment and order as question, putting or calling the Self into question—questioning as being questioned as indissociable from the ethical—is understood, not as a region of metaphysics alongside theology and cosmology, but as *prima philosophia*, as "First Philosophy" which, in its absolute and irreducible singularity, always precedes, for Levinas, the generality and indifference of ontology.

The ethical is not a regional discipline founded on the comprehension, the truth, and the meaning of Being, but rather arises in and through the singular and irreducible commandment of the transcendent Other electing the Self to an infinite responsibility. Ethics as "First Philosophy," for Levinas, is irreducible to any form of classification, categorization, or taxonomy within a systematic ensemble of regions or fields. Preceding all *logoi* (epistemology, anthropology, ontology, theology, psychology, cosmology, etc.), the ethical, for Levinas, marks an immemoriality from which is expressed the demand and the commandment of an infinite responsibility *beyond* and *before* the autonomy, the sovereignty, and the spontaneity or free will of subjectivity.

Ethics as "First Philosophy" opens and engages a Self which never settles for its "for-itself" and is always and already elected for the Other by the Other:

> A calling into question of the Same—which cannot occur within the egoist spontaneity of the Same—is brought about by the Other. We name this calling into question of my spontaneity by the presence of the Other, ethics. The strangeness of the Other, his irreducibility to the I, to my thoughts and my possessions, is precisely accomplished as a calling into question of my spontaneity, as ethics. Metaphysics, transcendence, the welcoming of the Other by the Same, of the Other by me, is concretely produced as the calling into question of the Same by the other, that is as the ethics that accomplishes the critical essence of knowledge.[97]

Following the radicality of this philosophical gesture which precedes and exceeds the theoretical and the practical, Levinasian ethics engages an incessant questioning of the Self's self-assurance and self-perseverance, egoity and spontaneity, decision and judgment, will and autonomy, as it entails nothing less than the undoing and the dismantling of the Self's pretention and self-identity. Indeed, Levinas engages a profound critique of the Self's rational sovereignty and identity throughout his entire philosophical thinking and writing. Which also means: the Self is incessantly elected to the ethical *before* and *beyond* reason, understanding, will, autonomy, sovereignty, freedom. The ethical arises elsewhere than from subjective free will and autonomy, rational universality, and moral normative imperatives. The ethical means the election, *beyond* and *before* the sovereignty of reason, of a Self irremediably and unescapably responsible for the Other.

Levinas thinks the utmost radicality of the ethical when marking in which manner the Self encounters the face of the Other as commandment and demand always exceeding the universal moral norms emanating from the subject's autonomy and practical rationality. Wholly other, the Other commands the Self to an infinite responsibility *beyond* and *before* any intersubjective contractualism or universalism. The ethical is always exceptional and marks the exceptionality of the Other. The ethical as "First Philosophy" engages the exceptionality of the alterity of the Other *before* and *beyond* the intersubjective recognition of the Other or the ontological comprehension of "being-with" the Other.

This extraordinary approach of the ethical, Levinas typifies it as the dissymmetry of a *diachrony*. Indeed, the ethical marks the non-reciprocal, non-reconciliatory, non-mutual relation to the Other. The ethical reveals *beyond* manifestation and presentation the irreducible *height* and *primacy* of the Other. This non-reciprocity, non-reconciliation, non-mutuality incessantly opens, for Levinas, the Self to a response of responsibility for the Other *beyond* and *before* the capabilities and the sovereignty of the Self and irreducible to the logic of the Sameness and totality of Being implied in intersubjectivity and recognition, universality, and commonality.

The ethical implies thus a "resistance" to the violence of the Same and the indifference and anonymity of Being. That is: the ethical expresses the transcendent infinity of the Other as face which "resists possession, resists my powers. In its epiphany, in expression, the sensible, still graspable, turns into total resistance to the grasp. This mutation can occur only by the opening a new dimension."[98] Ethically, the Self does not expect or demand of the Other the reciprocity of a contract or the mutuality of an economical, calculable, or even equitable relationship. All to the contrary, the ethical informs a relationship where the Self is always and already committed to the

Other, irreplaceably and singularly elected and awakened as ethical for the Other. The ethical, for Levinas, names the infinite responsibility for the Other, and thus remains irreducible and infinitely transcendent to the Greek idea of *ethics* either as "place" (*ethos*) of a common and unified gathering between beings *or* as the inherent dispositions of the Self to a "Good life" attuned to the normativity of a shared and common reason or universality. The ethical cannot and does not settle for a common or unified gathering of Self and Other, nor for an accordance with a universal ideal of the Good, of sociality or community, nor can it contend with the autonomy of each practical subject culminating in an idea of recognition in which the Self and the Other are seen within the confines of an intersubjectivity, a Sameness reciprocally engaging one with the Other. Levinas questions precisely these ethical references: from the Greeks to Kantian morality—grounded on the idea of a moral categorical imperative revealed by the rational autonomy of the subject—and Hegelian ethics—founded on the idea of recognition and reconciliation—to the Heideggerian's typification of an "original ethics"[99] expressing itself, before the theoretical and practical, as the meaning and truth of Being where community is determined by the unsubstitutable "being-toward-death" of each *Dasein* and the "essential sacrifice each *Dasein* must take on for itself without which there would never be camaraderie."[100]

Levinas engages the ethical as exposition and election of the Self *before* and *beyond* the Self to and by the heteronomy of the commandment expressed in the face of the Other. This shift is however not a simple reversal from autonomy of the Self to heteronomy of the Other. Levinas' gesture is rather to think a *wholly other source of signification* for the ethical, outside the binarism of autonomy and heteronomy, immanence and transcendence, identity and difference: an ethical responsibility emanating from a *diachrony* which singularly elects the Self to respond *before* the commandment of the Other and *beyond* what the Self can or could respond for the Other as well as *beyond* what the Other can expect or suppose of the Self's response.

Levinas orients thinking toward a *hyperbolical ethics before and beyond phenomenology*. This *before and beyond phenomenology* deploys itself as *language*. Indeed, the ethical means the hyperbolical possibility of *expressing* a responsibility *before* the unconditional spontaneity of the subject's freedom and *beyond* what its universal normativity could institute for it as an autonomous and rational being. Otherwise said, Levinas engages toward a *hyperbolical* responsibility which entails an ethical Self responding *diachronically*: elected to respond *before* recognizing the call of the Other and at the same time *beyond* what it, the Self, does, can or could respond in its responsibility for the Other. As Levinas indeed marks it in *Otherwise than Being, or Beyond Essence*:

> Ethical language, which phenomenology resorts to in order to mark its own interruption, does not come from an ethical intervention laid out over descriptions, it is the very meaning of approach, which contrasts with knowing. No language other than ethics could be equal to the paradox which phenomenological description enters when, starting with the disclosure, the appearing of a neighbor, it reads it in its trace, which orders the face according to a diachrony which cannot be synchronized in representation. A description that at the beginning knows only being and *beyond* being turns into ethical language. The enigma in which transcendence comes to flesh has to be distinguished from arbitrariness and illusions. The exteriority of Illeity, refractory to disclosure and manifestation, is a having-to-be in the face of another. In it there is announced not a *Sollen*, which is always asymptotic, but *glory*.[101]

Evil (*Mal*)

Contrarily, to a determined tradition in the history of philosophy, Levinas does not define evil as a privation, a lack, an absence, a diminution, or a deficiency. Rather, evil is thought as unjustifiable and unsurpassable violence: that of effacing and negating the Other as Other, reducing the absolute alterity of the Other to the Sameness of the general, the universal, the ontological totality of identity. In this sense, evil is defined as the full presence and suffocating essence of Being which always and already reduces, negates and annihilates the singularity of the Other. In this sense, evil, for Levinas, means to eradicate the Otherness of the Other in the Sameness of Being and thereby reduce the Other to an ontological and historical indifference, anonymity, comprehension, and grasp always purporting Sameness and identicalness. Evil is therefore, for Levinas, always associated with ontology, the indifference of Being, the Sameness of the Same, the anonymity of essence, identity as concept, where are always comprehended and reconciled, and thus annulled and annihilated, the Otherness of the Other into an all-encompassing and all-embracing totality of meaning and signification.

Evil is thereby manifest as the presence and historical perseverance of Being, its whole and totalizing truth, which also implies and symbolizes the effacement of the Other in the ontological Sameness where alterity is grasped and seized in the indifference of a generalized uniformity and homogeneousness.

For Levinas, Being is *without* limit and thus has no exteriority, no outside, no Other which could break or rupture its plenitude, its auto-affirmation and essential projection of itself by itself. This essence of Being embodies, for Levinas, the *positivity of evil*: "Being is evil, not because it is finite, but rather because it is without limits."[102] This is also why Levinas marks evil as a complete depersonalization and, in this sense, as the reification of the Other within the indifference and anonymity of Being.

In *Useless Suffering*,[103] which engages a radical critique of theodicy, Levinas situates evil in the pure suffering of the Other. Unassumable and unjustifiable, this pure evil provokes the question of "salvation," that is, of escaping or evading the asphyxiating presence and essence of Being: "Is not the evil of suffering—extreme passivity, impotence, abandonment and solitude—also the unassumable and thus the possibility of a half opening and, more precisely, the possibility that wherever a moan, a cry, a groan or a sigh happen there is the original call for aid for curative help, for help from the other whose alterity, whose exteriority promises salvation?" Retrieving and reinterpreting the *Book of Job*, Levinas marks the *uselessness* of evil as *useless* suffering, that is, the radical impossibility of converting evil into a meaningful moment in the composition, constitution, or institution of a historical narrative. It is precisely at the point of this impossibility for evil to be converted and sublimated in the determination of a general historical economy of meaning, that Levinas points toward a *beyond* theodicy, *beyond* the narrative of reason in History: "For pure suffering, which is intrinsically meaningless and condemned to itself without exit, a *beyond* takes shape in the inter-human."[104] Indeed, for Levinas, this *beyond* engages a wholly other relation to the Other human. And thereby, also a distinction between the Self and the Other:

> of nameless sufferings, but in which the suffering of suffering, the suffering for the useless suffering of the other person, the just suffering in me for the unjustifiable suffering of the Other, opens upon suffering the ethical perspective of the inter-human. In this perspective a radical difference develops between suffering in the Other, which for me is unpardonable and solicits me and calls me, and suffering in me, my own adventure of suffering, whose constitutional or congenital uselessness can take on a meaning, the only meaning to which suffering is susceptible, in becoming a suffering for the suffering—be it inexorable—of someone else. It is this attention to the Other which, across the cruelties of our century—despite these cruelties, because of these cruelties—can be affirmed as the very bond of human subjectivity, even to the point of being raised to a supreme ethical principle—the only one which it is not possible to contest—a principle which can go so far as to command the hopes and practical discipline of vast human groups.[105]

It is important to note here how and why the experience of suffering as unjustifiable evil is here marking the Self's responsibility for the unbearable suffering of the Other: that is, the ethical Self's infinite responsibility—ethical—for the Other's singular suffering.

> To envisage suffering, as I have just attempted to do, in the inter-human perspective—that is, as meaningful in me, useless in the Other does not consist in adopting a relative point of view on it, but in restoring it to the dimensions of meaning outside of which the immanent and savage concreteness of evil in a consciousness is but an abstraction. To think suffering in an inter-human perspective does not amount to seeing it in the coexistence of a multiplicity of consciousnesses or in a social determinism, accompanied by the simple knowledge that people in society can have of their neighbourliness or of their common destiny. [. . .] Properly speaking, the inter-human lies in a non-indifference of one to another, in a responsibility of one for another. The inter-human is prior to the reciprocity of this responsibility, which inscribes itself in impersonal laws, and becomes superimposed on the pure altruism of this responsibility inscribed in the ethical position of the self as self. It is prior to every contact which would signify precisely the moment of reciprocity where it can, to be sure, continue, but where it can also attenuate or extinguish altruism and disinterestedness. The order of politics—post-ethical or pre-ethical—which inaugurates the "social contract" is neither the sufficient condition nor the necessary outcome of ethics.[106]

Thinking evil as the full and fulfilled presence of Being engages an upheaval and an urgency: that of *escaping* and *evading* the ontological indifference and anonymity, reciprocity, and disinterestedness of the Same by responding to the exceptional and singular commandment of the Other whose call, plea, and address suspends and interrupts the "*il y a*" of Being and elects, that is, individualizes the Self to the ethical *beyond* Being, that is, to the *Good otherwise than Being*.

For Levinas, the ethical refuses, through the address and the commandment of the Other, to grasp the alterity of the Other as a moment or an instance of ontological Sameness or historical normative universality. In this sense, evil is understood as the annihilating reduction of the Other to the Same which constitutes the fundamental orientation, according to Levinas, of Western philosophy and theodicy. Levinas writes indeed: "Western philosophy has most often been an ontology: a reduction of the Other to the Same by the interposition of a middle and neutral term that ensures the comprehension of Being."[107]

To escape this reduction means to liberate the *Good beyond Being*, an *otherwise than Being* which, far from an egology, far from thematization and conceptualization always engaging the "suppression and the oppression of the Other"[108] opens to what Levinas calls the "nakedness of the face" which is "not presented to me because I disclose it" but "supplicates and commands, that can supplicate only because it demands, deprived of everything because entitled to everything, and which one recognises in giving": "the epiphany of the face as a face. The nakedness of the face is destituteness. To recognise the Other is to recognise a hunger. To recognise the Other is to give. But it is to give to the master, to the lord, to him whom one approaches as You in a dimension of height."[109]

Expiation (*Expiation*)

The idea of expiation is evoked and developed in *Otherwise than Being, or Beyond Essence* and is closely related to the modality of substitution. Levinas indeed often couples substitution for the Other with expiation—and thereby opens, through these two ideas, a certain form of ethical disposition *beyond* Being, *before* the Self's autonomy and self-determination, and thus resolutely engaged in and toward a novel source of significance, wholly other than identity or Sameness and which embodies the "One-for-the-Other" as "Other-in-the-Same."

The idea of expiation is to understand in line with Levinas' redefinition of forgiveness and pardon. Indeed, expiation never means pardon of a fault committed, of a wrong caused, of an injury enacted. Rather, for Levinas, expiation engages the possibility of carrying the Other's vulnerability *before* and *beyond* one's Self. Expiation thereby entails the infinitization of a responsibility for the Other which is elected as ethical *before* and *beyond* the commandment of the Other. Expiation for the Other means thus to respond to the Other *before* the call of the Other and always exceeding, always beyond the demand of the Other. In other words, expiation engages the ethical as *support* of the Other *before* the Other and *beyond* what the Self can give to the Other. Expiation thereby means to give *beyond* giving and *before* being asked to give for the Other—*before* the Other *beyond* the Other. For Levinas, expiation engages an *incessance of expiation*—and indeed, in this *diachrony* of the ethical Self always responding *before* the Other and *beyond* what the Other can expect from the Self, lies a perpetual pleading and reiteration of forgiveness. As if the ethical Self incessantly expressed in its *infinitizing* responsibility for the Other: *forgive me for responding too late, always too late to your call, while precisely responding before your commandment.*

Here lies the extraordinary aspect in Levinas' ethics as "First Philosophy": how and why expiation, while engaging an incessance of the plea for forgiveness, also and at the same time proposes to think the possibility of an expiation, that is, a certain type of forgiveness *without* conciliation or reconciliation or, otherwise said, an *irreconciliation* as infinite responsibility for the Other. Expiation, "originary expiation,"[110] as Levinas writes, means: a forgiveness *without* conciliation or reconciliation as infinite responsibility for the Other incessantly responding *before* the call of the Other and *beyond* what the Other can expect in response—that is, also, *before* and *beyond* the Self's sovereignty and autonomy.

Is opened here nothing less than an hyperbolic response of responsibility where the ethical Self is never with itself, "in itself" and "for itself," and thus always and already engaged, elected, taken, obsessed by the Other for the Other, always at once asking for forgiveness and yet always giving more to the Other than forgiveness: expiation *without* conciliation or reconciliation, that is, mending, caring, incessant givenness *beyond* and *before* what can be termed or fixed, determined or projected, planned or consigned. As Levinas marks:

> In expiation, on a point of the essence there weighs the rest of the essence, to the point of expelling it. The self, the subjection or subjectivity of the subject, is the very over-emphasis of a responsibility for creation. Responsibility for the other, for what has not begun in me is responsibility in the innocence of being a hostage. My substitution for another is the trope of a sense that does not belong to the empirical order of psychological events, an *Einfuhlung* or a compassion which signify by virtue of this sense.[111]

For Levinas, expiation engages an interruption and suspension of the tropes of conciliation and reconciliation and thus marks where the ethical Self is elected as a creature already engaged in creating an infinitizing responsibility for the Other. Which means: expiation for the Other translates the *diachrony* of the ethical where the Self always responds *before* its autonomy and *before* the commandment of the Other *as* already *beyond* its own capacities and *beyond* what could be demanded by the Other. Expiation means thus to incessantly respond to the Other for the Other, *before* and *beyond* the Self's identity and *before* and *beyond* the Other's calling or commandment.

This is precisely why, for Levinas,

> The ego is not an entity 'capable' of expiating for the others: it is this *original expiation*. This expiation is involuntary, for it is prior to the will's initiative (prior to the origin). It is as though the unity and uniqueness of the ego were already the hold on itself of the gravity of the other. In this sense the self is goodness, or under the exigency for an abandon of all having, of all one's own and all /or oneself, to the point of substitution. Goodness is, we have said, the sole attribute which does not introduce multiplicity into the One that a subject is, for it is distinct from the One. If it showed itself to

> the one, it would no longer be a goodness in it. Goodness invests me in my obedience to the hidden Good. The individuation or superindividuation of the ego consists in being in itself, in its skin, without sharing the eonatus essendi of all beings which are beings in themselves. It consists in my being faced with everything that is only because I am by regard for all that is. It is an expiating for being. The self is the very fact of being exposed under the accusation that cannot be assumed, where the ego supports the others, unlike the certainty of the ego that rejoins itself in freedom.[112]

Expression (*Expression*)

The face of the Other is expression: the face of the Other *expresses, beyond* phenomenality, *beyond* words and signs, its immemorial commandment: "*Thou shalt not kill*" to which the ethical Self responds "*Here I am for the Other*." Levinas insists on the face of the Other as irreducible expression *beyond* presentation and unassimilable to intentionality. Expression *informs* and, as pure unconditional signifier, calls *beyond* the intentionality of a sign toward an ethical relation, that is, an alliance between the Law, language, and the face of the Other:

> Expression manifests the presence of Being, but not by simply drawing aside the veil of the phenomenon. It is of itself presence of a face, and hence appeal and teaching, *entry into relation* with me—the ethical relation. And expression does not manifest the presence of being by referring rom the sign to the signified; it presents the signifier. The signifier, he who gives a sign is not signified. It is necessary to have already been in the society of signifiers for the sign to be able to appear as a sign. Hence, the signifier must present himself before every sign, by himself—present a face.[113]

Expression, for Levinas, is the occurrence of the face of the Other which incessantly commands *beyond* intention and whose commandment overwhelms thematization, signification, judgment, and categorization. Expression of the Other as face—that is, as ethical commandment *beyond* phenomenality—occurs as rupture, suspension, interruption of the *play* between the signifier and the signified. The expression of the Other engages, for Levinas, the exceptionality of a response *beyond* and *before* the Self's autonomy or sovereignty. It engages, as election, an ethical Self which singularly expresses its response *without* reserve, *without* restraint, urgent and immediate, a response of infinite responsibility as substitution and expiation for the Other.

The notion of expression, for Levinas, marks the excess of the face of the Other always and already surpassing the order of manifestation and signification. The face of the Other expresses its commandment *beyond* phenomenality as interruption of manifestation and signification: it expresses itself *without* mediation calling the Self immediately to the ethical. Which is why, for Levinas, expression remains irreducible to signification and, as rupture of the phenomenal order, marks the "primordial event of signification" before the order of signification: the Other.

This is why, for Levinas, the face of the Other as expression is not a moment inscribed in and within a general intentionality of signification. In this sense, Levinas maintains that the face of the Other, its expression as immemorial commandment, is more ancient than the signification of the sign.

Why and how? As expression, argues Levinas, is the *givenness* of a commandment incessantly overwhelming the possibility of its comprehension engaging, calling, demanding of language an excess of its own expressivity: *this excess is the ethical*. Expression is givenness of signification. And in this sense, expression is always the *excess of expressivity*: the commandment of the Other, the plea of the face of the Other which demands not its inscription in the general economy of meaning and signification but rather and wholly otherwise: the interruption and rupture of the dynamic play between the signified and the signifier. That is, the ethical suspension of the general economy, anonymous and indifferent, of meaning and signification.

This is why, for Levinas, expression always opens toward a thinking of the *excess* as ethical demand and commandment in the face of the Other. Indeed, expression as that which commands *beyond* sign and signification and yet inscribes itself in the occurrence of the face of the Other, elects the Self to escape the play of signification between signifier and signified and thus awakens the Self to evade the classical relation between a commandant and a commanded, between heteronomy and autonomy. It is precisely this escape which engages the ethical as an incessant expression arising from a *before* the binarism of presence and absence, immanence and transcendence, law and love—the expression of the Other as commanding *before* all binarisms and, at the same time, as engaging toward an incessant excess of responsibility for the Other in the face of the vulnerability and defenselessness of the Other.

Expression *says* the vulnerability and the singularity of the Other *beyond* words and *before* signs—it calls onto an infinite responsibility, a response *without* reserve incessantly outdoing the possibilities of taming, converting or subduing it. Expression instills the commandment and demand, appeal and plea, *beyond* and *before* thematization or categorization, to a responsibility *without arché* or *telos*. Expression is thus always and already *of the Other* in that it emanates *from the Other* as irreducible and unthematizable commandment of responsibility *for the Other*.

Expression is testimony of an ethical *beyond*, the face of the Other, irreducible to thematization and which nonetheless offers, renders and allows, from its *beyond*, for the possibility of thematization and categorization.

Which Levinas understands as teaching (*enseignement*) where the face of the Other orients *beyond* the significance of the sign and yet toward the responsibility, the care for the significance of the sign:

> The infinite, against which every definition stands out, is not defined, does not offer itself to the gaze, but signals itself, not as a theme but as thematizing, as him starting from *whom* everything can be fixed in its identity. But also he signals himself by attending the work that signals him; he does not only signal himself, but speaks—is a face.[114]

Expression expresses the nakedness and defenselessness of the face of the Other, its vulnerability and fragility which always, for Levinas, entails an excess of givenness *beyond* signification and engages a response irreducible to measure, evaluation, judgment—an infinite responsibility incessantly giving more than it can for the Other.

For Levinas, expression means an ethical excess engaging the ethical Self to an infinite expression as response incessantly expressing more than what can be expressed: responsibility—expiation and substitution—for the Other: "The proximity of the Other, the proximity of the neighbor, is in being an ineluctable moment of the revelation of an absolute event (that is, disengaged from every relation) which expresses itself. His very epiphany consists in soliciting us by his destitution in the face of the Stranger, the widow, the orphan."[115]

Exteriority (*Extériorité*)

The word appears in the title of Levinas first major philosophical oeuvre, *Totality and Infinity. An Essay on Exteriority*. The idea of exteriority is thus central in Levinas' philosophical project, that of redefining the ethical as "First philosophy."

Exteriority however does not mean, for Levinas, that which "stands outside," that which is "out there," that which is "outer" or "external," an object exterior to a subject, an "externality" or an "outwardness." Furthermore, Levinas does not define exteriority by opposing it to interiority and thus by constrasting it with that which is "inner," "inside," and by extension to the "innermost," the "inward," the "inmost intimacy" of the Self or of the subject.

Nor does exteriority mean, for Levinas, a pure positivity or heteronomy which traditionally implies an imposition, an outer determination, a domination or dominion as a given which befalls and controls the Self. Exteriority is not, for

Levinas, a givenness (Natural or Historical) which would fixate and determine, consume, and expend the subject in the simple acceptation or espousal of a heterogeneous and heteronomous determination.

Rather, Levinas employs the term "exteriority" to firstly insist on the irreducible and absolute alterity of the Other as an *antecedent* transcendence informing and awakening the Self *before* objectification and representation, autonomy or self-determination. In this sense, the Other as exteriority marks at once the impossibility of identifying, categorizing, judging, or conceptualizing the Other as part of a whole, as moment of a totality, or as an instant in a historical narrative or becoming of rationality or Being. Exteriority marks an impossibility to define the Other as a category within an enclosed horizon of meaning or intentionality. Which means that exteriority reveals the irreducible otherness of the Other to context, to signification and thus the retraction, withdrawal, non-inclusivity of the Other from presence, representation, manifestation, or phenomenality.

Exteriority, in this sense, marks the Other as singularity, unique, and irreplaceable and thus as separation, differentiation, dissociation from the Self's intuition or understanding, representation or will, prehension, or comprehension. In this sense, exteriority, for Levinas, marks an absolute transcendence to totality and totalization and thus as that which remains separated and dissociated from the immanence of Being, from the comprehension of signification, from the unifying order of presence or the wholeness and Sameness of identity or identification.

However, and far from denegating Being, signification, presence or identity, far from negating the Self or crushing it under the weight of an incomprehensible, heteronomous, and heterogeneous positivity, the exteriority of the Other, its infinite and absolute transcendence, *awakens* and *elects* the Self as Self to an ethical response and responsibility which always expresses more than it can express, gives itself *beyond* what it could determine and *before* its will or self-resolve.

In this sense, exteriority, far from negating or crushing the Self, elects the ethical in the Self by expropriating the Self toward the Other, *before* autonomy and *beyond* judgment, and as irrepressible responsibility for the Other.

This is why Levinas defines exteriority positively as that which, from the absolute transcendence of the Other, promotes the ethical in the Self and thereby animates and awakens a responsibility unhinged by universality or judgment, normativity, or decision: a responsibility incessantly stretching itself outwards toward the Other for the Other—trace of the absolute exteriority and irreducible transcendence of the Other:

> Exteriority is true not in a lateral view appercieving it in its opposition to interiority; it is true in a face-to-face that is no longer entirely vision, but goes further than vision. The face-to-face is established starting with a point

> separated from exteriority so radically that it maintains itself of itself is me; every other relation that would not part from this separated and therefore arbitrary point (but whose arbitrariness and separation are produced in a positive mode as me), would miss the—necessarily subjective—field of truth. The true essence of man is presented in his face, in which he is infinitely other than a violence like unto mine, opposed to mine and hostile, already at grips with mine in a historical world where we participate in the same system. He arrests and paralyses my violence by his call, which does not do violence and comes from on high. The truth of being is not the *image* of being, the *idea* of its nature; it is the being situated in a subjective field which *deforms* vision, but precisely thus allows exteriority to state itself, entirely command and authority: entirely superiority. This curvature of the intersubjective space inflects distance into elevation; it does not falsify being, but makes truth first possible.[116]

Exteriority engages the superiority of transcendence which commands the election and the awakening of the Self to the ethical in responsibility for the Other. This is why Levinas always defines exteriority in and through a language which incessantly surpasses the comprehension of signification. Indeed, exteriority means the awakening of the Self as *infinitizing* responsibility for the Other. As Levinas remarks:

> We have broached the exteriority of being not as a form that being would eventually or provisionally take on in dispersion or in its fall, but as its very existing—inexhaustible, infinite exteriority. Such an exteriority opens in the Other; it recedes from thematisation. But it refuses thematisation positively because it is produced in a being who expresses himself. In contradistinction to plastic manifestation or disclosure, which manifests something *as* something, and in which the disclosed renounces its originality, its hitherto unpublished existence, in expression the manifestation and the manifested coincide; the manifested attends its own manifestation and hence remains exterior to every image one would retain of it, presents itself in the sense that we say of someone that he presents himself by stating his name, which permits evoking him, even though he remains always the source of his own presence. A presentation which consists in saying "It's me" and nothing else to which one might be tempted to assimilate me. This presentation of the exterior being nowise referred to in our world is what we have called the face. And we have described the relation with the face that presents itself in speech as desire—goodness and justice.[117]

Face (*Visage*)

The alterity of the Other expresses itself through the face of the Other: as the ethical infinite *beyond* and *before* manifestation or representation, *beyond* and *before* measure, cognition, or recognition. Which means, for Levinas: the face of the Other expresses an irreducible transcendence, which commands singularly, announces itself uniquely, and occurs unconditionally as ethical demand: "*Thou shall not kill*".

In this sense, the face of the Other is irreducible to a plastic image or embodied materiality; it "is" *irrepresentable* as such. The face of the Other thereby breaks and interrupts the intentional horizon from which phenomenality appears as it ruptures the anonymity of totality and indifference of Being. The face of the Other "is" always and already *beyond* phenomenality as it penetrates phenomenality to suspend the horizon of its intentionality and order of its very presentation. In this sense, for Levinas, the face of the Other, irreducible to phenomenality and objectivity, occurs as that which *breaks* phenomenality *in* phenomenality and thus fissures the context of phenomenality while erupting through phenomenality.

For the face of the Other is the expression or the announcement of the Infinite, incessantly disrupting the intentionality of phenomenality in its transcendent *Saying*. And its *Saying* is the *ethical*. It commands and demands from the absolute height of its transcendence which marks the radical separation between the Self and the Other:

> The relation with the Other does not nullify separation. It does not arise within a totality of comprehension or commonality nor does it establish a totality of meaning, integrating within its own-most sameness and identity the Self and the Other. Nor does the "face-to-face" conjuncture presuppose the existence of universal truths in which subjects would be indifferently absorbed in a reciprocal relation of communion, community, commonality, intersubjectivity, Sameness and identity. Rather, here, the converse thesis must be maintained: the relation between the Self and the Other commences in the *inequality*: infinite transcendence of the Other *inspiring* the Self to an ethical responsibility already responding *before* the Other's plea and always *beyond* the Other's demands. That is, also, before and beyond the Self's will. The Other qua Other is transcendent height and of abasement—*glorious* abasement; the Other demands and commands as "the poor, the stranger, the widow and the orphan, and at the same time, of the master called to invest and justify my freedom.[118]

The face of the Other in its defenselessness and nakedness defies the categories of understanding and the forms of intuition: the face of the Other breaks and overwhelms the totality of truth as adequation, overflows *logos* as "gathering" or "bringing together," suspends the wholeness of comprehension as conciliation or reconciliation by commanding from an irrepresentable and absolute transcendence. The face commands a response unaccountable by these ontological tropes of signification. The face of the Other, *beyond* and *before* phenomenality and suspending conceptualization and intentionality, incessantly eluding its own manifestation and essentialization, "is" expression *without* mediation, diction *without* contradiction: absolute ethical commandment. In this sense, and as expression, the face of the Other "is" the concrete singular intrusion of an exposed and vulnerable existent commanding an ethical response overflowing and exceeding comprehension or measure. It expresses the infinite transcendence of the Other speaking *beyond* and *before* all context and contextualization and thereby, as commandment and in its absolute vulnerability, defenselessness, mortality, nakedness, opens to the ethical—an hyperbolical ethics erupting *without* ground or foundation and which cuts through and pierces all horizon of intentionality as well as perceptive. As Levinas writes:

> The presence of the face coming from *beyond* the world, but committing me to human fraternity, does not overwhelm me as a numinous essence arousing fear and trembling. To be in relationship while absolving oneself from this relation is to speak. The Other does not only appear in his face, as a phenomenon subject to the action and domination of a freedom; infinitely distant from the very relation he enters, he presents himself there from the first as an absolute. The I disengages itself from the relationship, but does so within relationship with a being absolutely separated. The face with which the Other turns to me is not reabsorbed in a representation of the face. Less, for the face summons me to my obligations and judges me. The being that presents himself in the face comes from a dimension of height, a dimension of transcendence, whereby he can present himself as a stranger without opposing me as obstacle or enemy. The Other who dominates me in his transcendence is thus the stranger, the widow, and the orphan, to whom I am obligated.[119]

It is from the height of this absolute transcendence of the face of the Other that Levinas insists on its inherent duality *without* paradox: irrepresentable and irreducible to presence, always wholly other than Being, the order of manifestation, absolute transcendence and height *beyond* and *before* the Self and its categories *while already and at the same time*, the face of the Other is also the most exposed and vulnerable of all events erupting and occurring in phenomenality by interrupting, breaking, rupturing the order of phenomenality. In this sense, the face of the Other occurs as disruption, excess *beyond* presence *in* presence and representation. To the point of *overturning* and *overwhelming*, *overbearing*, and *exceeding* the very possibility of manifestation and the order of presentation and phenomenalization.

The face of the Other, undoing its own form, calls the visible to contravene itself; such is why it also bears the name of a *counter-phenomena*: the face erupts *in* phenomenality as an encounter which *counters* phenomenality. The face of the Other occurs thus as wholly irreappropriable by phenomenality and as incessantly breaking, rupturing, fracturing the intentional order of phenomenality. At once the closest neighbor and absolute stranger, the face of the Other subjects the spontaneity of the Self and thus incessantly *puts into question* the sovereignty and the autonomy of the Self, thereby opening it to the dimension of a signification *wholly other* than intentionality: the ethical signification of a responsibility *without* ground or foundation and, hence, always exceeding and superseding self-determination toward and for the Other:

> The infinite in the finite, the more in the less, which is accomplished by the idea of Infinity, is produced as Desire—not a Desire that the possession of the Desirable slakes, but the Desire for the Infinite which the desirable arouses rather than satisfies. A Desire perfectly disinterested—goodness. But Desire and goodness concretely presuppose a relationship in which the Desirable arrests the "negativity" of the I that holds sway in the Same—puts an end to power and emprise. This is positively produced as the possession of a world I can bestow as a gift on the Other—that is, as a presence before a face. For the presence before a face, my orientation toward the Other, can lose the avidity proper to the gaze only by turning into generosity, incapable of approaching the Other with empty hands. This relationship established over the things henceforth possibly common, that is, susceptible of being said, is the relationship of conversation. The way in which the other presents himself, exceeding *the idea of the other in me*, we here name face. This mode does not consist in figuring as a theme under my gaze, in spreading itself forth as a set of qualities forming an image. The face of the Other at each moment destroys and overflows the plastic image it leaves me, the idea existing to my own measure and to the measure of its *ideatum*—the adequate idea. It does not manifest itself by these qualities, but *kath auto*. It *expresses itself*.[120]

The face of the Other, as irreducible to the order of vision, "appears" as exteriority which appeals and commands as awakening and electing the Self in responsibility for the Other. Unmediated injunction, the face of the Other reveals its expression by interrupting, turning over, upheaving the order of representation and calls onto the singularity of the Self, electing the Self as if the Self called were unique to respond to the Other for the Other. This election to ethical responsibility, Levinas marks it as an *urgency* which postpones and rescinds the obligations the Self could determine for itself and toward itself:

> The face of a neighbor signifies for me an unexceptionable responsibility, preceding every free consent, every pact, every contract. It escapes representation; it is the very collapse of phenomenality. Not because it is too brutal to appear, but because in a sense too weak, non-phenomenon because less than a phenomenon. The disclosing of a face is nudity, non-form, abandon of self, ageing, dying, more naked than nudity. It is poverty, skin with wrinkles, which are a trace of itself. My reaction misses a present which is already the past of itself. This past is not in the present, but is as a phase retained, the past of this present, a lapse already lost which marks ageing, escaping all retention, altering my contemporaneousness with the other. It reclaimed me before I came. The delay is irrecuperable. "I opened . . . he had disappeared." My presence does not respond to the extreme urgency of the assignation. I am accused of having delayed.[121]

Always *too late* in responding to the face of the Other which is always *beyond* the order of vision, phenomena, and objectivity, its occurrence preserves its exteriority from which the imperative commandment elects an irrevocable responsibility for the Other. For Levinas, the face of the Other is a *Saying without universalization or normativity*: it *expresses* an ethical command *before* autonomy or self-determination electing the Self to an ethical *beyond* what it can normatively condition for itself; the face of the Other speaks to the Self *before* the Self by engaging the Self *beyond* itself for the Other. It is in this sense that the face of the Other is *beyond* phenomenality, de-structuring phenomena; as nakedness irreducible to representation, the "face is not what is presented to me because I disclose it [. . .]. The face has turned to me and this is its very nudity. It *is* by itself and not by reference to a system."[122] Which means, as Levinas explicates: "The Other continues to face me, to reveal himself in his face."[123]

To encounter the face of the Other is to *hear* a demand and an order irreducible to a universalizable norm; it is to *hear without vision* a commandment demanding and ordering an infinite responsibility. This exceptionality of the face of the Other marks it *beyond* phenomenality overwhelming manifestation as vulnerability and defenselessness—that is, as the mortality of the Other. The face of the Other always carries the death of the Other. This is why Levinas insists on how and why the face of the Other always exposes the Self to the primacy of the death of the Other, to that death always occurring *before* the Self's own mortality. The face of the Other reveals *beyond* manifestation and phenomenality *its* mortality as primary and initial, as always anterior and already disrupting the Self's ownmost concern for its own mortality. Levinas not only seeks here to think how the face of the Other interrupts the *Dasein*'s "resolute anticipation" through the *Dasein*'s engagement in its "utmost possibility not to be outstripped" revealed in its "Being-toward-death"—which Heidegger famously develops in Section II of *Being and Time*—but also, and more profoundly, he seeks to show why the face of the Other *exceeds* the primacy of the Self's relation to *its own* death. The face of the Other, by and through its ethical *Saying* as commandment, expresses *its* death and marks the primacy of *its* death *before* the mortality of the Self. Which opens to a further ethical responsibility: that of responding from *always surviving* the death of the Other. This *ethics of always surviving* the death of the Other—that death which is always primary—opens, for Levinas, to a responsibility where the Self—*before* autonomy and sovereignty—takes the Other upon itself—substitution and expiation—where taking the Other upon one's Self means to never abandon the Other to *its* death:

> A face is a trace of itself, given over to my responsibility, but to which I am wanting and faulty. It is as though I were responsible for his mortality, and guilty for surviving. A face is an anachronous immediacy more tense than that of an image offered in the straightforwardness of an intuitive intention. In proximity the absolutely other, the stranger whom I have "neither conceived nor given birth to," I already have on my arms, already bear, according to the Biblical formula, "in my breast as the nurse bears the nurseling." He has no other place, is not autochthonous, is uprooted, without a country, not an inhabitant, exposed to the cold and the heat of the seasons. To be reduced to having recourse to me is the homelessness or strangeness of the neighbor. It is incumbent on me.[124]

Responsible for the Other's mortality *before* tending to one's own death, Levinas also presents how the face of the Other can present itself as a call to murder, and thus as the source for the desire to murder the Other. The Other, through the face and its commandment, can also spur on a certain inversion of this call—*it can prompt all the contrary than responsibility*, and thus awaken an will to annihilate the Other. This is why the "Other inseparable from the very event of transcendence is situated in the region from which death, possibly murder comes."[125] Indeed, for Levinas: "To approach the Other is to put into question my freedom, my spontaneity as a living being, this impetuosity of the current to which everything is permitted, even murder."[126]

The imminence of murder, which is also lodged in the occurrence of the Other, for Levinas, *calls*–and such is the ethical *before* and *beyond* evil–for an *inversion*. To murder the Other is always to annihilate the face of the Other. But this is precisely "what" the face of the Other interrupts and suspends: the desire to annihilate the face of the Other. In this sense, the face of the Other in its ethical Saying interrupts the desire of murder as it occurs *before* this will to power and thus to overpower the Other. The face of the Other interrupting the desire to murder the Other opens to the demand of an infinite responsibility for the Other. Which means: the Self is awakened and elected *as* ethical Self in reversing the imminence of the murder of the Other into the care and responsibility for the death of the Other. An inversion which is radicalized in *Otherwise than Being, or Beyond Essence*, where the ethical Self is transmuted into *obsession* and *trauma* in the face of the mortality of the Other—persecution, hostage, substitution, and expiation for the Other.

Face-to-face (*Face-à-face*)

The face-to-face relation signifies the transcendence of the ethical *beyond* Being as rupture and interruption of the totality, the identity, and the Sameness, generality, indifference, anonymity of essence. In this sense, the face-to-face relation marks, for Levinas, the primary structure of sociality. This ethical structure indicates and depicts the irreducible asymmetry ofthe transcendent Other and thus marks the impossibility to synchronize, conciliate, or reconciliate the absolute transcendence of the Other in a symmetry *between* the Self with the Other or the Other with the Self.

The face-to-face relation is irreducible to intersubjectivity. Levinas, in the opening pages of *Totality and Infinity*, indeed marks it unequivocally:

> The Same and the Other can not enter into a cognition that would encompass them; the relations that the separated being maintains with what transcends it are not produced on the ground of totality, do not crystallize into a system. [. . .] The conjuncture of the Same and the Other, in which even their verbal proximity is maintained, is the *direct* and *full face* welcome of the Other by me. This conjuncture is irreducible to totality; the "face-to-face" position is not a modification of the "along side of. . ." Even when I shall have linked the Other to myself with the conjunction "and" the Other continues to face me, to reveal himself in his face.[127]

The face-to-face relation means thus the separation and the irreducible transcendence of the Other as heteronomous which awakens the Self to the ethical as infinite responsibility for the vulnerability and defenselessness of the Other.

The face-to-face ethical structure and relation is developed by Levinas in *Totality and Infinity*.

Indeed, Levinas characterizes the asymmetrical relation from the Other to the Self, that is, from the face of the Other *commanding* the Self to an infinite responsibility for the Other. And indeed, the relation of the Other to the Self remains radically irreducible to a common "we," a commonality or community of subjects where the Other is always recognized as an *alter-ego*, and thus where the Other is always standing *next* to the Self, *side-by-side* with the Self and where the Other and the Self form a reciprocal, intersubjective space of mutual recognition based on Sameness or identicalness.

Levinas' hyperbolical ethics supposes a break of reciprocity, recognition, intersubjectivity, community, conciliation, and reconciliation. Indeed, the ethical occurs in the unique relation from a singular Other calling, commanding, demanding, expressing itself as commandment, toward a unique Self called to respond, summoned to responsibility, ordered to answer "*Here I am for the Other*" without reciprocity or mutuality, without Sameness or identity. Such a *sociality* (which Levinas distinguishes from community) implies an irreducible asymmetry which, from the commandment expressing itself through the face of the Other, engages nothing less than an unilateral response of responsibility *without* limit or limitation, *without* finality or fulfillment for the Other.

Otherwise said, the ethical face-to-face marks a heteronomous relation where the singular Other, *without* reciprocity or conciliation, singularly demands and commands a unique responsibility always exceeding the Self's capacities, understanding and intuition, autonomy and free will.

This is why the Levinasian face-to-face relation is not reducible to a Buberian "I and Thou" reciprocity—rather it marks, for Levinas, an irreducible asymmetry where the Self is always commanded by the Other and through this heteronomous commandment already awakened and elected as wholly exposed, passivity more passive than all passivity, incessantly responding more than what it can in a responsibility always furthering itself, extending itself and offering itself *beyond* what it could give for the Other. This is why, for Levinas, the ethical Self, elected by the Other to an infinite responsibility for the Other, always responds *without* reserve and *without* return, *without* exigency of Sameness, conciliation, reconciliation, identification, or commonality with the Other.

Levinas repeatedly describes the face-to-face as the ethical situation which marks the asymmetry of the Other electing the Self *before* autonomy and sovereignty, singularly commanding the Self to the point of overwhelming the Self to respond as unsubstitutable responsibility *beyond* any contract or subjective decision for the Other.

This heteronomy and asymmetry however—and Levinas insists on this most significantly—is not understood as a sovereign supremacy of the Other over the Self, a domination or a control of the Self by the transcendent Other. Rather, the heteronomy and asymmetry of the transcendent Other awakening and electing the Self to its infinite responsibility in the face-to-face relation is indissociable from the immeasurable suffering, mortality, vulnerability and defenselessness of the Other: its abandonment, poverty, misery, weakness, call for help and assistance, demand of care and attention. It is this abandonment, poverty, misery, weakness, call for help and assistance, demand of care and attention expressed by the Other which commands the Self in its urgent demand and appeal, electing the Self, individuating the Self to the ethical and as respondent, carer, and guardian of the Other for the Other. In this sense, the commandment of the Other expressed in the face-to-face relation is always and already *ethical* and demands, from its singular weakness and fragility as height and transcendence, the Self to its ethicality by already deposing and dispossessing the Self from its own autonomy, propriety, and sovereignty. The Self is awakened and elected to itself as ethical and in this election responds as infinite responsibility—substitution and expiation—to the call and the demand of the Other.

The exceptionality of the face-to-face relation is thus to be distinguished from empathy toward the Other, recognition of the Other, intersubjectivity, or community between the Self and the Other founded on an essential Sameness or identity of Self and Other. For Levinas, these modalities of thinking toward the Other are all, each specifically, *reductions* of the absolute and transcendent alterity of the Other to the Sameness of Being or the totality of essence. The face-to-face relation engages a sociality *beyond* recognition, and where the commandment of the Other—"*Thou shall not kill*"—demands an infinite responsibility for the Other—"*Here I am for the Other*"—a responsibility not to be outstripped, singular and inescapable, which incessantly exceeds all prevision, contract, or economy and in which the Self "sees itself" at once and simultaneously as *host* and *hostage* of and for the Other.

It is here also important to note that the face-to-face relation as sociality also suggests and implies—Levinas indeed underlines this point as early as *Totality and Infinity* before radicalizing it in *Otherwise than Being, or Beyond Essence*—the presence of the Third party (*le tiers*) which introduces a *certain* measure and equality, parity, and symmetry in the irreducible asymmetry of the Other's commandment to the Self's infinite responsibility for the Other. The third party implies, in this sense, a certain pacification of the radical transcendence of the face of the Other commanding, calling, demanding the Self to its unique and singular, urgent, and irrevocable response of responsibility. And, following Levinas, the Third party indeed pacifies the infinite distance of the transcendent Other, the singularity of the call and commandment of the Other, the hyperbolical heterogeneity of its expression. Why? For the Other *also* carries an *other Other*, and ultimately conveys the Other of the Other: the Others.

> As Levinas marks in *Totality and Infinity*: Language as the presence of the face does not invite complicity with the preferred being, the self-sufficient "I-Thou" forgetful of the universe; in its frankness it refuses the clandestinity of love, where it loses its frankness and meaning and turns into laughter or cooing. The third party looks at me in the eyes of the Other—language is justice. It is not that there first would be the face and then the being it manifests or expresses would concern himself with justice; the epiphany of the face qua face opens humanity. The face in its nakedness as a face presents to me the destitution of the poor one and the stranger; but this poverty and exile which appeal to my powers, address me, do not deliver themselves over to these powers as givens, remain the expression of the face. The poor one, the stranger, presents himself as an equal. His equality within this essential poverty consists in referring to the Third party, thus present at the encounter, whom in the midst of his destitution the Other already serves.[128]

Which means, at least: the "presence" of the Third party, of the Other of the Other, of all the Others, presupposes the asymmetrical face-to-face relation and inversely, but without reciprocity, the face-to-face relation already testifies and witnesses the occurrence of the Third party, all the Others. Which opens to an *aporia* incessantly informing the ethical, that is, incessantly inspiring it to exceed itself: at once and simultaneously, the Other already testifies, in its hyperbolical commandment, of the all the Others *and* also, always marks the singular commandment of an infinite responsibility for the Other.

This *aporetic* situation, far from immobilizing the ethical Self, inspires it to incessantly *exceed* its responsibility, substitution and expiation for the Other *as well as* for all Others.

This further complexification, and thus the entry of the Third party as always and already "present" in the face-to-face relation, is one of the, *perhaps the*, most complex development in Levinas' thinking, and is highly significative in the passage from *Totality and Infinity* to *Otherwise than Being, or Beyond Essence*. As Levinas also indicates in *Otherwise than Being, or Beyond Essence*:

> All the others that obsess me in the other do not affect me as examples of the same genus united with my neighbor by resemblance or common nature, individuations of the human race, or chips of the same block, like the stones metamorphosed into men by Deucalion, who, behind

> his back, had to collect into cities with their hearts of stone. The others concern me from the first. Here fraternity precedes the commonness of a genus. My relationship with the other as neighbor gives meaning to my relations with all the others. All human relations as human proceed from disinterestedness. The One-for-the-Other of proximity is not a deforming abstraction. In it justice is shown from the first, it is thus born from the signifyingness of signification, the-one-for-the-other, signification. This means concretely or empirically that justice is not a legality regulating human masses, from which a technique of social equilibrium is drawn, harmonizing antagonistic forces. That would be a justification of the State delivered over to its own necessities. Justice is impossible without the one that renders it finding himself in proximity. His function is not limited to the "function of judgment," the subsuming of particular cases under a general rule. The judge is not outside the conflict, but the law is in the midst of proximity. Justice, society, the State and its institutions, exchanges and work are comprehensible out of proximity. This means that nothing is outside of the control of the responsibility of the One-for-the-Other. It is important to recover all these forms beginning with proximity, in which being, totality, the State, politics, techniques, work are at every moment on the point of having their center of gravitation in themselves, and weighing on their own account. In no way is justice a degradation of obsession, a degeneration of the for-the-other, a diminution, a limitation of anarchic responsibility, a neutralization of the glory of the Infinite, a degeneration that would be produced in the measure that for empirical reasons the initial duo would become a trio. But the contemporaneousness of the multiple is tied about the diachrony of two: justice remains justice only, in a society where there is no distinction between those close and those far off, but in which there also remains the impossibility of passing by the closest. The equality of all is borne by my inequality, the surplus of my duties over my rights. The forgetting of self moves justice.[129]

The idea of justice, as Levinas indicates, is not a simple *pacification* of the face-to-face relation: it rather marks the *diachrony* of the ethical. In this sense, the event of the Third party always occurring in the face-to-face relation does not mean a reduction of the hyperbolical ethics of responsibility. All to the contrary! First, for Levinas, the face-to-face relation is indissociable from the occurrence of the Third party and, in this sense, the Third party is always and already required by the face-to-face relation and indeed is necessary to the face-to-face relation, preventing it thus from befalling into a closed and self-enclosed "I-Thou" relation where no exteriority would or could occur to disrupt it, and hence would or could vivify and animate it ethically.

But also, and secondly, it is only as face-to-face relation incessantly calling on the Self to rise to its-Self as hyperbolical responsibility for the Other, unquieted and irreducible, that the occurrence of the Third party can also be "seen," and thus "seen" as opening to a *wholly other* relation than one of neutral intersubjectivity, anonymous, and impersonal community grounded in Sameness, original identity, and identification or identicalness of differences:

> The pre-original, anarchic saying is proximity, contact, duty without end, a *Saying* still indifferent to the *Said* and *Saying* itself without giving the *Said*, the-one-for-the-other, a substitution. It requires the signification of the thematizable, states the idealized *Said*, weighs and judges in justice. Judgments and propositions are born in justice, which is putting together, assembling, the being of entities. Here with a problem begins the concern for truth, for the disclosure of being. But it is for justice that everything shows itself, and to the extravagance of substitution is superimposed, through the exigencies for responsibility itself which substitution is, a rational order, the ancillary or angelic order of justice, and the very fact of seeing, seeing everywhere clearly and recounting everything.[130]

Fecundity (*Fécondité*)

The term appears most significatively in *Existence and the Existents* and in *Totality and Infinity*. In both texts, Levinas thinks fecundity as a central aspect of the relation to or toward the Other. Through and in fecundity, for Levinas, the Other—the child, the new-born, and thus the promise of a futurity—marks the possibility and the actuality of a plurality, multiplicity, and the creation of alterity *beyond* the Self, *beyond* the self-enclosed identity of the Self.

Fecundity means, for Levinas, a relation to the Other which, emanating in the Self, succeeds and surpasses the Self. Hence through fecundity, Levinas rethinks the inherent possibility in the Self to extend itself *beyond* itself and toward that which remains irreducible and irretrievable to and by the Self: the Other. The Self is therefore, for Levinas, not a simple and static self-enclosed monad, an entity closed in on itself and for itself. Rather, the Self is that existent from which the plural and the multiple is opened and comes forth as an incessant possibility *to come*. The Self is, in this manner, always and already inhabited by that which exceeds it, by alterity and an otherness toward which it is extended and for which it is superseded.

Most particularly in the early texts and up to *Totality and Infinity*, Levinas portrays the Self as a self-enclosed entity, and thereby as a substance—that which possesses itself, appropriates itself for itself and in itself. Fecundity however reverses or inverses this monadic identity and deploys, engages, and extends the Self in a suspension of its self-enclosure, an interruption of the Self as a sovereign, autonomous, independent entity, always recognizing itself through the appropriation of itself. Fecundity engages *another* idea of the Self where the Other occurs to the Self in the Self as irreducible difference extending *beyond* the Self. For Levinas, thus, fecundity shows the Other already growing and always exceeding the Self. Fecundity marks, in this sense, a break in the self-identical narrative of the Self appropriating and recognizing itself as Self in itself and for itself. For it marks an irreducible exposition to the Other which, occurring in the Self, nonetheless ruptures the unity of its ownmost identical being and transposes, transfers, awakens or elects the Self to an-Other transcending the Self, an alterity which is at once inseparable from the Self and yet which remains irreducibly Other tothe Self:

> In fecundity the I transcends the world of light—not to dissolve into the anonymity of the *there is*, but in order to go further than the light, to go *elsewhere*. [. . .] The relation with the son in fecundity does not maintain us in this closed expanse of light and dream, cognitions and powers. It articulates the time of the absolutely other, an alteration of the very substance of him who can—his trans-substantiation. [. . .] Transcendence is time and goes unto the Other. But the Other is not a term: he does not stop the movement of Desire. The other that Desire desires is again Desire; transcendence transcends toward him who transcends—this is the true adventure of paternity, of the trans-substantiation which permits going *beyond* the simple renewal of the possible in the inevitable senescence of the subject. Transcendence, the for the Other, the goodness correlative of the face, founds a more profound relation: the goodness of goodness. Fecundity engendering fecundity accomplishes goodness: above and *beyond* sacrifice that imposes a gift, the gift of the power of giving, the conception of a child. Here the Desire which in the first pages of this work we contrasted with need, the Desire that is not a lack, a Desire that is the independence of the separated being and its transcendence, is accomplished—not in being satisfied and in thus acknowledging that it was a need, but in transcending itself, in engendering Desire.[131]

Femininity (*Féminité*)

Certainly one of the most controversial and ambiguous terms in Levinas' philosophical corpus. Famously, Simone de Beauvoir criticized, in *The Second*

Sex,[132] Levinas' characterization and analyses, phenomenological descriptions and determinations of the feminine and femininity. Indeed, de Beauvoir argued that for Levinas the feminine is framed as secondary to the masculinity of paternity and filiality.

Different but also notable critical appraisals, and indeed objections, can be found in Derrida,[133] Irigaray,[134] and Chalier.[135]

The concept of femininity has considerably evolved in Levinas' writing. The first occurrence of the feminine is in *Time and the Other*. However, it is in *Totality and Infinity* that the feminine and feminity are deployed within the general philosophical framework of Levinas' thought through the infamous analyses grouped under the title *Beyond the Face* (Section IV).

In *Time and the Other*, femininity, through the erotic, is conceived as an original relation to transcendence. *Eros* opens the subject to the *beyond* of transcendence, to the alterity of the Other and engages subjectivity to incessantly exceed itself toward the Other as the feminine. For Levinas, this transport or transference, this extension of the Self *beyond* itself in the erotic relation, is a modality of escape and evasion, tearing the Self away from the indifference and anonymity of Being toward a *wholly other* source of signification than the self-enclosure of egoism and sovereignty. The erotic relation offers the possibility of exceeding the "*il y a*" and thereby of rupturing the immanence of Being toward a wholly other disposition, that is: toward the transcendent Other irreducible to the Sameness and indifference of Being or essence, irreducible thus to the anonymity and indifference of Being and essence.

For Levinas, the feminine and femininity figure this irreducible Other occurring to the Self as incessantly irreappropriable and ungraspable in and within the proximity of the erotic relation. Which means: the *beloved* occurs to the *lover without* the *lover* ever being capable of enclosing the *beloved* in its grasp and comprehension. The *beloved*, the feminine, is beloved by the lover in the infinite distance of a relation irreducible to Sameness and identity. Indeed, and certainly retrieving the difference between the *lover* (*Amant*, which is masculine) and the *beloved* (*Aimée*, which is feminine) from Rosenzweig and most particularly from Section II, "Revelation", in the *Star of Redemption*,[136] the *lover* never appropriates the *beloved*, the masculine never transforms the feminine into an object as it, the *beloved*, the feminine, always remains irretrievable, irreappropriable to the *lover*, the masculine. Furthermore, the masculine, the *lover*, always exceeds itself in its desire for the feminine, the *beloved*. Incessantly transcending itself toward the ungraspable, the *lover* in the erotic relation breaks the will to dominate by substituting power for passion and compassion for the Other, the *beloved*. The mark of this substitution from domination and objectivation to passion and compassion is, for Levinas, expressed as the *caress*. Levinas writes:

> The movement of the lover before this frailty of feminity, neither pure compassion nor impassiveness, indulges in compassion is absorbed in the complacence of the caress. The caress, like contact, is sensibility. But the caress transcends the sensible. It is not that it would feel *beyond* the felt, further than the senses, that it would seize upon a sublime food while maintaining, within its relation with this ultimate felt, an intention of hunger that goes unto the food promised, and given to, and deepening this hunger, as though the caress would be fed by its own hunger. The caress consists in seizing upon nothing, in soliciting what ceaselessly escapes its form toward a future never future enough, in soliciting what slips away as though it *were not yet*. It *searches*, it forages. It is not an intentionality of disclosure but of search: a movement unto the invisible. In a certain sense it *expresses* love, but suffers from an inability to tell it. It is hungry for this very expression, in an unremitting increase of hunger. It thus goes further than to its term, it aims *beyond* an existent however future, which, precisely as an existent knocks already at the gates of being. The desire that animates it is reborn in its satisfaction, fed somehow by what *is not yet*, bringing us back to the virginity, forever inviolate of the feminine. It is not that the caress would seek to dominate a hostile freedom, to make of it its object or extort from it a consent. *Beyond* the consent or the resistance of a freedom the caress seeks *what is not yet*, a "less than nothing", closed and dormant *beyond* the *future*, consequently dormant quite otherwise than the *possible*, which would be open to anticipation.[137]

This description of the erotic relation as caress, and thus of the relation between the *masculine* toward the transcendent *feminine*, the *lover* toward the *beloved*, the Self toward the Other as possibility of escaping the suffocating immanence of Being, marks, for Levinas, an exceptionality which not only critically dismantles the idea of immanent fusion or reciprocity, and even of recognition and reconciliation, but also engages a novel thinking of love as irreducible separation and incessant exposition to the absolute and irreducible transcendence of the Other. Facing the feminine and feminity in *eros* means thus, for Levinas, to expose one's Self to the absolute transcendence of the Other, and thus to the irreducible otherness of the Other.

Furthermore, and always in *Totality and Infinity*, Levinas will radicalize this breakthrough and engage the concept of femininity not only as an irreducible alterity, futurity and inviolable transcendence absolutely Other, but also as host, hospitality, welcome and reception. The feminine *receives* the Other and thereby opens to the possibility *beyond* Being of a *passivity* of exposition, of hospitality of the Other as singular and unique.

Levinas proceeds in marking the feminine and feminity as the inauguration of the interiority and the intimity of the "*chez soi*," that is the intimacy of *being at home as being with one's own self always and already open to the Other. Indeed,* through the feminine and feminity Levinas will thereby think separation and severance in dwelling as exposition to the Other in *being at home as being with one's ownmost self for the welcoming of the Other*. In this sense, thus, the feminine and feminity also embody the always open hospitality as reception and welcome, greeting, and address *beyond* the ontological determinations of Sameness and identity.

Throughout *Totality and Infinity*, femininity is thus thought as hospitality, receptivity, and as the *possibility* of all relation to the transcendence of the Other. The feminine and feminity names the relation to the Other which escapes the ontological reciprocity of Sameness and identicalness. The feminine and feminity always *receives* the Other, greeting and hosting the Other *beyond* and *before* an intersubjective normativity and judgment between Self and Other instills itself which would always, for Levinas, reduce the otherness of the Other to the sameness of the Self. Indeed, the feminine and feminity is *openess* to the transcendence of the Other as always singular, unique, and thus as hospitality to defenselessness of the face of the Other.

Femininity also appears in Levinas' description of the erotic as the *equivocity* and *ambiguity* of *profanation*. That is: the incessant double play of the secret and the manifest, of the covered and the uncovered, of concealedness and revelation. Which marks for Levinas, the feminine and feminity as Otherness *beyond* form and formalization and thus as the opening of a relation, the erotic relation, of incessant non-indifference. The feminine is, in this sense, irreducible to the formal alterity of a term in an ensemble: the feminine figures *equivocity, ungraspability*, and *unseizability*, fragility *wholly other* than intuition and understanding.

As always, Levinas approaches feminity through the relation of separation between the *lover* and the *beloved*:

> To love is to fear for another, to come to the assistance of his frailty. In this frailty as in the dawn rises the Loved, who is the Beloved. An epiphany of the Loved, the feminine is not added to an object and a Thou antecedently given or encountered in the neuter. The epiphany of the Beloved is but one with her *regime* of tenderness. The *way* of the tender consists in an extreme fragility, a vulnerability. It manifests itself at the limit of being and non-being, as a soft warmth where being dissipates into radiance, like the "pale bush" of the nymphs in the *Afternoon of a Faun*, which "leaps in the air drowsy with thick slumbers", relieving itself of its own weight of being, already evanescence and swoon, flight into self in the very midst of its manifestation. And in this flight the other is other, foreign to the world too coarse [. . .] *The essentially hidden throws itself toward the light, without becoming signification*. Not nothingness—but what is not yet. This unreality

> at the threshold of the real does not offer itself as a possible to be grasped: the clandestinity does not describe a gnoseological accident that occurs to a being. "Being not yet" is not a this or a that; clandestinity exhausts the essence of this non-essence. In the effrontery of its production this clandestinity avows a nocturnal life not equivalent to a diurnal life simply deprived of light; it is not equivalent to the simple *inwardness* of a solitary and inward life which would seek expression in order to overcome its repression. It refers to the modesty it has profaned without overcoming. The secret appears without appearing, not because it would appear half-way, or with reservations, or in confusion. The simultaneity of the clandestine and the exposed precisely defines *profanation*. It appears in equivocation. [. . .] The simultaneity or the equivocation of this fragility and this weight of non-signifyingness [non-significance], heavier than the weight of the formless, we shall term *femininity*.[138]

At the heart of this analysis, Levinas points out not only a risk, but a certain concatenation of the erotic relation. Indeed, Levinas marks how and why a certain reduction which also disfigures and defaces the face of the Other can occur, does indeed occur, in the erotic relation. For Levinas, the ultra-materiality of the erotic *inverts* the relation between the Self and the Other into one of presence and presentation where both Self and Other are reduced to the economy of enjoyment and pleasure which draws to a forgetfulness or oblivion of the ethical responsibility for the Other. The erotic relation through femininity *can* open toward the absolute transcendence of the Other, but it *can also* close itself up in the economy of enjoyment and in the forgetfulness of the Other's transcendence. In this sense, for Levinas, where femininity opens to a certain break of the ontological toward a wholly other relation, one of address and hospitality toward the face of the Other, the erotic *can also* transform and transfigure this relation into the unethical oblivion of the Other by and through the economy of enjoyment, transforming the ambiguity of eros into a relation of power, objectification, and materiality.

Filiality (*Filialité*)

As fecundity, filiality liberates and frees the Self from the immanence, indifference, and anonymity of Being. The idea of filiality marks, for Levinas, a model of the ethical relation in that it incessantly testifies of the eruption of Otherness in the immanence of identity. Indeed, for Levinas, the very possibility of filiality—the possibility of the *son* (Levinas marks the link in French between *fils* (son) and *filiation* (filiation))—delivers the Self from itself, frees the Self from its ownmost identity, liberates the Self from a self-centered Selfhood confined to itself alone. Filiality breaks the immanence of the Self as it ruptures its internment in its self-enclosedness.

For Levinas, the father, through the son, is extended *beyond* itself toward the Other as irreducible and irreappropriable. And this point is indeed capital for Levinas: the son is not another Self; the son is Other than the Self erupting from the Self. And thus, the son embodies an alterity which, related to the Self, also breaks and ruptures this relation. Certainly, the son does not negate or abolish the identity or the ipseity of the father—the son rather incessantly introduces its otherness as irreducible separation within this relation.

Which means, for Levinas, the son is irreducibly singular and unique and the relation between the father and the son is one of discontinuity in and through continuity—a relation of Otherness affecting the Same as irreducible to the Same:

> The I breaks free from itself in paternity without thereby ceasing to be an I, for the I *is* its son. The converse of paternity, filiality, the father-son relationship, designates a relation of rupture and a recourse at the same time. As rupture, repudiation of the father, commencement, filiality at each moment accomplishes and repeats the paradox of a created freedom. But in this apparent contradiction and in the form of the son being *is* infinitely and discontinuously, historical without fate. [. . .] But the son's relation with the father across fecundity is not effected only in recourse and the rupture which the I of the son accomplishes as an I already existing. The I owes its unicity as an I to the paternal *Eros*. The father does not simply cause the son. *To be* one's son means to be I in one's son, to be substantially in him, yet without being maintained there in identity. Our whole analysis of fecundity aimed to establish this dialectical conjuncture, which conserves the two contradictory movements. The son resumes the unicity of the father and yet remains exterior to the father: the son is a unique son. Not by number; each son of the father is the unique son, the chosen son. The love of the father for the son accomplishes the sole relation possible with the very unicity of another; and in this sense every love must approach paternal love. But this relation of the father with the son is not *added* to the already constituted I of the son, as a good fortune. The paternal *Eros* first invests the unicity of the son; his I qua filial commences not in enjoyment but in election.[139]

The idea of filiality marks thus a singular ethical relation: that of election, where the alterity of the elected son incessantly suspends the Sameness and the identity of relationality. Going to the limit of this description, one could say, with Levinas, that the son as elected Other singularizes the relation by breaking and rupturing incessantly the relationality and the commonality of the relation. Which, for Levinas, intends the following: this relation *without* relation, extending *beyond* identity and genealogy, never re-instores itself as an egoisitc rivality. On the contrary, the father/son relationship, for Levinas, indicates the possibility of responding for the Other *beyond* and *before* the Self, gratuity and generosity, gift without measure or finality, from the Self (father) toward the Other (son) and through the suspension and interruption of any identity or sameness between the Self and the Other. The father is *for* the son as the son is irreducibly other than the father engaging, thus an ethical relation as filiality and filiation which incessantly ruptures the logic of fusion, identicalness and thereby totality.

In this sense, filiality is paradigmatic of the ethical: it implies a responsibility toward the Other as an incessant giving to the Other for the Other and which presupposes the creation of a separation, a suspension, an interruption from the father toward the son. Which means: filiality indicates how and why the Other always *exceeds* the Self, the son *exceeds* irretrievably the father. Such a paradigmatic relation proposes a temporality entirely pointing to the *futurity* of the Other irrecuperable by the Self—the incessant event of the Other commanding a separation, a suspension, an interruption, and through this separation, suspension, interruption, the eruption of a responsibility for the Other as *giving beyond* the Self for the Other.

Forgiveness (*Pardon*)

The idea of forgiveness or pardon is central in Levinas' philosophy, and most particularly in the Levinasian analysis of temporality. Indeed, it is in Sub-section G, entitled *The Infinity of Time* (Section IV, *Beyond the Face*) of *Totality and Infinity*, that Levinas inscribes the question of forgiveness or pardon as *diachrony* and thus as the *dis-jointment* of time as temporal continuity. Forgiveness or pardon is thought, by Levinas, as undoing and dismantling the essential stability and synchronicity, gathering, or *bringing-together* of temporality with itself.

Which entails that the idea of forgiveness or pardon is also thought as *fecundity* and *filiality*: possibility of time as *creation*, "absolute youth" which opens to a "futurity" and a "recommencement" always *arriving* (*à-venir*) from and of the Other:

> The discontinuous time of fecundity makes possible an absolute youth and recommencement, while leaving the recommencement of a relation with the recommenced past in a free return to that past (free with a freedom

> other than that of memory), and in free interpretation and free choice, in an existence as entirely pardoned. This recommencement of the instant, this triumph of the time of fecundity over the becoming of the mortal and aging being is a pardon, the very work of time.[140]

Forgiveness or pardon means, for Levinas, the incessant *re*-birth of a "futurity" which, *otherwise* than as memory, recollection or retention, *repairs* the past by projecting it toward a renewal, a regeneration, a restoration—that is, a *redemption*. It is important to note here that this "redemptive" forgiveness or pardon does not engage a reconciliation, a reconciliatory temporality whereby the past would be dialectically "put to the past," surpassed, interiorized, and relieved, comprehended, and healed. Indeed, and contrarily to the dialectic of *Evil and its Forgiveness* in Hegel's *Phenomenology of Spirit*[141] where forgiveness or pardon always embody the speculative reconciliation of the Law *with* love, of the particular judgment of justice within the infinity of mercy through which "the wounds of Spirit heal, and leave no scars behind"[142] in the absolute *comprehension* of knowledge as History always and already converting the "negative" historical moment into the meaning of "truth as whole", truth as inclusive totality, identity of identity and difference, Sameness, Levinas underlines the inherent and irreducible *paradoxality* of forgiveness or pardon. Indeed, the paradox of pardon lies in its "retroaction," that is, in the modality of revealing that which remains *irreappropriable*, impossible to interiorize, and thus *irreconcilable*. For Levinas indeed, History is *irreconciliable* with itself: incessantly spurring on possibilities of *redemption* from its absolute irreconcilability and thereby which create occurrences of concrete repair, mending, restoring. This is why forgiveness or pardon is always, for Levinas, marking not a reconciliatory movement or modality of comprehension, but rather the always oblique and singular occurrence of a historical recovering *without* reconciliation—that is, *justice*. Which means, for Levinas, that forgiveness or pardon does not innocent or acquit. Nor does it consign to the past in forgetfulness. Indeed, Levinas here situates the exceptionality of a forgiveness and a pardon *without* forgetfulness and *without* resolution as *without* reconciliation: where "forgetting nullifies the relations with the past, pardon conserves the past pardoned" where "the pardoned being is not the innocent being."[143]

In this sense, forgiveness or pardon marks the *irreconciliation* of an incessance of temporality as recommencement of the past in a futurity. It marks thus the extension of the past into a futurity unresolved and uniquely committed to the absolute otherness of the Other. Forgiveness is thus always and already futural; it marks the futural possibility always renewed, always reasserted, always reinvented of healing the past *without* reconciliation or conciliation with the past:

> The paradox of the pardon refers to pardon as constitutive of time itself. The instants do not link up with one another indifferently, but extend from the Other unto me. The future does not come to me from a swarming of indistinguishable possibles which would flow toward my present and which I would grasp; it comes to me across an absolute interval whose other shore the Other absolutely other—though he be my son—is alone capable of marking and of connecting with the past. But then the Other is alone capable of retaining from this past the former Desire that animated it, which the alterity of each face increases and deepens ever more profoundly. [. . .] time no longer expresses the unintelligible dispersion of the unity of being, wholly contained in the first cause as substance, in an apparent and phantasmal series of causes and effects; time adds something new to being, something absolutely new. But the newness of springtimes that flower in the instant (which, in good logic, is like the prior one) is already heavy with all the springtimes lived through. The profound work of time delivers from this past in a subject that breaks with his father. Time is the non-definitiveness of the definitive, an ever recommencing alterity of the accomplished—the "ever" of this recommencement. The work of time goes *beyond* the suspension of the definitive which the continuity of duration makes possible. There must be a rupture of continuity and continuation across this rupture. The essential in time consists in being a drama, a multiplicity of acts where the following act resolves the prior one. Being is no longer produced at one blow, irremissibly present. Reality is what it is, but will be once again, another time freely resumed and pardoned.[144]

In this sense, and as incessant re-beginning, recreation, *diachrony* rupturing and interrupting of synchrony, futurity as utmost possibility of repairing and mending the past for the future, opening in the past a *beyond* its irreversibility as infinte exigency of reparation; forgiveness, and pardon *without* reconciliation opening toward the incessant reiteration of an ethical exigency to redeem the past in the name of futurity—what Levinas also names "resurrection."[145]

This *redemption* as *resurrection* constitutes and institutes a "messianic time" wholly riveted to an absolute futurity as an absolute transcendence of the Other irreducible to presence, incarnation, embodiment, or fulfillment. Far from a logic of reconciliation in which redemption would embody itself as a fulfilled salvation, Levinas here marks how forgiveness and pardon engage an incessant

> recommencement in discontinuous time brings youth and thus the *infinition* of time. Time's infinite existing ensures the situation of judgment, condition of truth, behind the failure of the goodness of today. By fecundity I dispose on an infinite time, necessary for truth to be told, necessary for

> the particularism of the apology to be converted into efficacious goodness, which maintains the I of the apology in its particularity, without history breaking and crushing this allegedly still subjective concordance. But infinite time is also the putting back into question of the truth it promises. [. . .] The completion of time is not death, but messianic time, where the perpetual is converted into eternal. Messianic triumph is the pure triumph; it is secured against the revenge of evil whose return the infinite time does not prohibit.[146]

Levinas marks thus how and why forgiveness and pardon always project by overwhelming the present *outside* and *beyond* presence, *outside* and *beyond* resolution, fulfillment or accomplishment of History. Forgiveness and pardon open to a *diachrony* through which the immemorial past commands a futurity always to further as responsibility always to engage for the Other, a futural *Saying* as incessant messianic imperative of reviving an *otherwise than the present*, an *otherwise than presence*; and thus an incessantly renewed and recreated, re-engaged and reiterated substitution and expiation *without* end, *telos* or *principle* in responsibility for the Other. Incessantly responding *before* and *beyond* the present for the Other, the ethical Self is elected in always responding "*Here I am for the Other*" which sustains an infinite responsibility *without* reserve, already engaged further than what can be expected or determined. In this sense, for Levinas, forgiveness or pardon means *to always give more than what can be given*—an infinite responsibility *beyond* and *before* the logic of the gift, the fulfilment of givenness, of donation for the Other.

Otherwise said, forgiveness or pardon, as an original structure of temporality, marks for Levinas the *creation* and *re-creation*—redemption *as* resurrection, mending and healing—of the present *as* response and responsibility *before* and *beyond* the presence of the present and toward an immemorial past always occurring as pure futurity—absolute otherness of the Other. And Levinas to propose this question in closing the reinterpretation of forgiveness and pardon as a temporal modality, eternity, of the *messianic*: "Is this eternity a new structure of time or an extreme vigilance of the messianic consciousness? The problem exceeds the bounds of this book."[147] Certainly this question will be retrieved in *Otherwise than Being, or Beyond Essence*, notably through the ideas of substitution and expiation, and where Levinas will suggest how and why the "eternity of the messianic," irreducible to presence as essence of temporality and Being, is at once a "new structure of time" and an "extreme vigilance": "new structure of time" as incessant re-creation, recommencement, renewal; "extreme vigilance" as the incessant *creation* and *re*-creation of a justice for the singularity of the Other *without* conciliation, reconciliation, comprehension.

Freedom (*Liberté*)

The idea of freedom is pivotal in Levinas' philosophy. Which also means that the meaning of freedom is profoundly redefined by Levinas. Indeed, Levinas identifies freedom as an integral and constitutive concept of European civilization and Western philosophy. In the opening pages of *Totality and Infinity*, Levinas—after having showed how and why Western philosophy "has most often been an ontology: a reduction of the Other to the Same by interposition of a middle and neutral term that ensures the comprehension of Being"[148]—situates the birth of the idea of freedom in the Socratic *maieutic*:

> This primacy of the Same was Socrates's teaching: to receive nothing of the Other but what is in me, as though from all eternity I was in possession of what comes to me from the outside—to receive nothing, or to be free. Freedom does not resemble the capricious spontaneity of free will; its ultimate meaning lies in this permanence in the Same, which is reason. Cognition is the deployment of this identity; it is freedom. That reason in the last analysis would be the manifestation of a freedom, neutralizing the Other and encompassing him, can come as no surprise once it was laid down that sovereign reason knows only itself, that nothing other limits it. The neutralization of the Other who becomes a theme or an object—appearing, that is, taking its place in the light—is precisely his reduction to the Same. [. . .] The ideal of Socratic truth thus rests on the essential self-sufficiency of the Same, its identification in ipseity, its egoism. Philosophy is an egology.[149]

Levinas marks, in this sense, how the central concept of the history of Western philosophy, Being, implies an idea of freedom wholly and entirely founded and grounded in the *ego* and thus on the structure of Sameness by and through which is deployed meaning and signification, position and sovereignty. It is however important here to note that the idea of freedom, for Levinas, is not simply or solely referred to the will or volition. Indeed, Levinas seeks to reveal a deeper structure preceding the very instance of will, volition, autonomy of the Self. Levinas seeks to also reveal an irreducible *antecedence* to the structure of the Same as the fundamental ontological order by which and through which the will can draw its possibility and actuality. As Levinas indicates, by reference to Heidegger's "fundamental ontology":

> If freedom denotes the mode of remaining the same in the midst of the Other, knowledge, where an existent is given by interposition of impersonal Being, contains the ultimate sense of freedom. It would be opposed to

> justice which involves obligations with regard to an existent that refuses to give itself, the Other, who in this sense would be an existent par excellence. In subordinating every relation with existents to the relation with Being the Heideggerian ontology affirms the primacy of freedom over ethics. To be sure, the freedom involved in the essence of truth is not for Heidegger a principle of free will. Freedom comes from an obedience to Being: it is not man who possesses freedom; it is freedom that possesses man. But the dialectic which thus reconciles freedom and obedience in the concept of truth presupposes the primacy of the Same which marks the direction of and defines the whole of Western philosophy.[150]

The idea of freedom is here understood by Levinas as the essence of a fundamental Sameness from which the *ego* draws and derives, constitutes and institutes thereby, its ontological meaning and significance. The *ego* is tributary of Being, responding, engaged, attuned to the ontological Sameness of Being. Furthermore, it is in and within this Sameness that its freedom can deploy itself, give what it is to give, express what it is to express, pose and propose its ownmost meaning through its act and activity.

Which means: the Sameness of the Same orders and determines the idea of freedom which is in turn only comprehensible by and through an irrepressible reference to identity. Otherwise said, the totality of Being encompasses the individuality of the *ego* where the latter's freedom and the former's meaning both signify and are signified by the same essential Sameness. Which Levinas will also qualify as the "*il y a*": the indifference, anonymity, commonality of the Self as *same* as the Other, of the Other as *same* as the Self in and within the significance of Being.

But Levinas marks a radical rupture and break with this ontology of freedom.

Indeed, and still referring to the "ideal of Socratic truth" and the Platonic distinction between the objective order of truth and the rationality of the existent, Levinas suggests that the modality of this *maieutic* always and already presupposes, albeit unbeknown, the alterity of the Other:

> Plato maintains the difference between the objective order of truth, that which doubtlessly is established in writings, impersonally, and reason *in* a living being, "a living and animated discourse", a discourse "which can defend itself, and knows when to speak and when to be silent." This discourse is not the unfolding of a prefabricated internal logic, but the constitution of truth in a struggle between thinkers, with all the risks of freedom. The relationship of language implies transcendence, radical separation, the strangeness of the interlocutors, the revelation of the Other to me. In other words, language is spoken where community between the terms of the relationship is wanting, where the common plane is wanting

> or is yet to be constituted. It takes place in this transcendence. Discourse is thus the experience of the absolutely foreign, a *pure* "knowledge" or "experience", a *traumatism of astonishment*.[151]

Prefiguring the traumatism—obsession, substitution, expiation—which animates the entirety of *Otherwise than Being, or Beyond Essence*, Levinas marks the following: the Other *precedes* and thus *instructs, commands* and *awakens, elects, informs* the freedom of the Self. And thus the idea of freedom does not lie or rely on the Sameness of the Same between Self and Other, but rather announces itself through the absolute transcendence of the Other electing the Self to the ethical. For Levinas, freedom occurs to the Self *from the Other*, that is, *freedom is awakened and elected in the Self from the Other*, opening thus *to the ethical before will or willfulness, autonomy, or auto-determination*:

> The absolutely foreign alone can instruct us. And it is only man who could be already foreign to me—refractory to every typology, to every genus, to every characterology, to every classification—and consequently the term of a 'knowledge' finally penetrating *beyond* the object. The strangeness of the Other, his very freedom! Free beings alone can be strangers to one another. Their freedom which is "common" to them is precisely what separates them.[152]

Which is precisely why, for Levinas, freedom will signify being *invested* by the Other *before* autonomy or decision, judgment, or sovereignty of the Self spurring on an incessant excess of responsibility *beyond* what the Self can determine and fulfill for the Other. And for Levinas, this implies that freedom cannot justify itself in itself or for itself—it is always and already elected and awoken by and through the occurrence and the commandment, the calling and demand of the Other. Freedom means thus to have always and already *been put into question* by the Other and thus being elected as Self, exposed *before* autonomy, or volition, in responding *beyond* any contract between the Self and the Other as infinite responsibility to and for the Other.

Which thus entails that to be free in autonomy is *not yet* freedom—for the justification of this autonomous freedom lies and relies "in arbitrariness."[153] That is, it lies and relies on individualism, egoism, and an economy of possessiveness. Levinas marks in this sense how and why the Self in freedom—that is, as elected, unique, irreplaceable—always and already *presupposes* the call and the commandment of the Other. And to go to the limit: the ethical Self expresses *its* freedom only as response to the call and the commandment of the Other, that is, as infinite responsibility for the Other.

Which is why, for Levinas,

> freedom is not justified by freedom. To account for being or to be in truth is not to comprehend nor to take hold . . . , but rather to encounter the Other without allergy, that is in justice. To approach the Other is to put into question my freedom, my spontaneity as a living being, my emprise and possession over the things, this freedom of a "moving force", this impetuosity of the current to which everything is permitted, even murder. The 'You shall not commit murder' which delineates the face in which the Other is produced submits my freedom to judgment.[154]

Ultimately, Levinas defines freedom as the "difficult" response of responsibility for the Other, and thus as being subjected to justice, that is, to the commandment and the demand of the Other as Law: "*Thou shall not kill*", "*You shall not commit murder*." The freedom of the Self is *wholly* oriented toward that which—*before* and *beyond* the ontology of freedom, *before* and *beyond* the ontological structure of the Sameness of the Same from which the Self draws its identity thereby reducing the Other to a *same* order of identity and identification, cognition and recognition, intersubjectivity or community—calls and commands from *elsewhere*: the exteriority as the absolute transcendence electing the Self to a the responsibility *without* term or finality in the name of a justice for the singularity of the Other:

> Freedom is not justified in the consciousness of certitude, but in an infinite exigency in regard to oneself, in the overcoming of all good conscience. But this infinite exigency with regard to oneself, precisely because it puts freedom in question, places me and maintains me in a situation which I am not alone, in which I am judged. This is the primary sociality: the personal relation is the rigor of justice which judges me and not in love that excuses me.[155]

And thus freedom is *inspiration—being inspired* by the Other as unique and irreplaceable substitution and expiation for the Other. As Levinas remarks, in *Otherwise than Being, or Beyond Essence*:

> But in the irreplaceable subject, unique and chosen as a responsibility and a substitution, a mode of freedom, ontologically impossible, breaks the unrendable essence. Substitution frees the subject from ennui, that is, from the enchainment to itself, where the ego suffocates in itself due to the tautological way of identity, and ceaselessly seeks after the distraction of games and sleep in a movement that never wears out. This liberation is not an action, a commencement, nor any vicissitude of essence and of ontology, where the equality with oneself would be established in the form of self-consciousness. An anarchic liberation, it emerges, without being

> assumed, without turning into a beginning, in inequality with oneself. It is brought out without being assumed, in the undergoing by sensibility beyond its capacity to undergo. This describes the suffering and vulnerability of the sensible as the other in me. The other is in me and in the midst of my very identification. The ipseity has become at odds with itself in its return to itself. The self-accusation of remorse gnaws away at the closed and firm core of consciousness, opening it, fissioning it. [. . .] The recurrence in the subject is thus neither freedom of possession of self by self in reflection, nor the freedom of play where I take myself for this or that, traversing avatars under the carnival masks of history. It is a matter of an exigency coming from the other, beyond what is available in my powers, to open an unlimited "deficit," in which the self spends itself without counting, freely. All the suffering and cruelty of essence weighs on a point that supports and expiates for it.[156]

God (*Dieu*)

Levinas refers to the absolute transcendence and separation, infinite distance and non-manifest Otherness as that *through which* the idea of God "comes to mind." God is thus never understood as a perfect, all-knowing, all-powerful sovereign Being, immanent presence, or unconditional cause. The idea of God never refers to a supreme substance, a *causa sui* and/or as the author or designer of Being and beings. The idea of God in Levinas' philosophical thinking and writing is, in this manner, radically distinguished from the traditional philosophical conceptions of God.

God, for Levinas, remains irreducible to *reason* as well as to its classical or traditional opposite, *faith*. God lies *outside* the *binarism* of reason and revelation, *beyond* knowledge and faith. In this sense, the idea of God is signified, for Levinas, only as a transcendent exceptionality and singularity absolutely ungraspable, irrepresentable and undiscoverable *Illeity*.

This radical and absolute *Illeity* of God also means the suspension and the interruption of the "incarnation" of God. Which signifies: the transcendent separation of God as absolute Other intends to awaken a singular and irreducible relation to the Other which remains always and already irretrievable and irrecuperable in the order of presence, representation, recognition, historical becoming or embodiment.

God occurs *outside* presence, essence, substance, cause or freedom, thematization or categorization and thereby lies *beyond* the economies of reason *and* faith, immanence *and* transcendence, identity *and* difference, conciliation or reconciliation of the finite and the infinite. For Levinas, God is the absolute *beyond* which *commands* the Self to an unescapable and ineffaceable relation to the Other as ethical responsibility for the Other *before* and *beyond* its fulfilment in an immanence of comprehension and appropriation.

In this sense, for Levinas, God is irreducible to a being, an entity, or an existent—God is *without* Being as *otherwise than Being*—wholly Other than the immanent horizon of Being.

Which is also why the subject, for Levinas, immersed in Being and essence within the world is characterized as *atheism*. The subject *in* and *within* the world, *within* the immanence of Being and signification is atheism as forgetfulness of the transcendence of God. However, for Levinas, the atheism of the subject remains, in its obliviousness of the radical transcendence and otherness of God, always and already attached and allied to this very absolute transcendence. Indeed, atheism *also* attests and testifies to the transcendence of God. Which entails nothing less than, for Levinas: religion, as alliance to the radically transcendent, presupposes atheism and supposes the separation or separatedness the Self inscribes between its "being *in* the world" and the absolute transcendence of God. In other words, religion as relation to transcendence is *desire* of the transcendent which presupposes a Self who always and already refers to God not as "incarnation" or "embodiment," but as the transcendent Law *beyond* presence, *beyond* Being where is opened the concreteness of the ethical as wholly *otherwise* than presence and Being: that is, as an infinite responsibility toward that which is inassimilable and irreappropriable to the Self's knowledge or intuition, comprehension or representation.

The idea of God, in that it remains irreducible to substance or presence, marks thus the opening of a relation as ethical responsibility toward an irrepresentable and irreducible transcendence: *Illeity*. This ethical responsibility, as an attestation and a testimony of separation and transcendence, what Levinas will also call Holiness (*sainteté*) or the Holy (*saint*), engages the Self for the Other where the face of the Other commands more than an intersubjective respect or a universal moral normativity—commands from its absolute transcendence to an infinite responsibility, *beyond* presence, *beyond* Being, *beyond* the anonymity and indifference of Being *qua* Being, for the Other.

We must here therefore remark how, for Levinas, the absolute transcendence of God, irrepresentability, the *otherwise* than presence, *otherwise* than Being opened in the irreducible Height of a commanding Otherness, God or the Law, is far from projecting the Self in a mystical oblivion of the ethical. All to the contrary! For Levinas, the absolute transcendence of God engages the Self into its concrete responsibility toward the Other, thereby inscribing the Self in the inescapable response of responsibility to the Other for the Other. This is why the ethical means "loving the Torah more than God." And thus, as Levinas remarks in his commentary on this Talmudic phrase:

> Man's real humanity and gentle nature enter into the world with the harsh words of an exacting God. Spirituality is offered up not through a tangible substance, but through absence. God is real and concrete not through incarnation but through Law, and His greatness is not inspired by His sacred mystery. His greatness does not provoke fear and trembling, but fills us with high thoughts.[157]

That is, *elects* the Self to the ethical for the Other as Law. Toward which "heading"? To the point of substitution and expiation for the Other always and already commanding the Self from the irreducible and irrepressible transcendence of the ethical.

Good (*Bien*)

The idea of the Good traverses the entirety of Levinas' thinking and writing. Levinas thinks toward an idea of the Good *outside* the totality of meaning and meaningfulness, *outside* the "philosophy of unity" which has always sought to "suppress separation" and where "the separated being traverses on the way of its return to its metaphysical source, a moment of a history that will be concluded by union."[158]

However, Levinas does not simply condone the history of Western philosophy or metaphysics as having negated the otherness of the Other and thereby suppressed the idea of the Good in a totalizing immanence of meaning and Being. Reading also in this history an *other orientation*, Levinas marks very judiciously how

> Greek metaphysics conceived the Good as separate from the totality of essences and in this way it caught sight of a structure such that the totality could admit of a *beyond*. The Good is Good *in itself* and not by relation to the need to which it is wanting; it is a luxury with respect to needs. It is precisely in this that it is *beyond* being. When, above, disclosure was contrasted with revelation, in which truth is expressed and illuminates us before we sought it, the notion of the Good in itself was already being taken up anew. Plotinus returns to Parmenides when he represents the apparition of the essence from the One by emanation and by *descent*. Plato nowise deduces being from the Good: he posits transcendence as surpassing the totality. Alongside of needs whose satisfaction amounts to

> filling a void, Plato catches sight also of aspirations that are not preceded by suffering and lack, and in which we recognize the pattern of Desire: the need of him who lacks nothing, the aspiration of him who possesses his being entirely, who goes *beyond* his plenitude, who has the idea of Infinity. The Place of the Good above every essence is the most profound teaching, the definitive teaching, not of theology, but of philosophy.[159]

Levinas underlines this *other orientation* within the history of the Same by engaging and presenting a certain paradoxality, the "paradox of the an Infinity admitting a being outside of itself which it does not encompass, and accomplishing its very infinitude by virtue of this proximity of a separated being—in a word the paradox of creation."[160] Which means: the Infinite is irreappropriable in the totality of the meaning of Being as it opens to a *wholly other* engagement, discourse and modality than the reappropriation in the Same, in the Sameness of the Same, in the ontological indifference of an essence which always and already reduces the transcendence of the Other to the immanence and unifying totality of Being.

To the ontological modality of the indifference incessantly reappropriating and reducing the Other to the Same, Levinas proposes another call opening to a *wholly other* ethical disposition:

> This relation is Desire, the life of beings that have arrived at self-possession. Infinity thought concretely, that is, starting with the separated being turned toward it, *surpasses* itself. In other words, it opens to itself the order of the Good. In saying that infinity is *thought* concretely starting with the separated being turned toward it we are nowise taking a thought that starts with the separated being to be relative. Separation is the very constitution of thought and interiority. Infinity is produced by withstanding the invasion of totality, in a contraction that leaves a place for the separated being.[161]

At the "antipodes of Spinozism," writes Levinas, the idea of the Good opened through the transcendent Infinity of the Other engages the "surpassing of phenomenal existence"[162] which projects a relation *beyond* recognition or intersubjectivity: an ethical relation which consists in giving the Other "one's being" and thus where "to be oneself is to express oneself, that is already to serve the Other."[163] Which Levinas qualifies: "The ground of expression is goodness. To be *kath auto* is to be good."[164]

In this sense, the idea of the Good wholly outside the grasp of Being, transcending and exceeding the essence of the Same where the Self and the Other are reduced to a middle element from which their Sameness embodies their singularities and unicities, elects the Self to an infinite responsibility for the Other. And for Levinas, the Goodness of the Good is always *prior* to

Being, *anterior* to the indifference and anonymity of the "*il y a*." This anteriority however does not refer to an origin, an originary place in which the ethical would be fixed and determined, substantially defined and consigned. All to the contrary, for Levinas, the *anteriority* and *precedence* of the Goodness of the Good exceeds all fixation and determination—anarchically—and thus projects the relation between the Self and the Other *beyond* the totalization of meaning and presence, comprehension and essence, commonality and identicalness. Always *before* Being and already *beyond* Being, the idea of the Good in its Goodness, that is also in its incessant Desire of the Other, a "desire engendering Desire" means to subvert the meaning and the truth of Being as "being for the Other."[165] That is, the Good subverts the truth of Being as always marking *before* and *beyond* the totalizing meaning of Being the election of the *Self as already for the Other* where this *for the Other* does not mean the negation or the effacement of the I but rather its awakening to its own unsubstituable ethicality: as oriented and called to the Goodness of the Good which

> is not regulated by the principles inscribed in the nature of a particular being that manifests it (for thus it would still proceed from universality and would not respond to the face), nor in the codes of the State. It consists in going where no clarifying—that is, panoramic—thought precedes, in going without knowing where. An absolute adventure, in a primal imprudence, goodness is transcendence itself. Transcendence is the transcendence of an I. Only an I can respond to the injunction of a face.[166]

Levinas, in the concluding pages of *Totality and Infinity*, and precisely where he interprets the Goodness of the Good as that by which Being is transcended and exceeded into the wholly irreducible ethical election of the *Self for the Other*, further qualifies this movement as "pluralism." Indeed, the ethical as *called* to the responsibility for the Other also reveals the Third party, the Other of the Other, and thus the plurality of Others engaging hence a thinking of pluralism—a pluralism which refuses and repudiates the universal indifference of multiplicity where all are "engulfed in the universal."[167] Rather Levinas marks a pluralism as *peace* irreducible to simple conciliation, reconciliation, fusion, identity or Sameness. Otherwise said, peace here engages a responsibility of testimony toward the infinite transcendence of the Goodness of the Good. As Levinas marks:

> transcendence or goodness is produced as pluralism. The pluralism of being is not produced as a multiplicity of a constellation spread out before a possible gaze, for thus it would be already totalised, joined into an entity. Pluralism is accomplished in goodness proceeding from me to the Other,

> in which first the Other, as absolutely Other, can be produced, without an alleged lateral view upon this movement having any right to grasp of it a truth superior to that which is produced in goodness itself. One does not enter into this pluralist society without always remaining outside by speech (in which goodness is produced)—but one does not leave it in order to simply *see oneself* inside. The unity of plurality is peace and not the coherence of the elements that constitute plurality. Peace therefore cannot be identified with the end of combats that cease for want of combatants, by the defeat of some and the victory of the others, that is, with cemeteries or future universal empires. Peace must be my peace, in a relation that starts from an I and goes to the Other, in desire and goodness, where the I both maintains itself and exists without egoism.[168]

In *Otherwise than Being, or Beyond Essence*, Levinas will considerably radicalize the idea of the Good, of the Goodness of the Good by insisting on the antecedence of responsibility for the Other to the point of substitution and expiation for the Other. That is, on the election of a responsibility *before* the autonomy and at the same time always and already *beyond* the capacities of the Self for the Other. Indeed, for Levinas in *Otherwise than Being* or *Beyond Essence*, the idea of the Good as Goodness of the Good engages the ethical Self in a *diachronial* responsibility where the Self always responds *before* the call of the Other as *before* the Self's autonomy or decision *and beyond* the expectations of the Other as incessant excess of the Self's responsibility for the Other—hostage of the Other as elected unicity *before* any choice or decision, immemorially obedient to the Goodness of the Good for the Other. This *diachrony* of responsibility marks the ethical Self's immemorial commitment to the Goodness of the Good orienting it *wholly otherwise* than Being and *already beyond* essence. As Levinas writes:

> If ethical terms arise in our discourse, before the terms freedom and non-freedom, it is because before the bipolarity of good and evil presented to choice, the subject finds himself committed to the Good in the very passivity of supporting. The distinction between free and non-free would not be the ultimate distinction between humanity and inhumanity, nor the ultimate mark of sense and nonsense. To understand intelligibility does not consist in going back to the beginning. There was a time irreducible to presence, an absolute unrepresentable past. Has not the Good chosen the subject with an election recognizable in the responsibility of being hostage, to which the subject is destined, which he cannot evade without denying himself, and by virtue of which he is unique? A philosopher can give to this election only the signification circumscribed by responsibility for the other. This antecedence of responsibility to freedom would signify

> the Goodness of the Good: the necessity that the Good choose me first before I can be in a position to choose, that is, welcome its choice. That is my pre-originary susceptiveness. It is a passivity prior to all receptivity, it is transcendent. It is an antecendence prior to all representable antecedence: immemorial. The Good is before being. There is diachrony: an unbridgeable difference between the Good and me, without simultaneity, odd terms. But also a non-indifference in this difference. The Good assigns the subject, according to a susception that cannot be assumed, to approach the other, the neighbor. This is an assignation to a non-erotic proximity, to a desire of the non-desirable, to a desire of the stranger in the neighbor. It is outside of concupiscence, which for its part does not cease to seduce by the appearance of the Good. In a Luciferian way it takes on this appearance and thus claims to belong to the Good, gives itself out to be its equal, but in this very pretention which is an admission it remains subordinated. But this desire for the non-desirable, this responsibility for the neighbor, this substitution as a hostage, is the subjectivity and uniqueness of a subject.[169]

For Levinas, the idea of the Good as Goodness of the Good *before* and *beyond* Being *without* origin or fixed determination dismantles the nihilism of the genealogy of values as much as it undermines the subjectivist ground of universal moral ethics. Indeed, for Levinas, the idea of the Good announces itself as irreducible transcendence of an absolute Law which immemorially elects the Self to an infinitely exceeding responsibility for the Other, and thus to the ethical *before* autonomy or judgment as unsubstitutable substitution and expiation for the Other: As Levinas writes:

> From the Good to me, there is assignation: a relation that survives the "death of God." The death of God perhaps signifies only the possibility to reduce every value arousing an impulse to an impulse arousing a value. The fact that in its goodness the Good declines the desire it arouses while inclining it toward responsibility for the neighbor, preserves difference in the non-indifference of the Good, which chooses me before I welcome it. It preserves its *Illeity* to the point of letting it be excluded from the analysis, save for the trace it leaves in words or the "objective reality" in thoughts, according to the unimpeachable witness of the Descartes' Third Meditation. That in the responsibility for another, the ego, already a self, already obsessed by the neighbor, would be unique and irreplaceable is what confirms its election. For the condition for, or the unconditionality of, the self does not begin in the auto-affection of a sovereign ego that would be, after the event, "compassionate" for another. Quite the contrary: the uniqueness of the responsible ego is possible only in being obsessed by another, in the trauma suffered prior to any auto-identification, in an

unrepresentable before. The one affected by the other is an anarchic trauma, or an inspiration of the one by the other, and not a causality striking mechanically a matter subject to its energy. In this trauma the Good reabsorbs, or redeems, the violence of non-freedom. Responsibility is what first enables one to catch sight of and conceive of value.[170]

"Here I am" ("Me voici")

"Here I am," Levinas retrieves the Biblical and prophetic phrase which, throughout the project of an ethics as "First Philosophy," opens and engages toward an hyperbolical ethics for the Other *before* the Self can constitute or institute itself as autonomy, freedom, will, and sovereignty. For Levinas, this Abrahamic response (cf. *Genesis*) is emblematic of the response *without* measure, *without* reserve, *without* evaluation, to the call and the commandment of the Other. "Here I am" engages what Levinas also calls a "freedom invested," and, in this sense, marks the election of the Self to the ethical subjecting it and awakening it *before* its own self-determination to an infinite responsibility for the Other. It is also in this sense that through the "Here I am" of the ethical Self lies the witnessing of the infinite transcendence of the Other. For Levinas, "Here I am for the Other" means a certain ethical individuation as election of the Self. Indeed, the ethical Self is not a substantial or sovereign subjectivity, but *before* and *beyond* autonomy, exposition, passivity, more passive than all passivity, responsibility for the Other—and thus exposition which, as elected and awakened as ethical Self, incessantly exceeds its responsibility for the Other, substitution and expiation:

The glory of the Infinite is the anarchic identity of the subject flushed out without being able to slip away. It is the ego led to sincerity, making signs to the other, for whom and before whom I am responsible, of this very giving of signs, that is, of this responsibility: "here I am." The saying prior to anything said bears witness to glory. This witness is true, but with a truth irreducible to the truth of disclosure, and does not narrate anything that shows itself. Saying is without noematic correlation in the pure obedience to glory that orders. It is without dialogue, in the passivity from the first subordinate to the "here I am." The distance that is enlarged in the measure that proximity narrows, the glory of infinity, is the inequality between the same and the other, the difference that is also the non-indifference of the same for the other and the substitution which, in its turn, is a nonequality with oneself, a non-recovering of self by self, a dispossession of self, the self leaving the clandestinity of its identification. It is already a sign made to another, a sign of this giving of signs, that is, of this non-indifference, a sign of this impossibility of slipping away and being replaced, of this identity, this uniqueness: "here I am". The identity aroused thus behind identification is an identity by pure election. Election traverses the concept of the ego to summon me as me through the inordinateness of the other. It extracts me from the concept in which I continually take refuge, for I find in it the measure of an obligation which is not defined in the election. Obligation calls for a unique response not inscribed in universal thought, the unforseeable response of the chosen one. This identity is pre-original, anarchic, older than every beginning. It is not self-consciousness attaining itself in the present, but the extreme exposure to the assignation by the other, already realized behind consciousness and freedom.[171]

"Here I am" means thus "for the Other"—that is, the awakening of the Self through the hyperbolical ethical commandment which singularly elects an obedience for the Other *before* the commandment of the Other, *before* the recognition or the intersubjective relation with the Other and *beyond* all decision, freedom, commonality and moral normativity. The exceptionality of this response and responsibility, "Here I am," marks the Self as always and already responding for the Other in substitution and expiation. Accusative, obsessed, persecuted by the Other, the Self is elected to respond for the Other as wholly responsible of death of the Other. It is here that, for Levinas, the ethical Self witnesses the Infinite commandment through the *Illeity* as the immemorial past of a transcendent alterity: God. Which means for Levinas that the urgency of the responsibility for the Other always precedes the devotion or the faith in God. What Levinas names the gratitude of the gift as responsibility, substitution, expiation for the Other—responsibility, substitution, expiation which does not suppress or step *beyond* the Law but are engaged in an idea of justice *before* truth, a justice *toward* the singularity of the Other:

> Infinity is not announced in the witness given as a theme. In the sign given to the other, by which I find myself torn up from the secrecy of Gyges, "taken by the hair" from the bottom of my obscurity in the saying without the said of sincerity, in my "here I am," from the first present in the accusative, I bear witness to the Infinite. The Infinite is not in front of its witness, but as it were outside, or on the "other side" of presence, already past, out of reach, a thought behind thoughts which is too lofty to push itself up front. "Here I am, in the name of God," without referring myself directly to his presence. "Here I am," just that! The word God is still absent from the phrase in which God is for the first time involved in words. It does not at all state "I believe in God." To bear witness God is precisely not to state this extraordinary word, as though glory would be lodged in a theme and be posited as a thesis, or become being's essence. As a sign given to the other of this very signification, the "here I am" signifies me in the name of God, at the service of men that look at me, without having

anything to identify myself with, but the sound of my voice or the figure of my gesture—the Saying itself. This recurrence is quite the opposite of return upon oneself, self-consciousness. It is sincerity, effusion of oneself, "extraditing" of the self to the neighbor. Witness is humility and admission; it is made before all theology; it is kergyma and prayer, glorification and recognition. But what is proper to all the relations that are thus unfolded—and what a deception for the friends of truth that thematizes being, and of the subject that effaces itself before Being!—is the fact that the return is sketched out in the going, the appeal is understood in the response, the "provocation" coming from God is in my invocation, gratitude is already gratitude for this state of gratitude, which is at the same time or in turn a gift and a gratitude. The transcendence of the revelation lies in the fact that the "epiphany" comes in the saying of him that received it. The order that orders me does not leave me any possibility of setting things right side up again with impunity, of going back from the exteriority of the Infinite, as when before a theme one goes back from the signifier to the signified, or as when in a dialogue one finds in "you" a being. It is in prophecy that the Infinite escapes the objectification of thematization and of dialogue, and signifies as Illeity, in the third person. This "thirdness" is different from that of the third man, it is the third party that interrupts the face-to-face of a welcome of the other man, interrupts the proximity or approach of the neighbor, it is the third man with which justice begins.[172]

Holy (*Saint*)

Traditional Judaism names the Holy (*saint*) the absolute separation between humanity and God. The Holy refers to and thereby bears witness to the absolute and irreducible transcendence of God. Levinas retrieves this idea and by it radicalizes the separation, the distinction, the differentiation of the otherness, the absolute alterity, the irreducible separation of the *Otherwise than Being* as *beyond* and *before* Being as always and already *beyond* and *before* truth and meaning, totality and essence, presence and representation, identity and unification, Sameness and commonality. *Otherwise than Being* means irreducible separation *beyond* and *before* Being, *beyond* and *before* the intentional structure from which beings or entities can appear and be manifest. *Before* and *beyond* Being as the ethical. It is this holiness of God, its absolute separation, which Levinas translates as the "desirable", as that which incessantly motivates, animates, awakens desire toward the Other and which it will never capture, comprehend, appropriate, consume, or absorb in an immanence of meaning. Indeed, for Levinas, as holiness, as absolute and transcendent separation, the Other incessantly absolves itself from its appropriation by the Self and, in this sense, always aggravates, exacerbates, intensifies, and deepens the separation and its own *ab*solution. Levinas always engages this movement of holiness which sees desire infinitely tending toward the Infinite as infinitely tending itself *without* end or *telos* toward the Other and thus as *infinitization* of the ethical Self's responsibility for the Other.

Distinguished from the *sacred* (*sacré*) which consecrates idolatry and defines idolization, and in this sense constitutes paganism itself, the Holy calls to the human in the human, that is to the transcendent in the Self *beyond* and *before* the Self who, responsible *before* any call or commandment, responds already *beyond* its will or judgment, always overwhelming and exceeding the universal norms of morality, autonomy, or intersubjective recognition, community, "being-together."

This distinction between the *sacred* and the Holy is emphasized in the volume of the Talmudic readings and lectures entitled *Du sacré au saint.*[173] For Levinas, the *sacred*, sacrality and sacralization, engage a reduction of the Holy, a materialization and "incarnation" of the absolute transcendence of the Other. The *sacred* is, in this sense, a synonym for perjury, treason, and transgression as it pretends to embody the transcendence of the the Holy but in truth reduces its absolute Height to an object, a material embodiment, and immanence in the Sameness of the Same. The *sacred* engages an identity between the materiality of the thing and the ideality of the idea in which the transcendence of the Other is always and already nullified and annihilated in a whole comprehension and totalizing reappropriation of identification. The *sacred* inscribes the transcendence of God in and within Nature, equates God with the Natural as fulfilled materiality, and thus consolidates an identification between the absolute transcendence of the Law and the essential immanence of manifestation, phenomenality, presentation, presence.

Levinas rather insists on Holiness, the Holy as infinite Height occurring, calling, commanding as justice in and through the face of the Other. Indeed, the absolute and irreducible transcendence of the Holy opens and engages an ethical relation where the Self is always obliged and obsessed, already called to its Self by the Other as response and responsibility, always and already required by the Other for the Other *without* the possibility of escape and thereby *without* end, *without* finality, *without* being able to "call it even" with the Other.

The Holy implies thus a radical interruption of phenomenality, materiality, presence, embodiment, or incarnation. That is the Holy commands from its absolute separation—and demands in its heterogeneous commandment a rupture and a *caesura* with the order of manifestation in opening an *anarchic* ethical responsibility for that which remains irreducible to presence or manifestation: the Other.

It is however important to mark how and why, for Levinas, the Holy implies a radical critique of sacralization and thus engages a *de-sacralization* of the ethical. Indeed, for Levinas, the ethical is not a sublime posture, a pure gratuity or givenness of charity, benevolence, mercy, forgiveness, self-sacrifice. Ethics as "First philosophy" does not mean or engage the empty moralism of an ideal and superlative exposition to the Other. Levinas' ethics always refers at once and simultaneously to the Law and to responsibility in the face of the commandment of the Other—which is also always of the Law, expressed as the Law, "Thou shall not kill." In this sense, the Holy for Levinas means the *de-sacralization* of the simple altruistic postures and sublime or sublimating postures of ideals, posturing as ethical—such as the postures of self-sacrifice as renunciation and simple abdication of the Self, charity as pure givenness, forgiveness as reconciliation. Levinas always claims to the inescapability of the Law as incessant recall of responsibility for the Other as the critical dismantling and incessant questioning of the accomplished and fulfilled logics of self-sacrifice, charity, forgiveness—that is, of the theological and ontological dynamics where *love* would be given *without* and *beyond* the justice of the Law.

Home (*Chez-soi*)

In recalling Heidegger's analyses in *Being and Time*, and most particularly on the "mineness" (*Jemeinigkeit*) of the *Dasein* and its "in view of oneself" as authenticity in being one's self through its ownmost existential *solus ipse*,[174] Levinas poses the question:

> The Heideggerian analyses of the world have accustomed is to think that the "in view of oneself" that characterizes *Dasein*, care in situation, in the last analysis conditions every human product. In *Being and Time* the home does not appear apart from the system of implements. But can the "in view of oneself" characteristic of care be brought about without extraterritoriality—without *being at home with oneself*?[175]

This question posed to Heidegger's "fundamental ontology" engages precisely another analysis of *being at home with oneself*. Levinas indeed seeks to undermine the ontological appropriation and reappropriation of the Self by itself through its engagement and attunement in and by Being. Far from deploying the essence of a *dwelling* in the essence and within the truth of Being, Levinas marks the irreducible otherness of the Other overwhelming the ontological Sameness of the truth of Being, the impredictable occurrence of the Other as disturbance, displacement, disorder always and already overcoming the determined frontiers of the "home," the inexhaustible errancy of the alterity of the Other suspending and interrupting the proper and identifiable identity and Sameness of the Self's homecoming:

> I can indeed recollect myself in the midst of my life, which is life from . . . . However, the negative moment of this *dwelling* which determines possession, the recollection which draws me out of submergence, is not a simple echo of possession. We may not see in it the counterpart of presence to things, as though the possession of things, as a presence to them, dialectically contained the withdrawal from them. This withdrawal implies a new event; I must have been in relation with something I do not live from. This event is the relation with the Other who welcomes me in the Home, the discreet presence of the Feminine. But in order that I be able to free myself from the very possession that the welcome of the Home establishes, in order that I be able to see things in themselves, that is, represent them to myself, refuse both enjoyment and possession, I must know how *to give* what I possess. Only thus could I situate myself absolutely above my engagement in the non-I. But for this I must encounter the indiscreet face of the Other that calls me into question. The Other—the absolutely other—paralyses possession, which he contests by his epiphany in the face. He can contest my possession only because he approaches me not from the outside but from above. The same can not lay hold of this other without suppressing him. But the untraversable infinity of the negation of murder is announced by this dimension of height, where the Other comes to me concretely in the ethical impossibility of committing this murder. I welcome the Other who presents himself in my home by opening my home to him.[176]

In this sense, the home means first, for Levinas, *hospitality* for the Other, the welcome as exposition, to the commandment of the Other to the point where the home is always inhabited and roused by the Other irreducible to the Self, the Same, the wholeness of the totality of one's identity with one's self. The home thus marks a certain *being-taught* by an irreducible transcendence and exteriority: "This voice coming from another shore teaches transcendence itself. Teaching signifies the whole infinity of exteriority. And the whole infinity of exteriority is not first produced, to the teach: teaching is its very production. The first teaching teaches this very height, tantamount its exteriority, the ethical."[177] It is important here to mark that, for Levinas, teaching is not domination or dominion. Levinas does not engage the domination or the dominion of the Other over the Same. Rather, he marks a novel modality of hospitality to the transcendence of the Other—a relation which never demotes or reduces the ethical Law of the Other. That is: to teach means to always inscribe the relation of the Self to the Other and of the Other commanding the Self as the instantiation of the Law, of justice, and thus of the interdiction of murder—of the annihilation of the Self *or* the murder of the Other. To teach means to awaken and elect toward a responsibility and not the hegemony of an abdication or a renunciation of the Self. To teach means to reveal, *beyond* and *before* the universality of the moral norm, the singularity of a responsibility *without* measure or reserve:

> In this commerce with the infinity of exteriority or of height the naïveté of the direct impulse, the naïveté of the being exercising itself as a force on the move is ashamed of its naïveté. It discovers itself as a violence, but thereby enters into a new dimension. Commerce with the alterity of infinity does not offend like an opinion; it does not limit a mind in a way inadmissible to a philosopher. Limitation is produced only within a totality, whereas the relation with the Other breaks the ceiling of the totality. It is fundamentally pacific. The other is not opposed to me as a freedom other than, but similar to my own, and consequently hostile to my own. The Other is not another freedom as arbitrary as my own, in which case it would traverse the infinity that separates me from him and enter under the same concept. His alterity is manifested in a mastery that does not conquer but teaches. Teaching is not a species of a genus called domination, a hegemony at work within a totality, but is the presence of infinity breaking the closed circle of totality.[178]

Hostage (*Otage*)

The idea of hostage traverses Levinas' *Otherwise than Being, or Beyond Essence* and marks how and why, paradoxically, the ethical Self is elected and always and already responding, how and why the ethical Self is liberated in its Selfhood through its inescapable and undeniable responsibility for the Other. Far from engaging in an ethics of self-sacrifice, Levinas deploys how the ethical Self is elected to a responsibility for the Other—a responsibility which repudiates self-abnegation as much as it engages the ethical *before* and *beyond* the autonomy of the moral subject posing through its own freedom the universality of a rational moral norm. For Levinas, it is always and already through the responsibility for the Other claiming the Self to the ethical *before* and *beyond* the autonomy of its will which engages its liberation, its "difficult freedom." Which means: the liberation of the Self *beyond* and *before* the claim of its sovereignty expresses the ethical Self as hostage of the Other for the Other in responsibility. What Levinas also marks as the exposedness of the subject to the Other, passivity more passive than all passivity—infinite trauma of responsibility for the Other *before* and *beyond* the comprehension of subjectivity in and as being-there or being-present of its self-determination:

> This passivity is, to be sure, an exposedness of the subject to another, but the passivity of the subject is more passive still than that which the oppressed one determined to struggle undergoes. The most passive, unassumable, passivity, the subjectivity or the very subjection of the subject, is due to my being obsessed with responsibility for the oppressed who is other than myself. Due to it the struggle remains human, and passivity does not simulate essence through a recapture of the self by the ego, in a will for sacrifice or generosity.[179]

This is why Levinas' ethics as "First Philosophy" always implies to think the ethical Self as a liberation from the anonymity of Being and escape from the indifference of essence. A liberation as hostage of responsibility for the Other. In this sense, through responsibility for the Other, the Self does not occur or come to be by and from its own self-determination or self-affirmation, but as assigned, elected, commanded, awoken by the Other. The Self emerges by the Other for the Other—as hostage of responsibility for the alterity of the Other. Which entails that the primacy of the ethical implies the primordiality of always and already being-for-the-Other, uniquely and singularly elected to being the hostage of a responsibility for the Other. And again, this election to being the hostage of the Other in and through responsibility is irreducible to a self-sacrificial posture. It opens the Self to a certain abandonment of the subject's sovereignty, pretention, will, where, in this abandonment, is liberated the acute and exceptional possibility of responding *without* reserve as infinite responsibility for the Other.

Which is why, for Levinas, "Subjectivity is being hostage." And furthermore, as Levinas explicates:

> This notion reverses the position where the presence of the ego to itself appears as the beginning or as the conclusion of philosophy. This coinciding in the same, where I would be an origin, or, through memory, a covering over of the origin, this presence, is, from the start, undone by the other. The subject resting on itself is confounded by wordless accusation. For in discourse it would have already lost its traumatic violence. The accusation is in this sense persecuting; the persecuted one can no longer answer it. More exactly, it is accusation which I cannot answer, but for which I cannot decline responsibility. Already the position of the subject is a deposition, not a *conatus essendi*. It is from the first a substitution by a hostage expiating for the violence of the persecution itself. We have to conceive

> in such terms the de-substantiation of the subject, its de-reification, its disinterestedness, its subjection, its subjectivity. It is a pure self, in the accusative, responsible before there is freedom.[180]

The idea of hostage opens to the "difficult freedom" of the ethical Self as responsibility for the Other *before* and *beyond* the rational autonomy of practical freedom and as unsurpassable and irremediable election for the Other. It is in this manner, thus, that the idea of the ethical Self as hostage of the Other for the Other is always allied to another major trope of *Otherwise than Being, or Beyond Essence*, that of *substitution*: "This responsibility for the neighbor, this substitution as a hostage, is the subjectivity and uniqueness of a subject."[181]

The idea of substitution marks, for Levinas, how and where the ethical Self is always responsible for the Other, already responding more, and more responsibly than what would or could be demanded or expected. In other words, substitution means to be always responding, responding *before* and *beyond* the commandment of the Other, by already exceeding in responsibility through responsibility for the Other. Responsibility exceeding responsibility, and thus responsibility *without* measure or end, *without* relying on a universal principle of moral action, and, in this sense, already overwhelming, hyperbolically surpassing all norms or judgment for the Other and in the name of the singularity of the Other. Which is why Levinas, in *Otherwise than Being, or Beyond Essence*, remarks: the ethical Self is always and already a hostage of responsibility for the Other, hostage of the Other in responding as infinite responsibility for the Other. That is, the exceptionality of the ethical Self is liberated by and through the inescapable and unsubstitutable responsibility—exceptionality of being hostage of responsibility—for the Other.

Through responsibility the Self adheres to the ethical and thus is elected to its ethical Self. For the Other, always and already responding *before* and *beyond* the call and the demands of the Other individualizes the Self to the ethical as non-interchangeable, unique, and thus exclusively for the Other as hostage in response and responsibility. Such is thus the exceptionality of Levinas' ethics as "First Philosophy": the Self rises to itself as ethical by and through the Other, responding always and already *before* the call of the Other to the point of substitution and expiation—that is as hospitality for the Other to the point of responding as responsibility, exposedness, trauma, passivity more passive than all passivity—as irremediable, irreplaceable and irrevocable hostage of the Other—what Levinas also calls *inspiration*:

> The responsibility for another, an unlimited responsibility which the strict book-keeping of the free and non-free does not measure, requires subjectivity as an irreplaceable hostage. This subjectivity it denudes under

the ego in a passivity of persecution, repression and expulsion outside of essence, into oneself. In this self, outside of essence, one is in a deathlike passivity! But in responsibility for the other for life and death, the adjectives unconditional, undeclinable, absolute take on meaning. They serve to qualify freedom, but wear away the substrate, from which the free act arises in essence. In the accusative form, which is a modification of no nominative form, in which I approach the neighbor for whom, without having wished it, I have to answer, the irreplaceable one is brought out. This finite freedom is not primary, is not initial; but it lies in an infinite responsibility where the other is not other because he strikes up against and limits my freedom, but where he can accuse me to the point of persecution, because the other, absolutely other, is another one. That is why finite freedom is not simply an infinite freedom operating in a limited field. The will which it animates wills in a passivity it does not assume. And the proximity of the neighbor in its trauma does not only strike up against me, but exalts and elevates me, and, in the literal sense of the term, inspires me.[182]

Human (*Humain*)

For Levinas, the human—and humanism—carries at least two meanings where the first is superseded by the second. Indeed, the classical definition of the human is critically questioned and redefined. Levinas undermines the classical and traditional determination of the human and re-orients the idea of human and concept of humanism to a *wholly other* orientation: *beyond* Being and essence, *beyond* reason and volition, *beyond* moral autonomy and determination. In its classical and traditional definition, the human means and signifies the individual as a member of the genus to which it can be identified and categorized. The human is understood as a substantial subject or subjectivity endowed with free will, autonomy, rationality, theoretical and practical judgment, and consequently as embodying and exemplifying a moral responsibility as universal duty within an intersubjective commonality. This classical definition of the human, ground and foundation of humanism, Levinas will undoubtedly engage it in a critical questioning, at times even retrieving elements of the "anti-humanist" critique of humanism. Indeed, Levinas will mark the need to renew the idea of the human and consequently of humanism from that of a *humanism of the Other*, and thus of the *Other human*. In this sense, indeed, Levinas retrieves the "anti-humanist" critique of humanism by indicating how and why the first dismantles and deconstructs the centrality of the human as privileged measure of all things, ground and foundation of existence and sole being among beings capable of determining the truth, the value, the norm, the meaning, the essence of Being, and consequently intersubjective "being-with" others. However, Levinas does not simply mark through this retrieval the effacement of the human. Rather, returning anti-humanism against itself, in a certain manner, Levinas suggests in *Humanism of the Other* that classical humanism is *not* sufficiently human and thus not sufficiently humanist in that it remains too circumscribed by an economy of judgment and normativity founded on the universality of reason and thereby on an intersubjectivity where Self and Other are equated, brought to the Same, identified in the immanence of an equilibriated relation and commonality. Classical humanism does not rise to its own ideal as it does not, pursues Levinas, reveal the human in the human, that is, does not reveal the irreducible alliance of the human to that which transcends human reason and self-determination: the Other.

Levinas thus calls onto an opening in humanism to a *beyond* humanism where the occurrence of the face of the Other as commandment and appeal elects the ethical Self *before* the normativity and universality of humanism—that is, *before* autonomy or sovereignty, judgment or intentionality, universality or morality, and thereby *before* the opposition between passivity and activity, possibility and necessity, theoretical reason and practical reason. Levinas' humanism of the Other is a humanism entirely turned into an infinite responsibility for the Other because already summoned, commanded, ordered by the transcendence of the Other. It marks and opens an ethical responsibility *without* norm and *without* reserve, arising as *anarchy*—*without* origin, *without* finality, *without* principle—in its infinite orientation—substitution and expiation—for the Other.

This is why, for Levinas, the human always "implies fraternity" where

> fraternity is radically opposed to the conception of a humanity united by resemblance, a multiplicity of diverse families arisen from the stones cast behind by Deucalion, and which, across the struggle of egoisms, result in a human city. Human fraternity has then two aspects: it involves individualities whose logical status is not reducible to the status of ultimate differences in a genus, for their singularity consists in each referring to itself. On the other hand, it involves the commonness of a father, as though the commonness of race would not bring together enough. Society must be a fraternal community o be commensurate with the straightforwardness, the primary proximity, in which the face of the Other presents itself to my welcome. Monotheism signifies this human kinship, this idea of a human race that refers back to the approach of the Other in the face, in a dimension of height, in responsibility for the Other.[183]

Hypostasis (*Hypostase*)

The term, from the Greek *hupostasis*, designates firstly and foremostly that which stands under, foundation or ground, basic and unitary structure of Being. The term is defined by Plotinus before being retrieved, as well as redefined, in Christian theology. For Plotinus, and the Neo-platonists, hypostasis is a divine principle: it signifies, through the unicity and uniqueness of the Divine, the modality by which this unicity and uniqueness deploys itself. It marks the concretion of the unicity and uniqueness of the Divine which Plotinus structures and hierarchizes in three stages. Indeed, for Plotinus, the hypostases of the unicity and the uniqueness of the Divine are: the absolute *One* from which emanates the *Intellect* and from which emerges the *Soul* (*Psyché*) engaged and embedded in and within the materiality of the *World*. The *Soul of the World* constitutes, in this sense, the ascending movement of a conversion from the human subject, entrenched in contingence, to the unicity of the One which redeems it. The term is re-interpreted in Christian theology for which it designates the difference between God and its creation which is re-unified, through the Incarnation and the Passion of Christ, the hypostasic alliance and comprehension of the human and God.

For Levinas, hypostasis marks the self's individuation and singularity. Indeed, Levinas seeks to show, as early as *Time and the Other* and *Existence and Existents*, how a radically solitary existent can come to its individuation and singularity *against* the anonymous and indifference of the "*il y a*," *against* the suffocating and asphyxiating presence and immanence of Being. The solitude of the existent is not merely a particular characteristic—for Levinas, it marks the basic ontological condition of the existent: to exist means to be enveloped and entrapped in the solitude of a monad, comprehended, and encompassed in the generality of the "there is," submerged in the indifference, anonymity, impersonality of the "night":

> There is, in general, without it mattering what there is, without our being able to fix a substantive to this term. There is an impersonal form, like in it rains, or it is warm. Its anonymity is essential. . . . What we call the I is itself submerged by the night, invaded, depersonalized, stifled by it. The disappearance of all things and of the I leaves what cannot disappear, the sheer fact of being in which one participates, without having taken the initiative, anonymously. Being remains, like a field of forces, like a heavy atmosphere belonging to no one.[184]

For Levinas, the indifference of the "*il y a*" needs and requires to be transcended, escaped and evaded by the existent. It is precisely here that the existent, absorbed in the anonymity of Being, immersed in the "*il y a*," *bears a name*. The name of the existent reverses and inverses the anonymity of the "*il y a*." Indeed, as Levinas remarks, the "*il y a*" is unnameable, impersonal neutrality, element which suffocates and smothers all existents in its generality and indistinction. The hypostasis means and signifies the "turn" from this anonymity into "substantives."[185] The anonymity of Being is inversed and inverted through an hypostasis and is engaged thereby in a transcending, an exceeding *beyond* itself out of itself to the point where, as Levinas marks, "beings are capable of bearing names."[186] This "exceptional situation" defines precisely the hypostasis: "[T]he present brings about the exceptional situation where we can give to an instant a name, and conceive it as a substantive. Not by an abuse of language, but in virtue of an ontological transmutation, an essential equivocation."[187]

The hypostasis engages the positing and positioning, in the anonymity of Being, of an existent and thus of a subjectivity or a Self incessantly transcending the indifference and impersonality of the "*il y a*." Inversion of Being, the hypostasis marks the spontaneous emergence *from existence to an existent*, and thus, in its "instant" as "a rip in the infinite beginningless and endless fabric of existence," opens, *beyond* the "*il y a*" of bare, brute, anonymous existence, a "beginning"[188]—an individuation of the irreducible singularity of the Self. It is important to note how, for Levinas, the hypostasis as a "beginning" is incessantly reiterated—the existent individuates itself incessantly *beyond* the impersonality, indifference and anonymity of Being. Otherwise said, as soon as the existent *comes-to-be*, the *existent exists*. And at the instant the existent emerges, *beyond* the "*il y a*" of Being, as an existent, its existence is unsubstitutable; the existent possesses itself. Which means that the existent needs to incessantly reiterate its individuation—needs to incessantly engage its hypostasis, its transcending *from* the anonymity of existence *to* its being a singular existent.

The analysis of the hypostasis of the existent is furthered by a question which finds its clearest expression in *Time and the Other*: "How, in the alterity of a you, can I remain I, without being absorbed or losing myself in that you? How can the *ego* that I am remain myself in a you, without being nonetheless the *ego* that I am in my present—that is to say, an ego that inevitably returns to itself? How can the *ego* become other to itself?"[189] Indeed, the movement of hypostasis transcends the "*il y a*" thereby individualizing an existent *beyond* Being, *beyond* the anonymity and the indifference, however does it not also immure the existent in its own existentiality, in its own materiality, in its own embodiment? Otherwise said, the materiality of the hypostasized subject makes it possible for the *ego* to grasp itself as a possession but also does it not also enclose the *ego* for itself and as *my own self?* For Levinas, however, the subject transcending Being through its hypostasis, the existent finds itself and *yet* still needs "become other to itself," needs to *transcend* its own existentiality, its materiality, its embodiment toward itself as other.

In *Time and the Other*, Levinas remarks that the possibility of this transcending hypostasis of the hypostasized subject is engaged in filiality and fecundity, most specifically, in paternity and the birth of a son: the transcending of the Self in an Other than the Self *beyond* the Self. Filiality and fecundity is the very modality by which the singularity of the Self is engaged in its own transcending toward the Other: the existent is singularized through the further hypostasis engaged in *filiation*: the Self transcending itself in the creation of an Other which is always also allied to the Self. The father, the Self, transcends itself in the son as Other whose separate hypostasis opens up the Self's own hypostasis giving thereby the Self the hope that death is not the only way of escaping or evading Being. To be the Other *without* including the Other in the Self is to "introduce a duality into existence, a duality that concerns the very existing of each subject. Existing itself becomes double."[190] Fecundity and filiality does not reduce the duality of existing to a unity, to an identification or a totalization. Rather fecundity, filiality possibilizes the individual through the separateness of the hypostasized existent to an escape—from the encompassing and inclosing of its material self-encumbrance and entrapment in oneself to the Other *beyond* the material enclosure of the Self; the son *beyond* the father.

In Levinas' later work, and most particularly in *Otherwise than Being, or Beyond Essence*, the modality of hypostasis is carried over. However, Levinas moves away from the idea of filiation, filiality and paternity to entirely reformulate how the Self can become *other* without being annihilated as a Self and reappropriated within the comprehension of the Same, identity, Sameness. It is in *Otherwise than Being, or Beyond Essence* that Levinas marks how and why the Self is always inhabited and inspired by the Other, how and why the Self is already for the Other, anarchically affected by the irreducible alterity of the Other. Which means, for Levinas, hypostasis will mean the incessant transcending of the Self *for* the Other as substitution and expiation. Substitution and expiation do not indicate a simple exchange between two terms—as if the Self replaces itself for the Other or reciprocally. All to the contrary: Levinas argues that the *irreplaceability* of the Self occurs, is awakened and elected as singularity by substituting itself for a singular Other. The Self and the Other are not the Same, nor is their difference collapsed. Rather, substitution and expiation as deployment of the modality of hypostasis marks the break and rupture of the Same by the irreducible transcendence of the Other and as the perpetual and incessant election of the Self for the Other, of the Self perpetually and incessantly exceeding itself *before* and *beyond* itself toward the absolute alterity of the Other.

For the Levinas of *Otherwise than Being, or Beyond Essence*, substitution and expiation as apex of the hypostasis, animates and elects the Self to its ethical responsibility as unsubstitutable singularity and unicity for the Other. Indeed, the individuation of the hypostasized subject as substitution and expiation entails the movement where the Self is "in itself already outside of itself" and "expelled into itself outside of being."[191] Which means: the Self exceeds itself *beyond* and *before* itself out of Being, in a way that both concentrates its selfhood into a single point and also into an incessant suspension of this point, giving over the Self as ethical to the Other, *without* any identity to hold onto except as orientation always and already for the Other. Indeed, the ethical Self *before* autonomy or sovereignty is elected as always and already committed and obligated beyond itself by the Other for the Other. The ethical Self is—*before* consciousness, self-consciousness, recognition of the Other—already *beyond* itself for the Other. The Self is already responsible for the Other—substitution and expiation—as irreplaceable and unsubstitutable. Levinas marks thus the ethical Self as always and already singularly for the Other and uniquely elected, awakened, engaged—prior to its for-itself—as obsession and response for the Other:

> It is by this hypostasis that the Self, as an identity unjustifiable by itself [. . .]. An identity prior to the for-itself, which is not the reduced or germinal model of the relationship of oneself with oneself that cognition is. Neither a vision of oneself by oneself, nor a manifestation of oneself to oneself, the oneself does not coincide with the identifying of truth, is not stable in terms of consciousness, discourse and intentionality. The unjustifiable identity of ipseity is expressed in terms such as *ego*, I, oneself, and, this work aims to show throughout, starting with the soul, sensibility, vulnerability, maternity and materiality, which describe responsibility for others. The "fulcrum" in which this turning of being back upon itself which we call knowing or mind is produced thus designates the singularity par excellence.[192]

Otherwise than Being, or Beyond Essence marks the anarchic exposure as incessant hypostasis of the ethical Self as singularity for the Other—singularity as already electing the Self to the ethical and where the ethical Self is a singularity "prior to the distinction between the particular and the universal. It is, if one likes, a relationship, but one where there is no disjunction between the terms held in relationship."[193]

Illeity (*Illéité*)

Absolute Otherness, the term "Illeity" means an "absolute *He*" and refers to the irreducible separation of the transcendence of the "Very High" ("*le Très-Haut*") marking the alterity of the ethical *beyond* and *before* the immanent presence of Being and its identity always comprehending "in itself and for itself difference," differentiation and alteration. Which means: Illeity signifies, for Levinas, the absolute Otherness transcendence of the Other *beyond* and *before* the simple binary and traditional distinctions: of the manifest and the concealed, of presence and absence, of identity and difference, of Being and non-Being or nothingness, of diction and contradiction.

For Levinas, Illeity as absolute Otherness remains irreducible to phenomenality as well as to non-phenomenality. As above marked, Illeity means, for Levinas, the pure transcendence and irreducible otherness of the Other. In this sense, Illeity signifies the immemoriality of a past, a past that has never been present and thus irreducible to a rememorable or retrievable past. Hence, Illeity is not apprehensible as a *Thou* nor is it assimilable to the face of the Other which commands and elects the ethical Self. Illeity, for Levinas, testifies of the absolute transcendent alterity, and, in this sense, opens to think *beyond* the "consciousness of . . ." and thereby *beyond* the constitution of intentionality. Illeity means the Infinite as Infinitely transcendent Other:

> The trace left by the infinite is not the residue of a presence; its very glow is ambiguous. Otherwise, its positivity would not preserve the infinity of the infinite any more than negativity would. The infinite wipes out its traces not in order to trick him who obeys, but because it transcends the present in which it commands me, and because I cannot deduce it from this command. The infinite who orders me is neither a cause acting straight on, nor a theme, already dominated, if only retrospectively, by freedom. This detour at a face and this detour from this detour in the enigma of a trace we have called '"Illeity."[194]

Without settling for the apophatic logic of negative theology, Levinas insists on the *positivity* of the absolute transcendence of the Illeity. That is, Levinas insists on how Illeity expresses itself in and through the face of the Other. In this sense, for Levinas, there lies always *in* the exteriority, the transcendence, the absolute otherness of the face of the Other a *further otherness*, an otherness of the Other expressing itself through the face of the Other in *its* order and commandment "Thou shall not kill." Illeity signifies the otherness absolutely Other, the transcendent otherness in and through the Other, irreducibly heterogeneous and immemorially heteronomous transcendence where and in which occurs the face of the Other:

> What is exceptional in this way of being signalled is that I am ordered toward the face of the other. In this order which is an ordination the non-presence of the infinite is not only a figure of negative theology. All the negative attributes which state what is *beyond* the essence become positive in

> responsibility, a response answering to a non-thematizable provocation and thus a non-vocation, a trauma. This response answers, before any understanding, for a debt contracted before any freedom and before any consciousness and any present, but it does answer, as though the invisible that bypasses the present left a trace by the very fact of bypassing the present. That trace lights up as the face of a neighbor, ambiguously him before whom (or to whom, without any paternalism) and him for whom I answer.[195]

For Levinas, Illeity implies not only an irreducibility to phenomenality, presence, or representation. It also marks an absolute transcendence, absolutely transcending itself and thereby surpassing all possible categorization or typification, *topos* or *logos.* Illeity as the Otherness always other than the face of the Other expressing itself, from its absolute transcendence, through the face of Other's commandment opens to an idea of justice. Incessantly re-affirmed as absolute Otherness *beyond* the face of the Other and simultaneously expressing itself *in* the commandment of the face of the Other orders, *without* presence, the immemoriality of a past as trace which is the tracing of justice. In this sense, Illeity means a certain enigma—the enigma of an immemoriality, and furthermore of the immemoriality of justice from which erupts the hyperbolical singularity of the ethical.

Furthermore, the absolute transcendence of the Illeity reaffirms incessantly the "paradox" or the *aporia* of the hyperbolical responsibility for the Other. This "paradox" or *aporia* is indissociable from the *positivity* of this responsibility. Indeed, the Illeity commanding through the face of the Other marks the *diachrony* of the ethical—and thus, the ethical Self's response or responsibility *before* the commandment of the Other and yet always *too late* on the demand of the Other:

> Illeity lies outside the "thou" and the thematization of objects. A neologism formed with (*he*) or *ille*, it indicates a way of concerning me without entering into conjunction with me. To be sure, we have to indicate the element in which this concerning occurs. If the relationship with Illeity were a relationship of consciousness, "he" would designate a theme, as the "Thou" in Buber's I—Thou relation does, probably—for Buber has never brought out in a positive way the spiritual element in which the I-thou relationship is produced. The Illeity in the *beyond-being* is the fact that its coming toward me is a departure which lets me accomplish a movement toward a neighbor. The positive element of this departure, that which makes this departure, this *diachrony*, be more than a term of negative theology, is my responsibility for the others. Or, one may say, it is the fact that the others show themselves in their face. There is a paradox in responsibility,

> in that I am obliged without this obligation having begun in me, as though an order slipped into my consciousness like a thief, smuggled itself in, like an effect of one of Plato's wandering causes. But this is impossible in a consciousness, and clearly indicates that we are no longer in the element of consciousness. In consciousness this "who knows where" is translated into an anachronical overwhelming, the antecedence of responsibility and obedience with respect to the order received or the contract. It is as though the first movement of responsibility could not consist in awaiting nor even in welcoming the order (which would still be a quasi-activity), but consists in obeying this order before it is formulated. Or as though it were formulated before every possible present, in a past that shows itself in the present of obedience without being recalled, without coming from memory, being formulated by him who obeys in his very obedience.[196]

It is highly important for Levinas to think through the idea of Illeity as absolute transcendence of the Other expressing itself and traced in the face of the Other engages the *diachrony* of responsibility as the incessant excess of responsibility in the ethical Self, *before* and *beyond* its own for-itself, *before* and *beyond* its autonomy, wholly exposed for the Other:

> Illeity, which does not simply designate an oblique presentation to a squinting look, may indeed first signify such a disposition of personages. But we must go all the way. The Infinite does not signal itself to a subjectivity, a unity already formed, by its order to turn toward the neighbor. In its being subjectivity undoes essence by substituting itself for another. *Qua one-for-another*, it is absorbed in signification, in saying or the verb form of the infinite. Signification precedes essence. It is not a stage of cognition calling for the intuition that would fulfill it, nor the absurdity of non-identity or of impossible identity. It is the glory of transcendence.[197]

Beyond presence and absence, *beyond* cause and effect, irretrievable and irreappropriable in a modality of rememoration or retention, Illeity opens to the incessant reiteration of the *diachrony* of responsibility as ethical:

> The way the Infinite passes the finite and passes itself has an ethical meaning is not something that results from a project to construct the "transcendental foundation" of "ethical experience." The ethical is the field outlined by the paradox of an Infinite in relationship with the finite without being belied in this relationship. Ethics is the breakup of the originary unity of transcendental apperception, that is, it is the *beyond* of experience. Witnessed, and not thematized, in the sign given to the other, the Infinite signifies out of responsibility for the other, out of the-one-for-the-other, a

> subject supporting everything, subject to everything, that is, suffering for everyone, but charged with everything, without having had to decide for this taking charge, which is gloriously amplified in the measure that it is imposed. Obedience precedes any hearing of the command. The possibility of finding, anachronously, the order in the obedience itself, and of receiving the order out of oneself, this reverting of heteronomy into autonomy, is the very way the Infinite passes itself. The metaphor of the inscription of the law in consciousness expresses this in a remarkable way, reconciling autonomy and heteronomy. It does so in an ambivalence, whose diachrony is the signification itself, an ambivalence which, in the present, is an ambiguity. The inscription of the order in the for-the-other of obedience is an anarchic being affected, which slips into me 'like a thief through the outstretched nets of consciousness. This trauma has surprised me completely; the order has never been represented, for it has never been presented, not even in the past coming in memory, to the point that it is I that only says, and after the event, this unheard-of obligation. [. . .] The unheard-of saying is enigmatically in the anarchic response, in my responsibility for the other. The trace of infinity is this ambiguity in the subject, in turns beginning and makeshift, a diachronic ambivalence which ethics makes possible.[198]

Illeity, as immemoriality, Infinite otherness of the Other, irrepresentable and irreducible, traced through the face of the Other, expresses, *beyond* manifestation, the *diachronical* excess of responsibility as the irreducible justice and Law *beyond* and *before* economy and universality, wholly *singular* and solely oriented by and toward *singularity*. Illeity engages, through the idea of a justice for *singularity*, that is in the incessant recurrence of a Self who responds always in excess of responsibility for the *singularity* of the Other and *before* being for-itself, accused and obedient *before* its autonomy or decision. What Levinas also marks as substitution and expiation for the Other. Indeed, Levinas points toward an Illeity as that which, from the transcendence of its absolute otherness and as the Infinite *beyond* presence and absence, traces itself in the commandment of the face of the Other as irreducible and irremediable justice for the Other—substitution and expiation for the Other:

> Substitution operates in the entrails of the self, rending its inwardness, putting its identity out of phase and disrupting its recurrence. Yet this occurs in the impossibility for me to evade substitution, which confers uniqueness on this ever failing identity of the oneself. Substitution is a communication from the one to the other and from the other to the one without the two relations having the same sense. It is not like the reversibility of the two way road open to the circulation of information, where the direction is indifferent. We have shown above this dissymmetry of communication in the analysis

of proximity. It is the proximity of the Third party that introduces, with the necessities of justice, measure, thematization, appearing and justice.[199]

"Il y a"

The "*il y a*," translated as "there is," retrieves the meaning of the German *es gibt*, the donation of the pure fact of Being *as* Being, event of Being as givenness of presence. The "*il y a*" signifies Being in itself and for itself, distinct from beings or entities, and thus marks the impersonal, indifferent, neutral, anonymous character of Being as immanent presence and existence.

The "*il y a*," for Levinas, means the impersonality, anonymity, indifference, fulfilled presence of Being, of the "is" *that* "is," and thus the totalizing meaning of the Same and Sameness, identity and identicalness where difference is always reappropriated and reduced in and within the fulfilled identity, immanence of Being and existence.

Certainly, Levinas using the term "*il y a*" is recalling Heidegger's typification, in *Zeit und Sein*, where the German philosopher defines the "*il y a*" as "*es gibt*," donation as *event* (*Ereignis*) appropriating and exappropriating the co-belonging and gathering of Time *and* Being as unifying truth of essence.

Levinas retrieves Heidegger's description and deploys the "*il y a*" as the fulfillment and appropriation of presence as Being *and* Time whose density reverts to emptiness, indifference, and anonymity. This is precisely why Levinas, in his own active reinterpretation of Heidegger's "*es gibt*," will mark the illimitness of Being, Being *without* limit, fulfilled presence *without* transcendence, and thus *without* Otherness. In this sense, Levinas does not contest the presence of alterity or otherness in Heidegger's "fundamental ontology." Rather, Levinas remarks how and where the other in the horizon of Being is always brought back to presence, that is to the fulfilled presence of Time *and* Being where the other is already inscribed and included, integrated and incorporated in the essence and the truth of Being. Nothing occurs or can occur from *outside* or *beyond* the essence of Being: which means, it is always and already Being *giving itself* as Being, as Being *there* in the *there* of presence, essence, indifference, anonymity. Which always means, for Levinas, that nothing can interrupt Being's presence and fulfillment, nothing can suspend the plenitude of its auto-affirmation, and thus no one responds to the singular suffering of the Other without already inscribing this suffering into the narrative of the truth of Being. The transcendence of the Other is entirely consigned to the fulfillment of presence in Being which comprises no openings, no escape, and which ultimately suffocates and smothers the Other within the pure impersonal presence of indifference and anonymity.

Levinas will characterize this suffocation and smothering of the Other in the pure presence of indifference and anonymity as *evil*. Indeed, Being as "*il y a*" is evil. As Levinas writes in *Time and the Other*: "Being is evil not because it is finite but because it is limitless."[200] This affirmation gives rise to one of the most radical interpretations of evil in the history of philosophy. Evil is thought as not only destructive or simply as an absence or a negation of the Good. Evil is here thought as condemning human existence to the impossibility of escaping or evading, transcending the unbearable weight, suffocating and asphyxiating, anonymous indifference of Being.

This is also why, for Levinas, Being in its anonymous indifference as evil marks the *urgency* to flee the ontological climate, the fulfilled presence of the ontological, toward a *wholly other* significance *beyond* and *before* Being—the ethical. Which engages the significance of an ethical Self never assured of itself, never grounded or founded, but incessantly awakened, elected, called to respond infinitely, perpetually exceeding itself in responsibility: infinite responsibility always responding *before* and *beyond* universal norms, autonomous morality measurable values or judgments, decision or evaluation—an hyperbolical responsibility for the Other.

Immemorial (*Immémorial*)

The idea of immemoriality—intolerable, says Levinas, for a "consciousness as consciousness for . . ."—opens to the *diachronic* temporality of an hyperbolical responsibility for the Other as an ethics of singularity. Indeed, the immemorial as past which never was consigned in a present and irretrievable as a past-present, thus immemorable and irreappropriable, testifies of the Infinite, of the Illeity, of the absolute transcendence of Otherness tracing itself through the face of the Other human through its commandment and address, demand and plea. The immemorial occurs to the Self *without* having ever been a present, past *without* present, and thus as always and already futural, always and already *to-come, trace heterogeneous to the present of presence*, irreducible to any temporal determination, categorization, interiorization, that is, wholly heterogeneous to its comprehension in a time-consciousness. The immemorial occurs as irreducible to the *ecstacies* of temporality—past, present, future—and irreducible to the essential co-belonging of temporality in presence past, present, and future in presence.

With the idea of immemoriality, Levinas introduces a certain rupture of temporal synchrony and inscribes a splicing, a break, suspension, or interruption, of the gathering essence of temporality within which events are appropriated and comprehended. Which entails: the immemorial occurs as already Other than presence: the *passing* and *passage*, the tracing and trace of transcendence incessantly exceeding the grasp, the comprehension, the representation and thereby the consciousness of an intentional subjectivity. Levinas opens through immemoriality of a past which has never consigned itself in a present to the idea of the Infinite, Illeity—irrepresentable and unrecognizable which has always engaged the Self in the irreducible and unsatiable excess of responsibility for the Other—what Levinas marks as the *diachrony* of responsibility for the Other. Indeed, the immemorial past means and marks, for Levinas, the *diachronic* exposition of the ethical Self as both *host* and *hostage* of the Other.

The *diachrony* of responsibility, opened through the passage and the trace of the immemorial past *without* present always and already calling the Self to the ethical, entails thereby how the Self is incessantly engaged in responding for the Other in responsibility, a responsibility *always out of joint* with itself. Which means: always and already exceeding its response for the Other *before* and *beyond* what it can or could give or provide. And indeed, for Levinas the ethical Self always and already responds *too late* on the call of the Other while also and already responding *before* hearing the demand of the Other. Here lies the extraordinary and aporetic impulsion of the immemorial commandment of this hyperbolical ethics as "First philosophy": the *diachrony* of the ethical Self as incessantly responding in responsibility *before* hearing the call of the Other and yet always *too late* on the call of the Other. Which marks an ethical temporality irreducible to its comprehension by a "time-consciousness" and irreducible to presence: a temporality of responsibility always and already engaged *before* and *beyond* its own self-determination, *before* any decision and *beyond* all fulfilment.

The immemorial commandment of the Infinite as Illeity engages a response of responsibility always in excess of what the ethical Self can or could respond for the Other. Indeed, the immemorial subjects the ethical Self to respond in a responsibility incessantly exceeding itself for the Other and where no other can respond for the Self: election and awakening of the Self to the ethical *without* reserve, *before* and *beyond* all economy of recognition or community, intersubjectivity and commonality. Exceptional ethics of singularity as signification of a Self "in itself already outside of itself" "expelled into itself outside of being," in "exile or refuge in itself"[201] and always responsible for the Other. Already and always responsible for the Other engages a responsibility incessantly interrupting the identity of the Self while at the same time always singling out the Self as a unique respondent—irreducibly and ineluctably Self as inescapably *for* the Other. The ethical Self is "one and irreplaceable, one inasmuch as irreplaceable in responsibility."[202] The singularity of the ethical Self always responding singularly to the singularity of the Other arises from the immemorial otherness of the Other as engaging the ethical Self to its perpetual excess of responsibility—substitution and expiation—for the Other. It is in this sense that the immemorial otherness of the Other as commandment destitutes the subject as self-determination, as autonomy, as being-for-one's self toward an elected ethical Self as*otherwise* than Being, *otherwise* than presence, other than indifference, or the anonymity of ontology which also means *otherwise* than moral or rational normativity. The elected ethical Self responds to an immemorial past incessantly occurring from its irreappropriable past as irreducible futurity, as a responsibility always exceeding itself, *before* and *beyond* its own Self for the Other.

Infinity (*Infini*)

Levinas explains the "in" of infinity not as a negative or a negation. *In*-finity does not refer to a *non*-finite or to that which would *negate* finitude. *In*-finity, for Levinas, expresses and affirms the transcendence of the Other as irreducibly other to presence, comprehension, representation, and categorization. Otherwise said, the Infinite marks the absolute otherness which incessantly breaks and interrupts the proliferation and perseverance, immanence, totality, anonymity and indifference of Being. Infinity inscribes a rupture in Being from its radical otherness to Being. Suspending the immanence and totality of Being which always consists in gathering and reappropriating itself with itself, assimilating, comprehending and integrating, interiorizing, recognizing by internalizing, ultimately reducing the Other to the Same, and thus to the anonymity of essence, Infinity always entails an excess, surplus, overabundance of the Other over and above the Sameness of Being. Infinity always and already interrupts and suspends the Sameness of Being and which is nowhere "visible" but in its supererogatory movement itself—excess of excessiveness, surplus of surplus, overwhelming incessantly overflowing the grasp and the comprehension, the totalization or interiorization of judgment, categorization, representation.

The Infinity of the Other overwhelming the Sameness of Being as totality of comprehension is not a simple heteronomous positivity which heterogeneously befalls on the Self, predetermining it to a simplistic obedience or compliance and which would crush and annihilate the Self under an incomprehensible and irrepresentable transcendence. For Levinas, the idea of the Infinite opens to a *wholly different exposition* of the Self—an exposition electing the Self to the ethical, that is, irrevocably awakening the Self to an *infinitizing* ethical responsibility for the Other.

Wholly different than the submission of the subject to the heteronomy of the Law (as in Kant, (cf. the *Religion Within the Limits of Simple Reason*[203]) who interprets the "historical revelation" or the "revealed Law" in Judaism as an untranslatable singularity impossible to rationalize and universalize in a "pure moral religion" or as in Hegel (cf. *The Spirit of Christianity and its Fate*[204]), who understands the Judaic Law as a subjection of the Self to the "positivity" of an irrepresentable and thus unknowable or invisible heteronomic and transcendent God[205], for Levinas the Infinity of the Other expresses the absolute transcendence and exteriority of the face of the Other, calling and commanding the Self to the *infinitization* of *its* ethical responsibility for the Other. That is, the Infinity of the Other engages not a negation or an abnegation of the Self but rather the *diachrony* of responsibility in which the ethical Self is engaged, *before* and *beyond* itself, elected to respond in responsibility, substitution and expiation, for the Other.

This *diachrony* animating, electing, awakening, and calling the Self *before* its autonomy to rise to the ethical by being already engaged in the *infinitization* of responsibility for the Other, Levinas inscribes it entirely in the Infinite transcendence of the Other commanding a responsibility incessantly exceeding itself, overwhelming the sovereignty of the subject for the Other. Indeed, the Self "is" ethical in this incessant excess and overwhelming of its responsiveness as responsibility for the Other.

By breaking and rupturing the synchrony of a temporality entirely ordered and constituted by presence, the infinity of the Other "shows" itself in *Totality and Infinity* as *desire* for the Other, and later, in *Otherwise than Being, or Beyond Essence* as trauma, obsession—being traumatized and being obsessed by the irreducible singularity of the Other demanding a response of responsibility—substitution and expiation—infinitely exceeding itself *beyond* measure or fulfiment and *before* categorization and self-determination.

In *Totality and Infinity*, Levinas associates the idea of infinity with the absolute transcendence in the face of the Other:

> transcendence in the face of the Other. The rigorously developed concept of this transcendence is expressed by the term infinity. This revelation of infinity does not lead to the acceptance of any dogmatic content, whose philosophical rationality cannot be argued for in the name of the transcendental truth of the idea of infinity. [. . .] The relation with infinity cannot, to be sure, be stated in terms of experience, for infinity overflows the thought that thinks it. Its very infinition is produced precisely in this overflowing. The relation with infinity will have to be stated in terms other than those of objective experience; but if experience precisely means a relation with the absolutely other, that is, with what always overflows thought, the relation with infinity accomplishes experience in the fullest sense of the word. [. . .] The idea of infinity is not an incidental notion forged by a subjectivity to reflect the case of an entity encountering on the

> outside nothing that limits it, overflowing every limit, and thereby infinite. The production of the infinite entity is inseparable from the idea of infinity for it is precisely in the disproportion between the idea of infinity and the infinity of which it is the idea that this exceeding of limits is produced. The idea of infinity is the mode of being, the *infinitization* of infinity. Infinity does not first exist, and then reveal itself. Its *infinitization* is produced as revelation, as a positing of its idea *in* the Self, *before* and *beyond* the Self. It is produced in the improbable feat whereby a separated being fixed in its identity, the Same, the I, is always and already preceded by what it can neither contain nor receive solely by virtue of its own identity. Subjectivity realizes these impossible exigencies—the astonishing feat of containing more that it is possible to contain. [. . .] The idea of infinity (which is not a representation of infinity) sustains activity itself.[206]

Levinas also inscribes the idea of the Infinite in a reinterpretation of Descartes' *Meditations on First Philosophy*. Naturally, this filiation is not developed in order to fix the idea of the Infinite in a determined conceptual order and context. All to the contrary, Levinas retrieves the Cartesian idea of the Infinite to show how the Infinite always overflows, surpasses, overwhelms the subject by exceeding its self-determination and thereby outdoing the economies of comprehension, fulfillment, accomplishment of immanence, totality, and Sameness. In this sense, Levinas thinks the Infinite as a calling incessantly exceeding the *ego* and, by dismantling and suspending the structures and orders of judgment and self-determination, elects it, awakens it, projects it *before* its self-determination to a *beyond* all self-projection in and hyperbolical infinitizing responsibility for the Other.

Infinity gives itself as the "experience" *before* and *beyond* experience and as that which always and already overwhelms experience. That is, the Infinite dismantles conceptuality and categorization which always and already encompasses the transcendent alterity of the Other in and within its order and totalizing horizon of intentionality. The Infinity always gives itself as *revelation*, which does not signify, for Levinas, an uncovering or an unconcealment, but rather a commandment incessantly exceeding itself and impossible to appropriate, apprehend, interiorize as a norm and which animates, elects the Self *before* its self-determination to an *infinitization* of responsibility, and thus to an *infinite supplement* of responsibility extending itself already *more* than its determination and categorization toward the Other. Furthermore, it is precisely in this impossible appropriation and incessant supplement *beyond* judgment and measure, *before* autonomy and self-determination that the idea of the Infinite *comes to mind*. That is, Infinity comes to mind in its incessant overflowing of the Self's possibilities of conceiving it, appropriating or interiorizing it. This is why, for Levinas, Infinity is never reducible to a substance or an essence: the Infinite is the "experience" of a break, an overflowing, a perpetual excess of response and responsibility toward the Other irreducible to presence and representation and which, in the same gesture, burrows the Self, *before* and *beyond* its own Selfhood, toward the ethical as *infinitizing* response of responsibility for the Other.

Infinity marks the incessant surplus *beyond* Being as "expression," "discourse," and thereby engages the Self *before* its self-determination in an *infinitization* of responsibility for the Other. The Infinite transcendence of the Other commands and expresses the *infinitization* of a responsibility *without* beginning and *without* finality. It requires an incessant excess of responsibility for the Other: an ethical Self always and already responding *before* and *beyond* the commandment of the Other which it never contains nor comprehends in the horizon of a universal morality: ethics of singularity *beyond* and *before* universalist morality, ethics as "First Philosophy" for the unique singularity of the absolute transcendence of the Other:

> Infinity presents itself as a face in the ethical resistance that paralyses my powers and from the depths of defenseless eyes rises firm and absolute in its nudity and destitution. The comprehension of this destitution and this hunger establishes the very proximity of the other. But thus the epiphany of infinity is expression and discourse. The primordial essence of expression and discourse does not reside in the information they would supply concerning an interior and hidden world. Its expression a being presents itself; the being that manifests itself attends its manifestation and consequently appeals to me. This attendance is not the neutrality of an image, but a solicitization that concerns me by its destitution and its Height. To speak to me is at each moment to surmount what is necessarily plastic in manifestation. To manifest oneself as a face is to *impose oneself* above and *beyond* the manifested and purely phenomenal form, to present oneself in a mode irreducible to manifestation, the very straightforwardness of the face-to-face, without the intermediary of any image, in one's nudity, that is, in one's destitution and hunger. In *Desire* are conjoined the movements unto the Height and unto the Humility of the Other. [. . .] Thus in expression the being that imposes itself does not limit but promotes my freedom, by arousing my goodness. The order of responsibility, where the gravity of ineluctable being freezes all laughter, is also the order where freedom is ineluctably invoked.[207]

In *Otherwise than Being, or Beyond Essence*, Levinas defines the Infinite, Infinity, as *inspiration* which never conforms to substance or essence, which never translates itself as the foundational being of the subject capable of comprehending its own source or origin. Infinity incessantly burrows and excavates the Self, thereby electing it *before* and *beyond* its own self-determination toward the Other. This is why the Infinite for Levinas is wholly different than a "bad Infinity" (cf. Hegel's *Science of Logic, Doctrine of Being,* Section "Quantity"[208] and *Encyclopedia Logic,* §§ 94-95[209]) where "bad infinity" is defined as the unaccomplished tendency and propensity, task and project of the finite subject toward an ungraspable and incomprehensible transcendent ideality and which marks a radical separation between finitude and infinitude, understanding and reason, the subject and substance: the Infinite does not condemn the Self to an unfulfilled resolution of its own-most appropriation and identity in Absolute Knowledge, but rather elects the Self, *before* and *beyond* its self-determination, to the ethical as incessant awakening for the Other. That is: as incessant Desire for the Other as inspiration by the Other—precisely where the Other is inassimilable and irreducible to the Sameness of the Same, of the *ego* or the Self: "*Beyond* the bad infinity of the *Sollen* it increases infinitely, living infinity, an obligation more and more strict in the measure that obedience progresses and the distance to be crossed untraversable in the measure that one approaches. The giving then shows itself to be a parsimony, the exposure a reserve, and holiness guilt. It is life without death, the life of the Infinite or its glory, a life outside of essence and nothingness."[210]

Which means: the Infinite inspires the sincerity of the ethical Self for the Other—that is, a sincerity which expresses a responsibility *without* beginning, *without* finality, *before* and *beyond* autonomy, decision, self-determination, sovereignty: "Here I am for the Other" as pure exposition, passivity more passive than all passivity, and thus as being elected to the ethical *before* and *beyond* the Self as always and already engaged in an hyperbolical, ineluctable, irremissible, inescapable responsibility *before* and *beyond* the singular call of the Other. Precisely what Levinas also names the "Glory of the Infinite," the witnessing of the Glory which testifies of a significance as commandment *beyond* and *before* truth, disclosure, discovery, unconcealment—this significance as commandment *beyond* and *before* truth marks, for Levinas, an irreducible and transcendent idea of justice and Law of an infinitizing responsibility for the Other to the point of substitution and expiation:

> Glory is but the other face of the passivity of the subject. Substituting itself for the other, a responsibility ordered to the first one on the scene, a responsibility for the neighbor, inspired by the Other, I, the same, am torn up from my beginning in myself, my equality with myself. The Glory of the Infinite is glorified in this responsibility. It leaves to the subject no refuge in its secrecy that would protect it against being obsessed by the Other, and cover over its evasion. Glory is glorified by the subject's coming out of the dark corners of the "as-for-me," which, like the thickets of Paradise

in which Adam hid himself upon hearing the voice of the eternal God traversing the garden from the side from which the day comes, offered a hiding-place from the assignation, in which the position of the ego at the beginning, and the very possibility of origin, is shaken. The Glory of the Infinite is the anarchic identity of the subject flushed out without being able to slip away. It is the *ego* led to sincerity, making signs to the Other, for whom and before whom I am responsible, of this very giving of signs, that is, of this responsibility: "here I am." The *Saying* prior to anything *Said* bears witness to Glory. This witness is true, but with a truth irreducible to the truth of disclosure, and does not narrate anything that shows itself. *Saying* is without noematic correlation in the pure obedience to Glory that orders. It is without dialogue, in the passivity from the first subordinate to the "*here I am*." The distance that is enlarged in the measure that proximity narrows, the Glory of Infinity, is the inequality between the Same and the Other, the difference that is also the non-indifference of the Same for the Other and the substitution which, in its turn, is a nonequaility with oneself, a non-recovering of Self by Self, a dispossession of Self, the Self leaving the clandestinity of its identification. It is already a sign made to another, a sign of this giving of signs, that is, of this non-indifference, a sign of this impossibility of slipping away and being replaced, of this identity, this uniqueness: "*here I am*". The identity aroused thus behind identification is an identity by pure election. Election traverses the concept of the ego to summon me as me through the inordinateness of the Other."[211]

Insomnia (*Insomnie*)

The term insomnia is defined differently and divergently in Levinas' early and late writings. However, despite the differences and divergences between the early conception of insomnia and its later reformulation, Levinas will always maintain, throughout his philosophical writing how insomnia designates a certain vigilance and watchfulness, that is, a wake and wakefulness exceeding consciousness. In this sense, insomnia excepts consciousness from the state of a self-consciousness, engaging the Self to an ethical disposition inassimilable to the intentional structure of "consciousness for or consciousness of . . . ," that is, irreducible to the *ego*'s attention and intention to and toward the objectivity of objects.

Insomnia means, throughout Levinas' writing and thinking, to guard and watch over, by extension to peruse and care for, to put in check, and to oversee. And indeed, Levinas thematizes both senses of this "experience" which affects subjectivity in always exceeding itself out of itself and *beyond* the horizon of its intentional aim or order of understanding.

In the early writings, and most notably in *Existence and Existents*, Levinas presents a phenomenological analysis of insomnia where this "experience" is described as the Self's complete exposition to the anonymity and indifference of Being, which is also described as "the night of Being," and where the Self is entirely plunged in the "horror" that "strips consciousness of subjectivity" and projects it in the "undetermined menace of space itself." Insomnia is thought thus as an exposition to the immanence of Being, the undetermined space where the possibility of naming different existents in their differences is voided and hollowed out. This is why insomnia, in Levinas' early thinking, is also coupled with the notion of the "*il y a*." Levinas indeed writes: "It is not that there is *my* vigilance in the night; in insomnia, it is the night itself that watches. It watches. In this anonymous nightwatch where I am completely exposed to being, all thoughts of insomnia are suspended on *nothing*." Insomnia is, in this sense, ontological. Irreducible to Heidegger's typification of anxiety—which opens toward the authenticity of Dasein's existence in the resolute project and resolution of posing the question pertaining to the meaning of Being—the experience of insomnia in Levinas' early interpretation is that of the pure void incessantly showing itself as the indifference and anonymity of Being. It marks thus a certain paralysis, a wakeness *without* intentional content or projection. Which is precisely why insomnia is an "experience" *without* awakening, an "experience" in nothing to nothing and of nothing: that is, a remaining awake in the void of Being, a staying awake within the horror of the indifference of Being. Insomnia is thus an "experience" of the plenitude and the plentifulness of absence and emptiness where no existents stand out and the anonymity, the bare fact of the presence indissociable from the nothingness—indifference—of Being engulfs all existents into its ownmost Sameness.

However, in the Levinas' later writing, and most specifically in *Otherwise than Being, or Beyond Essence* and *Of God who Comes to Mind*, insomnia will take on, for Levinas, the meaning of an awakening, *beyond* intentionality and *before* the intentional structure of consciousness as consciousness of . . . , and thus of a wake and irepressible wakefulness toward the singular and inescapable suffering of the Other. Insomnia is no longer thought of as the "experience" of remaining awake or staying awake in the plentiful nothingness and suffocating indifference of the "*il y a*", but as the awakening to an infinite responsibility for the Other. Insomnia marks thus the exposition of the ethical Self *caring* for the Other and attending to the Other *beyond* and *before* recognition or intersubjectivity; a *vigilance* toward the Stranger who is also the neighbor, that is toward the suffering and commanding Other.

Insomnia means here the "experience" of a watchful responsibility *without* limit incessantly awakening the Self *before* and *beyond* its egoism, identity, and sovereignty for the Other.

There is thus a turn and a considerable shift in Levinas' interpretation of insomnia. As ontological, insomnia is this continuous situation of a remaining awake *without* escape, *without* awakening. This "experience" of insomnia is the monstration of a constant state of indifference: the indifference and anonymity of Being. But this "experience"—and this is where Levinas will supplement this early interpretation, supplement to the point of substitution and expiation—will also break and interrupt this continuous paralysis of Being in Being to awaken the Self to an incessant responsibility for the Other. For the later Levinas thus, insomnia means the tireless incessance of a responsibility for the Other. And this persistent and irreducible awakening out of the paralysis of Being and the indifference of the "*il y a*", marks, for Levinas, the most human in the human. The "experience" of insomnia for the Other, as having been awakened for an incessantly novel sobering-up from its self-presence and self-perseverance marks, for the ethical Self, the humanity of the human, a humanism *beyond* humanism, a humanism of the Other for the Other.

Inspiration (*Inspiration*)

"Obliged *without* this obligation having originated in me"[212]: this phrase indicates, for Levinas, a subjection to a commandment and an obligation which never coincides with self-consciousness as "being-present," never concurs within an intersubjective recognition or "being-with" the Other in the sameness or the identicalness of a community, a commonality, a sociality.

For Levinas, this obligation obliges as an election the Self to the ethical *before* and thereby *beyond* community, contract, intersubjectivity. Obliges to a responsibility for the Other *before* any wrongdoing or fault, autonomy or decision, sovereignty or dominance. The Self as ethical is obliged by the Other for the Other *before* the Self's identity and freedom—such is the ethical *in* and thereby *inspiring* the Self *before* the Self, orienting the Self *beyond* what the Self can circumscribe or determine as ethical or responsible.

Inspiration *beyond* intuition and obligation and *before* any identity and self-determination, the ethical Self is elected by the Other and turned toward the Other for the Other—immemorially inspired by the Other for the Other *before* its sovereignty and autonomy, *before* recognizing the Other, *before* hearing the call and the commandment of the Other. And thus, always and already *before* any community, commonality or intersubjectivity with the Other, the ethical Self is inspired as host and hostage by the irrepresentable, the uncategorizable, the unrepresentable trace of the Infinite expressing itself in and through the face of the Other as commandment, demand, plea, which, irreducible to the moral norm, incessantly appeals to the Self *before* and *beyond* its own Self toward the Other as irrecusably responsible for the Other.

The idea of inspiration, literally "breathing in," does not indicate, for Levinas, how or why the Other could motivate the Self to act in such and such a manner. Rather, it marks the heteronomy of the ethical, and furthermore, how the obligation toward the Other always and already precedes the autonomy of the Self and thereby orients the Self in responsibility for the Other. Indeed, responsibility for the Other is commanded incessantly and *in spite of* the Self—that is, *without* reference to a self-instituted or constituted selfhood. In this sense, Levinas marks inspiration as that which elects the Self *before* self-determination to the ethical and thus to a responsibility for the Other *beyond* what the Self can constitute and institute as its moral autonomy. Inspiration means, for Levinas, the ethical Self as response and responsibility *before* and *beyond* autonomy—always and already responding to the Other for the Other. Inspiration means thus the ethical obligation for the Other awakening the Self where this election for the Other always and already precedes a moral universality based on a free practical rational will.

Levinas here marks through inspiration how and why the ethical Self engages its responsibility for the Other *before* the commandment of the Other as precedence and antecedence of all cognition, recognition, thematization, hearing, or intuiting the call, the address, the demand of the Other. Which brings Levinas to mark the *diachrony* of the ethical Self: *it is through the responsibility for the Other that the commandment, the call, the address of the Other can be heard.* Which means: the ethical Self always responds to the Other, for the Other—hyperbolically, infinitely as exceeding itself incessantly—*before* the commandment of the Other and thereby *beyond* what could be expected of the Self in its response of responsibility for the Other. This obligation toward the Other preceding the call of the Other to always stretch out *beyond* what is determinable and which is only heard in the unconditional and infinite responsibility for the Other, Levinas marks it as a *pneumatology*—inspiration of the Self by and through the Other, election by the Other for the Other *before* the Self's assuredness and constitution, institution, self-determination and sovereignty.

The idea of inspiration, for Levinas, thus marks a *diachrony* irreducible to presence or representation and which inscribes, as the very awakening of the ethical Self for the Other and *before* the commandment of the Other, an election whereby the Self becomes, in a certain manner, the always and already inspired "author" of its obligation and responsibility for the Other. *Without* autonomy, *without* sovereignty, the ethical Self "authors" its response in always renewing its awakening for the Other *before* any call, commandment, address, or plea is formulated or heard, expressed or voiced. Which is why Levinas also insists on how and why, *before* any representation of the Other as calling the Self to responsibility, the ethical Self testifies or witnesses the call or the commandment only by having *already* responded and always having been *engaged* in its response as infinite responsibility for the Other.

The idea of inspiration informs Levinas' ethics as a *pneumatology*. The ethical interpretation of the idea of inspiration marks for Levinas how inspiration of the Self by the Other means the ethical awakening and election of the Self through the Other, the animation of a responsibility *without* limit incessantly designated *before* choice or decision for the Other. As inspiration precedes expiration and arouses respiration, the "pneuma of psychism," the Other gives the Self its respiration and breath, and thus its awakening, its election, both invisible, imperceptible, unthematizable, and ungraspable, while, at the same time, giving life to the Self by prying it open to itself through and by its election for the Other in an *infinitizing* responsibility.

For Levinas, the ethical as pneumatology means the Other penetrating the Self and electing the Self to life, animation, and awakening as response, responsibility, care to the extreme point of substitution and expiation for the Other. Always and already exposed to the Other for the Other, the Self breathes in the transcendence of the Other as an incessant de-substantialization and de-centering of its own Self which incessantly in-forms and elects the Self to the ethical. And thus the Self lives by the Other as response of responsibility always exceeding itself for the Other. The ethical Self is always inspired by the Other marks thus how and why the Self is, for Levinas, already de-substantialized and exposed to the Other for the Other. Inspiration means the de-structuration of the Self as autonomy and sovereignty which inspires a thinking of the Self as response and responsibility *without* finality, *without* ground or foundation, exposition to a responsibility for the Other *without telos* or *eschaton*. The ethical Self is inspired by the Other for the Other:

> breathing is said more simply in terms of biology: answering a fundamental need for energy, it brings to the tissues the oxygen necessary for the functioning of the organism, and eliminates the waste. Air and the oxygen it contains are then treated like wood and iron; air can be healthy or unhealthy, conditioned air or liquid air; oxygen is carried in the baggage of astronauts like fresh water on ships. But the relationship to air by which the experiences expressed in these truths are formed and stated is not in its turn an experience, despite the status of objectivity it acquires even in the philosophical language that describes the signification of these experiences by going behind these experiences, or reducing them to the horizon of their thematization. But in reducing the said to the saying, philosophical language reduces the said to breathing opening to the other and signifying

> to the other its very signifyingness. This reduction is then an incessant unsaying of the said, a reduction to the saying always betrayed by the said, whose words are defined by non-defined words; it is a movement going from said to unsaid in which the meaning shows itself, eclipses and shows itself. In this navigation the element that bears the embarkation is also the element that submerges it and threatens to sink it. Philosophy is perhaps but this exaltation of language in which the words, after the event, find for themselves a condition in which religions, sciences and technologies owe their equilibrium of meaning. An openness of the self to the other, which is not a conditioning or a foundation of oneself in some principle, a fixity of a sedentary inhabitant or a nomad, but a relation wholly different from the occupation of a site, a building, or a settling oneself, breathing is transcendence in the form of opening up. It reveals all its meaning only in the relationship with the other, in the proximity of a neighbor, which is responsibility for him, substitution for him. This pneumatism is not nonbeing; it is disinterestedness, excluded middle of essence, besides being and non being.[213]

Israel (*Israël*)

The word Israel in Levinas' thinking is extremely complex as it engages every aspect of Levinas' oeuvre. Indeed, Israel means both and at the same time the absolute hyperbolical ethics of the Other as infinite responsibility for the singularity of the Other *and* the advent of this extraordinary ethical demand in the actuality of History. Furthermore, the word "Israel" works in Levinas' thinking *both* as an ethical orientation and a concrete political reality. Indeed, and despite both the ethical and political significations of Israel being at work in all instances of Levinas' oeuvre, the same Levinas engages with the word Israel itself in a relatively small number of writings.[214] We could even go so far as to say that the word Israel is not the object of a sustained and confirmed thematization in Levinas' oeuvre. For Israel embodies a question for Levinas, that is that toward which we are called to respond. What could be this question? In which manner does Levinas engage with the question of Israel?

One example of this question is given in a short text from *Difficult Freedom. Essays on Judaism*, entitled "Judaism": "What does the voice of Israel say and how can it be translated?"[215] Of course, Levinas understands very well the impossible task prompted by his very question. Indeed, the word "Israel" concentrates a multitude of significations throughout its history: a people, a Nation, a community, a religion, a descendance, a struggle, a prophetic promise and messianic calling, at once a millenary attachment to a land and a lived condition of exile, since 1948 a sovereign State. And thus, what does Levinas mean when he calls onto and names the "voice of Israel"?

Although it is impossible to fully and completely determine its exact definition—perhaps the exactitude of a determination is precisely that which the word "Israel" seeks to question—the word Israel in Levinas' writings and thinking engages a search and a task. Israel means the *creation* of a certain passage from an ethical commandment, the transcendent Law of the Other, into the political, that is, into its concrete instantiation in the becoming of History. In this sense, Israel for Levinas remains always and already *to create*, that is an urgent responsibility *already inherited* and *always yet to come*. The word Israel indeed embodies the *aporia* of a messianic promise and the disjointment of presence its temporality entails: at once and simultaneously *in* History and also *beyond* History.

Levinas thinks the "voice of Israel" as both the immemorial messianic and the prophetic ideal and Law *and* how this Law speaks through its concrete political and historical instantiations. This is why, Israel, for Levinas, far from simply defining or constituting an abstract transcendent ideal or a pure ethical position, engages concretely the absolute transcendence of the ethical to also construct and institute itself in the immanence of History, that is, in the political. Which means: for Levinas, Israel signifies the absolute transcendence of the ethical incessantly awakening the historical and the political *otherwise* and *beyond* the historico-political horizon of intentionality or significance. That is, the hyperbolical transcendent ethical commandment incessantly electing the historico-political to exceed its determination toward a *wholly other heading*. Indeed, for Levinas, the "voice of Israel" does not resonate in an empty sky of pure abstraction: it inscribes itself in its historical and political translation as that which irreducibly activates the historical and the political to express *other performatives* than those it embodies *in* its historical concretion. Indeed, the "voice of Israel" marks the ethical commandment of the Other to incessantly inscribe in the concreteness of the political the promise always reiterated of a *wholly other* instantiation for the political—that is, where the ethical commands the political to *stretch beyond* its classical and traditional meaning as sovereignty, identity, nationality to reiterate a further responsibility and responsibilization, an excess of justice for the Other and through the Other for all the Others.

First point therefore to mark and which is spurred on by the word "Israel" in Levinas' thinking and writing: the political is never simply reducible to political rationality or sovereignty. Rather, the political, *without* ever negating the concrete necessity of the political (that is also of the State and its rationality and normativity in sustaining equality among subjects as citizens) incessantly searches for a further expression of responsibility than that founded and grounded in its sovereignty. Which leads to the second point to be made:

for Levinas, the political remains always and already preceded and thereby animated by the absolute transcendence of the ethical. Indeed, for Levinas, the political always need to reach *beyond* the determination of the political by being always and already engaged in the transcendence of the ethical Law as responsibility *without* limit, hyperbolical responsibility for the singularity of the Other, and, through this singular responsibility, for all the Others. In this sense, the political is never *just* political, for Levinas, nor does it simply settle for the political. Which means: the political cannot remain solely political. It must incessantly be inspired and awakened by the transcendence of the ethical if it is not to succumb to the propagation of violence and the evil which Levinas always associates to the indifference of Being and the anonymity of totality, immanence, sameness, and identicalness. Otherwise said, the *transcendence of the ethical in the immanence of the political* as the "Other-in-the-Same," for Levinas, means the transcendence of the ethical suspending and interrupting each time singularly the political in its perseverance and persistence, its order and organization within its own rationality and intentionality—suspension and interruption which, as *justice*, disrupts incessantly the drift the political can take toward its ontological determination, definition, categorization, comprehension.

This irreducible ethical exigency electing the concreteness of the political *beyond* itself, Levinas also inscribes it and reveals it—that is, sees it emerge out of the history of the "Jewish people among the nations." Indeed, the history of the Jewish people reveals a certain distance and abstraction from the fascination and enchantment of a particular territory. Levinas reads into this Judaic "identity" the engagement in nothing less than a radical questioning of political rationality through which are determined the identity of the indigeneous and thereby the foreignerness of the foreigner and thus which operates by including those who are deemed the "same" and excluding those who are marked as "foreign." The political grounded on the "awareness of sovereignty that is assumed by well-settled nations firmly installed on their lands, whose self-affirmation is sustained by the firmness of the land beneath their feet, by this certainty, this original experience of the immovable"[216] can only manifest itself in the effacement of the Other in the figure of the foreigner. And it is *against* this effacement of the Other (which Levinas also sees as the concretion of antisemitism) that the "voice of Israel" is engaged in by inspiring incessantly the political to exceed itself beyond itself toward hospitality and thus as responsibility for the Other. The "voice of Israel" speaks precisely in the "difficult freedom" of incessantly questioning the political determinations of identity, sovereignty, patriotism, and nationalism from the hyperbolical ethical commandment and demand of infinite responsibility for the Other and, through this infinite responsibility, for all the Others. That is, Israel, for Levinas, forces in the political its openness toward the urgency of an hyperbolical ethics, response as infinite responsibility, wholly oriented toward the singularity, call and commandment, demand and order, of the Other and through this hyperbolical responsibility for the singular Other toward the creation of a justice for all the Others. Which entails how and why this "difficult freedom" as incessant ethical questioning of identity, sovereignty, patriotism, or nationalism ought not to mean, for Levinas, that the relationship between the transcendence of the ethical and the immanence of the political can simply be outstripped by simplistically clinging onto a purely, idealistic, diasporic character or imaginary of an exilic ethics wholly removed from its concretion in the political. Levinas marks all to the contrary how and why the "voice of Israel" also *must* never undermine the necessity of the political and its concrete exercise. Such is the reason why Levinas, quoting Hegel's "beautiful souls" reminds us that the pure angelism of morality can also foster and produce the unethical. As Levinas remarks:

Already the place—or the Diaspora, or the migrations—of the Jewish people among the nations, its antiquity as one people across the diverse and contradictory periods of History, should call into question the excluding nature of political conceptualization. Interiority is perhaps simply this. An interiority that would no longer be the imaginary dimension of "beautiful souls" should no doubt be measured in terms of this antiquity, whether it is founded on fidelity to memories or a book. A prophetic book, in the event, made up of subversive discourses that defy kings and the grandees without fleeing into clandestinity. A book that bears within it this disputed land more deeply than do the geological strata of its depths. A fidelity that encourages, certainly, but, more surely, denotes an impassiveness in the face of the world's clamorous outbursts, its wars, glories and hegemonies. This guarantees that, in the melee, of men and events, hypothetical imperatives do not conceal their conditioning nor impose themselves categorically. This represents an ethical destiny, one without *anachoresis*, or isolation, the distance necessary for judgement. It is the difficult freedom of Israel, which is not to be treated as an ethnographic curiosity but as one extreme limit of human potential. Such a potential disturbs and irritates the awareness of sovereignty that is assumed by well-settled nations firmly installed on their lands, whose self-affirmation is sustained by the firmness of the land beneath their feet, by this certainty, this original experience of the immovable.[217]

The "voice of Israel" thereby insists on the exigency of thinking through a certain "contradiction"[218] between the transcendence of the ethical and the immanence of the political, and thus of marking in which manner the transcendence of the ethical Law, *without* reducing itself to the Sameness of community or commonality, intersubjectivity or recognition, immanence of normativity, can *awaken* and inspire the political out of its determination and orient it toward an idea of justice which responds to the singularity of the

Other and furthermore seeks, that is, *creates*, through this singular response for the Other, an *infinitizing* responsibility for all Others.

Israel represents for Levinas the potential, the possibility and the necessity, for such a *creation*.

How? There is *always* a "contradiction"[219] between the ethical and the political. Put very schematically: the ethical is always for the Other, whereas the political is already grounded in the Same. The question which emanates thus from this "contradiction" between the ethical and the political can be formulated as follows: In which manner can the hyperbolical responsibility for the Other translate itself into the political sphere of alliances and interests? Or said otherwise, how can the ethical inspire the political to incessantly exceed and surpass itself *beyond* itself? Levinas sees in the "voice of Israel," the possibility of a translation from transcendence into immanence which, far from reducing the transcendence of the Other, demands of the political to incessantly surpass and exceed its own-most determination. Otherwise said, the ethical—and here lies the radicality of the idea of justice as Third party, as responsibility for the Others of the Other, the multiple Others already commanding through the singular Other—orders and commands the ontological totalizing element of the political to respond *otherwise* and engage in a *wholly other* responsibility, an incessant excess of responsibility, in the name of justice for the singularity of all alterities. This is why, far from simply undermining the relation between the ethical and the political, this "contradiction" animates and awakens the possibility of thinking *together* an ethical politics or a political ethics differently and thereby as the incessant inspiration of the transcendence of the ethical commandment demanding of the immanence of the political to extend itself *beyond* itself and *toward* the singularity of all alterities. The "voice of Israel" means here, for Levinas, the creation of a movement between the ethical and the political *without* elevating the ethical to a pure abstract and idyllic idealism *and* without reducing the political to a simplistic self-assured and sovereign *Realpolitik*.

It is in this "contradiction" between the ethical and the political—a "contradiction" animating from the ethical the political *beyond* its own-most determination—that Levinas sees the space in which and from which erupts the possibility and the expression of Zionism. Why Zionism? For Zionism is, for Levinas, the political engagement which contains an "ethical justification,"[220] that is, embodies very particular situations. First, that of expecting Judaism to not secure itself in its own-most identity, circumscribed and confined in the pretention of its distinctiveness as other and foreign to the political, other than the other Nations, a "beautiful soul" outside History and its complexities, concreteness, difficulties. Second, as the expectation for the ethical, and thus the ethical Law of Israel as well, to risk itself in the difficult and yet necessary translation of the ethical *in* the political. In other words, Levinas marks the "ethical justification" of Zionism as that commandment by which Judaism is called to "end its arbitrariness," and thus its pretention and its posture, by engaging concretely with the political. That is, take the risk of translating the transcendent ethical calling of its Book, its Law, which it has carried throughout its lived history into the concrete becoming of the political. Indeed, as Levinas says in response to S. Malka and in discussion with A. Finkielkraut in the interview above quoted, to refuse the "temptation of innocence," that is, refuse the abstract temptation of simply expressing an ethical ideal without ever engaging it concretely in the difficulties of the political:

> I think that there's a direct contradiction between ethics and politics, if both these demands are taken to the extreme. It's a contradiction which is usually an abstract problem. Unfortunately for ethics, politics has its own justification. In mankind, there is a justification for politics. The Zionist idea, as I now see it, all mysticism or false immediate messianism aside, is nevertheless a political idea which has an ethical justification. It has an ethical justification insofar as a political solution imposes itself as a way of putting an end to the arbitrariness which marked the Jewish condition, and to all the spilt blood which for centuries has flowed with impunity across the world. This solution can be summed up as the existence, in conditions which are not purely abstract, that is, not just anywhere, of a political unity with a Jewish majority. For me, this is the essence of Zionism.[221]

Which means: the "essence of Zionism" is a commandment addressed to Judaism to expose itself to the political by always engaging the political to a surplus and an excess of responsibility as justice. This is precisely why Levinas marks how and why Israel and its political translation through Zionism is always subjected, and justly so, to an excess of responsibility. Indeed, in response to S. Malka's opening question in the interview above quoted, "Emmanuel Levinas, first of all I'd like to ask you whether Israel is innocent or responsible for what happened at Sabra and Chatila?" Levinas responds:

> Let me begin with our immediate reactions on learning of this catastrophe. Despite the lack of guilt here—and probably there, too—what gripped us right away was the honor of responsibility. It is, I think, a responsibility which the Bible of course teaches us, but it is one which constitutes every man's responsibility toward all others, a responsibility which has nothing to do with any act one may really have committed. Prior to any act, I am concerned with the Other, and I can never be absolved from this responsibility. To use an expression close to my heart, "Even when he does not regard me, he regards me". Consequently, I shall speak of the responsibility of those "who have done nothing", of an original responsibility

> of man for the other person. It is all the more overwhelming and direct for existing in the space between two people who are regarding one another. This is the responsibility of those we call innocent! But it is no more light or more comfortable for all that; it doesn't let you sleep any the easier. I would insist on this responsibility, even if I am not speaking of direct guilt. I have always thought of Jewish consciousness as an attentiveness which is kept alert by centuries of inhumanity and pays particular attention to what occasionally is human in man: the feeling that you personally are implicated each time that somewhere—especially when it's somewhere close to you—humanity is guilty.[222]

Which means Israel must engage with an incessant responsibilization of the political *before* and *beyond* the attribution of fault or guilt. That is also, *before* and *beyond* innocence. Which is why Levinas redefines the idea of "innocence" by marking how "innocence" is not "the zero degree of conscience." That is, innocence does not remove one from the ethical and its political instantiation. All to the contrary! Innocence, for Levinas, engages one *further* into the ethical, and thus, by this engagement, calls for the ethical to inspire ceaselessly the political to exceed its determination and respond always in excess of responsibility for the Other, for all Others. Which implies that Levinas' ethics as "First Philosophy," and thereby the "voice of Israel" is not confined to a simple non-political or a-political stand, a purely abstract ethical position removed from the concreteness of History. Going to the limit of Levinas' position here would mark: innocence does not exempt but rather engage further the Self into ethical responsibility in the political, that is to always and already be "more" responsible for the Other and thereby for all the Others. Indeed, for Levinas, innocence would be betrayed if it only remained in the simple ethical posture of guiltlessness, and thus would be empty if it did not engage itself in the concreteness of the political. For Levinas, innocence commands always a supplement of responsibility and thus demands to bring the ethical in its incessant confrontation with the political to force the political to express itself *otherwise* than through its ownmost identity and determination and thus inspire the political to always further responsibility for the singular Other as all the Others. The "voice of Israel" and the essence of Zionism is thus seen as a certain passage, necessary, from the ethical to the political; that is, as that which engages the ethical *in* the political *without* reducing the transcendence of the ethical by interminably engaging the political in the urgency of expressing itself *otherwise more justly*, exceeding and further its responsibility *beyond* the simple determinations of sovereignty and national identity.

This redefinition of innocence implies that the ethical needs to be always more responsible than its determined definition by calling onto the political to engage itself *beyond* itself, that is, by furthering responsibility *beyond* what it can or will. In this sense, what is most important in this dynamic between the ethical and the political is how Levinas refuses the ethical and the political to ever fix and fixate responsibility in a predetermined value or valuation. Which is why Levinas thinks the relation between the ethical and the political *beyond* the simple and simplistic binarism of "victim and offender." That is, Levinas understands very well how the victim can manipulate its victimhood and thereby become the offender as easily as the offender can show itself as a victim in its offense. And Levinas is here extremely radical. Indeed, he insists on questioning both the ethical and the political by marking how and why the simple status of victim can never solely justify an excuse for any ethical wrong or political evil. Which means, for Levinas, that to be a victim also means to assume and engage further in responsibility both ethically and politically. This is why the necessity of the ethical is to always engage further in responsibility for the Other precisely where this engagement also creates its relation with the political in always forcing the political to a surplus and a supplement of responsibility for the Other and thereby for all the Others. As Levinas remarks:

> Innocence is not the zero degree of conscience, but merely an exalted state of responsibility, which is perhaps the final nodal point of the Jewish conscience, among all those symbolized by the knots of our *tzitzit*: the more innocent we are, the more we are responsible. But this is not to forget the Holocaust. No-one has forgotten the Holocaust, it's impossible to forget things which belong to the most immediate and the most personal memory of every one of us, and pertaining to those closest to us, who sometimes make us feel guilty for surviving. That in no way justifies closing our ears to the voice of men, in which sometimes the voice of God can also resound. Evoking the Holocaust to say that God is "with us" in all circumstances is as odious as the words "*Gott mit uns*" written on the belts of the executioners. I don't at all believe that there are limits to responsibility, that there are limits to responsibility in "myself." My self, I repeat, is never absolved from responsibility towards the Other. But I think we should also say that all those who attack us with such venom have no right to do so, and that consequently, along with this feeling of unbounded responsibility, there is certainly a place for a defence, for it is not always a question of "me," but of those close to me, who are also my neighbours. I'd call such a defence a politics, but a politics that's ethically necessary.[223]

Israel engages, for Levinas, an incessant ethical questioning of the political to the point where it, the political, responds *beyond* what it determines as politically just. Which also means, and without ever undermining the meaning and significance of the political, and most specifically the value and significance of the State, and here of the State of Israel, Levinas insists on the ethical urgency to not let the political settle for the political. This is why Levinas indicates, continuing from what he claimed on the "essence of Zionism":

> It signifies a State in the fullest sense of the term, a State with an army and arms, an army which can have a deterrent and if necessary a defensive significance. Its necessity is ethical—indeed, it's an old ethical idea which commands us precisely to defend our neighbours. My people and my kin are still my neighbours. When you defend the Jewish people, you defend your neighbour; and every Jew in particular defends his neighbour when he defends.[224]

The neighbor always means for Levinas the singular Other, irrepresentable and irreducible alterity of the Other. In this sense, what Levinas marks in this passage is how the State is always and already obliged to respond *beyond* what it determines and thus as always exceeding in responsibility for the Other, and thereby all the Others. By no means does Levinas here entail—as it has often been misrepresented—a form of responsibility only in the identicalness of a group: as if the State of Israel were here only to "defend" its own kinship. Rather, Levinas affirms the contrary: that the State marks the ethical responsibility of exceeding its own identity and responding in responsibility for the Other and all the Others. Which is precisely why Levinas inscribes the "contradiction" between the ethical and the political and its limits in the concrete events of History and not in the abstract "reflections of philosophers":

> However, there is also an ethical limit to this ethically necessary political existence. But what is this limit? Perhaps what is happening today in Israel marks the place where ethics and politics will come into confrontation and where their limits will be sought. Unfortunately, contradictions like those at play between morals and politics are not only resolved in the reflections of philosophers. It takes events, that is, human lived experience. And perhaps this is where we might find the solution to the universal human problem of the relationship between ethics and politics; the people "engaged" (*engagé*) in this "contradiction" and for whom, despite the war, it is an everyday thought, is a people with a long ethical tradition. The events over there, which we would rather hadn't happened, will therefore take on a significance for the general history of the mind. Perhaps that's where some light will be shed on the matter, in the concrete consciousness of those who suffer and struggle.[225]

That is, the political need confront a certain limit. It needs to confront the imposition of a limit in its very exercise. What Levinas thereby indicates here is how the relation from the ethical to the political cannot extract itself from History and singular historical events. And thus, the relationship from the ethical to the political must confront the problem of violence, and thus must measure itself against the occurrence of the enemy.

The scene of this question is often portrayed and indeed set up in academic scholarship on Levinas by reference to the interview already quoted above, conducted by S. Malka with Levinas and A. Finkielkraut. The geopolitical context of this interview is the aftermath of the brutal and horrific Sabra and Shatila massacre of Palestinians refugees perpetrated by Christian Phalangist militias. The interview was recorded two weeks after the massacre in which were indiscriminately murdered an estimated 850 to 3,500 Palestinian children, women, and men. This interview is haunted by one daunting question, posed by S. Malka to Levinas. The question: "Emmanuel Levinas, you are the philosopher of the 'other.' Isn't history, isn't politics the very site of the encounter with the 'other,' and for the Israeli, isn't the 'other' above all the Palestinian?"[226] To this highly *political* question, posed in the wake of the unjustifiable massacre of Palestinian refugees in Lebanon perpetrated by Christian Phalangist militias and which occurred under the watch of the Israeli military, Levinas responds as follows:

> My definition of the other is completely different. The other is the neighbour, who is not necessarily kin, but who can be. And in that sense, if you're for the other, you're for the neighbour. But if your neighbour attacks another neighbour or treats him unjustly, what can you do? Then alterity takes on another character, in alterity we can find an enemy, or at least then we are faced with the problem of knowing who is right and who is wrong, who is just and who is unjust. There are people who are wrong.[227]

Levinas' response to S. Malka's question occasioned serious, objectionable, and even abhorrent commentaries and interpretations, firstly sketched by M. Jay,[228] and furthered by J. Butler,[229] both claiming that Levinas was here, in this interview, stating and affirming that the Palestinian is "*faceless*". This extremely grave misrepresentation and distortion of the entirety of Levinas' ethics as "First Philosophy" is formulated by a series of misquotes of Levinas' writings, and in particular of the here quoted interview. J. Butler, most probably founding her reading on M. Jay's previous skewed interpretation, levels against Levinas the highly condemning charge and accusation that the hyperbolical ethics negates and nullifies the Palestinian to only value an ethical commitment to "those who were bound together by his version of Judeo-Christian and classical Greek origins."[230] These readings of Levinas are highly ideological and thereby intellectually as well as academically dishonest. They stem from a predetermined prejudice against Zionism and the foundation, as well as the historical becoming, of the State of Israel. These ideological readings of Levinas' ethics fail to engage with the incessant complexities—complexities which animate the relationship between the ethical and the political in Levinas' thought, and most specifically wholly misrepresent the central modality of Levinas' ethico-political thinking, and thus fail to see at work in this thinking the incessant movement of the ethical *calling* the political to perpetually exceed its responsibility each time singularly for the Other, and—as Levinas always marks—through the singularity of the Other *also for all Others*.

Beyond these misrepresentations and grave distortions, Levinas' response marks the exact contrary of what these falsifications have suggested. Indeed, Levinas marks how and why the Other is irreducible to a definition, a determination, a characterization, an image, a name, a nationality—the Other is always and already *other* than presentation, representation, identity, nationality. Indeed, the Other, for Levinas, is the "neighbour"—that which is most close and at the same time that which is irreducible to being the Same or confounded to a sameness or identicalness. Otherwise said, the Other as "neighbour" is always *wholly* Other and from this Otherness intimately animates and elects the Self to its ethical and infinite responsibility for the Other. The commandment and the demand of the irreducible alterity of the Other, commanding and demanding of the Self to respond as elected and awakened *before* and *beyond* its autonomy and decision in an *infinitizing* ethical responsibility for the Other, response of responsibility always and already furthering itself *beyond* what it can or could determine—a responsibility incessantly responding more than what it can or could for the Other. This is precisely what Levinas means in marking the ethical exceptionality of the Self. An exceptionality which does not and cannot settle in the heroism and/or the self-righteousness of self-sacrifice (which for Levinas is just another mark of self-satisfaction or self-glorification), but which incessantly engages the Self *beyond* and *before* its autonomy toward the Other in the *infinitization* of responsibility, in the ethical *diachrony* of responding *before* the commandment of the Other and *beyond* what the Self can determine or will for the Other. This hyperbolical ethics, translated in the dynamic and the distinction between the ethical and the political, means the ethical Law precedes and exceeds the political norm of universality and thus the political determination of sovereignty, identity, and nationality. The ethical precedes and exceeds the universality of reason as it marks a singular response to the singularity of the Other *before* and *beyond* what universality can ensure as morality. Otherwise said, the *transcendence of the ethical in the immanence political* means a certain *overwhelming* of the institutional categories and the rational constitution of the political toward a further responsibilisation of the political as justice.

This is why Levinas always marks the necessity to open to the ethical *before* the political and thus why the political means a certain *after* the ethical. The title of Levinas' text, "Politics After!"[231], hence, does not mean that the political is relegated to a secondary stance *after* the ethical. Rather, it underlines and implies how the political needs to be incessantly awakened *from* the ethical. And in this sense, the ethical occurs *before* the political as it engages the political *from* the ethical to ceaselessly inspire the political *beyond* the political, *beyond* what the political has fixed, constituted, and instituted as ethical and/or as political. Which is why the ethical seeks to bring to the political that which the political cannot exercise without undermining its meaning, essence, determination, and institution. And hence the ethical opens in the political a certain *messianic inspiration* engaging the political outside and *beyond* its own-most determination or definition.

The ethical inspiring the political would mean, for Levinas, an engagement of responsibility in which the Other is always and already commanding *before* and *beyond* the intersubjectivity of recognition or the moral universality determined by and through political rationality or equity, sovereignty, or identity. Here lies the force of Levinas' thinking through the "voice of Israel" indissociable from a Zionism always subjected to its critical questioning. The word Israel for Levinas marks such an ethical exigency brought to the political, and thus irreducibly commanding or ordering the political to engage *beyond* its own justification, *beyond* the universality of its own-most rationality, to orient it toward the exceptional singularity of the absolute Other, the "neighbour," the closest and the farthest, without denomination, in the name of a justice for all Others.

The "voice of Israel" means for Levinas the messianic calling the political *beyond* itself—perhaps even *beyond* the political configuration of the State. Certainly, for Levinas, the idea of the State contains and maintains a configuration by which and through which the transcendence of the ethical *can* develop and embody itself by forcing the political beyond its own-most determination. Otherwise said, the "voice of Israel" indicates and orients through the ethical a resolved engagement in the concrete questioning of the political, and thereby an incessant "mise en abîme" of the politics of identity and sovereignty, nationalism and patriotism which also entails the exigency of an idea of justice whereby the hyperbolical response of responsibility for the singular Other also commands a supplement and an excess of responsibility for all Others outside the determinations of universality, rational normativity or mutual recognition. And indeed, the "voice of Israel" means for Levinas the incessant insistence which, never abdicating the political, always commands it to measure itself to an idea of justice by which is opened the possibility of a responsibility incessantly exceeding and surpassing the exercise of the political.

Israel means for Levinas thus the ethical *in* the political *beyond* the political, that is the ethical incessantly calling the political to engage more than what it determines as ethical. However, this ethical exigency is also why Levinas will never relegate or devalue the institution of the State and thereby the political. The State *can* embody more than what the State determines as just—it *can* open to another excess and supplement of its response in the name of an irreducible idea of justice. Which means the State *can* respond to the name of a justice irreducible to the political and yet always already inspiring the State for the alterity of all the Others.

And furthermore, at a minimal level, Levinas will also never relegate or devalue the State as that through which the political can give *at least* a certain assurance of justice, or bare survival. That is, of protection, equality, togetherness—which, if following Levinas, are also each time ethical, or ethically inspired. Levinas indeed will never simply look over the protection the political and singularly democracy can give for the Other. Having said this however, Levinas also marks how and where the political, and the State, cannot not reduce the absolute singularity of the Other to a recognition, a sameness, a universal and horizontal plane of immanence by which the Other is also *equal* to all others. The political is thus the theatre of the inevitable reduction of singularity to universality, of the hyperbolical ethical responsibility for the Other to the intersubjective recognition of identities all equal under the normative horizon of an institutionalized justice of equity and judgment. And yet, perhaps here lies the "voice of Israel": it also can inspire otherwise, the State can incessantly be called and exposed, animated and awakened by the desire to engage otherwise with the Other, that is, as infinite responsibility for the Other *beyond* what is determined by the political. As Levinas marks in *Otherwise than Being, or Beyond Essence*:

> The way of thinking proposed here does not fail to recognize being or treat it, ridiculously and pretentiously, with disdain, as the fall from a higher order or disorder. On the contrary, it is on the basis of proximity that being takes on its just meaning. In the indirect ways of *Illeity*, in the anarchical provocation which ordains me to the other, is imposed the way which leads to thematization, and to an act of consciousness. The act of consciousness is motivated by the presence of a third party alongside of the neighbour approached. A third party is also approached; and the relationship between the neighbour and the Third party cannot be indifferent to me when I approach. There must be a justice among incomparable ones. There must then be a comparison between incomparables and a synopsis, a togetherness and contemporaneousness; there must be thematization,

> thought, history and inscription. But being must be understood on the basis of *being's other*. To be on the ground of the signification of an approach is to be with another for or against a third party, with the other and the third party against oneself, in justice. This way of thinking is against a philosophy which does not see beyond being, and reduces, by an abuse of language, *Saying* to the *Said* and all sense to interest. Reason, to which the virtue of arresting violence is ascribed, issuing in the order of peace, presupposes disinterestedness, passivity or patience. In this disinterestedness, when, as a responsibility for the other, it is also a responsibility for the third party.[232]

Indeed, for Levinas, the ethical always inspires the ontology of the political to exceed itself *beyond* itself in acting out a justice of responsibility for alterity—that is, a responsibility for all Others already commanding through the singular Other.

And yet—and such is the ethico-political question: how to respond when and if the "neighbour," the Other, engages in destroying, annihilating, obliterating the Self? To phrase it in Levinasian terms: What response, which responsibility can be awakened when the Other seeks to destroy the Self? Which response can the Self give at the instant when the Other does not command, or demand, elect or order, but rather seeks to annihilate and obliterate the Self? Which response, which responsibility can the Self engage in the face of an Other already determined not to awaken the Self to the ethical, but rather resolved to exterminate the Self?

The "voice of Israel" and the space in which and by which Zionism, as the political concretion of this voice, offers a certain response to this question. And Levinas engages precisely with this response. This response is not a justification of Zionism nor is it its negation. It suggests rather an incessant movement from the political to the promise of a *beyond the political*. Indeed, it marks the following: to each time singularly engage with the most radical affirmation of the political *against* the Other who expresses not "Thou shalt not kill!" but the contrary and commands destruction, demonstrates the desire to annihilate the Self, while each time singularly reserving the instant and the space, messianic and prophetic, for the possibility of exceeding the affirmation of the political toward another sphere of encounter. Otherwise said, the "voice of Israel," and thereby of Zionism, proposes for Levinas the dual possibility at once and simultaneously to protect the Self from its annihilation at the hands of the Other who seeks its destruction *and* to respond to the Other *otherwise* by infinitely giving the Other more than what the Self can will or determine. For Levinas, the "voice of Israel" marks, for Levinas, the dual engagement to both the ethical and the political—dual engagement *without* reconciliation and in the incessant excess—justice—of the ethical exceeding the political and the political infinitely tending in its exposition toward the ethical. What is capital in this dual engagement, for Levinas, and as he translates the "voice of Israel" in History is to never relegate the ethical Law to a the purity and gratuity of a giveness without Law. As Levinas radically marks in the concluding pages of *Otherwise than Being, or Beyond Essence*:

> The present study puts into question this reference of subjectivity to essence which dominates the two terms of the alternative brought out. It asks if all meaning proceeds from essence. Does subjectivity draw its own meaning from it? Is it brought out as a struggle for existence, to let itself be seduced by the power of powers, in the violences of nationalism, even when it hypocritically pretends to be only at the service of essence and not to will will? The true problem for us Westerners is not so much to refuse violence as to question ourselves about a struggle against violence which, without blanching in non-resistance to evil, could avoid the institution of violence out of this very struggle. Does not the war perpetuate that which it is called to make disappear, and consecrate war and its virile virtues in good conscience? One has to reconsider the meaning of a certain human weakness, and no longer see in patience only the reverse side of the ontological finitude of the human. But for that one has to be patient oneself without asking patience of the others—and for that one has to admit a difference between oneself and the others. One has to find for man another kinship than that which ties him to being, one that will perhaps enable us to conceive of this difference between me and the other, this inequality, in a sense absolutely opposed to oppression.[233]

Levinas proposes here at once and simultaneously the political protection of the State as a "resistance" against the barbarity of violence while *always* evoking and awakening the inspiration whereby the political, and the State in its political rationale of protection from violence, remain exposed, and thereby commanded, demanded, ordered to surpass and exceed itself *beyond* itself in the expression of an hyperbolical responsibility for the singular Other and through this singularity toward all Others in justice: a justice already capable of engaging a responsibility always exceeding the oppressive binarity and the binarism of the Self and the Other.

As Levinas himself marks, in response to questions asked when presenting in Hebrew language the text entitled "Ethics as Transcendence and Contemporary Thought" (modified version of "Ideology and Idealism"), in July 1972, at the *Summer Institute on Judaism and Contemporary Thought* at Nir Etzion, Israel: "Indeed, if there were only two of us in the world, I and one other, there would be no problem. The other would be completely my responsibility. But in the real world there are many others. When others enter, each of them external to myself, problems arise. Who is closest to me? Who is the Other? Perhaps something has already occurred between them. We must investigate carefully. Legal justice is required. There is need for a State. But it is very important to know whether the State, and power are required because man is a beast to his neighbor (*homo homini lupus*) or because I am responsible for my fellow. It is very important to know whether the political order defines man's responsibility or merely restricts his—bestiality. It is very important, even if the conclusion is that all of us exist for the sake of the state, the society, the law."[234] To which we must add and read at the same time, another response which concludes the "Ethics and Politics" interview, Levinas states:

> The truth of Israel ! It's because a profound attachment to Israel—and to the new mode of life we find there—can only be found precisely in conformity with the heritage of our scriptures. Not enough has been said about this, not enough has been said about the shock that the human possibility of the events at Sabra and Chatila—whoever is behind them—signifies for our entire history as Jews and as human beings. It's not only our thought that we must defend and protect, it's our souls, and that which upholds our souls: our books ! Yes, for Jews, this is an enormous question, and the supreme threat: that our books should be in jeopardy ! The books which carry us through history, and which, even more deeply than the earth, are our support [. . .] I'm not going to give a summing-up of our books . but here's a text that occurs three times in the Talmud . Let me recite it purely and simply: "Our masters have said: those that are offended, without giving offence, those who are defamed without defaming, those who obey in love and rejoice in suffering, are like the sun that rises in its glory." And this metaphor of the sun rising in its glory is borrowed by the Talmudic scholars from Judges, chapter 5, the verse which ends the glorious song of the military victory of Deborah, as if the true light of the sun of victory shone only on those who can "bear defamation without defaming". Or as if all Deborah's military combat simply stood for a moral combat. I'd also like to mention another Talmudic text, for the benefit of those who confuse Zionism—or the relationship to the world and to human beings that its message entails—with some sort of commonplace mystique of the earth as native soil. It is a text that deals with the condemnation of calumny. But the Talmud always says one thing in order to say another as well. Calumny is to be condemned. How do we know? We know it of course, from the Book, from a passage in Numbers, where Moses sends explorers to spy out the land the people of Israel must enter. But the explorers vilify that land. According to the text, they are punished with death. And here the Talmud asks: "What do we learn from this condemnation and this punishment of the explorers who have maligned the land?" Above all, it should teach us

the gravity of calumny concerning persons. For if calumny of that which is "but stones and trees" already merits death, then how serious, a fortiori, must be calumny relating to human beings. The argument—the *a fortiori* of it—is remarkable. A person is more holy than a land, even a holy land, since, faced with an affront made to a person, this holy land appears in its nakedness to be but stone and wood.[235]

Justice (*Justice*)

Justice is a central idea of Levinas' ethics as "First philosophy." And yet, this idea engages two distinct, and perhaps opposed, directions or orientations, at least interpretations, in his thinking and writing. Indeed, in *Totality and Infinity*, Levinas calls justice the asymmetry of the ethical relationship, the break, suspension, and interruption of reciprocity, Sameness, identilcalness and totality of comprehension which always and already reduces the Other to the Same and encompasses in its fulfilled commonality the Self and the Other in an essential identity of Being. In this sense, the idea of justice marks that from which the transcendence of the face of the Other calls and elects the Self to the ethical and thereby to an infinite response of responsibility for the Other.

In *Otherwise than Being, or Beyond Essence*, however, Levinas names justice the occurrence of the Third party (*Tiers*) in and within the radical and absolute asymmetry of the ethical relation. In this sense, Levinas calls justice, in *Otherwise than Being, or Beyond Essence*, the necessity to respond to the Others in and through the hyperbolical relation to the singular Other. And thus, the idea of justice implies a sociality revealed in the transcendent commandment of the Other which inscribes the singular and hyperbolical ethical relationship as infinite responsibility for the singular Other to *also* respond to *all Others*.

It is therefore necessary to propose an interpretation which can, in some manner, relate and bring together these two different approaches of the idea of justice in Levinas' writing and indeed demonstrate the continuity between the two major works, *Totality and Infinity* and *Otherwise than Being, or Beyond Essence*.[236]

The idea of justice in *Totality and Infinity* marks and typifies the ethical relationship itself; a relationship from the Self to the Other, of the Self for the Other which precedes both the foundation of an autonomous subjectivity as well as the establishment of a community, of a reciprocal recognition, of an informed intersubjectivity. In *Totality and Infinity*, the ethical commandment expressed in the face of the Other engages nothing less than a suspension of judgment and decision, representation, and determination and thereby means a relinquishment of the Self's autonomy, mastery, free will, and sovereignty in the name of an infinite responsibility for the Other. Justice indicates thus a radical exposition, passivity, and receptivity to the call and commandment of the Other.: that is, a complete hospitality and thereby openness for the Other in which the idea of justice engages an unsubstitutable responsibility for the Other. This is also why, and in the wake of the idea of God, Levinas also thinks justice as relation to the Infinite:

> A God invisible means not only a God unimaginable, but a God accessible in justice. Ethics is the spiritual optics. The subject-object relation does not reflect it; in the impersonal relation that leads to it the invisible but personal God is not approached outside of all human presence. The ideal is not only a being superlatively being, a sublimation of the objective, or, in the solitude of love, a sublimation of a Thou. The work of justice—the uprightness of the face-to-face—is necessary in order that the breach that leads to God be produced—and 'vision' here coincides with the this work of justice.[237]

As read in *Totality and Infinity*, the "work of justice" implies the idea of a radical and absolute transcendence, God, which immemorially calls the Self to the ethical "uprightness" for the Other and thus to the subjection of its autonomy and self-determination in the face-to-face commandment and address of the Other. This is also why Levinas marks how and why justice

> would not be possible without the singularity, the unicity of subjectivity. In this justice subjectivity does not figure as a formal reason but as individuality; formal reason is incarnate in a being only in the measure that it loses its election and is equivalent to all the others. Formal reason is incarnate only in a being who does not have the strength to suppose that, under the visible that is history, there is the invisible that is justice.[238]

The "work of justice" marks the exceptionality of the ethical Self always exceeding its response of responsibility for the Other *beyond* and *before* "formal" or "practical" reason. And indeed Levinas underlines and stresses this exceptional and hyperbolical singularity of the ethical Self always giving more than what it can for the Other:

> To be I and not only an incarnation of a reason is precisely to be capable of seeing the offense of the offended, or the face. The deepening of my responsibility in the commandment that is borne upon me is not of the order of universalisation: *beyond* the justice of universal laws, the I enters under the justice of the Good. Goodness consists in taking up a position in being such that the Other counts more than myself. Goodness thus

> involves the possibility for the I that is exposed to the alienation of its powers by death to not be for death.[239]

In this manner, Levinas inscribes a radical shift in the history of philosophy (and theology) by proposing that "truth presupposes justice,"[240] and thus that truth remains tributary of an irreducible justice as absolute transcendence of the ethical commandment, the demand and plea of the Other *before* the autonomy of the Self, that is mastery of the demanding and pleading Other from its defenselessness and nakedness, fragility and vulnerability to a response of responsibility *without* norm, *before* and *beyond* the universality of morality:

> Society does not proceed from the contemplation of the true; truth is made possible by relation with the Other our master. Truth is bound up with the social relation which is justice. Justice consists in recognizing in the Other my master. Equality amongst persons means nothing in itself; it has an economic meaning and presupposes money and already rests on justice—which, when well ordered begins with the Other. Justice is the recognition of his priviledge qua Other and his mastery, is access to the Other outside of rhetoric, which is ruse, emprise and exploitation. In this sense justice coincides with the overcoming of rhetoric.[241]

The idea of justice awakens and elects the Self for the Other *beyond* any rhetoric and *before* the establishment, institution, or constitution, of its Self-identity. Justice thereby means: responding to the Other for the Other where this response supposes a certain suspension and interruption, even an abandonment and relinquishment of the Self's sovereignty and autonomy.

Levinas entirely reformulates the classical and traditional understanding and conception of justice. Justice does not entail an equality or a symmetry between parties or entities, between the Self and the Other. The idea of justice does not suppose, for Levinas, the common space of shared responsibilities in accordance with a recognized institution where all are equal under the Law. For Levinas, justice marks the privilege, the irreducible height and absolute transcendence of the Other commanding an infinite responsibility for the Other. For Levinas therefore, and in *Totality and Infinity*, justice consists in responding to the Other for the Other and thereby implies an interruption of free will, of the standpoint of representing, categorizing, judging, the Other in a logic of recognition or intersubjectivity. In this sense, the idea of justice testifies to another approach of language where the essence of expression is not to establish an objective thematization and capture signification in speech or writing in the establishment and institution of a norm, but rather to *respond* to that which remains irretrievable and unrecognizable, secret, and irrepresentable in the Other for the Other. Discourse is justice when the Other speaks and calls *before* the autonomous Self and thereby commands the Self *beyond* its autonomy, freedom, decision as infinite responsibility *without telos, without arché*, substitution and expiation incessantly exceeding its self-determination for the Other.

Levinas introduces, particularly in *Otherwise than Being, or Beyond Essence*, another typification of the idea of justice. After designating justice as *un*-totalizable structure of sociality whereby the inescapable response of responsibility in the asymmetry of the ethical relation from the Self exposed and elected by the Other for the Other, Levinas indicates, in the 1974 text, a certain "*consciousness*"[242] of the asymmetrical and hyperbolical ethics of the face-to-face relation described in *Totality and Infinity*. Levinas marks, in *Otherwise than Being, or Beyond Essence*, how and why the Others of the Other, the Third party is always and already present in the face-to-face relation and indeed already announced and always speaking through the gaze and the transcendent commandment of the singular Other. Otherwise said, the Other is not alone for the Self, the Other also bestows on the Self the calling and commandment of multiple other Others. In this sense, and following *Otherwise than Being, or Beyond Essence*, the other Others already inhabiting the face-to-face relationship commanding and electing the ethical Self to an hyperbolical responsibility engage a renewed idea of justice. Which means: the always and already commanding and demanding Third party in the face of the Other does not mean a simple reduction of the hyperbolic hyperbolical ethical demand and commandment. The Third party does not engage a reduction of the hyperbolical ethics of responsibility to an abstract universality or moral rationality. The infinite ethical responsibility for the Other in the wake of the response to the Other's commandment is never reducible to an identity or a Sameness, and thus remains irreducible to the institution of an intersubjectivity, a community, or a sociality drowning or encompassing the singularity of the ethical in the universal moral order of norms. Rather, Levinas, and in the wake of the reversal he had opened in *Totality and Infinity*, "Truth presupposes justice,"[243] re-engages an idea of justice as each time singular and thereby as a novel, *wholly other thinking* which far from settling for universalism or moral normativity, commands an *each time singular responsibility* for the singularity of the Other and at the same time for the unicity of all Others. This is why Levinas insists in *Otherwise than Being, or Beyond Essence*:

> All the others that obsess me in the other do not affect me as examples of the same genus united with my neighbor by resemblance or common nature, individuations of the human race, or chips of the same block, like the stones metamorphosed into men by Deucalion, who, behind

> his back, had to collect into cities with their hearts of stone. The others concern me from the first. Here fraternity precedes the commonness of a genus. My relationship with the other as neighbor gives meaning to my relations with all the others. All human relations as human proceed from disinterestedness. The one for the other of proximity is not a deforming abstraction. In it justice is shown from the first, it is thus born from the signifyingness of signification, the-one-for-the-other, signification. This means concretely or empirically that justice is not a legality regulating human masses, from which a technique of social equilibrium is drawn, harmonizing antagonistic forces. That would be a justification of the State delivered over to its own necessities. Justice is impossible without the one that renders it finding himself in proximity. His function is not limited to the "function of judgment," the subsuming of particular cases under a general rule. The judge is not outside the conflict, but the law is in the midst of proximity. Justice, society, the State and its institutions, exchanges and work are comprehensible out of proximity. This means that nothing is outside of the control of the responsibility of the one for the other. It is important to recover all these forms beginning with proximity, in which being, totality, the State, politics, techniques, work are at every moment on the point of having their center of gravitation in themselves, and weighing on their own account. In no way is justice a degradation of obsession, a degeneration of the for-the-other, a diminution, a limitation of anarchic responsibility, a neutralization of the glory of the Infinite, a degeneration that would be produced in the measure that for empirical reasons the initial duo would become a trio. But the contemporaneousness of the multiple is tied about the diachrony of two: justice remains justice only, in a society where there is no distinction between those close and those far off, but in which there also remains the impossibility of passing by the closest. The equality of all is borne by my inequality, the surplus of my duties over my rights. The forgetting of self moves justice.[244]

It is in the name of an infinitizing responsibility for the Other and through the singularity of this responsibility incessantly exceeding itself *beyond* and *before* the face-to-face relation and expressing itself toward *all* Others that the idea of justice comes to mind as both Law *and* substitution and expiation, an idea of justice always and already engaged in the *vigilance* of the Law of the Other, the Law irreducibly commanding in and through the singular Other—"Thou shall not kill"—and, through this extreme *vigilance* of the Law, *also responds in infinite responsibility as substitution and expiation* for all other Others *before* and *beyond* the enunciation and expression of the Law. As Levinas indeed marks in the closing pages of *Otherwise than Being, or Beyond Essence*:

> The extraordinary commitment of the other to the third party calls for control, a search for justice, society and the State, comparison and possession, thought and science, commerce and philosophy, and outside of anarchy, the search for a principle. Philosophy is this measure brought to the infinity of the being-for-the-other of proximity, and is like the wisdom of love. But, come out of signification, a modality of proximity, justice, society and truth itself which they require, must not be taken for an anonymous law of the 'human forces' governing an impersonal totality. It is through its ambivalence which always remains an enigma that infinity or the transcendent does not let itself be assembled. Removing itself from every memorable present, a past that was never present, it leaves a trace of its impossible incarnation and its inordinateness in my proximity with the neighbor, where I state, in the autonomy of the voice of conscience, a responsibility, which could not have begun in me, for freedom, which is not my freedom. The fleeting trace effacing itself and reappearing is like a question mark put before the scintillation of the ambiguity: an infinite responsibility of the one for the other, or the signification of the Infinite in responsibility. There is an ambiguity of the order that orders to me the neighbor who obsesses me, for whom and before whom I answer by my ego, in which being is inverted into a substitution, into the very possibility of gift—and of an infinite illeity, glorious in the human plot hatched in proximity, the subversion of essence into substitution. In it I could not arise soon enough to be there on time, nor approach without the extraordinary distance to be crossed augmenting before every effort to assemble it into an itinerary. Illeity overflows both cognition and the enigma through which the Infinite leaves a trace in cognition. Its distance from a theme, its reclusion, its holiness, is not its way to effect its being (since its past is anachronous and anarchic, leaving a trace which is not the trace of any presence), but is its glory, quite different from being and knowing.[245]

Metaphysics (*Métaphysique*)

The history of philosophy counts numerous definitions and, at times, contradictory determinations of this central concept. Generally, the word metaphysics entails the study of the essence of Being, and thus of the fundamental, eternal, and first causes and principles of Being *qua* Being. In this sense, metaphysics, as "First Philosophy," studies the unchanging substantial predicates of Being in itself and for itself.

Initially, the word metaphysics, and before becoming a philosophical concept and further on a discipline or a domain at the root of the practice and exercise of philosophy, served a simple editorial function. Altogether absent from Aristotle's vocabulary and lexiconcthe Greek philosopher used the locution "First Philosophy" to name the "science of Being *as* Being" or "science of Being *qua* Being"—the word metaphysics was firstly attributed around 100 BC by the first editors of Aristotle's writings to classify an ensemble of works which were *ta meta ta physica*, that is: *coming after* Aristotle's treatise entitled *The Physics*. This ensemble of works were simply typified as works indexed *after* or *following* Aristotle's *Physics*. This ensemble comprises fourteen books posthumously ordered which deploy both an *ontology*, a "science of Being *qua* Being" as "First Philosophy," and a *theology*, an understanding of God (*theos*) as first cause and principle, eternal prime unmoved mover.

Unsurprisingly, this editorial definition was quickly superseded: indeed, as the prefix *meta*—an also mean *beyond*, and not only *after*—and as the nature of the works grouped *after* Aristotle's *Physics* engaged a thinking *beyond* physical reality in the understanding and comprehension of *that from which emanates* physical reality itself, its meaning and signification, its substantiality, essence, origin and presence—the word metaphysics began designating the foundational philosophical science explicating and deploying the grounding principles of "Being *qua* Being" *beyond* the order and the manifestation of entities, *beyond* reality and materiality.

Metaphysics is traditionally distinguished into two forms: a general form, a *metaphysica generalis* (ontology), and three special forms, the *metaphysicae specialis* (cosmology, anthropology or psychology, and theology).

For Kant, metaphysics signifies a supra-sensible knowledge and consequently a speculative engagement to think *beyond* the objectivity of experience and the limits of understanding. Metaphysics typifies therefore, and always for Kant, the *unknowable* for human understanding. Kant determines thereby three metaphysical notions or ideas: the *soul*, the *world*, and *God*. Certainly, for Kant, metaphysics engages thinking toward the primary foundations of knowledge, however these foundations remain *beyond* understanding and thus are to be thought only as hypothetical ideals of rationality toward which human finitude ought to tend. This critical appraisal of metaphysics will be retrieved by Husserlian phenomenology. Indeed, for the latter clearly inspired by Kant's critique, metaphysics, in its pretention to discover and uncover the ultimate root of Being completely loses sight of the real and thereby projects itself in purely abstract, illusory, and illusive, ideas. This critique of metaphysics certainly aimed to question and indeed dismantle the Hegelian pretense of reconciling identity and difference as Absolute and Absolute Knowledge through the infinite movement of comprehension deployed in and through speculative dialectic. Indeed, Hegel will seek, by surpassing the Kantian transcendental standpoint of finitude, to reconfigurate the idea of metaphysics as appropriation of the Absolute in itself and for itself. Hegel will engage philosophical thinking *beyond* the finitude of objective experience and moral autonomy and thereby reconciliate subject and substance in and through the absolute comprehension of Being, Essence, Spirit. Speculative dialectics marks the absolute comprehension as reconciliation of finitude and infinitude as "absolute knowledge" through History understood as the immanent becoming of reason which always signifies, for Hegel, the absolute presence of the Absolute. Metaphysics means thus the totality of meaning incessantly reconciliating and thereby recognizing, as its ownmost whole Truth, all oppositions and distinctions, differences and contradictions in the identity and unity of its essence.

Levinas will rethink the idea of metaphysics *beyond* each of these historical determinations. Otherwise said, *beyond* the critique of metaphysics or its absolute affirmation, Levinas defines metaphysics *otherwise*. Metaphysics implies and engages, for Levinas, a transgressive character: *meta* will thus mean *trans*, "*after*" and "*beyond*" as *to exceed* and *transcend*. The idea of metaphysics will thus entail for Levinas the *exceeding* and *transcending* in *surpassing, outdoing, overwhelming* the horizon of phenomenality and the ontological order of presence, manifestation and appearance. In this sense, for Levinas, the idea of metaphysics does not open to a unitary source, or project toward a unified or unificatory *origin* of meaning and presence: it engages a *transgression* as exceeding and transcending experience of the Infinite incessantly burrowing and excavating that which appears and shows itself, manifests itself in presence or the order of Being. This is why Levinas marks how and why the metaphysical relation, that relation which "is the dawn of humanity,"[246] is irreducible to mythical thinking: it is rather a relation to absolute transcendence as relation to the idea of infinity:

> Transcendence is to be distinguished from a union with the transcendent by participation. The metaphysical relation, the idea of infinity, connects with the noumenon which is not a numen. This noumenon is to be distinguished from the concept of God possessed by the believers of positive religions ill disengaged from the bonds of participation, who accept being immersed in a myth unbeknown to themselves. The idea of infinity, the metaphysical relation, is the dawn of a humanity without myths.[247]

Metaphysics designates, for Levinas, the dimension of excess and supplement transcending Being, ontology, presence, and phenomenality. A certain parallel can be established indeed: as the Other questions and puts into question the Same, metaphysics questions and puts into question the order of ontology. It is in this sense that Levinas rehabilitates the idea of metaphysics *after* Heidegger's typification of metaphysics as onto-theology. Contrarily to Heidegger's typification of metaphysics as that process which engages the *forgetfulness* of the meaning of Being to the ontical order, and thereby inaugurates a *shift* from the *fundamental* question of metaphysics pertaining to the meaning of Being to its *directing* question—what is the "highest entity"?—, Levinas redefines metaphysics as *relation* to that which projects thinking *beyond* and *before* ontology, *beyond* and *before* the foundational essence and meaning of ontology, that is as a thinking oriented by a relation to the absolute transcendence and separation of the Infinite as ethical commandment of the Other.

Levinas' renewed approach of the idea of metaphysics is not reducible to a theology: it calls onto God as the Infinite Other, absolute transcendence, which expresses and leaves its trace through the defenseless face of the Other in its ethical commandment, appeal, demand which consecrates an infinitizing responsibility for the Other and thereby for all Others as justice. In this sense, metaphysics implies an *atheism* as transgression of theology or blind faith, toward a concrete relation to the absolute transcendence of the Other through the commandment expressing itself in the face of the Other human, "the face of the Stranger, the widow, the orphan." As Levinas writes in *Totality and Infinity*:

> The dimension of the divine opens forth from the human face. A relation with the Transcendent free from all captivation by the Transcendent is a social relation. It is here that the Transcendent, infinitely other, the proximity of the neighbor, is in being an ineluctable moment of the revelation of an absolute presence (that is, disengaged from every relation), which expresses itself. His very epiphany consists in soliciting us by his destitution in the face of the Stranger, the widow, the orphan. The atheism of the metaphysical means, positively, that our relation with the Metaphysical is an ethical behavior and not theology, not thematization, be it a knowledge by analogy, of the attributes of God. God rises to his supreme and ultimate presence as correlative to the justice rendered unto men. The direct comprehension of God is impossible for a look directed upon him, not because our intelligence is limited, but because the relation with infinity respects the absolute transcendence of the Other without being bewitched by it, and because our possibility of welcoming him in the human goes further than the comprehension that thematises and encompasses its object. It goes further, for precisely it goes into Infinity. The comprehension of God taken as a participation in his sacred life, an allegedly direct comprehension, is impossible because participation is a denial of the divine, and because nothing is more direct than the face-to-face, which is straightforwardedness itself. A God invisible means not only a God unimaginable, but a God accessible in justice.[248]

In *Totality and Infinity*, where ontology is and informs totality, where Being means indifference and anonymity, the metaphysical testifies for Levinas of the Infinite transcendence of the Other, always rupturing and interrupting the totality of Being as indifference and anonymity, reduction of the Other to the Sameness of presence, comprehension, recognition. In this sense, the metaphysical means the incessant burrowing of ontological knowledge to pry open an orientation *before* and *beyond* Being, that is a *wholly other* and *irreducibly heterogeneous* dimension of signification: the Good. Metaphysics means thus the transcendence of the Infinite as the ethical, Good *beyond* and *before* Being, and which incessantly breaks and ruptures the ontological order of reconciling truth and immanent meaning, horizon of presence and anonymity of the Sameness of the Same. Which is why the infinite transcendence of the Good *beyond* and *before* Being incessantly rupturing the order of ontology precedes affirmation and negation, precedes the totality of the Same as comprehension of contradiction, and thereby awakens to a relation toward an infinite distance, the Other, where the relationship does not annul the distance nor inversely the infinite distance negate the relation. It rather creates a wholly other relationship, and thus a Saying as ethical commandment *before* and *beyond* the "being-with" the Other or intersubjectivity, recognition, commonality. As Levinas indeed writes:

> The relationship with a being infinitely distant, that is overflowing its idea, is such that its authority as an existent is already *invoked* in every question we could raise concerning the meaning and the truth of Being. One does not question oneself concerning him; one questions him. Always he faces. If ontology—the comprehension, the embracing of Being—is impossible it is not because every definition of Being already presupposes the knowledge of Being as Pascal had said and Heidegger refutes in the first pages of Being and Time; it is because the comprehension of Being in general cannot dominate the relationship with the Other. The latter relationship commands the first. I cannot disentangle myself from society with the Other when I consider the Being of the existent he is. Already the comprehension of Being is said to the existent who again arises behind the theme in which he is presented. This "saying to the Other"—this relationship with the Other as interlocutor, this relation with an *existent* [the Other] precedes all ontology. Ontology presupposes metaphysics.[249]

Murder (*Meurtre*)

Levinas proposes a highly original interpretation of murder which is always associated with the annihilation and effacement of the Other. Certainly, this interpretation is first sketched in *Is Ontology Fundamental?*, as well as retrieved and expanded in *Totality and Infinity* (cf. Section III, B, 2). Indeed, Levinas addresses the possibility of murder, the murder of the Other, in the analysis of ontological comprehension as totality, indifference and anonymity. As Levinas indicates it, the each time singular event of the face of the Other as absolute transcendence, commandment, plea, demand as it ruptures and breaks the ontology of the Same inevitably engages a *reaction* of the Self in the face of its occurrence. The face of the Other, its epiphany and absolute transcendence, resists all comprehension and reduction to the ontology of the Same. This means, for Levinas, that the face of the Other defies and thereby counters the power, the domination, the Self's will to power, the "power of my power" always seeking to control and appropriate, comprehend and grasp the Other in its clutch, representation, appropriation. Levinas marks how the face of the Other, "like the hardness of the rock against which the effort of the hand comes to naught, like the remoteness of a star in the immensity of space,"[250] exemplifies an "insurmountable resistance." Levinas thereby marks how and why the face of the Other breaks and ruptures the grasp of this comprehension and the power of the Self to reduce the Other in the totality and the indifference of its ontological comprehension: "The face breaks through the form that nonetheless delimits it. This means concretely: the face speaks to me and thereby invites me to a relation incommensurate with a power exercised, be it enjoyment or knowledge."[251]

However, the absolute transcendence of the Other also marks a certain ambiguity: the transcendence of the face, its irreducible epiphany, also, and inevitably so, emprisons it. Otherwise said, the face of the Other, from the height of its transcendence, commandment and demand, can also perjure itself and thereby embody itself in "caricature."[252] Levinas marks this ambiguity in showing how and why the absolute Otherness of the face also spurs on its annihilation and effacement. Which entails that as the epiphany of the face of the Other *defies* the powers of the Self, by the same token, so to speak, it also engages in the Self the wish and the will to negate the Other. Levinas indeed goes to the limit of this *aporia*; the face of the Other, from its height and thereby confronting the powers of the Self, exacerbates and aggravates these same powers to the extent of spurring on in the Self the will and desire of annihilating the Other. The face of the Other calls to transcendence, but its transcendent calling also always antagonizes and provokes the Self's will to power to incessantly smother the call, efface the Other, and foreclose its transcendent alterity—what Levinas will call the "murder of the Other":

> And yet this new dimension opens in the sensible appearance of the face. The permanent openness of the contours of its form in expression imprisons this openness which breaks up form in caricature. The face at the limit of holiness and caricature is thus still in a sense exposed to powers.

> In a sense only: the depths that opens in this sensibility modifies the very nature of power, which henceforth can no longer take, but can kill.[253]

Which means that murder always means the *murder of the face of the Other*, and thus the annihilation of the singular transcendence of the Other, the total negation of the Other's absolute alterity. And, for Levinas, murder is always *of* the Other: emanating and spurred on from the radical transcendence and irrepresentable otherness of the Other as well as always annihilating the singularity and unsubstitutability of the Other. Indeed, Levinas writes:

> Murder alone lays claim to total negation. Negation by labor or usage, like negation by representation, effect a grasp or a comprehension, rest on or aim at affirmation. To kill is not to dominate but to annihilate: it is to renounce to comprehension absolutely. Murder exercises a power over what escapes power. It is still a power for the face expresses itself in the sensible, but already impotency, because the face rends the sensible. The alterity that is expressed in the face provides the unique "matter" possible for total negation. I can wish to kill only an existent absolutely independent, which exceeds my powers infinitely, and therefore does not oppose them but paralyses the very power of power. The Other is the sole being I can wish to kill.[254]

It is in this manner that Levinas insists on the *exceptionality* of murder: murder means to annihilate transcendence through the negation of a singular being. Murder means to destroy the transcendence from which emanates the commandment of the Other. Which is precisely why, for Levinas, the Other

> can oppose to me a struggle, that is oppose to the force that strikes him not a force of resistance, but the very *unforeseeableness* of his reaction. He thus opposes to me not a greater force, an energy assessable and consequently presenting itself as though it were part of a whole, but the very transcendence of his being by relation to that whole; not some superlative of power, but precisely the infinity of his transcendence.[255]

Levinas distinguishes the ontological from the ethical, murder from responsibility precisely where ethical responsibility for the Other is always confronting the very possibility of murdering and annihilating the Other, its transcendent and infinite commandment. This is why, for Levinas, the ethical means precisely to suspend, stop and disrupt the will to kill the Other, most singularly to awaken the Self to an infinitizing responsibility through the face of the Other's extraordinary and overwhelming transcendence, demand, plea.

In this sense, the Other opposes to the will of murder and annihilation of its infinite transcendence "not a greater force", but "the very transcendence of his being," the "infinity of his transcendence." And Levinas marks: "This infinity, stronger than murder already resists us in his face, is his face, is the primordial *expression*, is the first word: *you shall not commit murder*."[256] For Levinas, the infinity of the transcendence of the Other while always arousing the will of murder, the will to kill the Other, the will to annihilate the transcendent face of the Other also and at the same time—and here lies the ethical—the fifth Biblical commandment: *Thou shall not kill*. The infinity of the Other also commands the suspension and the interruption of the will to murder by expressing, from its infinity, the rupture of the will of destruction and annihilation. "The infinite paralyses power by its infinite resistance to murder, which, firm and insurmountable, gleams in the face of the Other, in the total nudity of his defenceless eyes, in the nudity of the absolute openness of the Transcendent."[257]

The relation to the transcendent otherness of the Other implies and engages what Levinas calls "the resistance of what has *no resistance*: the ethical resistance"[258] which entails nothing less than an ethical disarming of the Self in the face of the Other's commandment "Thou shall not kill", ethical disarming of the Self's will to murder precisely at the instant where the temptation to murder the Other is at its most actual. As Levinas writes:

> The epiphany of the face brings forth the possibility of gauging the infinity of the temptation to murder, not only as a temptation to total destruction, but also as the purely ethical impossibility of this temptation and attempt. If the resistance to murder were not ethical but real, we would have a perception of it, with all that reverts to the subjective in perception. We would remain within the idealism of a consciousness of struggle, and not in relationship with the Other, a relationship that can turn into struggle, but already overflows the consciousness of struggle. The epiphany of the face is ethical.[259]

In this sense, and contrarily to Hegel's analysis of the *struggle for recognition* and the *Master and Slave dialectic*, developed in both the early Iena writings[260] and the *Phenomenology of Spirit* and where the idea of recognition, and thus of the recognition of the other, is conditioned on a primary struggle in the face of death and annihilation, Levinas engages the relation to the Other *outside* the context and the horizon of such a confrontation. Indeed, for Levinas, the relation to the Other does not depend on recognition nor does it imply a confrontation to death between the Self and the Other. The relation to the Other depends solely on the Infinity of the transcendence of the Other as *interruption* and *suspension* of murder and thereby of the death of the Other expressing thus an ethical resistance *against* death and which "paralyses my powers and from the depths of defenceless eyes rises firm and absolute in its nudity and destitution."[261] Which opens a wholly other ethical relation to the Other irreducible to recognition: a relation to the Other as as proximity, expression, discourse which, *before* and *beyond* spatiality or communication, engages, a "solicitation that concerns me by its [the Other's] destitution and Height."[262]

Obedience (*Obéissance*)

Levinas situates obedience in the ethical and thus defines it as an awakening and election of the Self to the ethical demand as response to the Other's suffering, defenselessness, fragility, and mortality. Response *before* and *beyond* autonomy or self-determination, service *without* servitude, obedience, for Levinas, is not a simple compliance and submission in the face of a heteronomical law which crushes or negates, alienates or suppresses the Self. All to the contrary, obedience does not repress the Self, but *elects* the Self as infinitizing responsibility for the Other. To be obliged means, for Levinas, to respond *as* responsibility to the face of the Other whose irrecusable and inescapable commandment does not proceed from a contract, a commonality, a norm or moral universalism, but from the primacy of the Other's mortality. This is why, for Levinas, in obedience as election of the ethical Self *before* autonomy and *beyond* judgment is heard the commandment of the Other: *Thou shall not kill the Other* as *Thou shall not abandon the Other to its death.* Which also entails that in obedience the ethical Self, as passivity more passive than all passivity, and thus as exposition to the Other for the Other, the absolute infinity of God, the glory of the Infinite, "comes to mind." Which for Levinas entails the extraordinary *aporia* of the ethical and which incumbs singularly on the elected Self for the Other: to respond *before* hearing the call and the commandment of the Other *beyond* what can be expected or determined, fulfilled or satisfied in responsibility for the Other:

> An obedience preceding the hearing of the order, the anachronism of inspiration or of prophecy is, for the recuperable time of reminiscence, more paradoxical than the prediction of the future by an oracle. "Before they call, I will answer" the formula is to be understood literally. In approaching the other I am always late for the meeting. But this singular obedience to the order to go, without understanding the order, this obedience prior to all representation, this allegiance before any oath, this responsibility prior to

> commitment, is precisely the Other-in-the-Same, inspiration and prophecy, the passing itself of the Infinite.[263]

Obedience as ethical occurs in and through the awakening and election of the Self. For Levinas, this entails the *aporetic* modality of the ethical which engages the exceptionality of an infinitizing responsibility for the Other—the *infinitization* of responsibility incessantly exceeding itself for the Other. This is why, through obedience, Levinas suggests "metaphorically" how the heteronomy of the Other's commandment *informs* the Self's individuation as singularly elected to the ethical and for the Other. This individuation of the Self for the Other never translates an autonomy. Rather, it incessantly exceeds and surpasses autonomy, freedom, will or self-determination. Levinas insists rather that the ethical individuation of the Self for the Other means the incessant excess of responsibility *before* and *beyond* what the subject can determine as its identity and thereby *before* and *beyond* what the autonomous subject rationally determines as its universal moral norm. Which also means, for Levinas, that the ethical is always an *inspiration* of that which, *without* origin or finality, commands and elects, demands and awakens the Self *before* and *beyond* its own Self, the *psyche* of the Self singularly for the Other. As Levinas writes:

> Obedience precedes any hearing of the command. The possibility of finding, anachronously, the order in the obedience itself, and of receiving the order out of oneself, this reverting of heteronomy into autonomy, is the very way the Infinite passes itself. The metaphor of the inscription of the law in consciousness expresses this in a remarkable way, reconciling autonomy and heteronomy. It does so in an ambivalence, whose diachrony is the signification itself, an ambivalence which, in the present, is an ambiguity. The inscription of the order in the for-the-other of obedience is an anarchic being affected, which slips into me "like a thief" through the outstretched nets of consciousness. This trauma has surprised me completely; the order has never been represented, for it has never been presented, not even in the past coming in memory, to the point that it is I that only says, and after the event, this unheard-of obligation. This ambivalence is the exception and subjectivity of the subject, its very psyche, a possibility of inspiration. It is the possibility of being the author of what had been breathed in unbeknownst to me, of having received, one knows not from where, that of which I am author. In the responsibility for the other we are at the heart of the ambiguity of inspiration. The unheard-of saying is enigmatically in the anarchic response, in my responsibility for the other. The trace of infinity is this ambiguity in the subject, in turns beginning and makeshift, a diachronic ambivalence which ethics makes possible.[264]

One-for-the-Other (*Un-pour-l'autre*)

As with the *Other-in-the-Same*, the *One-for-the-Other* marks a primary and prime modality of significance. Indeed, for Levinas, the *One-for-the-Other* is the *signifyingness of signification* which is not revealed as a mode of presence, representation or description, nor as the symbolic evocation of an absence, a makeshift or a failing of presence. One-for-the-Other means an *outdoing* of the meaning of Being and the essence of Truth opening thereby to a responsibility in the Self for the Other to the point of substitution and expiation—responsibility for the responsibility of the Other. One-for-the-Other implies thus and engages a responsibility *before* and *beyond* presence or representation, *before* and *beyond* the circumscribed unity, self-identity, and sovereignty as self-determination and moral autonomy of subjectivity. It opens the Self *before* and *beyond* itself and to an antecedence, anteriority, precedence and priority: being-commanded and ordered *by* the Other *for* the Other *without* possibility of denegation, abandonment, desertion. In other words, One-for-the-Other means always and already being elected by the Other for the Other. Here thus lies the uniqueness of the Self: in and through the ethical, the Self is elected as unique and singular through its infinite response of responsibility, *host* and *hostage* for the Other. A responsibility for responsibility, that is a responsibility for the Other and where no one else but the Self can or could respond in its place. This is why, for Levinas, the One-for-the-Other marks the immemorial, unrepresentable, invisible, impresentable commandment which orders as it elects, demands as it awakens the Self *before* its own autonomy or sovereignty to respond *beyond* its capacity or judgment for the Other and in the name of the irreducible singularity of the Other. Indeed, Levinas always insists in accentuating the Self's responsibility for the Other *beyond* any possible determination or fixation as already responsible *before* freedom or willingness: incommensurable and unescapable election for the Other in the *diachrony* of responding always *too late* and yet always *before* the call, the demand, the plea of the Other which far from immobilizing the Self animates and individuates it singularly to the ethical.

As Levinas marks in the opening pages of *Otherwise than Being, or Beyond Essence*:

> Immemorial, unrepresentable, invisible, the past that bypasses the present, the pluperfect past, falls into a past that is a gratuitous lapse. It can not be recuperated by reminiscence not because of its remoteness, but because of its incommensurability with the present. The present is essence that begins and ends, beginning and end assembled in a thematizable conjunction; it is the finite in correlation with a freedom. Diachrony is the

> refusal of conjunction, the non-totalizable, and in this sense, infinite. But in the responsibility for the Other, for another freedom, the negativity of this anarchy, this refusal of the present, of appearing, of the immemorial, commands me and ordains me to the other, to the first one on the scene, and makes me approach him, makes me his neighbor. It thus diverges from nothingness as well as from being. It provokes this responsibility against my will, that is, by substituting me for the other as a hostage. All my inwardness is invested in the form of a despite-me, for-another. Despite-me, for-another, is signification par excellence.[265]

Host and hostage, *host* to the point of being *hostage* of the Other, the ethical Self, for Levinas, is responsibility for the Other *before* and *beyond* the autonomy of reason or self-determining judgment. Always and already responsible, being host to the point of being hostage is not chosen nor willed. If there had been a choice, a decision, or a judgment, the Self would have marked the relation to the Other by and through its "for-itself" and its "being-with-itself." But the ethical Self, for Levinas, consists not in valuing or justifying its independence and thereby ensuring or determining its own ethical engagement with the Other based and founded on the autonomy of will, decision, and rational judgment. Rather, the ethical Self is elected to the ethical precisely where it supports the Other *before* its own selfhood, and thus where it responds to the Other *before* being for its own-self and *beyond* what its sovereignty or autonomy can determine:

> The conjuncture in which a man is responsible for other men, the ethical relationship, which is habitually considered as belonging to a derivative or founded order, has been throughout this work approached as irreducible. It is structured as the-one-for-the-other. It signifies outside of all finality and every system, where finality is but one of the principles of systematization possible. This responsibility appears as a plot without a beginning, anarchic. No freedom, no commitment undertaken in a present, a present among others, recuperable, is the obverse of which this responsibility would be the reverse, but no slavery is included in the alienation of the same who is "for the other." In responsibility the same, the ego, is me, summoned, provoked, as irreplaceable, and thus accused as unique in the supreme passivity of one that cannot slip away without fault. The models of being and the subject-object correlation, which are justifiable but derivative, do not depict signification, the-one-for-the-other.[266]

One-for-the-Other means an irreducible election for the Other *before* and *beyond* the Self's auto-constitution, self-determination and ownness. It marks and "makes possible relationship, and the point outside of being, the point of disinterestedness, necessary for a truth that does not wish to be pure ideology. But it is not what one means by 'committed subjectivity.'"[267]

One-for-the-Other precedes subjective commitment and engagement: it is the mark of being elected, responding *before* the commandment or the injunction to respond thereby responding *beyond* any possible fulfilment of the response: the awakening of the ethical Self:

> It is in a way very different from commitment that the one is implicated in the-one-for-the-other. It is not a question of a forsakenness in a world, a situation which is from the first its own reversal, in which I can settle and build myself a place, a situation that is produced and reverses into the representation of a diversity put in conjunction. It is a question of a signification in which the meaning of establishment and representation are indeed justified, but this signification signifies prior to any world, signifies the proximity of the same and the other, in which the implication of the one in the other signifies the assignation of the one by the other. This assignation is the very signifyingness of signification, or the *psyche* of the same. Through the psyche proximity is my approaching of the other, the fact that the proximity of the same and the other is never close enough. The summoned one is the ego—me.[268]

Which means, for Levinas: the ethical Self is always assigned to its signification by the Other for the Other. And thus: assigned by the anteriority of the Good *beyond* and *before* the totality and immanence, presence and proliferation of the meaning and the truth of Being. Which opens a radically other modality of significance, one which seeks *otherwise than Being* and *beyond essence* to think a certain idea of the Good which, without conciliation or reconciliation, engages a peace with the Other through one's infinite and infinitizing responsibility for the Other, or what Levinas also calls *proximity*:

> But proximity, conceived independently of this spiritualism of consciousness and recognized as signification or goodness, allows us to understand goodness in another way than as an altruistic inclination to be satisfied. For signification, the-one-for-the-other, is never an enough, and the movement of signification does not return. This is also not to conceive of it as a decision of the will, an act of consciousness beginning in the present of a choice, having an origin in consciousness, or in the present of a choice conditioned by inhabitation (which is the context of every origin!). Goodness in the subject is anarchy itself. As a responsibility for the freedom of the other, it is prior to any freedom in me, but it also precedes violence in me, which would be the contrary of freedom. For if no one is good voluntarily, no one is a slave of the Good. The plot of goodness and of the Good, outside of consciousness, outside of essence, is the exceptional plot of substitution, which the said in its dissimulated truths

> betrays, and conveys, before us. The I approached in responsibility is for-the-other, is a, denuding, an exposure to being affected, a pure susceptiveness. It does not posit itself, possessing itself and recognizing itself; it is consumed and delivered over, dis-locates itself, loses its place, is exiled, relegates itself into itself, but as though its very skin were still a way to shelter itself in being, exposed to wounds and outrage, emptying itself in a no-grounds, to the point of substituting itself for the other, holding on to itself only as it were in the trace of its exile. What verbs like "to deliver itself," "consume itself," "exile itself (*se livrer, se consumer, s'exiler*)," suggest by their pronominal form is not an act of reflection on oneself, of concern for oneself; it is not an act at all, but a modality of passivity which in substitution is *beyond* even passivity. To be oneself as in the trace of one's exile is to be as a pure withdrawal from oneself, and as such, an inwardness. Inwardness is not at all like a way of disposing of private matters. This inwardness without secrets is a pure witness to the inordinateness which already commands me, to give to the other taking the bread out of my own mouth, and making a gift of my own skin. It is not commitment that describes signification; it is signification, the-one-for-the-other characteristic of proximity, which justifies all commitment.[269]

As Levinas marks, proximity means a non-indifference which, as One-for-the-Other, always and already extends for the Other toward the Other and which thereby cannot satisfy itself, fulfill or contend itself in the assuredness or certainty of a community, a "being-with", a contractual intersubjectivity. The Other is always and already wholly Other and from the height of its transcendence incessantly awakens the Self *before* its own self-determination and *beyond* its moral autonomy toward an ethical responsibility irreducible to moral judgment or ontological comprehension. For Levinas, One-for-the-Other entails the absolute transcendence interrupting and suspending the process and processuality of immanence and thus engages an ethical thinking wholly oriented toward the transcendent Otherness of the Other—an ethical thinking wholly other than cognition, recognition, presentation or representation of the Other-in-the-Sameness, indifference and anonymity, of understanding and/or moral autonomy. As Levinas pursues:

> In the non-indifference to a neighbor, where proximity is never close enough, the difference between me and the other, and the undeclinability of the subject are not effaced, as they are in the situation in which the relationship of the one with the other is understood to be reciprocal. The non-indifference to the other as other and as neighbor in which I exist is something *beyond* any commitment in the voluntary sense of the term, for it extends into my very bearing as an entity, to the point of substitution. It is at the same time prior to commitments, for it disengages in this extreme passivity an undeclinable and unique subject. Responsibility, the signification which is non-indifference, goes one way, from

> me to the other. In the Saying of responsibility, which is an exposure to an obligation for which no one could replace me, I am unique. Peace with the other is first of all my business. The non-indifference, the saying, the responsibility, the approach, is the disengaging of the unique one responsible, me. The way I appear is a summons. I am put in the passivity of an undeclinable assignation, in the accusative, a self. Not as a particular case of the universal, an ego belonging to the concept of ego, but as I, said in the first person-I, unique in my genus. It is indeed true that this I has already become a universal in the present exposition itself. But I am capable of conceiving of a break with this universal, and the apparition of the unique I which always precedes the reflection which comes again (with an alternating which we find in the refutation and rebirth of skepticism) to include me in the concept—which I again evade or am torn up from. The uniqueness of this ego, this I, is not due to a unique trait of its nature or its character; nothing is unique, that is, refractory to concepts, except the I involved in responsibility. In signification I am disengaged as unique. In the saying in responsibility, the one is not concealed in itself, but denudes itself in recurrence, substituting itself for another on the hither side of its own identity for another. This is the only way for it to be not multiplied in this relationship, but for its unity to be brought out in it. The "never enough" of proximity, the restlessness of this peace, is the acute uniqueness of subjectivity. The subject arising in the passivity of unconditionality, in the expulsion outside of its being at home with itself, is undeclinable. This undeclinability is not that of transcendental subjectivity, is not an intentionality or openness upon the world, not even a world that overflows me, and in which the alleged ecstatic subjectivity is only dissimulated. Proximity, difference which is non-indifference, is responsibility. It is a response without a question, the immediacy of peace that is incumbent on me. It is the signification of signs. It is the humanity of man not understood on the basis of transcendental subjectivity. It is the passivity of exposure, a passivity itself exposed. Saying does not occur in consciousness nor in a commitment understood in terms of consciousness or memory; it does not form a conjuncture and a synchrony. Proximity is fraternity before essence and before death, having a meaning despite being and nothingness, despite concepts.[270]

Ontology (*Ontologie*)

Etymologically, the term means *discourse on* or *of* Being and is therefore taken to signify the philosophical study pertaining to the meaning and the essence of Being *qua* Being.

For Levinas, ontology is always understood as the indifference and anonymity of the presence of Being which, as truth and meaningfulness, totality and signification, already reduces and effaces, negates and denegates the absolute transcendence of the Other in and within its comprehension and through the Sameness of the Same, the essence of identity or identicalness it consecrates. Ontology is totality of meaning and presence, comprehension, and thereby domination as one and unique, univocal, unitary truth, reducing and leveling the Other in and within the embrace and supremacy of Sameness and identity. Ontology is thus the consigned exercise of power always and already negating the infinite transcendence of the otherness of the Other, annihilating the Height of the Infinite, and demoting the irrepresentable precedence of the ethical commandment into Sameness, indifference, indistinction, anonymity.

Levinas' critique of ontology is foremostly directed at Heidegger whom he sees as the culminating point of the predominance of ontology throughout the history of Western philosophy. In this sense, Levinas associates Heidegger's project of re-establishing a "fundamental ontology" capable of retrieving and recovering the "forgetfulness" of the meaning of Being *beyond* and *before* the history of onto-theology to yet a further philosophical reduction and indeed effacement, closure and foreclosure of the singular and absolute transcendence of the Other—reduction and effacement, closure and foreclosure of the irreducible otherness of the Other. For Levinas, ontology levels the Other to the meaning of an all-embracing totality and Sameness, indifference and anonymity by and through the immanent truth of Being. Levinas proposes thus to think, *before* and thus as well *beyond* the essence of Being as indifference and anonymity in and through the essence of its meaning and truth, toward the singularity of an irrepresentable and irreducible transcendence of the Other human which commands from a *wholly other demand* than that of truth, meaning, intersubjectivity, community; a *wholly other injunction* than that of the essential conjunction of Being *and* Time as *presence* in the event of their co-belonging (*Er-eignis*) and in which all that sustains itself and thereby perseveres by itself is the "*il y a*," the pure anonymity of *thereness* where the Other and the Self are brought to their identical nullifications.

This is why Levinas contends:

> The primacy of ontology for Heidegger does not rest on the truism: "to know an existent it is necessary to have comprehended the Being of existents." To affirm the priority of Being over existents is to already decide the essence of philosophy; it is to subordinate the relation with *someone* who is an *existent*, (the ethical relation) to a relation with the *Being of existents*, which, impersonal, permits the apprehension, the domination of existents (a relationship of knowing), subordinates justice to freedom. If freedom denotes the mode of remaining the same in the midst of the

> other, knowledge, where an existent is given by interposition of impersonal Being, contains the ultimate sense of freedom. It would be opposed to justice which involves obligations with regard to an existent par excellence. In subordinating every relation with existents to the relation with Being the Heideggerian ontology affirms the primacy of freedom over ethics. To be sure, the freedom involved in the essence of truth is not for Heidegger a principle of free will. Freedom comes from an obedience to Being: it is not man who possesses freedom; it is freedom that possesses man. But the dialectic which thus reconciles freedom and obedience in the concept of truth presupposes the primacy of the same, which marks the direction of and defines the whole of Western philosophy.[271]

Ontology as discourse of Being *qua* Being, as truth and meaning of the essence of Being in its historical deployment is, for Levinas, synonym of indifference, neutralization, and anonymity. Always for Levinas, ontology is thus the imposition of the order of identity, Sameness, uniformity, totality. It engages the annihilation of the alterity of the Other in its process of the totalization of meaningfulness as comprehension in and through immanent presence of Sameness. Here, for Levinas, the Other is reduced to "being-there":

> The neutralisation of the other who becomes a theme or an object—appearing, that is, taking its place in the light—is precisely his reduction to the same. To know ontologically is to surprise in an existent confronted that by which it is not this existent, this stranger, that by which it is somehow betrayed, surrenders, is given in the horizon in which it loses itself and appears, lays itself open to grasp becomes a concept. To know amounts to grasping being out of nothing or reducing it to nothing, removing from it its alterity.[272]

In this sense, for Levinas, Being, in its incessant reduction of the alterity of the Other and annihilation of the Other's transcendence is *evil*: totality, totalization, and even totalitarianism of the Same.

To this totalizing process and deployment inherent to the "primacy of ontology" and always associated and equated with the becoming of Western philosophy, Levinas asks: "Is ontology fundamental?" This infamous article, published in 1951, proposes nothing less than the undermining of this ontological tradition which, according to Levinas, stretches from Plato and culminates in Heidegger. Indeed, Levinas questions the predominance and the perseverance of ontology, the reign of the Same and totality, the deployment of the history of the truth of Being as *donation* of meaningfulness, all encompassing presence, throughout the history of Western philosophy. Otherwise said, Levinas challenges the primacy of the meaning and truth of Being as essence and presence, identity and comprehension by evoking *before* and *beyond* ontology, Being and essence, the irrepresentable antecedence and precedence of the transcendence of the Other. Setting his critical question *contra* Heidegger's "fundamental ontology" as the culmination of the history of ontological knowledge in Western philosophy, Levinas writes:

> One cannot prefer as the condition of ontology a relation with beings over the fundamental thesis that every relation with a being presupposes the intimacy or the forgetfulness of Being. From the moment that one engages in reflection and precisely for the very reasons which since Plato subject the sensation of the particular to knowledge of the universal, one is forced, it would seem, to subject relations between beings to structures of being, metaphysics to ontology, the existentiell to the existential. How, moreover, can the relation with being be, from the outset, anything other than its comprehension as being-present (*étant*), the fact of freely letting it be inasmuch as it is being-present (*étant*). Unless it is Other. Our relation with the other certainly consists in wanting to comprehend him, but this relation overflows comprehension. Not only because of the other requires, outside of all curiosity, also sympathy or love, ways of being distinct from impassible contemplation, but because in our relation to the Other, he does not affect us in terms of concept.[273]

Which entails that the relation to the transcendence of the Other—irreducible to ontology for occurring *before* the ontological comprehension of the Other as that being always and already in and within the horizon of the essence and Sameness of Being—is a relation to the Other's "invocation, where this invocation is not preceded by comprehension":[274] that is, "religion"[275] (which is "nothing theological, nothing mystical"[276] and where discourse is "prayer.")[277] Levinas opens thus to a *wholly other source of significance* than the ontological through the idea of *religion* as relation to the infinite, incomprehensible Illeity, and irrepresentable transcendence of the Other and *prayer* as discourse toward the alterity of the Other and which is distinguished from "thought aiming at an object [that is, ontology] from the tie with a person is that the latter is articulated in the vocative: what is named is at the same time that which is called."[278]

In this manner, Levinas marks the singularity of the Other *before* its comprehension in the horizon of an ontology and thereby toward which the Self must always and already respond *beyond* all ontological or moral determinations. Indeed, is opened here a regime of significance which lies not on the immanence of comprehension, of that which *brings together* and *unifies* beings or entities within the meaning and truth of Being. Rather is here engaged a responsibility toward the irrepresentable transcendence of an alterity irreducible to Being and from where occurs a commandment demanding each time singularly the ethical break and rupture, suspension and interruption of comprehension, that is each time singularly demanding the ethical overwhelming of ontological comprehension. As Levinas notes: "To comprehension and signification grasped within a horizon, we oppose the signifyingness of the face."[279]

Other (*Autre*)

Levinas' philosophical questioning is directed toward a dismantling of the classical ontological opposition between the "Same" and the "Other" in order to liberate a *wholly other* possibility of thinking toward an infinite ethical responsibility for the "Other absolutely Other." The impulse of this ethics as "First Philosophy" is affirmed in the opening of *Totality and Infinity*:

> The absolutely Other is the Other. He and I do not form a number. The collectivity in which I say "you" or "we" is not a plural of the "I." I you—these are not individuals of a common concept. Neither possession nor the unity of number nor the unity of concepts link me to the Stranger, the Stranger who disturbs that being at home with oneself.[280]

The Other, irreducibly heterogeneous to the Same and the Self, is neither graspable as an ontological or a logical category, nor comprehensible within a determined horizon of intentionality or intersubjectivity. The Other is irrepresentable and irreducible to knowledge and representation; *wholly other* to the totality or comprehension of Being, the Sameness of intersubjectivity, community, or commonality. Levinas engages a profound ethical redefinition of the Other irreducibly Other opening thus a resistance to the systematicity and identity, identification, unification of Being in Western philosophy and for which the Same always comprehends and already appropriates, reduces and negates the otherness of the Other.

For Levinas, the Other is always already Other and occurs as commandment, expression, demand, and call by and through which the Self is elected and awakened to an ethical responsibility *beyond* and *before* Being, meaning and truth, universality and normativity.

The Other is always and already *beyond* history *in* history, *beyond* the possibility of its reduction to a reason of History and yet always interrupting, suspending, rupturing the becoming of History. The Other calls and commands an incessant interruption and suspension of the narrative and pretention in philosophy to reduce and level out the otherness of the Other to its own immanent deployment of sense and signification. As Levinas indicates and remarks:

> To say that the other can remain absolutely other, that he enters only into the relationship as conversation, is to say that history itself, an identification of the same cannot claim to totalise the same and the other. The absolutely other, whose alterity is overcome in the philosophy of immanence on the allegedly common plane of history, maintains his transcendence in the midst of history. The same is essentially identification within the diverse, or history, or system. It is not I who resist the system as Kierkegaard thought: it is the other.[281]

The Other transcends infinitely the Same while inspiring, electing, commanding, and demanding of the Self to respond *beyond* and *before* its autonomy as infinite responsibility, response, *host* as *hostage* of the Other, substitution and expiation for the Other. This is why Levinas, poses the question: "Why does the other concern me? What is Hecuba to me? Am I my brother's keeper?" And answers:

> These questions have meaning only if one has already supposed that the ego is concerned only with itself, is only a concern for itself. In this hypothesis it indeed remains incomprehensible that the absolute outside-of-me, the other, would concern me. But in the "prehistory" of the ego posited for itself speaks a responsibility. The self is through and through a hostage, older than the ego, prior to principles. What is at stake for the self, in its being, is not to be. Beyond egoism and altruism it is the religiosity of the self. It is through the condition of being hostage that there can be in the world pity, compassion, pardon and proximity—even the little there is, even the simple "After you, sir." The unconditionality of being hostage is not the limit case of solidarity, but the condition for all solidarity. Every accusation and persecution, as all interpersonal praise, recompense, and punishment presuppose the subjectivity of the ego, substitution, the possibility of putting oneself in the place of the other, which refers to the transference from the "by the other" into a "for the other", and in persecution from the outrage inflicted by the other to the expiation for his fault by me. But the absolute accusation, prior to freedom, constitutes freedom which, allied to the Good, situates beyond and outside of all essence.[282]

The Other engages the election and awakening of the Self to the ethical, *before* and *beyond* the autonomy and sovereignty of the Self. Levinas indeed marks the irreducible transcendence as antecedence, precedence, anteriority of the Other already inhabiting the Self and thereby always inspiring the infinite responsibility for the Other, a responsibility *before* intersubjectivity and *beyond* what could be stipulated in a contract, *before* community and *beyond* judgment, or moral normativity. Levinas indeed marks:

> The responsibility for the Other can not have begun in my commitment, in my decision. The unlimited responsibility in which I find myself comes from

> the hither side of my freedom, from a "prior to every memory," an "ulterior to every accomplishment," from the non-present par excellence, the non-original, the anarchical, prior to or *beyond* essence. The responsibility for the other is the locus in which is situated the null-site of subjectivity, where the privilege of the question "Where?" no longer holds. The time of the said and of essence there lets the pre-original saying be heard, answers to transcendence, to a dia-chrony, to the irreducible divergency that opens here between the non-present and every representable divergency, which in its own way—a way to be clarified—makes a sign to the responsible one.[283]

Other-in-the-Same (*Autre-dans-le-même*)

For Levinas, the Other-in-the-Same, as modality of signification, remains irreducible to its dialectical appropriation or reappropriation where the Other would figure and appear within the intentional horizon of a Sameness or identity, totality, or whole. It marks transcendence, and the transcendence of the Other. In this sense, this modality of signification marks the incessant awakening of the Same toward and for the Other—an orientation which also supposes the interruption and suspension, break and rupture of ontology opening to the otherness of the Other. Which means: the Other-in-the-Same means the Other transcending incessantly the Same and thereby informing it to respond incessantly to the absolute otherness of the Other.

In this sense, the Other-in-the-Same means, firstly, the Other incessantly *awakening* the Same *out of its* self-sameness, self-determination, autonomy. The Other-in-the-Same does not mean the Other integrated or interiorized in the Same, or recognized or represented within the Same. It means the Other *inspiring* the Self *before* and *beyond* its self-sameness or identity and toward an infinite response of responsibility for the Other.

For Levinas, this principal modality of signification opens to the ineluctable and inescapable election of the Self as always and already respondent of and for the Other. Otherwise said, this modality of signification far from pacifying the relation with the Other incessantly marks the aggravation and intensification of responsibility for the Other. Marking that the Other is always and already primary—and in this sense always and already informing, inhabiting, haunting the Self *before* itself and *beyond* what the Self could represent or codify, determine, or comprehend—Levinas adds:

> The self in a being is exactly the not-being-able-to-slip-away-from an assignation that does not aim at any generality. There is no ipseity common

> to me and the others; "me" is the exclusion from this possibility of comparison, as soon as comparison is set up. The ipseity is then a privilege or an unjustifiable election that chooses me and not the ego. I am unique and chosen; the election is in the subjection. The conceptualization of this last refusal of conceptualization is not contemporaneous with this refusal; it transcends this conceptualization.[284]

Which entails how the Other-in-the-Same engages *in the* Same, and thus in the Self, an irreducible non-indifference toward the Other. Precisely the non-indifference of the Same for the Other and the substitution which, in its turn, is a nonequality with oneself, a non-recovering of self by self, a dispossession of self, the self leaving, as Levinas marks,

> the clandestinity of its identification. It is already a sign made to another, a sign of this giving of signs, that is, of this non-indifference, a sign of this impossibility of slipping away and being replaced, of this identity, this uniqueness: "here I am." The identity aroused thus behind identification is an identity by pure election. Election traverses the concept of the ego to summon me as me through the inordinateness of the other. It extracts me from the concept in which I continually take refuge, for I find in it the measure of an obligation which is not defined in the election. Obligation calls for a unique response not inscribed in universal thought, the unforeseeable response of the chosen one.[285]

Indeed, the Other-in-the-Same engages a non-identical Self whose ethical election as Self toward a hyperbolical responsibility which never accomplishes or fulfills itself in a contract or a norm. Responsibility incessantly calling for an excess and a supplement of responsibility *before* and *beyond* what the Self can propose and predict, the Other-in-the-Same awakens the Self as always and already testifying of the Illeity of the Other, that is the immemorial Good *before* and *beyond* Being. Which means the Self is elected and already and always engaged by the Infinite to an *infinitization* of responsibility for the irreducible alterity of the Other. An ethical Self awakened and elected to the point of substitution and expiation for the Other and in the name of the singularity of the Other:

> The ego stripped by the trauma of persecution of its scornful and imperialist subjectivity, is reduced to the "here I am," in a transparency without opaqueness, without heavy zones propitious for evasion. "Here I am" as a witness of the Infinite, but a witness that does not thematize what it bears witness of, and whose truth is not the truth of representation, is not evidence. There is witness, a unique structure, an exception to the rule of

being, irreducible to representation, only of the Infinite. The Infinite does not appear to him that bears witness to it. On the contrary the witness belongs to the glory of the Infinite. It is by the voice of the witness that the glory of the Infinite is glorified. No theme, no present, has a capacity for the Infinite. The subject in which the other is in the same, inasmuch as the same is for the other, bears witness to it. The difference of proximity is absorbed in the measure that proximity becomes closer, and by this very absorption is brought out gloriously, and accuses me always more. The same in its bearing as same is more and more extended to the other, to the point of substitution as a hostage. Expiation coincides in the last analysis with the extraordinary and diachronic reversal of the same into the other, in inspiration and the *psyche*.[286]

Otherwise than Being (*Autrement qu'être*)

The expression *otherwise than Being* or *beyond essence*, names and opens to the absolute and irreducible transcendence of the Infinite from which thinking is exposed to the call, commandment, plea of the Other for which the Self is elected and awakened in responsibility, substitution and expiation for the Other. This expression engages a radicalization of what Levinas himself had deployed in *Totality and Infinity* and which remained, in this last work, still too entrapped in an ontological language. *Otherwise than being* or *beyond essence* means to mark that which precedes ontology and calls from an irreducible antecedence before the Sameness, indifference, anonymity of Being as presence thereby engaging the Self always *to* respond *beyond* its self-determination, and thus *beyond* the determined and determining Sameness of intersubjectivity or community, commonality, identicalness. Otherwise than Being *opens to the irreducible alterity of the Other and thereby to* an ethical responsibility, substitution and expiation, *without* reserve for the Other.

The ontological horizon and intentional domain of essence is that of pure presence which always succeeds in comprehending all interval, difference, distance, or separation within its identicalness and Sameness. Indeed, Levinas marks: all *esse* is *inter-esse*. And Levinas also insists on how and why the reign or the order of essence, the homogenization of all differences and differentiation in its pure synchronism—also called *imperialism*—which always and already comprehends and captures, in itself and for itself, the Other's singularity, is *war*. Which entails, for Levinas, the urgency of escaping and evading the proliferation of war, that is the effacement of the Other in the predominance, comprehension, presence of the identicalness and the Sameness of essence. *Otherwise than Being* or *beyond essence* transcends thus the alternative between Being and non-Being and thereby exceeds the nothingness and the nothing (which for Levinas is always thought and thinkable in reference to Being): to be or not to be is *not* the question—the question is of the Other, of the *otherwise* than Being and *beyond* essence as infinite responsibility, substitution and expiation, for the Other.

Otherwise than being or *beyond essence* designates the Infinite as absolute transcendence and extraction from Being, from the identity and the Sameness of Being, presence, essence. In this sense, *otherwise than Being* or *beyond essence* remains always and already heterogeneous and irreducible to a *being otherwise*. *Otherwise than Being* or *beyond essence* inscribes a rupture and interruption of the very logic of Being and suspension of essence as presence, identity, Sameness, *inter-esse*, totality and through this rupture, interruption, suspension an opening toward a *wholly other* source of significance; an ethical significance engaging an infinite responsibility for the Other calling *before* and *beyond* the universality of morality based on the autonomy and sovereignty of the subject.

Making explicit the *otherwise than being* or *beyond essence* engages an extraction from the predominance and presence of Being; the Self extracting itself from Being by and through the Other, by and through the commandment, the plea, the call of the face of the Other. *Otherwise than being* or *beyond essence* marks the desire for the Other in responsibility and response to the call of the Other *before* and *beyond* Being. This response and responsibility *before* and a *beyond* the autonomy or sovereignty of freedom expresses substitution and expiation for the Other. In this sense, *otherwise than being* or *beyond essence* means the Self's bearing of a response and responsibility for the Other *before* autonomy and sovereignty, decision or judgment to the point of incessantly exceeding its responsibility in obsession, substitution, expiation, elected to being hostage for the Other.

Substitution and expiation for the Other in the name of the Other, the ethical Self is already called by the Other for the Other, commanded *before* its self-determination and already engaging the Self *beyond* its freedom, despite itself, to an incessant excess of exposition for the Other. The ethical Self is incessantly called as unique elected responsibility for the Other to the point of substitution and expiation of the Other—an ethical Self expressing itself always and already as *for the Other*, that is as *otherwise* than freedom, autonomy, contractual ethics, normativism, intersubjective recognition or moral equivalence or equality.

Peace (*Paix*)

Totality and Infinity opens with the infamous phrase: "Everyone will readily agree that it is of the highest importance to know whether we are not duped by morality."[287] This opening phrase, by which Levinas critically suggests how and where morality and universal moral norms could convey *all the contrary* than what it intends or proposes, is followed by a lengthy exposition and analysis of how "the visage of being that shows itself in war is fixed in the concept of totality which dominates Western Philosophy."[288] Levinas demonstrates, in these opening pages of *Totality and Infinity* how violence—a violence which reduces individuals to "being bearers of forces that command them unbeknown to themselves"[289]—deploys itself in and through the perseverance and presence of Being as identity, indifference, anonymity, Sameness. Which implies, as Levinas claims, that Being as totality promulgates a sacrificial[290] violence which annihilates existents in the affirmation and comprehension of an essential Sameness and identicalness always and already grasping in its deployment the singularity of existents. This analysis leads Levinas to mark how and why the violence of meaning purports *war* and thereby produces the effacement of existents in a totality of Being incessantly reducing the singularity of the Other and the unicity of the Self to an order of uniformity, univocity, and ultimately indifference and anonymity. In this sense, as Levinas also remarks, the peace here obtained is but a *simulacra* of peace, what he names a "peace of empires":

> "The peace of empires issued from war rests on war. It does not restore to the alienated beings their lost identity." For peace to occur, a peace in which the singularity of existents engages a thinking of plurality and thereby where the transcendence of the Other awakens the responsibility of the Self in the ethical, a peace therefore no longer tributary of a universalizing morality where recognition culminates in the leveling of the Other to the Same, Levinas insists on the urgency of an evasion, an escape, and thus on an "eschatology" which engages "a relationship with a *surplus always exterior to the totality*, as though the objective totality did not fill out the true measure of Being, as though another concept, the concept of *infinity*, were needed to express this transcendence with regard to totality, non-encompassable within a totality and as primordial as totality."[291]

This urgency of evasion and escape in search for an "eschatological" peace—a peace *wholly other* than the pacification through conceptualization and the determination, categorization, and universalization of totality as Sameness and thus a pacification always engaged in a certain form of violence, of war insofar as it imposes an effacement of the singularity of the Other and the unicity of the Self to the order of identicalness—will inform the *Conclusions* of *Totality and Infinity*. Indeed, in the last pages of the work, Levinas insists on approaching "morality" not as grounded on a universal rationality, moral norms, intersubjectivity, recognition or community, but as "First Philosophy," which means, for Levinas, *as* "being for the Other," or, *singularly being for the singularity of the Other*:

> But "being for the Other" is not the negation of the I, engulfed in the universal. The universal law itself refers to a face-to-face position which refuses every exterior "viewing". To say that universality refers to the face-to-face position is (against a whole tradition of philosophy) to deny that being is produced as a panorama, a coexistence, of which the face-to-face would be a modality. This whole work [*Totality and Infinity*] opposes this conception. The face-to-face is not a modality of coexistence nor even of the knowledge (itself panoramic) one term can have of another, but is the primordial production of being on which all the possible collocations of the terms are founded. The revelation of the Third party, ineluctable in the face, is produced only through the face. Goodness does not radiate over the anonymity of a collectivity presenting itself panoramically, to be absorbed into it.[292]

Peace means a pluralism which incessantly suspends the totality of the Same and of Sameness, interrupts the reduction of the transcendence of the Other to identity, and ruptures morality grounded in universality. Peace as plurality engages thus the uniqueness of a responsibility for the Other in the commandment erupting from the face of the Other, that is, a unity in which speaks firstly the absolute transcendence of the Other demanding, pleading, and addressing the Self to a responsibility *without* reserve, *without* beginning or end, anarchic: an eschatology which incessantly reinitiates its expectation, its Law, its aspiration for the Other *without* conciliation or reconciliation. As Levinas writes:

> Pluralism is accomplished in goodness proceeding from me to the Other, in which first the Other, as absolutely Other, can be produced, without an alleged lateral view upon this movement having any right to grasp of it a truth superior to that which is produced in goodness itself. One does not enter into this pluralist society without always remaining outside by speech (in which goodness is produced)—but one does not leave it in order to simply see oneself inside. The unity of plurality is peace and not the coherence of the elements that constitute plurality. Peace therefore cannot be identified with the end of combats that cease for want of combatants, by the defeat of some and the victory of the others, that is, with cemeteries or future universal empires. Peace must be my peace, in a relation that starts from an I and goes to the other, in desire and goodness, where the I both maintains itself and exists without egoism.[293]

Persecution (*Persécution*)

Ordinarily, the term persecution means a hostile and demeaning mistreatment of a person or a group of persons due to their membership to a determined and defined collective. Levinas, however, retrieves this term and shifts it from its immediate signification to mean an ethical disposition of the Self for the Other. Indeed, persecution informs, for Levinas, the ethical disposition of the "one-for-the-other" as passivity more passive than all passivity, that is: as absolute *exposition* to the Other. The ethical Self is always and already persecuted, that is obsessed, accused, and traumatized by the Other for the Other. Persecuted, and thus obsessed, accused, and traumatized by the commandment and the plea, the address and the demand of the Other on the Self—commandment, plea, address, demand which are each time singular and irreducible to any comprehension or categorization—electing the Self to the ethical, that is to an infinitization of responsibility to the point of substitution and expiation for the Other. In this sense, this persecution is not a fixation or a simple determination. Levinas indeed always describes persecution as incessantly electing and awakening the Self to the ethical, to a response and responsibility for the Other, an individuation of the Self as substitution and expiation for the Other. Levinas marks as persectution the opening of an hyperbolical ethical response and responsibility unconstrained by any norm or universal measure, *without* judgment or evaluation: *infinite* and always *infinitizing itself*—that is, always *exceeding* its response of responsibility, substitution and expiation—for the Other.

It is in *Otherwise than Being, or Beyond Essence* that Levinas radicalizes the responsibility for the Other summoned by and through the transcendent alterity of the Other to mean and signify the persecution, obsession, accusation, and trauma of the Self elected to the ethical *before* and *beyond* its own self-determination and autonomy and thereby expressing itself as substitution and expiation for the Other: "one-for-the-other". And it is also here where Levinas suggests how the anonymity and indifference of Being, the unbreathable horizon of presence, essence, meaning as identity entirely concentrated in the categories of understanding and categorizations of knowledge founded in the autonomy and the sovereignty of the subject, closes up this subjectivity and ultimately reduces it, suffocates it, and smothers it. Otherwise said, the repetition of Being as sole meaning, unique source of signification for the subject incessantly relapses it, the subject, into its own self-enclosed egoity and egoism, self-centeredness, and self-interested economy of domination.

And yet, at the same time, Levinas also marks how and where, in and within this "being thrown" in the anonymity and indifference of Being, identicalness and totality of essence, a certain shift or transfer *occurs*: a shift which transfers the "there is" or the "*il y* a" of Being, the order of categorial determination, the presence of essence as comprehension in the identity of meaning *toward* an irresolvable precedence, an anteriority, an Otherness inspiring, *before* the Self, toward a *beyond* the Self. *Before* and *beyond* Being occurs and questions, commands and demands the transcendence of the Other. Indeed, the otherness of the Other and from its precedence and antecedence, immemoriality, elects the Self to the ethical, *before* the autonomy and *beyond* the free will or self-determination of the rational subjectivity.

Levinas writes:

> In obsession the accusation effected by categories turns into an absolute accusative in which the ego proper to free consciousness is caught up. It is an accusation without foundation, to be sure, prior to any movement of the will, an obsessional and persecuting accusation. It strips the ego of its pride and the dominating imperialism characteristic of it. The subject is in the accusative, without recourse in being, expelled from being, outside of being, like the one in the first hypotheses of Parmenides, without a foundation, reduced to itself, and thus without condition. In its own skin. Not at rest under a form, but tight in its skin, encumbered and as it were stuffed with itself, suffocating under itself, insufficiently open, forced to detach itself from itself, to breathe more deeply, all the way, forced to dispossess itself to the point of losing itself.[294]

To which Levinas poses the question:

> Does this loss have as its term the void, the zero point and the peace of cemeteries, as though the subjectivity of a subject meant nothing? Or do the being encumbered with oneself and the suffering of constriction in one's skin, better than metaphors, follow the exact trope of an alteration of essence, which inverts, or would invert, into a recurrence in which the expulsion of self outside of itself is its substitution for the other? Is not that what the self emptying itself of itself would really mean?[295]

Levinas indeed liberates the ethical Self from the "recurrence" of the self-enclosed and self-enclosing transcendental, autonomous and sovereign subjectivity. Indeed, through the "recurrence" of this question always and already inhabiting the Self, Levinas marks a certain overwhelming of subjectivity by an irreducible antecedence as "obsessional and persecuting accusation": the alterity of the Other. Rather than losing itself in the void, the anonymity and indifference of Being and meaning, the Self is awakened and elected by an anteriority incessantly inspiring it to engage *otherwise* than in and through the appropriation of itself in its self-determination. Perhaps here lies what Levinas calls "ultimate secret of the incarnation of the subject":

> prior to all reflection, prior to every positing, an indebtedness before any loan, not assumed, anarchical, subjectivity of a bottomless passivity, made out of assignation, like the echo of a sound that would precede the resonance of this sound. The active source of this passivity is not thematizable. It is the passivity of a trauma, but one that prevents its own representation, a deafening trauma, cutting the thread of consciousness which should have welcomed it in its present, the passivity of being persecuted. This passivity deserves the epithet of complete or absolute only if the persecuted one is liable to answer for the persecutor. The face of the neighbor in its persecuting hatred can by this very malice obsess as something pitiful. This equivocation or enigma only the persecuted one who does not evade it, but is without any references, any recourse or help (that is its uniqueness or its identity as unique!) is able to endure. To undergo from the other is an absolute patience only if by this from-the-other is already for-the-other. This transfer, other than interested, "otherwise than essence," is subjectivity itself. "To tend the cheek to the smiter and to be filled with shame," to demand suffering in the suffering undergone (without producing the act that would, be the exposing of the other cheek) is not to draw from suffering some kind of magical redemptive virtue. In the trauma of persecution it is to pass from the outrage undergone to the responsibility for the persecutor, and, in this sense from suffering to expiation for the other. Persecution is not something added to the subjectivity of the subject and his vulnerability; it is the very movement of recurrence. The subjectivity as the Other-in-the-Same, as an inspiration, is the putting into question of all affirmation for-oneself, all egoism born again in this very recurrence. (This putting into question is not a preventing!) The subjectivity of a subject is responsibility of being-in-question in the form of the total exposure to offence in the cheek offered to the smiter. This responsibility is prior to dialogue, to the exchange of questions and answers, to the thematization of the said, which is superposed on my being put into question by the other in proximity, and in the saying proper to responsibility is produced as a digression[296]

Persecution means thus the incessant and irrevocable election of the Self for the Other. In this sense, the ethical Self is persecuted by the Other for the Other, host as hostage for the Other, always and already elected *before* its own in-itself and *beyond* what it can determine or decide for-itself. Which entails, for Levinas, that persecution as ethical engages the incessant excess, supplement, aggravation of responsibility—substitution and expiation—for the Other. As accusation, obsession, trauma engaging the ethical Self in the *infinitization* responsibility to the point of substitution and expiation for the Other, persecution marks the exceptional election, the unicity *beyond* normativity, and the singularity *before* self-determination of the ethical Self for the Other always and already commanded by the Good *beyond* and *before* Being:

> The uniqueness of the self is the very fact of bearing the fault of another. In responsibility for another subjectivity is only this unlimited passivity of an accusative which does not issue out of a declension it would have undergone starting with the nominative. This accusation can be reduced to the passivity of the self only as a persecution, but a persecution that turns into an expiation. Without persecution the ego raises its head and covers over the self. Everything is from the start in the accusative. Such is the exceptional condition or unconditionality of the self, the signification of the pronoun self for which our Latin grammars themselves know no nominative form. The more I return to myself, the more I divest myself, under the traumatic effect of persecution, of my freedom as a constituted, willful, imperialist subject, the more I discover myself to be responsible; the more just I am, the more guilty I am. I am "in myself through the others". The *psyche* is the Other-in-the-Same, without alienating the same. Backed up against itself, in itself because without any recourse in anything, in itself like in its skin, the self in its skin both is exposed to the exterior (which does not happen to things) and obsessed by the others in this naked exposure. Does not the self take on itself, through its very impossibility to evade its own identity, toward which, when persecuted, it withdraws? Does not a beginning rise in this passivity? The undeclinability of the ego is the irremissibility of the accusation, from which it can no longer take a distance, which it cannot evade. This impossibility of taking any distance and of slipping away from the Good is a firmness more firm and more profound than that of the will, which is still a tergiversation.[297]

Phenomenology (*Phénoménologie*)

Levinas refers to phenomenology as it was developed by Husserl and furthermore realigned and reworked by Heidegger. Indeed, Levinas firstly marks the phenomenological exigency, method, and questioning as primordial and primary philosophical *attitude* which implies to rethink critically, through suspension and bracketing, philosophical discourse itself, its breath, extent, history, effects in view of reformulating entirely the demands of the human condition. Levinas classically adopts the method of phenomenology explicated by Husserl as "return to the things themselves" and which consists in a *critical dismantling* and *undermining* of the speculative and idealist constructions of the traditional and classical metaphysical tradition. Levinas thereby sees in the Husserlian phenomenological method the possibility to rethink by and through a suspension of received determinations or traditional metaphysical definitions of what appears and thus as a novel and renewed disposition to that which is given in appearing, that is to *appearance itself appearing as such in and through intentionality*. By and through the phenomenological operation of the *epokhe*, the suspension and interruption of the what Husserl calls the "natural attitude"—that attitude which naturally, immediately and spontaneously poses beings as existing and manifest as such—Levinas always refers to phenomenology as an inaugural decision, an engagement in and for philosophy as *critique* and *questioning power* in the face of phenomenality and thereby as the possibility of *revealing beyond* the manifest or the apparent, *beyond* phenomenality itself, the intentional essence of manifestation, appearance, phenomenality. In this sense, and as *critique* and *questioning power*, Levinas always claimed a resolute fidelity to the phenomenology throughout his writings by marking how and where its method liberates thinking from the fixed determinations of ontological, rationalistic, speculative, or abstract philosophical constructions.

However, this faithfulness to phenomenology also requires, for Levinas, an *interruption* of phenomenology itself, an *epokhe* of the phenomenological *epokhe*, where is opened a thinking of the immemorial antecedence and precedence of the Infinite transcendence of the Other, the absolute alterity of the Other which incessantly overwhelms and exceeds the transcendental *ego*'s constitutive power and self-determination. Indeed, for Levinas, the transcendent face of the Other in its immemorial commandment supersedes and surpasses, exceeds and outdoes the phenomenological primacy of intentionality and thereby interrupt the phenomenological *epokhe* by already suspending the institution of the transcendental *ego* from which erupts the constitution of the horizon of intentionality from which occurs phenomenality, manifestation, appearance. The transcendence of the Other opens thus to a wholly other source of significance, the Good, irreducible to intentionality and heterogeneous to phenomenality, *always other* and commanding *otherwise* than how the Self constitutes itself in its autonomy and self-determination. In this sense, the source of ethical significance as excess of responsibility for the Other already outstrips and outdoes, dismantles and ruptures, breaks and interrupts the intentional context in which "beings" are always given and already appear as "intentional givens" through their appearance; that is always given and already appear as signified, comprehended, appropriated in and within a horizon of Sameness or identification.

From the outset, Levinas' writings, although claiming an indefectible kinship with Husserlian phenomenology, also engage a critical questioning of the phenomenological impulse. Levinas reproaches Husserlian phenomenology of not engaging as far as it ought to toward the ethical and the idea of the Good as transcendence and infinity, although it had, in a certain manner, opened the way and traced the course, engaged the orientation for and of thinking toward a certain *freedom* and *liberation* from the fixed determinations of ontology and/or categorial rationality. Indeed, Levinas always marks how and why Husserl, although opening a certain direction to think toward the alterity of the Other and the infinite transcendence of alterity, ultimately covers over and dissimulates this inaugural possibility and orientation. As Levinas stipulates, the attention to the specificity of each type of appearing and manifesting, and thus of the unicity of phenomenality, ultimately ends up in a *subordination* of *all* phenomena to the transcendental order of intentionality. Indeed, for Levinas, the phenomenological description of the unique modality of appearing proper to each singular phenomenon culminates in its appropriation within the consciousness of a constituting transcendental *ego* as sole and unique intentional pole.

Hence, it is true that Levinas retrieves, in a certain manner, Heidegger's criticism of Husserl and praises the former's manner of freeing meaning from the constitutive tutelage of a transcendental consciousness itself contained through and by a principle of intentionality and intentional horizon of Sameness and identicalness. However, for Levinas, and pursuing his own ethical orientation, Heidegger also remains trapped—albeit not in transcendental subjectivity—in the project of a "fundamental ontology" which purports the meaning of Being as *event* in which occurs the "presencing" for which entities are in and within the truth of Being. Hence, Heidegger entirely encompasses meaning within the givenness, the appropriating event of Being *and* time, which, for Levinas, consists in

> neutralising the existent in order to comprehend and grasp it. It is hence not a relation with the other as such but the reduction of the other to the same. Such is the definition of freedom: to maintain oneself against the other, despite every relation with the other to ensure the autarchy of an I. Thematization and conceptualisation, which moreover are inseparable are not peace with the other but suppression and possession of the Other. For possession affirms the other but within a negation of its independence. "I think" comes down to "I can"—to an appropriation of what is, to an exploitation of the other. Ontology as first philosophy is a philosophy of power.[298]

Levinas will further mark that this "philosophy of power" is a "philosophy of injustice."[299] That is, a philosophy which refuses any or all possibilities of suspending or interrupting the order of Being *and* time as essential presencing of all that is as all there is, as "*il y a*" ("there is") and thus proliferates as indifference, anonymity, impersonality. Which means, fundamental ontology remains deaf to the call and commandment of that which transcends the presencing of Being *and* time: the infinite and transcendent alterity of the Other. This is precisely why for Levinas, Heidegger, in the latter's reformulation of phenomenology through a "fundamental ontology," remains forever closed to the hyperbolical ethical demand of infinite responsibility for the Other and closes itself off in the "subordination of the relationship with the Other to the relation with Being in general, remains under obedience to the anonymous and leads inevitably to another power, to imperialist domination, to tyranny."[300]

Levinas retrieves from the phenomenological method, the *epokhe*, the suspension, and interruption of the abstract and metaphysical postulations and categorial suppositions of phenomenality as fixated substances which result in the occultation and dissimulation of the very movement of their manifestation, appearing, and "presencing." Levinas retains indeed the idea of the suspension and interruption of determined categorizations of phenomenality *without* inscribing this phenomenological task and gesture (as Husserl had himself stipulated) within the centralized position of the transcendental *ego* always constituting, through its acts of consciousness, the context of phenomenality and the intentionality of that which appears as Being. In this sense, Levinas retains the phenomenological method by *shifting* its orientation elsewhere and forcing it to also remain exposed to the possibility of an *excess* of meaning and a *supplement* which always and already counters and impedes all fixation of significance in petrified entities. This *excess* and this *supplement* occurring *before* and *beyond* phenomenology, intentionality, phenomenality, intentional horizon is the face of the Other:

> The face of a neighbor signifies for me an unexceptionable responsibility, preceding every free consent, every pact, every contract. It escapes representation; it is the very collapse of phenomenality. Not because it is too brutal to appear, but because in a sense too weak, non-phenomenon because less than a phenomenon. The disclosing of a face is nudity, non-form, abandon of self, ageing, dying, more naked than nudity. It is poverty, skin with wrinkles, which are a trace of itself. My reaction misses a present which is already the past of itself. This past is not in the present, but is as a phase retained, the past of this present, a lapse already lost which marks ageing, escaping all retention, altering my contemporaneousness with the other.[301]

The Levinasian gesture cannot settle for the order of phenomenality and its incessant search and research of intentionality, culminating in a constituting transcendental consciousness. Levinas also engages an interruption and a suspension of the onto-phenomenological order by opening the phenomenological decision to *another revendication* and a *wholly other* commandment capable of undoing and breaking, rupturing, and halting the reign of presence determined by Sameness and identicalness:

> The terms must be reversed. For the philosophical tradition the *conflict* between the same and the other are resolved by theory whereby the other is reduced to the same—or concretely, by the community of the State, where beneath anonymous power, though it be intelligible, the I rediscovers war in the tyrannic oppression it undergoes from the totality. Ethics, where the same takes the irreducible Other into account, would belong to opinion. The effort of this book [*Totality and Infinity*] is directed toward apperceiving in discourse a non-allergic relation with alterity, toward apperceiving Desire—where power, by essence murderous of the other, becomes, faced with the other and "against all good sense", the impossibility of murder, the consideration of the Other or justice.[302]

The idea of justice in *Totality and Infinity* as absolute exposition to the transcendence of the Other commanding an infinite excess of responsibility will be itself radicalized in *Otherwise than Being, or Beyond Essence*, and most particularly in Levinas' analysis of the Third party. Indeed, how are we to think the Other of the Other, that is the Others, and thus how to relate to the multiplicity of the Others other than the unique Other commanding and demanding an *infinitizing* responsibility of the elected ethical Self? How are we to think the idea of justice for humanity in all of its diversity, that is, for all the Others beyond the hyperbolical face-to-face ethical relation from the singular Other electing a singular Self in response and responsibility?

The question of the Third party will thus engage a radicalization of the idea of justice in Levinas' thinking and writing. And this radicalization will be deployed in and through the explication Levinas proposes of the relation between the *Saying* and the *Said* in *Otherwise than Being, or Beyond Essence*—that is, the relation between the "significance of signification," the exposition to the singular Other expressing its commandment and demand *before* and *beyond* all verbal sign, *anterior* to discourse and *beyond* what can be comprehended in a *logos and* the necessity for this irreducible transcendence of the singularity of the Other and the relation it commands and elects to be recognized in and within a sociality with *all* Others. Levinas:

> How does saying differ from an act commencing in a conquering and voluntary ego, whose signifying is an act being converted into being, and whose "for the other" takes root in identity? The for-the-other of responsibility

> for the other does not proceed from any free commitment, any present, in which its origin would germinate, or in which an identity identifying itself would catch its breath. That is so, but then there is a new dilemma. Responsibility without a prior commitment, without a present, without an origin, anarchic, is thus an infinite responsibility of the One-for-the-Other who is abandoned to me without anyone being able to take my place as the one responsible for him. Does this confer upon me a new identity, that of being the unique chosen one? Or does this exclusive election, as signification of the Infinite, reduce me to the status of an articulation in its divine economy? Are we reduced to humanity as an extreme possibility in being, where the substantiality of "supporting oneself" is de-substantified in a "supporting the other," "substituting oneself for him"? Or through this ipseity reduced to being irreplaceable hostage, is the self-equivalent to the entry of the subject into, the play or designs of the Infinite?[303]

This *reversal* of phenomenology, Levinas will also apply it to his own ethics as "First Philosophy" by reinscribing, as above said, the idea of phenomenology in the context of the Third party and the idea of justice. Indeed, Levinas also returns to phenomenology by and through a certain *recognition* of the necessity to *re-intentionalize*—but *wholly otherwise* than as intentionality—the relation with the singular Other as relation with *all Others* already appearing, present, manifest in the hyperbolical commandment of the singular Other. Levinas names this radicalization of the hyperbolical ethics in and through sociality, of the Other to all Others a *sociality of fraternity*. Levinas indeed marks as *sociality of fraternity* the antecedence and precedence of the ethical *before* the essence of a conciliation between the transcendental *ego* and its lived-world and as that which incessantly demands and commands the Self to escape and suspend, break, and bracket the *inter* of intersubjectivity, the common and commonality of any or all conciliation or reconciliation *between* the Self and the Other. Opening toward a wholly other source of significance than intentionality—a wholly other source of inspiration through which the Self comes to itself by already having been inspired and elected to respond and in responsibility by and for the Other and through this election also to all Others.

Levinas' thinking and writing always engaged profoundly *with* Husserl while also and at the same time thinking *wholly otherwise* than Husserl. Ethics as "First Philosophy" has, in this manner, inherited not only the phenomenological method, which it also put into question, but also the Husserlian inspiration, which it also radicalized, exposing the Self to the absolute transcendence of the Other. This is precisely why Husserl, and generally the spirit of phenomenology, remained more than a constant philosophical reference for Levinas, but that through which the very meaning of philosophy could occur as an incessant *renewal* of thinking, *before* and *beyond* philosophy: a thinking toward and for the Other.

Proximity (*Proximité*)

Proximity is not, for Levinas, reducible to a spatial contiguity between two or more points, entities, or things, standing close to one another. Proximity is not grounded or founded on location. Rather, for Levinas, proximity orients and directs toward the irrepresentable, irreducible, and absolute transcendence of the Other: "Proximity is non-indifference, non-coinciding, an arrhythmia in time, a *diachrony* refractory to thematization, refractory to the reminiscence that synchronizes the phases of a past [in narration]."[304] In this sense, proximity implies and entails the ethical relation, and engages to rethink *before* and *beyond* spatial definition and determination. Proximity commands, for Levinas, the obsessive commandment and plea of the Other which, irreducible to perception, representation, understanding, remains always and already *beyond* the grasp of the subject, urging and electing it to respond *before* its ownmost capabilities and capacities, autonomy, or judgment.

In this sense, proximity describes and explicates the *aporia* of obsession and trauma, that is, of "being obsessed" and "traumatized" by and through the transcendence of the Other's ethical demand and commandment. Obsessive and traumatizing commandment ordering through the face of the Other which always and already remains irreducibly other and foreign, transcendent and heterogeneous, to intention or intentionality, to presence and representation. This obsession and trauma incessantly inhabiting the ethical Self from the inapparent, infinite, absolute transcendence of the Other surpasses and exceeds the Self's self-determination to host the Other, and, in the urgency of the Other's call and commandment, subjects the Self to an infinite responsibility: a being hostage of the Other for the Other. This is why the proximity of the Other marks also and simultaneously its absolute distance which thereby commands the ethical Self *before* autonomy and sovereignty electing it to always respond *beyond* its self-determination and judgment, will or freedom.

The term proximity first appears in *Time and the Other*: "a distance that is also a proximity"[305] which already marks its inherent paradoxality: the proximity of the Other purports the distance of the Other. This paradoxality marks the absolute transcendence of the Other, transcending otherness of the commandment of the Other which spurs on an always and already exceeding responsibility of the ethical Self for the Other.

In *Totality and Infinity*, Levinas defines proximity as implied and supposed in the "face-to-face" as "one-for-the-other" in infinite responsibility for the

Other and in response to the call, commandment, and appeal of the Other. Levinas radicalizes this definition in *Otherwise than Being, or Beyond Essence* as "difference which is non-indifference, responsibility, response without question."[306]

The advent of the Other, already exceeding the order of presence and representation, *before* and *beyond* symmetry and balance, means, in this sense, the *infinite distance* of the Other which also commands, requires and orders from its absolute transcendence *beyond* and *before* presence and representation, a response and a responsibility *without distance*, as it requires and commands a *without* delay of this response in responsibility for the Other—an *irreducible proximity* of the Self for the Other. This is why proximity must firstly be understood as the incessant movement of the ethical Self *approaching* the Other, *approaching without finality*, and which always responds more than what it can, more than what it fulfills or accomplishes, incessant movement of *approaching* the Other through which is revealed the infinity of the Self's debt and responsibility for the Other. Proximity of the Self for the Other as incessant approach as always *being-one-for-the-Other* and where the Self is already implied in the excess of being engaged, elected *before* and *beyond* itself in the name of the transcendence of the Other.

Uncontestably, the idea of proximity is abundantly developed in *Otherwise than Being, or Beyond Essence* where it appears, together with "Sensibility," as a central section of the work leading to the central notion of "substitution."

The idea of proximity offers another manner of rethinking the *asymmetry* of the relation between the ethical Self and the transcendent Other which, taking its lead from the face-to-face encounter deployed in *Totality and Infinity* and retrieved in *Otherwise than Being, or Beyond Essence*, is described as obsession, trauma, persecution marking an absolute non-reciprocity and irreconcilability with the neighbor, the Other.

And indeed, for Levinas the distance of the Other, the infinite separation of the neighbor, animates and awakens the hyperbolical responsibility for the Other as proximity of the Other:

> Proximity, difference which is non-indifference, is responsibility. It is a response without a question, the immediacy of peace that is incumbent on me. It is the signification of signs. It is the humanity of man not understood on the basis of transcendental subjectivity. It is the passivity of exposure, a passivity itself exposed. Saying does not occur in consciousness nor in a commitment understood in terms of consciousness or memory; it does not form a conjuncture and a synchrony. Proximity is fraternity before essence and before death, having a meaning despite being and nothingness, despite concepts.[307]

Enriched by the analysis of sensibility—and described by Levinas as vulnerability, traumatism, obsession, affection by the non-phenomenality and non-manifested transcendence of the Other, contact in which the sentient Self is besieged *before* any autonomy or localization, *before* any faculty of representation or constitution, *host* as *hostage before* assuming its subjectity, and always and already commanded, elected, addressed, exposed by and to the irreducible alterity of the Other in which the Self *cannot not* respond as it is touched by the untouchable, the unrepresentable, the un-phenomenalizable transcendence of the Other—proximity means the restlessness of a responsibility toward the transcendence and infinite distance and absolute Height of the Other; a responsibility with no null site, no place of rest, no synchrony or appeasement with the Other:

> Proximity as a suppression of distance suppresses the distance of consciousness of . . . The neighbor excludes himself from the thought that seeks him, and this exclusion has a positive side to it: my exposure to him, antecedent to his appearing, my delay behind him, my undergoing, undo the core of what is identity in me. Proximity, suppression of the distance that consciousness of . . . involves, opens the distance of a diachrony without a common present, where difference is the past that cannot be caught up with, an unimaginable future, the non-representable status of the neighbor behind which I am late and obsessed by the neighbor.[308]

As signification, "proximity is not a configuration produced in the soul. [. . .] Nor is it fusion; it is contact with the Other."[309] Proximity is *approach incessantly approaching* the transcendence of the Other, a closeness with the Other which always seeks more closeness, exceeds itself *without* conclusion, and in which the "Other is inescapable in my responsibility" and "responsibility is irrecusable": "In proximity is heard a command as though from an immemorial past . . . which began in no freedom. This *way* of the neighbour is a face."[310] Proximity means an extreme exposure to the defenselessness, vulnerability, nakedness for the Other and thus as infinite approach of the Other for the Other, an approach burrowing and amplifying the distance between the Self and the Other to the point of suspending and interrupting the possible communion or community, intersubjective or Sameness where the Self resembles the Other, and the Other mirrors the Self. Approach thus engaging an anarchic responsibility from which the ethical Self cannot escape, cannot hide, cannot turn away from—the proximity of the Other means ultimately the incessant excess and exceeding of responsibility for the Other.

This is why, for Levinas, in the proximity of the absolutely Other as the stranger, the orphan, the widow whom the I has "neither conceived nor given birth to" the ethical Self is always and already responsible for the Other. Without contract or pre-established community, the ethical Self is elected to respond for the proximity of the Other—a proximity which cannot be measured or evaluated as it is always amplifying the distance of the Other—as incessantly exceeding in its responsibility for the Other. The ethical Self is engaged and elected to a pre-philosophical responsibility where the Other—uprooted, homeless, hungry, exposed in its vulnerability and nakedness—is always and already commanding the Self *before* the Self *beyond the Self*, incessantly overwhelming and exceeding the Self by orienting it prior to its own Self:

> Signification as proximity is thus the latent birth of the subject. Latent birth, for prior to an origin, an initiative, a present designatable and assumable, even if by memory. It is an anachronous birth, prior to its own present, a non-beginning, an anarchy. As a latent birth, it is never a presence, excluding the present of coinciding with oneself, for it is in contact, in sensibility, in vulnerability, in exposure to the outrages of the other. The subject is the more responsible the more it answers for, as though thedistance between it and the other increased in the measure that proximity was increased. The latent birth of the subject occurs in an obligation where no commitment was made. It is a fraternity or complicity for nothing, but the more demanding that it constrains without finality and without end. The subject is born in the beginninglessness of an anarchy and in the endlessness of obligation, gloriously augmenting as though infinity came to pass in it. In the absolute assignation of the subject the Infinite is enigmatically heard: before and beyond.[311]

Religion (*Religion*)

Levinas understands the word "religion" from the latin *religare* and thus as a relation and consequently as a bond which allies the Same and the Other *without* however concluding in their totality, reconciliation, or conflation. Religion marks therefore separation and separateness between the Same and the Other, between the immanence of the Same and the absolute transcendence of the Other. The idea of religion here marked by Levinas entails a radical distinction between finitude and infinity which never settles for their reconciliatory or speculative identity or identification—which for Levinas would amount to indifference and reduction of the transcendence of the Other to the immanence of the Same.

This is also why, for Levinas, the idea of the Infinite incessantly overflows, overwhelms and exceeds all presence, categorization, representation, phenomenality. The infinity of the Other is irreducible and does not let itself be appropriated or integrated in a subjective consciousness, intuition, or understanding. It impedes any totalization as well as repudiates any image, imagination, and remains thus incessantly distant, transcendent, *wholly* other as absolute alterity.

The idea of religion opens, in this sense, to the *meta*-physical—that is, to the *beyond* physicality, phenomenality, representation or presence—and hence to the possibility of opening a relation between the Same and the Other *without* fulfilling or accomplishing, comprehending, or completing this relationship in an ontological unification, identity or essence, gathering or commonality. For Levinas, the idea of religion also opens *meta*-physics to a concrete discourse which incessantly retracts from the establishment, constitution, or institution of a substantial identicalness between Self and Other and thereby awakens a Self as responsibility *before* and *beyond* Sameness, totality, or unification—that is, toward the ethical as the infinitizing responsibility awakened in the Self for the Other. Indeed, for Levinas, the idea of religion engages a concrete discourse as ethical responsibility for the absolutely transcendent Other.

And in this sense, religion is thought as a relation *without* relation, and thus as an incessant ethical rapport to the irreducible "Height" of the Other. This hyperbolical ethical relation marks—contrarily to "fundamental ontology" (and thus irreducible to what Heidegger had termed, in the *Letter on Humanism*[312], an "originary ethics"[313] which, preceding the "theoretical" and the "practical," determines itself as the *place* (*ethos*) whereby the clearing of Being brings together, unifies, appropriates and conjoins by and through the appropriating event (*Ereignis*) that from which the history and truth of Being deploys itself and comes to manifestation, come to presence and presentification)—the impossibility of a totalization or comprehension, identification or presentation of the Self *with* the Other. The idea of religion opens to the ethical relation as election of the Self to and by the absolute transcendence of the Other and where this relation remains always heterogeneous and heteronomous to any resorption or reduction in identity, identicalness or Sameness, essence or commonality.

The idea of religion opens to the ethical Self as always preceded by the Other and where the Self is *created* through its facing the absolute transcendence of the Other and thereby exposed to responding and engaged in an infinite responsibility for the Other. For Levinas, the idea of religion implies the idea of the Infinite passing, tracing, immemorially commanding a responsibility *without* beginning or finality, anarchic and without reserve or fulfilment, satisfaction, contractualisation. And thus marks the impossibility for the ethical to settle for a communion or a community between Self and Other; rather, religion means a relation where the Self and the Other are engaged in an asymmetry and separation where the Self responds *before* any confirmed or recognized relation with the Other and thus where the Self *before* its own Self is already engaged to respond *beyond* its self-determination for the absolute transcendence of the Other:

> In the concrete [. . .] having the idea of infinity is discourse, specified as an ethical relation. For the relation between the being here below and the transcendent being that results in no community or communion of concept or totality—a relation without relation—we reserve the term religion. [. . .] Totality and the embrace of Being, or ontology, does not contain the final secret of being. Religion, where relationship subsists between the same and the other despite the impossibility of the Whole—the idea of Infinity—is the ultimate structure. The same and the other cannot enter into a cognition that would encompass them; the relations that the separated being maintains with what transcends it are not produced on the ground of totality, do not crystallize into a system. Yet do we not name them together? The *formal* synthesis of the word that names them together is already part of a discourse that is of a conjuncture of transcendence, breaking the totality. The conjuncture of the same and the other, in which even their verbal proximity is maintained, is the direct and full face welcome of the other by me. This conjuncture is irreducible to totality; the "face-to-face" position is not a modification of the "along side of . . ." Even when I shall have linked the Other to myself with the conjunction "and" the Other continues to face me, to reveal himself in his face. *Religion* subtends this formal totality.[314]

Responsibility (*Responsabilité*)

Prior to autonomy and preceding all social or normative contract, responsibility, for Levinas, is always and already for the Other and, in this sense, signifies an ethical response *without* ground, foundation, not based on a judgment. Always and already responding to the fragility and the defenselessness of the Other, to the demand and the plea of the Other, responsibility does not mean, for Levinas, *taking on one's responsibilities* in accordance with one's own convictions or contractual pledges or promises for one's deliberate actions. Responsibility means responding in the face of the Other to the commandment of the Other for the Other's suffering, misery, and faults *before* the institution or the constitution of a decision, autonomy, self-determination. In this sense, responsibility arises from the Other by the Other as it individualizes, inspires and elects the ethical Self always and already *before* its self-determination or freedom of will. Responsibility is being preceded by the demand and the plea of the Other, always animating, awakening, electing the Self in its response for the Other. For Levinas, the Self is thus responsible for that which has not originated in the Self, nor is it a response to or for the faults the Self has or could have committed. Accused *before* all guilt or culpability, responsibility means being awakened, being inspired, being elected, through an immemorial commandment *without* any wrongdoing and norm, to respond as infinite responsability to the Other for the Other. Response *before* the autonomy of the sovereign self-determining subject, preceding its will and decision, anterior to any engagement, commitment, judgment, responsibility means, for Levinas, the inescapable and irreducible, unsubstitutable and irreplaceable ethical response from the Self—*before* its constitution as a free subject, *before* the institution of an intersubjective recognition between the Self and the Other—to the Other for the Other.

For Levinas, and contrarily to the entire philosophical tradition which situates responsibility as emanating from an ethical norm justified either by a rational moral imperative proper to an autonomous subject or through a societal intersubjective relationship between equal subjects, responsibility means responding for the Other to the Other, responding to the singular call, address, and plea of the Other *before* the institution or the constitution of a free subject. In this sense, responsibility always means, for Levinas, exposition to the Other, suffering for the Other, and hence *proximity—before* any engagement and prior to all ontological structure of "being-with-the-others"—to the transcendent and inescapable commandment of the Other.

Responsibility, which for Levinas always commits the Self to a concrete and urgent response in the wake of the commandment of the Other, in the face-to-face relation with the Other and where the Other expresses its demand *before* the Self can institute itself as an autonomous subjectivity capable of circumscribing its universal moral horizon, is prevalent throughout Levinas' entire philosophy. Most particularly, responsibility means, for Levinas, to engage the ethical Self in a response preceding its will and freedom which also entails an ethical Self incessantly exceeding in responsibility for the Other. Indeed, responsibility for the Other marks a responsibility of "being host" of the Other to the point of "being hostage" of the Other. *Before* the sovereignty of the subject always capable of determining its autonomy and decision by which the ethical can be measured and assessed, calculated and estimated, responsibility, for Levinas, rather engages the impossibility of not responding to the call of the Other, of not putting one's Self in the place of the Other, of not suffering for the Other's suffering. As Levinas marks:

> The responsibility for another, an unlimited responsibility which the strict book-keeping of the free and non-free does not measure, requires subjectivity as an irreplaceable hostage. This subjectivity it denudes under the ego in a passivity of persecution, repression and expulsion outside of essence, into oneself. In this self, outside of essence, one is in a deathlike passivity! But in responsibility for the other for life and death, the adjectives unconditional, undeclinable, absolute take on meaning. They serve to qualify freedom, but wear away the substrate, from which the free act arises in essence. In the accusative form, which is a modification of no nominative form, in which I approach the neighbor for whom, without having wished it, I have to answer, the irreplaceable one is brought out (*s'accuse*). This finite freedom is not primary, is not initial; but it lies in an infinite responsibility where the other is not other because he strikes up against and limits my freedom, but where he can accuse me to the point of persecution, because the other, absolutely other, is another one (*autrui*). That is why finite freedom is not simply an infinite freedom operating in a limited field. The will which it animates wills in a passivity it does not assume. And the proximity of the neighbor in its trauma does not only strike up against me, but exalts and elevates me, and, in the literal sense of the term, inspires me. Inspiration, heteronomy, is the very pneuma of the psyche. Freedom is borne by the responsibility it could not shoulder, an elevation and inspiration without complacency. The for-the-other characteristic of the subject can be interpreted neither as a guilt complex (which presupposes an initial freedom), nor as a natural benevolence or divine "instinct," nor as some love or some tendency to sacrifice. This is quite the opposite of the Fichtean conception, where all suffering due to the action of the non-ego is first a positing of this action of the non-ego by the ego.[315]

To respond to the vulnerability and defenselessness of the Other *before* knowing or comprehending this vulnerability and defenselessness engages the ethical Self in a responsibility always increasing itself, exceeding and infinitizing itself, incessantly supplementing and overwhelming itself for the Other:

> Truth takes form in this response to a summons. The summons exalts the singularity precisely because it is addressed to an infinite responsibility. The infinity of responsibility denotes not its actual immensity, but a responsibility increasing in the measure it is assumed; duties become greater in the measure that they are accomplished. The better I accomplish my duty the fewer rights I have; the more I am just the more guilty I am. The I, which we have seen arise in enjoyment as a separated being having apart, in itself, the center around which its existence gravitates, is confirmed in its

> singularity by purging itself of this gravitation, purges itself interminably, and is confirmed precisely in this incessant effort to purge itself. This is termed goodness. Perhaps the possibility of a point of the universe where such an overflow of responsibility is produced ultimately defines the I.[316]

It is through this infinitizing responsibility as irrecusable and irreplaceable election for the Other that Levinas defines the Self. The ethical Self "is" wholly and entirely responsibility for the Other, responsibility for the responsibility of the Other, that is, *subjection* to the Other as infinitely responding as responsibility, care, substitution, and expiation for the Other. In this sense, this hyperbolical responsibility is always and already *non-indifference* to the Other and thereby *passion*, *obsession*, and *trauma*, where the ethical Self incessantly responds to the singular occurrence of the Other—a singularity by which the Other exposes the ethical Self to the point of substitution and expiation for the Other. This is why, always for Levinas, responsibility is irreducible to a kinship, intersubjectivity or even a community, a *being-together* or a *being-with* coordinating the Self *and* the Other and framing the *in-between* the "I" and the "Thou": the ethical Self is *subjected* to the unsubstitutable call and commandment of the Other—*subjected* to all Other as well as all Others, that is, infinitely responsible for all and to all irreducibly and inescapably. The ethical Self as *sub-jectum*—subjected as already responding, *before* autonomy or sovereignty, for the Other:

> It is an offering oneself which is not even assumed by its own generosity, an offering oneself that is a suffering, a goodness despite oneself. The "despite" cannot be decomposed into a will contraried by an obstacle. It is life, ageing of life, and unexceptionable responsibility, saying. The subjectivity of subjection of the self is the suffering of suffering, the ultimate offering oneself, or suffering in the offering of oneself. Subjectivity is vulnerability, is sensibility. Sensibility, all the passivity of saying, cannot be reduced to an experience that a subject would have of it, even if it makes possible such an experience. An exposure to the other, it is signification, is signification itself, the-one-for-the-other to the point of substitution, but a substitution in separation, that is, responsibility.[317]

This *subjection* as offering and incessant giving does not negate or succumb the Self—all to the contrary. It *individualizes* and *elects* the Self *before* the Self and, at the limit of the ethical, *before hearing* the call of the Other entailing thus a response of responsibility always and already exceeding itself *beyond* the Self's duty or autonomous freedom and moral normativity. It is precisely this *diachrony*, always and already occurring as the ethical Self, always and already electing the Self *before* the autonomy of the Self and *before* hearing the call of the Other, which orients the Self toward a hyperbolical responsibility for the Other, a *giving always beyond* what the Self can satisfy or fulfill, can give or offer:

> I am responsible, of this very giving of signs, that is, of this responsibility: "*here I am*." The *Saying* prior to anything *Said* bears witness to glory. This witness is true, but with a truth irreducible to the truth of disclosure, and does not narrate anything that shows itself. *Saying* is without noematic correlation in the pure obedience to glory that orders. It is without dialogue, in the passivity from the first subordinate to the "*here I am*." The distance that is enlarged in the measure that proximity narrows, the glory of infinity, is the inequality between the same and the other, the difference that is also the non-indifference of the same for the other and the substitution which, in its turn, is a nonequality with oneself, a non-recovering of self by self, a dispossession of self, the self leaving the clandestinity of its identification. It is already a sign made to another, a sign of this giving of signs, that is, of this non-indifference, a sign of this impossibility of slipping away and being replaced, of this identity, this uniqueness: *here I am*. The identity aroused thus behind identification is an identity by pure election. Election traverses the concept of the *ego* to summon me as me through the inordinateness of the other. It extracts me from the concept in which I continually take refuge, for I find in it the measure of an obligation which is not defined in the election. Obligation calls for a unique response not inscribed in universal thought, the unforeseeable response of the chosen one.[318]

Before the Self and *before* hearing the call of the Other, the ethical Self is elected to an hyperbolical and diachronical responsibility for the Other: *elected to giving always more than it can or could, beyond what it can or could* for the Other. In this sense, responsibility as election means to respond for the Other to the Other by being subjected to the point of substitution and expiation in the name of the Other: incessantly *giving* in excess of what *can* be given, gift of the Self *without* self-destruction or self-sacrifice, negation or denial of the Self: hyperbolical givenness *without* principle nor finality, *without* reserve or economy.

Responsibility means being Self *of the* Other as *subjected* to the Other for the Other. Levinas radicalizes this responsibility to the point of substitution and expiation for the Other which presupposes an *always giving more* of the Self than the Self can or could determine for the Other, elected to giving *before* and *beyond* the Self for the Other. As Levinas marks:

> In the non-indifference to a neighbor, where proximity is never close enough, the difference between me and the other, and the undeclinability

> of the subject are not effaced, as they are in the situation in which the relationship of the one with the other is understood to be reciprocal. The non-indifference to the other as other and as neighbor in which I exist is something *beyond* any commitment in the voluntary sense of the term, for it extends into my very bearing as an entity, to the point of substitution. It is at the same time prior to commitments, for it disengages in this extreme passivity an undeclinable and unique subject. Responsibility, the signification which is non-indifference, goes one way, from me to the other. In the saying of responsibility, which is an exposure to an obligation for which no one could replace me, I am unique. Peace with the other is first of all my business. The non-indifference, the saying, the responsibility, the approach, is the disengaging of the unique one responsible, me. The way I appear is a summons. I am put in the passivity of an undeclinable assignation, in the accusative, a self. Not as a particular case of the universal, an ego belonging to the concept of ego, but as I, said in the first person-I, unique in my genus. It is indeed true that this I has already become a universal in the present exposition itself. But I am capable of conceiving of a break with this universal, and the apparition of the unique I which always precedes the reflection which comes again (with an alternating which we find in the refutation and rebirth of skepticism) to include me in the concept—which I again evade or am torn up from. The uniqueness of this ego, this I, is not due to a unique trait of its nature or its character; nothing is unique, that is, refractory to concepts, except the I involved in responsibility. In signification I am disengaged as unique. In the saying in responsibility, the one is not concealed in itself, but denudes itself in recurrence, substituting itself for another on the hither side of its own identity for another. This is the only way for it to be not multiplied in this relationship, but for its unity to be brought out in it. The "never enough" of proximity, the restlessness of this peace, is the acute uniqueness of subjectivity. The subject arising in the passivity of unconditionality, in the expulsion outside of its being at home with itself, is undeclinable. This undeclinability is not that of transcendental subjectivity, is not an intentionality or openness upon the world, not even a world that overflows me, and in which the alleged ecstatic subjectivity is only dissimulated.[319]

This hyperbolical *infinitization* of the ethical as responsibility for the Other is not reducible to *eros*. Indeed, responsibility is that which exceeds *eros* and *enjoyment*. It engages a response for the Other *without* return to the Self, *without* economy, gratification, or *jouissance*. Without return to the Self, the *infinitization* of the ethical responsibility marks the Self as infinite approaching of the Other by incessantly giving itself more than itself for the Other. It means, for Levinas, a proximity as non-indifference for the Other—that is, an exigency of peace with the Other *beyond* the ontology and economy of war which always reduces the singularity of the Other to indifference and anonymity. Indeed, proximity as peace means and entails a responsibility always exceeding the capacities and capabilities of an autonomous and sovereign subjectivity—proximity in responsibility for the Other, which Levinas also calls "fraternity":

> Proximity, difference which is non-indifference, is responsibility. It is a response without a question, the immediacy of peace that is incumbent on me. It is the signification of signs. It is the humanity of man not understood on the basis of transcendental subjectivity. It is the passivity of exposure, a passivity itself exposed. Saying does not occur in consciousness nor in a commitment understood in terms of consciousness or memory; it does not form a conjuncture and a synchrony. Proximity is fraternity before essence and before death, having a meaning despite being and nothingness, despite concepts.[320]

This is also why responsibility for the Other means to respond *without* contract, and thus *before* decision or judgment. Furthermore, responsibility for the Other means to respond *before* any scene of intersubjectivity between the *ego* and the alter-*ego*, and thus *respond to the Other for the Other from the immemoriality of a commandment before the Self's self-determination* and *beyond the Self's self-understanding.* Always and already *before* recognition of the Other's command or plea, *before* and also *beyond* any community between the Self and the Other, responsibility opens to an "outside of essence" and "conveys the infinite. It inverses relationships and principles, reverses the order of interest: in the measure that responsibilities are taken on they multiply. This is not a *Sollen* commanding the infinite pursuit of an ideal. The infinity of the infinite lives in going backwards. The debt increases in the measures that it is paid. This divergency perhaps deserves the name glory. The positivity of the infinite is the conversion of the response to the infinite into responsibility, into approach of the other. The Infinite is non-thematizable, gloriously exceeds every capacity, and manifests, as it were in reverse, its exorbitance in the approach of a neighbor, obedient to its measure. Subjectivity, prior to or *beyond* the free and the non-free, obliged with regard to the neighbor, is the breaking point where essence is exceeded by the infinite."[321]

The ethical Self is accused *before* and *beyond* culpability or blame. The ethical Self responds in spite of its own autonomous subjectivity to the Other for the Other to the point of responding *before* the commandment or the plea of the Other. This is also why responsibility for Other is precisely not grounded or justified in a kinship or with the Other. Responsibility rather means for

Levinas an immemorial response, *before* any autonomy or sovereignty, where to be a Self means to always have responded and always be engaged in responding to the Other for the Other—not as a free autonomous decision, but rather as election, being elected, impossibility not to be called uniquely and singularly to respond to the Other's commandment and plea; impossibility not to substitute the Self for the Other; impossibility not to suffer for the Other *before* any recognition, judgment, or decision.

The Other is Other as unique and absolute transcendence: *beyond* genus and irretrievable through a genealogy, the Other is encountered in its human uniqueness and singularity, irreducible, and where its commandment demands a non-indifference as election to an infinite response of non-transferrable and unsubstitutable responsibility. The ethical Self is elected to a responsibility *before* and *beyond* morality—a responsibility, unique, *without* end, anarchic, and undeclinable, irreplaceable, exceptional: "Here I am" for the Other and uniquely for the Other as unique. The ethical Self is responsible *without* mediation: elected as an ethical Self, as an *I* and not another—where this "not another" entails a response of responsibility incessantly burrowing itself and in which the ethical Self is singularly for the Other—to the point of substitution and expiation, responsible *before* decision or freedom, *beyond* its capacity or self-determination:

> In substitution and expiation my being that belongs to me and not to another is undone, and it is through this substitution that I am not "another," but me. The self in a being is exactly the not-being-able-to-slip-away-from an assignation that does not aim at any generality. There is no ipseity common to me and the others; "me" is the exclusion from this possibility of comparison, as soon as comparison is set up. The ipseity is then a privilege or an unjustifiable election that chooses me and not the ego. I am unique and chosen; the election is in the subjection. The conceptualization of this last refusal of conceptualization is not contemporaneous with this refusal; it transcends this conceptualization. This transcendence separating itself from the consideration that conceptualizes it, the diachrony of subjectivity, is my entry into the proximity of the neighbor. Subjectivity is being hostage. This notion reverses the position where the presence of the *ego* to itself appears as the beginning or as the conclusion of philosophy. This coinciding in the same, where I would be an origin, or, through memory, a covering over of the origin, this presence, is, from the start, undone by the other. The subject resting on itself is confounded by wordless accusation. For in discourse it would have already lost its traumatic violence. The accusation is in this sense persecuting; the persecuted one can no longer answer it. More exactly, it is accusation which I cannot answer, but for which I cannot decline responsibility. Already the position of the subject is a deposition,

> not a conatus essendi. It is from the first a substitution by a hostage expiating for the violence of the persecution itself. We have to conceive in such terms the de-substantiation of the subject, its de-reification, its disinterestedness, its subjection, its subjectivity. It is a pure self, in the accusative, responsible before there is freedom.

The ethical Self is *substituted* for the Other as irreplaceable election in the incessant reiteration of its ethical excess as responsibility to the point of *expiation* for the Other. This expiation means a forgiveness always given to the Other and yet never accomplished as reconciliation, never fulfilled as forgiveness. Which entails a forgiveness incessantly furthering itself for the Other, *before* autonomy and *without* end, *always forgiving ad infinitum* the Other and yet incessantly exceeding this gift of forgiveness by reiterating yet a further plea of forgiveness, furthering its plea for forgiveness as gift giving itself *without* reconciliation and *without* conciliation: infinitely affianced in yet a further, always further, reiterated plea for forgiveness. Which means: the gift of a reiterated gift for the Other—the enigma of a responsibility *without* term, a

> gaping open of an abyss in proximity, the infinite which blinks, refusing speculative audacities, is distinguishable from pure and simple nothingness by the committing of the neighbor to my responsibility. But it is also distinguishable from the *Sollen*, for proximity is not a simply asymptotic approach of its "term." Its term is not an end. The more I answer, the more I am responsible; the more I approach the neighbor with which I am encharged the further away I am. This debit which increases is infinity as an infinition of the infinite, as glory.[322]

Sacrifice (*Sacrifice*)

Levinas never sacrificed the possibility of sacrifice and at the same time, and throughout his philosophical writing, he emits a profound and radical *critique*, suspicion and suspiciousness of self-sacrifice in ethics and *a fortiori* in politics. In the opening pages of *Totality and Infinity*, Levinas indeed associates sacrifice with the modality by which the totality of war marks the cadence of a teleology founded on the effacement and annihilation of individualities and singularities in the name of a common and communal meaning, reason, spirit, identity, identicalness and origin of History. Sacrifice—sacrifice of the Other and self-sacrifice as obliteration of singular existences—is the essential movement in which Being shows itself as war, foreclosure, effacement, annihilation of difference in the immanent indifference of Sameness, and anonymity. Thereby, sacrifice is wholly in service of the proliferation of a totality of meaning and totalization of identity and identicalness:

> The visage of Being that shows itself in war is fixed in the concept of totality, which dominates Western philosophy. Individuals are reduced to being bearers of forces that command them unbeknown to themselves. The meaning of individuals (invisible outside of this totality) is derived from the totality. The unicity of each present is incessantly sacrificed to a future appealed to bring forth its objective meaning. For the ultimate meaning alone counts; the last act alone changes beings into themselves. They are what they will appear to be in the already plastic forms of the epic.[323]

In this sense, Levinas exercises a profound suspicion—of course, drawing also from Rosenzweig's critique of philosophical teleology in the opening pages of *The Star of Redemption*—of the sacrificial logic which animates and empowers, engages and deploys itself as and in the speculative dialectic of "Reason in History" (Hegel[324]). Furthermore, Levinas also questions the sacrificial element in Heidegger's[325] deployment of the History of the meaning of Being always reducing and appropriating the singularity of the transcendence of the Other in the essential gathering and clearing of the "presencing" of the truth of Being. In this sense, Levinas questions the *operation* of sacrifice which always annihilates and negates the singularity of the existent by appropriating, reappropriating its uniqueness in the presence, Sameness and anonymity, indifference and immanence of Being. The *operation* of sacrifice and self-sacrifice informs the movement, the element, the immanence of Being by annihilating the singularity of existences and "elevating" them to the totality and comprehension of an essential historical meaning through which the Self and the Other are brought to a Sameness and identicalness in the mutual negation of their singularity; the operation of sacrifice thus, Levinas always understood it as a certain embodiment of sacredness, a form of paganism, already reducing the absolute transcendence of the Other, the Height of the Holy (*Saint*), the *Saying* of an immemorial justice to a comprehension in the immanence and the completion in reconciliation, unification, gathering, essential identicalness which always means, for Levinas, in indifference and anonymity through a totalizing appropriation of Being. To phrase it by using the terms of *Otherwise than Being, or Beyond Essence*, sacrifice is the essentializing modality of the *Said* which incessantly negates the *Saying* by reconciling the Same and the Other in an indifference and anonymity through their mutual sacrificial abnegation. Levinas indeed abhors the exaltation of sacrifice for sacrifice which, in a short text on the French military trial held in

1954 in Metz on the Struthof concentration and extermination camp guards, the philosopher sees as the "permanent origin of Hitlerism."[326]

Sacrifice, for Levinas, means *to sacralize* the movement of Sameness, the indifference and anonymity of Being and essence. Which is precisely why Levinas' ethics as "First Philosophy" insists on a *de-sacralization* and thereby on the opening of a possibility in thinking toward the ethical *without* the essentializing modality and operation of sacrifice, that is, *without* the abnegation of self-sacrifice and furthermore *without* the accomplishment and resolution of a sacrificial logic which has always informed Western ethics and morality. In a certain sense, Levinas engages the ethical possibility of extracting sacrifice from the ethical, that is, purports the possibility of a certain *deconstruction* of sacrifice in the name of an idea of justice for and in the name of the irreplaceability of singularity.

What we have here called Levinas' *deconstruction* of sacrifice is developed most specifically in *Otherwise than Being or Beyond Essence*. This *deconstruction* of sacrifice however does not mean a simple negation of the meaning and the idea of sacrifice. Levinas marks indeed how the hyperbolical ethics is also engaged in the *possibility* of sacrifice for the Other. As above said, Levinas never sacrifices the *possibility* of sacrifice. And, through the radicalization of the ethics of responsibility as substitution and expiation for the Other, Levinas *does* mark this possibility:

> Responsibility for the other, in its antecedence to my freedom, its antecedence to the present and to representation, is a passivity more passive than all passivity, an exposure to the other without this exposure being assumed, an exposure without holding back, exposure of exposedness, expression, saying. This exposure is the frankness, sincerity, veracity of saying. Not saying dissimulating itself and protecting itself in the said, just giving out words in the face of the other, but saying uncovering itself, that is, denuding itself of its skin, sensibility on the surface of the skin, at the edge of the nerves, offering itself even in suffering—and thus wholly sign, signifying itself. Substitution, at the limit of being, ends up in saying, in the giving of signs, giving a sign of this giving of signs, expressing oneself. This expression is antecedent to all thematization in the said, but it is not a babbling or still primitive or childish form of saying. This stripping *beyond* nudity, *beyond* forms, is not the work of negation and no longer belongs to the order of being. Responsibility goes *beyond* being. In sincerity, in frankness, in the veracity of this saying, in the uncoveredness of suffering, being is altered. But this saying remains, in its activity, a passivity, more passive than all passivity, for it is a sacrifice without reserve, without holding back, and in this non-voluntary—the sacrifice of a hostage designated who has not chosen himself to be hostage, but possibly elected by the Good,

> in an involuntary election not assumed by the elected one. For the Good can not enter into a present nor be put into a representation. But being Good it redeems the violence of its alterity, even if the subject has to suffer through the augmentation of this ever more demanding violence.[327]

Levinas in this passage unequivocally associates the hyperbolical responsibility, its *diachrony* and *infinitization* of responsibility as substitution and expiation for the Other, to a "sacrifice *without* reserve." The question however is: what is meant by this "sacrifice" lodged in the very movement of the hyperbolical and *diachronical* responsibility for the Other which incessantly transcends the immanence, indifference and anonymity of Being, that is, transcends the sacrificial logic and operativity of the ontological and the teleological?

Levinas qualifies the "sacrifice *without* reserve" as the culmination of a hyperbolical responsibility for the Other by marking how and why "these words take on their strong sense when, instead of only designating the lack of certainty, they express the gratuity of sacrifice. In a fine risk to be run, the word 'fine' has not been thought about enough. It is as antithetical to certainty, and indeed to consciousness, that these terms take on their positive meaning, and are not the expression of a makeshift."[328] Indeed, and with these words, Levinas signifies the hyperbolical ethics of responsibility in substitution and expiation for the Other as the "gratuity" of sacrifice. In this sense, sacrifice *without* reserve as gratuitous givenness for the Other—givenness of the Self, exposition *before* autonomy and passivity more passive than all passivity or Passion of responsibility—marks precisely what Levinas also signifies as the very "meaning of the human adventure."[329]

Firstly, and again to reiterate what we named above Levinas' suspicion and suspiciousness toward the sacralization of sacrifice, and thus toward the exaltation, and sublime heroism inherent in the operation of sacrifice: Levinas indeed also points out, in *Otherwise than Being, or Beyond Essence*, that the hyperbolical ethics of responsibility as substitution and expiation for the Other is *not* an ethics of sacrifice, and thus does not engage a self-sacrifice for the Other. Levinas' ethics as "First Philosophy" is *not* sacrificial. Indeed, as Levinas marks in the following, as an example of numerous such passages in *Otherwise than Being, or Beyond Essence*:

> the for-the-other characteristic of the subject can be interpreted neither as a guilt complex (which presupposes an initial freedom), nor as a natural benevolence or divine "instinct," nor as some love or some tendency to sacrifice. This is quite the opposite of the Fichtean conception, where all suffering due to the action of the non-ego is first a positing of this action of the non-ego by the ego.[330]

Following this point, we are to pose again our leading question: what could Levinas mean when marking the hyperbolical ethics of responsibility, substitution and expiation for the Other, as gratuitous "sacrifice *without* reserve" for the Other?

By sacrifice, Levinas does not mean self-abnegation, but rather *approach* of the Other. Indeed, when Levinas uses the term sacrifice, he is in truth translating the Hebrew word for sacrifice, *korban*, which also means *to draw near*, and thus *to approach*. Levinas sees in sacrifice, the *approach* of the Other. Indeed, for Levinas, sacrifice means *to approach* the absolute transcendence of the Other. Far from self-sacrifice, far from an ethics of self-sacrifice, as a sublime moral posture, far from a teleological determination of meaning and "Reason in History" signifying sacrifice as the modality by which and through which can be had and appropriated a conciliation and a reconciliation of History with itself and thus the essence of community between the Self and the Other through the comprehension and hence indifferenciation of their singularities, Levinas means, through sacrifice, the *approach of*, the *approaching*, the *drawing near* the absolute transcendence of the Other. That is: an *approach always approaching*, a *drawing near always moving towards* the Other and thereby always transcending the Self's identity and self-determination in expiation and substitution for the Other. Levinas in this sense, opens a possibility of an ethics as responsibility as infinite *approaching* of the Other and thereby as incessantly *suspending* and *interrupting, differing and deferring* the actuality, the actualization, the accomplishment and fulfilment of self-abnegation.

This incessant *approaching* of the Other as an interminable relationship toward the absolute transcendence of the Other means the passivity of an exposition as obedience and thereby responsibility for the Other *before* the autonomy of the subject and *beyond* the normativity it could or would determine. This is why, for Levinas, the hyperbolical ethics of responsibility for the Other means an election to a passivity more passive than all passivity *as* incessant *reiteration* of responsibility for the Other. In this sense, the ethical Self is never *sacrificing itself to the Other* but always *approaching the Other as infinitizing responsibility, substitution and expiation for the Other*, that is, elected to *approach infinitely* the Other, always and already *exceeding* and *furthering* its *approaching* toward the absolute transcendence of the Other *before* and *beyond* the commandment of the Other; responsibility given *before* the commandment of Other and *beyond* what the Self can or could give for the Other. Levinas insists repeatedly in *Otherwise than Being or Beyond Essence* on this reversal of *pronominality* from its activity to a passivity more passive than the opposition between activity and passivity and which engages a specific manner of *positively* responding, through passivity, to and for the vulnerability, defenselessness, helplessness of the Other. Levinas writes: "The passivity of the exposure responds to an assignation that identifies me as the unique one, not by reducing me to myself, but by stripping me of every identical quiddity, and thus of all form, all investiture, which would still slip into the assignation. The *Saying* signifies this passivity; in the saying this passivity signifies, becomes signifyingness, exposure in response to . . . , being at the question before any interrogation, any problem, without clothing, without a shell to protect oneself, stripped to the core as in an inspiration of air, an ab-solution to the one, the one without a complexion. It is a denuding *beyond* the skin, to the wounds one dies from, denuding to death, being as a vulnerability. It is a fission of the nucleus opening the bottom of its punctual nuclearity, like to a lung at the core of oneself. The nucleus does not open this depth as long as it remains protected by its solid crust, by a form, not even when it is reduced to its punctuality, for it identifies itself in the temporality of its essence, and thus covers itself over again. The limit of the stripping bare, in the punctual core, has to continue to be torn from itself. The one assigned has to open to the point of separating itself from its own inwardness, adhering to *esse*; it must be dis-interested. This being torn up from oneself in the core of one's unity, this absolute noncoinciding, this diachrony of the instant, signifies in the form of *one-penetrated-by-the-other*. The pain, this underside of skin, is a nudity more naked than all destitution. It is sacrificed rather than sacrificing itself, for it is precisely bound to the adversity or suffering of pain. This existence, with sacrifice imposed on it, is without conditions. The subjectivity of a subject is vulnerability, exposure to affection, sensibility, a passivity more passive than any passivity, an irrecuperable time, an unassemblable diachrony of patience, an exposedness always to be exposed the more, an exposure to expressing, and thus to saying, thus to giving."[331]

Sacrifice as *approach* of the Other and where this *approach* means the *incessant excess* and *furthering* of responsibility for the Other by and through the elected ethical Self responding always *before* its autonomy and already *beyond* its capacities—substitution *as* expiation. Indeed, through this *approach* as *sacrifice without* reserve and in its gratuity, Levinas means, the incessant substitution *as* expiation of the ethical Self for the Other. Substitution *as* expiation, whose very kernel lies in the "one-*for* the Other" as "One-*hostage*-of-the-Other," marks how the Self is wholly given over for the Other as unsubstitutable, unique, inimitable, irreplaceable and thus infinitely responsible, infinitely exceeding and furthering its responsibility for the Other where this *infinitization* of responsibility is always and already inescapable, irremediable, irreversible. The ethical Self, elected to responsibility through substitution *as* expiation, responds as *host* and *hostage* of the Other where no other can substitute one's Self for *my* Self for the Other. No other Self can substitute itself for myself in my substitution *as* expiation for the Other. Which means: substitution *as* expiation occurs through the exposition of the Self as singularly irreplaceable for the singularity of the Other. And thus substitution *as* expiation means a passivity more passive than all passivity in the ethical Self's exposition in the infinite responsibility, the *infinitization* of responsibility, never fulfilled nor fulfillable, unaccomplished and always furthering *its* responsibility, *its* approach and approaching, *its* "sacrifice" for the Other. Precisely where: "Through substitution for others, the oneself escapes relations. At the limit of passivity, the oneself *escapes* passivity or the inevitable limitation that the terms within relation undergo. In the incomparable relationship of responsibility, the other no longer limits the same, it is supported by what it limits. Here the overdetermination of the ontological categories is visible, which transforms them into ethical terms. In this most passive passivity, the self-liberates itself ethically from every other and from itself. Its responsibility for the other, the proximity of the neighbor, does not signify a submission to the non-ego; it means an openness in which being's essence is surpassed in inspiration. It is an openness of which respiration is a modality or a foretaste, or, more exactly, of which it retains the aftertaste. Outside of any mysticism, in this respiration, the possibility of every sacrifice for the other, activity and passivity coincide."[332]

Sacrifice indeed will animate for Levinas substitution *as* expiation. Through substitution *as* expiation, Levinas engages the Self in a responsibility *before* and *beyond* activity and passivity, and through this *diachrony*, a responsibility *beyond* and *before* any intersubjectivity or community between the Self and the Other. Otherwise said, substitution *as* expiation engages the singularity of the ethical Self as always and already singularly called and invested *before* and *beyond* its own Self as response *before* the Other's commandment and *beyond* what such a commandment could command or demand. The ethical Self responds *before* its own Self *beyond* its self-determination for the Other *before* the Other *beyond* the Other. In this sense, when Levinas marks that substitution *as* expiation means "to take the place" of the Other or "to respond for the Other, in place of the Other," he deploys how substitution *as* expiation engages a *diachrony* of responsibility where the Self exceptionally and unescapably responds *before* its self-determination and *before* hearing the commandment of the Other as already *beyond* that which the Self can respond and *beyond* what the Other could demand of the Self. Incessant excess, *infinitization* of the Infinite as responsibility through substitution *as* expiation, the ethical opens to that which, *without* conciliation or reconciliation, exceedingly elects the Self *before* the Self and *before* the Other to respond *beyond* the Self and *beyond* the Other. Substitution *as* expiation here means to be engaged in the incessant excess in the response of responsibility, *infinitization* of responsibility where neither the Self nor the Other can rationalize or come to terms, fulfill or accomplish the ethical responsibility, substitution *as* expiation, in a contract, a commonality, a judgment and community.

This *infinitizing* responsibility through the elected singularity and uniqueness of the Self for the unique and singular Other, always awakened in a Self as *creature* and thus irreducible to an *ego* capable of grounding its action in the universality of its scope or in the autonomous respect of its posited universal moral law, repudiates any identification or transubstantification with the Other. One-for-the-Other as One *host as hostage* of the Other, substitution *as* expiation, elected singular response as infinite responsibility *before* and *beyond* the Self never means, for Levinas, communion, community, conciliation or reconciliation, fusion, recognition or identification with the Other. Substitution *as* expiation means the incessance of temporal interruptions, the incessant reiteration of separation by which and through which a forgiveness *without* reconciliation reveals itself. Substitution opens thus toward the *incessance of an expiation* for the Other as the gift given each time singularly and which, *without* communion, conciliation or reconciliation between the Self and the Other, *creates* in and as History *irreducible breaks* and *scansions, fissures,* and *fractures,* through which a *communication* that is also a *temporality* of *singular instants of mending* are revealed.

This is why Levinas calls onto another word to think this *diachrony* as incessant *creation* at the heart of the one-for-the-Other as One *host and hostage* of the Other—another word than empathy, sympathy, or *being-with-the-other.* Another word which Levinas marks precisely when indicating the meaning of *approaching* the Other, and thus of *communication* with the Other.

Which could be this other word which also expresses the "fine risk" of which Levinas says is "always something to be taken in philosophy"? Levinas:

> Communication is an adventure of a subjectivity, different from that which is dominated by the concern to recover itself, different from that of coinciding in consciousness; it will involve uncertainty. It is by virtue of its *eidos* possible only in sacrifice, which is the *approach* of him for which one is responsible. Communication with the other can be transcendent only as a dangerous life, a fine risk to be run. These words take on their strong sense when, instead of only designating the lack of certainty, they express the gratuity of sacrifice. In a fine risk to be run, the word "fine" has not been thought about enough. It is as antithetical to certainty, and indeed to consciousness, that these terms take on their positive meaning.[333]

The "gratuity of sacrifice" as that "fine risk" which philosophy has yet to take and which *Otherwise than Being, or Beyond Essence* has ventured into and in order to rethink, *before* and *beyond* recognition or community, the *approach* of the Other in substitution *as* expiation for the Other and through its *diachrony* engages yet a further movement in that it marks how and why substitution *as* expiation also involves and implicates a sacrificial movement which Levinas sustains throughout the writing of *Otherwise than Being or Beyond Essence*. Indeed,

> Responsibility goes *beyond* being. In sincerity, in frankness, in the veracity of this saying, in the uncoveredness of suffering, being is altered. But this saying remains, in its activity, a passivity, more passive than all passivity, for it is a sacrifice *without* reserve, *without* holding back, and in this non-voluntary—the sacrifice of a hostage designated who has not chosen himself to be hostage, but possibly elected by the Good, in an involuntary election not assumed by the elected one. For the Good cannot enter into a present nor be put into a representation. But being Good it *redeems* the violence of its alterity, even if the subject has to suffer through the augmentation of this ever more demanding violence.[334]

We are already hearing the idea of *redemption* in this highly condensed passage. But what does Levinas understand here by the "gratuity of sacrifice," "sacrifice *without* reserve," sacrifice "*without* holding back"? Sacrifice as *approach* of the Other—*approach* with that through which the Good can *redeem* violence. Following this development of substitution *as* expiation which culminates in sacrifice as communication, as *approach* through the *diachrony* of responsibility for the Other we are to understand the "gratuity of sacrifice" precisely *not* as that *operation* in which the ethical Self would negate and abnegate itself, transform, through this self-renunciation, its responsibility for the Other in its ownmost Self as the "heroic" and sovereign gift of its Self. In other words, and as Levinas always allies sacrifice with *inspiration, psychism*, "respiration," the "gratuity of sacrifice" engages not the fulfillment of sacrifice, the accomplishment of self-sacrifice for the Other and the disclosure and presentation of its sacrificial gift, the representation and the performance of its givenness, of the gift of the Self as gift by the Self of itself. Rather and perhaps this is the *revelation* which Levinas points toward: the "gratuity of sacrifice" means the *interruption* and *suspension* of sacrifice where this *interruption* engages incessantly to always and already *give more than giving one's Self in sacrifice* and thus be *elected* to *incessantly approach the Other* in an incessant aggravation of a *separation* with the Other and where this *approach in separation* means an incessance of responsibility for the Other, a *responsibilization of responsibility* more than what the fulfillment of sacrifice or self-sacrifice could signify or symbolize.

For Levinas, the *embodiment of sacrifice and actualization of self-sacrifice* would imply an *abnegation* of responsibility for the Other in the representation of the accomplishment in the consecrated and reduced meaning of the ethical to an economy, to a *Said* foreclosing its *Saying*.

Levinas' insistence on "sacrifice" for the Other, the incessance and "without reserve" of this sacrifice for the Other, this always acute and active "possibility of sacrifice"[335] as "human adventure," engages—and in order not to reduce the ethical itself, in order for the ethical to remain always reconducted to a *Saying* awakening the *said*, a *Saying* at once overwhelming and animating the *said before* and *beyond* itself, and indeed where could occur the *promises* of a *redemption of the said* from its self-enclosure—the *reiteration* of a *suspension* and an *interruption* of sacrifice, of self-sacrifice, of the operativity of sacrifice and its conciliatory and reconciliatory essence. For Levinas, sacrifice means suspension and interruption of sacrifice which in the incessance of responsibility for the Other is *elected* a Self to an *excess of approaching* the Other, an *approach always approaching* the Other *further* than what the Self could ever express in the abnegation a self-sacrifice. That is, always and already *approaching* the singularity of the Other. The gratuity *without* reserve of sacrifice, this hyperbolical *infinitzation* of sacrifice for the Other renders and reveals the *incessance* of an *otherwise than sacrifice*, a *without sacrifice*, that is, a *without the realization of sacrifice*. Levinas here marks an interruption of self-sacrifice in and through the infinite reiteration of sacrifice as the *infinitizing approaching* in responsibility for the Other. An incessant *sacrifice of sacrifice*, always exposing more and already repudiating its termination in an accomplished sacrifice or self-sacrifice as if this accomplishment would only present itself as nothing less and nothing more than what Levinas also labels a *hypocrisy*. In this sense, the "Here I am for the Other" would also, *before* and *beyond* the Self, mean a *Here I am in sacrifice* as *also* interrupting and suspending the realization and fulfillment of sacrifice and where the *incessance* of sacrifice for the Other would also and at the same time *break* and *fracture* its accomplishment revealing thus the *infinitizing approaching* as interminable and unfulfillable *excess* of responsibility for the Other.

Saying (*Dire*)

The opposition between the *Saying* (*Dire*) and the *Said* (*dit*) is central and primordial in Levinas' late work, *Otherwise than Being, or Beyond Essence*.

Indeed, this irreducible opposition marks and defines the *exposition* to the Other, the *for* in *one-for-the-Other* through which the ethical Self as infinite and *infinitizing* responsibility given thus *without* reserve as substitution and expiation.

Always *prior* to any linguistic or semantic sign, to thematization or categorization, the *Saying* characterizes the *exposition* as *vulnerability to the*

Other for the Other. This exposition, passivity more passive than all passivity, occurs *before* the engagement of the subject in a sociality, a community, or an intersubjective relation and spurs on this Self as ethical to respond *beyond* any determination, self-determination, moral norm or normativity. Exposition to the Other *before* the recognition of the Other and anterior to the constitution and determination of the Self animating and electing the Self to the ethical response of responsibility *beyond* the fulfillment or accomplishment in accord to a norm or a normativity for the Other. The *Saying* precedes all word or wording, expresses itself *beyond* signification and as witness and testimony of the immemoriality of the Infinite transcendence of the Other; it inaugurates, for Levinas, the "significance of signification", that is the ethical *before* and *beyond* Being, *wholly otherwise* than essence.

The *Saying* is irreducible to presentation or representation, imagination or categorization, and, as that which marks a certain interruption and suspension of the order of intentionality, it always and already expresses an irreducibility—the ethical *before* and *beyond* Being—wholly oriented toward the Other. Which means: the *Saying* marks the incessance of the ethical Self's exposition as vulnerability and passivity in responsibility always and already exceeding itself, surpassing and overwhelming itself in its givenness of responsibility, substitution *as* expiation, for the Other.

For Levinas, the *Saying* marks the hyperbolical and exceptional irreducibility of the ethical:

> Saying uncovers, *beyond* nudity, what dissimulation there may be under the exposedness of a skin laid bare. It is the very respiration of this skin prior to any intention. The subject is not in itself, at home with itself such that it would dissimulate itself in itself or dissimulate itself in its wounds and its exile, understood as acts of wounding or exiling itself. Its bending back upon itself is a turning inside out. It's being "turned to another" is this being turned inside out. A concave without a convex. The subject of saying does not give signs, it becomes a sign, turns into an allegiance. Here exposure has a sense radically different from thematization. The one is exposed to the other as a skin is exposed to what wounds it, as a cheek is offered to the smiter. On the hither side of the ambiguity of Being and entities, prior to the *Said*, saying uncovers the one that speaks, not as an object disclosed by theory, but in the sense that one discloses oneself by neglecting one's defenses, leaving a shelter, exposing oneself to outrage, to insults and wounding. But saying is a denuding of denuding, a giving a sign of its very signifyingness, an expression of exposure, a hyperbolic passivity that disturbs the still waters, in which, without saying, passivity would be crawling with secret designs. There is denuding of denuding, without this 'reflection' or this iteration having to be added afterwards to the denuding.

> The passivity of the exposure responds to an assignation that identifies me as the unique one, not by reducing me to myself, but by stripping me of every identical quiddity, and thus of all form, all investiture, which would still slip into the assignation. The saying signifies this passivity; in the saying this passivity signifies, becomes signifyingness, exposure in *response to* . . . , being at the question before any interrogation, any problem, without clothing, without a shell to protect oneself, stripped to the core as in an inspiration of air, an ab-solution to the one, the one without a complexion. It is a denuding *beyond* the skin, to the wounds one dies from, denuding to death, being as a vulnerability. It is a fission of the nucleus opening the bottom of its punctual nuclearity, like to a lung at the core of oneself. The nucleus does not open this depth as long as it remains protected by its solid crust, by a form, not even when it is reduced to its punctuality, for it identifies itself in the temporality of its essence, and thus covers itself over again. The limit of the stripping bare, in the punctual core, has to continue to be torn from itself. The one assigned has to open to the point of separating itself from its own inwardness, adhering to *esse*; it must be dis-interested.[336]

Always prior to the *Said*, the *Saying* expresses nothing else than the immemorial commandment of the Other which calls the Self to the ethical urgency of a response, and thus to its awakening and election as an ethical Self—subjugation and subjection to the Other, persecution, obsession, accusation, and trauma by the Other to the point of substitution and expiation for the Other. The ethical Self is always and already responsible for the Other, responsible of its responsibility for the Other, that is thus responsible *before* and *beyond* its own Self, its own self-determination and incessantly exceeding, furthering, reiterating more than what it can or could respond for the Other.

The *Saying* is whole and radical exposition to the Other as inescapable and irrevocable responsibility and thus substitution *as* expiation for the Other. This is why, for Levinas, the *Saying* (which always exceeds the *Said* and thereby remains irreducible to the *Said*) expresses the singularity of the plea, the cry, the desperate and irreplaceable appeal in the face (*visage*) of the Other commanding, persecuting, obsessing the Self to an infinite responsibility, *infinitizing* responsibility, for the Other. Wholly other than the *Said*—which always designates, for Levinas, a thematization, a categorization, a typification and thus finds a stabilization and an equilibrium in a *shared logos* itself signified by a mutual understanding, entailing an identification, a recognition, a commonality with the Other—the *Saying* expresses absolute heteronomy, the event of a signification suspending and interrupting signification, breaking and splicing the stability, universality, and constancy of categorization and typification. The *Saying* elects, *before* all commitment or decision, the Self to an inalterable and unescapable ethical responsibility as substitution and expiation, as substitution *as* expiation:

> Saying is a denuding, of the unqualifiable one, the pure someone, unique and chosen; that is, it is an exposedness to the other where no slipping away is possible. In its sincerity as a sign given to another, it absolves me of all identity, which would arise again like a curd coagulating for itself, would coincide with itself. This absolution reverses essence. It is not a negation of essence, but a disinterestedness, an "otherwise than being" which turns into a "for the other," burning for the other, consuming the bases of any position for oneself and any substantialization which would take form in this consummation, consuming even the ashes of this consummation, in which there would be a risk that everything be born again. Here identity lies in the total patience of the one assigned, who, patient, despite himself, dies continually, lasts in his instant, "whitens under the harness." The reverting of the ego into a self, the de-posing or de-situating of the ego, is the very modality of dis-interestedness. It has the form of a corporeal life devoted to expression and to giving. It is devoted, and does not devote itself: it is a self despite itself, in incarnation, where it is the very possibility of offering, suffering and trauma. Then the for-the-other involved in saying must not be treated in terms of consciousness of . . . , thematizing intentionality, nor in terms of commitment. The signifyingness of saying does not refer to commitment; for commitment presupposes saying. How then are we to understand the *despite oneself*.[337]

The *Saying* is thus irreducible to the *Said* which always indicates a certain perjury or betrayal of the *Saying*. Indeed, the *Said* entails a reduction of the *Saying*. The *Saying without Said* expresses itself *beyond* content or form, *beyond* universality or particularity, *beyond* affirmation or negation. The *Saying*, as expression, reaches and stretches out toward the Other *without* possession or recognition, *without* appropriation or comprehension, *without* reappropriation or proprietorship. In this sense, the *Saying* is non-theoretical and expresses an irreducible antecedence to diction and contradiction. And yet, the *Saying* expresses itself from this *beyond* and, from this immemoriality, interrupts and suspends the ontological, immanent, totalizing *Said* to awaken it, the *Said*, toward the singular and unique otherness of the Other: irreducible orientation and inspiration *beyond the Said in the Said* toward an hyperbolical ethics of responsibility for the Other.

As often in Levinas' writing, the dynamic between the *Saying* and the *Said* is introduced by a series of questions each leading toward the opening of an antecedence irreducible to *logos* and thereby engaging *before* autonomy and sovereignty, *before* Being toward an *otherwise* than Being into the *hyperbolia* of the ethical. Levinas will name this incessant dynamic which always and already inspires the Said to turn toward the Other than itself, and thus toward the transcendent ethical *Saying*, "the enigma of a God speaking in man and of man not counting on any God":

> How does saying differ from an act commencing in a conquering and voluntary ego, whose signifying is an act being converted into being, and whose "for the other" takes root in identity? The for-the-other of responsibility for the other does not proceed from any free commitment, any present, in which its origin would germinate, or in which an identity identifying itself would catch its breath. That is so, but then there is a new dilemma. Responsibility without a prior commitment, without a present, without an origin, anarchic, is thus an infinite responsibility of the One-for-the-Other who is abandoned to me without anyone being able to take my place as the one responsible for him. Does this confer upon me a new identity, that of being the unique chosen one? Or does this exclusive election, as signification of the Infinite, reduce me to the status of an articulation in its divine economy? Are we reduced to humanity as an extreme possibility in being, where the substantiality of "supporting oneself" is de-substantified in a "supporting the other", "substituting oneself for him"? Or through this ipseity reduced to being irreplaceable hostage, is the self-equivalent to the entry of the subject into, the play or designs of the Infinite? But is not this dilemma rather an ambivalence, and the alternative an enigma? The enigma of a God speaking in man and of man not counting on any god?[338]

The *Saying* always expresses itself in the *Said* as that which at once and simultaneously loses itself in the *Said* and yet incessantly awakens the *Said* to phrase itself *otherwise* than according to its ownmost affirmation. In this sense, the *Saying* signifies the hyperbolical ethical commandment always transcending its comprehension while already stipulating, expecting, ordering *more than what can be given*—excess and surplus—for the Other. The *Saying* thus expresses the excess of the ethical in Being: the excess of a responsibility for the Other, *without* return or pacification, in the *Said*. The *Saying* and from its immemorial verbality incessantly disturbs and overwhelms the *Said*, activating its nominality *before* and *beyond* itself, its self-determination. This is why the distinction between *Saying* and *Said*, engaged by Levinas, is irreducible to the ontological difference between Being and entities—for the first marks an irreducible antecedence, a dynamic wholly oriented by the transcendent and immemorial Illeity *before* and *beyond*, infinitely outside, exterior, heterogeneous and transcending presence, truth, meaning, history. Indeed, Levinas insists: to remain in the play of the ontological difference, and thus in the horizon of presence and presentification, is to remain deaf to the call and the commandment of an *otherwise* than Being or a *beyond* essence. It is to remain deaf to the transcendent call and commandment of the Other in remaining riveted to the play entirely contained in the binarism between presence and absence, unconcealment and concealment, presentation and retraction. It is to remain deaf to the "enigma of the Infinite" and the *diachrony* of infinite responsibility for the Other:

> The enigma of the Infinite, whose saying in me, a responsibility where no one assists me, becomes a contestation of the Infinite. By this contestation everything is incumbent on me, and there is produced my entry into the designs of the Infinite. The enigma separates the Infinite from all phenomenality, from appearing, thematization and essence. In re-presentation, the Infinite would be belied without ambiguity, as though it were an infinite object which subjectivity tries to approach, but misses. The plot of the Infinite is not elaborated according to the scenario of being and consciousness. The extraordinary Illeity, in its diachrony of which the present is incapable, is not an extrapolation of the finite, is not the invisible taken to be behind the visible. The refusal that the infinity opposes to assembling by reminiscence does not come to pass in the form of a veiling and does not exhaust its meaning in terms of consciousness: clarity and obscurity, or distinctness and confusion, known and unknown. The not-known and the unknowable would still refer to a present, would form a structure in it, would belong to order. Diachrony is not a difference amounting to relations between the known and the unknown, where the dissimulated and the knowable would already share the thematizable plane of essence. The transcendence of the Infinite is an irreversible divergency from the present, like that of a past that was never present. A difference of the irrecuperable, it is not a "further" than the given, belonging still to the order of the given. A face is not a presence announcing a "non-said," which will be said from behind it. Substitution, responsibility without recallable commitment, without beginning, infinite approach in the proximity of another-is not an attitude taken in regards to a being.[339]

Certainly, and as marked above, the *Said* can only betray the *Saying*, reduce the hyperbolic ethical *Saying* to the order of presence and manifestation, immanence and essence. However it is always and already the *Saying* which inspires, awakens, arouses the *Said* to always say itself *otherwise*, to transcend itself incessantly in yet another formulation, exceed itself toward a surplus and a supplement of justice *beyond* and *before* truth. Levinas, as always, radicalizes what we have also labeled the *aporia of the ethical* or its *diachrony*: the incessant betrayal of the *Saying* in the *Said* also interrupts and suspends the *Said* by engaging it to yet a further reformulation of itself, a transcending *impetus* where the *Said* also witnesses, obliquely and indirectly, the hyperbolical commandment of the ethical expressed in the *Saying*. This is precisely why, for Levinas, skepticism is not a negative determination in the history of Western philosophy: it is *transformative* as it reworks and persistently engages the *Said* in *alterations* which open to a *beyond* transcendent to its nominal form and formalism. For Levinas, skepticism *unsays* the *Said* and, through this activity of *unsaying*, reveals and unravels that which always lies *beyond* the *Said*: the ethical transcendence of the *Saying*. This is why the *Saying* is never removed, despite its irreducible transcendence, from the *Said*. The *Saying*, aporetically, through its betrayal in the *Said* engages the *Said* in its own *unsaying* by orienting it toward that which is wholly other than the *Said*: the hyperbolical ethical *Saying*. As Levinas remarks:

> What shows itself thematically in the synchrony of the *said* in fact lets itself be *unsaid* as a difference of what cannot be assembled, signifying as *the-one-for-the-other*, from me to the other. The very exhibition of the difference goes diachronically from the *said* to the *unsaid*. The very discussion which we are at this moment elaborating about signification, diachrony and the transcendence of the approach *beyond* being, a discussion that means to be philosophy, is a thematizing, a synchronizing of terms, a recourse to systematic language, a constant use of the verb being, a bringing back into the bosom of being all signification allegedly conceived *beyond* being. But are we being duped by this subreption? The objections are facile, like those that, since the birth of philosophy, are thrown at skepticism. What about our discussion, narrating, as though they were fixed in themes, the anarchy and the non-finality of the subject in which the Infinite would pass? They are thus found to answer in the end not with responsibility, but in the form of theoretical propositions, to the question "What about . . .?" They do not answer the proximity of the neighbor. The discussion thus remains onto-logical, as though the comprehension of being ordered all thought and thinking itself. By the very fact of formulating statements, is not the universality of the thematized, that is, of being, confirmed by the project of the present discussion, which ventures to question this universality? Does this discourse remain then coherent and philosophical? These are familiar objections![340]

And further onwards in *Otherwise than Being, or Beyond Essence*, Levinas indicates how this *non*-dialectical dynamic between the *Saying*, the *Said*, and the *unsaying* of the *Said* is always and already ordered by the infinite transcendence of the Other, and thus by a certain "ambiguity in which the anarchy of the Infinite resists the univocity of an originary or a principle." That is: the movement by which the idea of God comes to mind, can arrive at our intellection as trace and tracing of the Infinite, a *before* and *beyond* Being, the *Other-in-the-Same* as *One-for-the-Other*.

Levinas thus writes:

> That the ontological form of the said could not alter the signification of the *beyond* being which shows itself in this said devolves from the very contestation of this signification. How would the contestation of the pretension *beyond* being have meaning if this pretension were not heard? Is there a negation in which the sense of which the negation is a negation is not conserved? The contradiction which the signification of the *beyond* being-which evidently is not-should compromise is inoperative without a second time, without reflection on the condition of the statement that states this signification. In this reflection, that is, only after the event, contradiction appears: it does not break out between two simultaneous statements, but between a statement and its conditions, as though they were in the same time. The statement of the *beyond* being, of the name of God, does not allow itself to be walled up in the conditions of its enunciation. It benefits from an ambiguity or an enigma, which is not the effect of an inattention, a relaxation of thought, but of an extreme proximity of the neighbor, where the Infinite comes to pass. The Infinite does not enter into a theme like a being to be given in it, and thus belie its *beyond* being. Its transcendence, an exteriority, more exterior, more other than any exteriority of being, does not come to pass save through the subject that confesses or contests it. Here there is an inversion of order: the revelation is made by him that receives it, by the inspired subject whose inspiration, alterity in the same, is the subjectivity or psyche of the subject. The revelation of the *beyond* being is perhaps indeed but a word, but this 'perhaps' belongs to an ambiguity in which the anarchy of the Infinite resists the univocity of an originary or a principle. It belongs to an ambiguity or an ambivalence and an inversion which is stated in the word God, the apex of vocabulary, admission of the stronger than me in me and of the 'less than nothing' nothing but an abusive word, a *beyond* themes in a thought that does not yet think or thinks more than it thinks.[341]

This is why Levinas insists on marking how the *Saying*, by expressing the truthfulness and sincerity of the face (*visage*) of the Other, its transcendent commandment *before* the autonomy of the subject projecting it *beyond* intersubjectivity, recognition, "being-with-the-other," inspires the *Said* in its *unsaying*, in its interruption and suspension as *diachrony*, where can be revealed the ethical orientation: substitution *as* expiation for Other *beyond* the immanence of the *Said*. The very idea and task of philosophy will here be entirely refocused and redefined as wholly ethical *before* and *beyond* Being:

indeed, philosophy will engage in the possibility to incessantly awaken, through its *unsaying*, the *Said* to the *Saying*, elect the *Said beyond* thematization, meaning, categorization—*beyond* and *before* itself.

But "why philosophy?" Why this exigency to inscribe the *Saying* in the *Said* when the *Saying* in its "anarchy" remains always irreducible to the *Said* and ungraspable by it? Or again, why the necessity to translate the *Saying in the Said* and thereby perjure and betray the *Saying* in the immanence of the *Said*? Or again, and as Levinas phrases the question: "Why would proximity, the pure signification of saying, the anarchic one-for-the-other of *beyond* being, revert to being or fall into being, into a conjunction of entities, into essence showing itself in the said? Why have we gone to seek essence on its empyrean? Why know? Why is there a problem? Why philosophy?"[342]

Levinas answers: as the face-to-face relation is also inhabited by the Third party, the other of the Other, and thus of all the others. Indeed, for Levinas, the translation of the hyperbolic and *diachronic* ethical *Saying* into the immanence and synchrony of the *Said* incessantly calling the *Said* to perfect itself *beyond* itself is necessary as it also opens to a wholly novel dimension, that of justice for all others. Otherwise said, Levinas engages not only a responsibility *without* limit or finality for the singular Other but also, and through the necessary treason, betrayal, perjury of the hyperbolical *Saying* in the synchrony of the *Said* is revealed the novel possibility of thinking toward an idea of justice *for others beyond* and *before* the singular face-to-face relation from the Other toward the Self; a novel possibility of thinking toward an idea of justice which, through the singularity of the ethical responsibility for the singular Other, responds to all the *others of the Other*.

Levinas deploys through this necessary perjury or translation of the *Saying* in the *Said* a novel possibility of justice as *sociality*: a justice *beyond* the face-to-face relation—hyperbolic responsibility for the Other—which requests an incessant correction, perfectibility, exigency of rectification in the Sameness, the indifference, the anonymity of Being as a *redemption* as mending of *sociality* always and already seeing itself entirely oriented by singularity *before* and *beyond* universality, uniqueness *before* and *beyond* Sameness, exceptionality *before* and *beyond* generality, uniformity, identicalness. This novel possibility of justice as interruption and suspension of the *Said* through the incessant inspiration of the *Saying* which at once *unsays* the *Said* as projecting the Said to its incessant excess of itself for the Other does not negate the hyperbolical ethics of responsibility, does not foreclose the ethical election of an infinite responsibility. On the contrary! For Levinas, the idea of justice as responsibility in regard to all others of the Other, in regard to the Third party already inhabiting the face-to-face relation with the transcendence of the Other is thereby elected from the hyperbolic ethical commandment of the Other and inspires a furthering of responsibility toward all others of the Other. As Levinas marks:

All the others that obsess me in the other do not affect me as examples of the same genus united with my neighbor by resemblance or common nature, individuations of the human race, or chips of the same block, like the stones metamorphosed into men by Deucalion, who, behind his back, had to collect into cities with their hearts of stone. The others concern me from the first. Here fraternity precedes the commonness of a genus. My relationship with the other as neighbor gives meaning to my relations with all the others. All human relations as human proceed from disinterestedness. The one-for-the-Other of proximity is not a deforming abstraction. In it justice is shown from the first, it is thus born from the signifyingness of signification, the-one-for-the-other, signification. This means concretely or empirically that justice is not a legality regulating human masses, from which a technique of social equilibrium is drawn, harmonizing antagonistic forces. That would be a justification of the State delivered over to its own necessities. Justice is impossible without the one that renders it finding himself in proximity. His function is not limited to the "function of judgment," the subsuming of particular cases under a general rule. The judge is not outside the conflict, but the law is in the midst of proximity. Justice, society, the State and its institutions, exchanges and work are comprehensible out of proximity. This means that nothing is outside of the control of the responsibility of the One-for-the-Other. It is important to recover all these forms beginning with proximity, in which being, totality, the State, politics, techniques, work are at every moment on the point of having their center of gravitation in themselves, and weighing on their own account. In no way is justice a degradation of obsession, a degeneration of the for-the-other, a diminution, a limitation of anarchic responsibility, a neutralization of the glory of the Infinite, a degeneration that would be produced in the measure that for empirical reasons the initial duo would become a trio. But the contemporaneousness of the multiple is tied about the diachrony of two: justice remains justice only, in a society where there is no distinction between those close and those far off, but in which there also remains the impossibility of passing by the closest. The equality of all is borne by my inequality, the surplus of my duties over my rights. The forgetting of self moves justice.[343]

Sensibility (*Sensibilité*)

In *Totality and Infinity*, Levinas approaches sensibility by referring it principally to enjoyment (*jouissance*). Enjoyment however is not an experience fulfilled or satisfied by the possession or the grasp of an object. Rather Levinas thinks enjoyment as the "quasi-eternal immemoriality of the element":[344] that is, an event *without* substance, an occurrence *without* essence, a happening *without* fulfillment or satisfaction. Which entails, for Levinas, that sensibility indicates an *exposition* to that which retracts from presence, to that which remains irreducible to "being-there," and thus to that which incessantly remains *beyond* one's grasp, categorization, appropriation. In this sense, for Levinas, sensibility opens to a certain contact or proximity which does not seek to comprehend, appropriate or reappropriate. Sensibility engages rather a certain suspension of comprehension and interruption of recognition: "Sensibility does not aim at an object, however rudimentary. [. . .] its proper work consists in enjoyment, through which every object is dissolved into the element in which enjoyment is steeped."[345] Which entails that sensibility relates, before reason and rationality, presentation and representation, to an exteriority *without* concept and thus marks the incessant transcending of the *ego* toward an ungraspable and unrepresentable Other. Sensibility enacts separation through which the I incessantly "transcends itself": "But sensibility is not a blind reason or folly. It is prior to reason; the sensible is not to be ascribed to the totality to which it is closed. Sensibility enacts the very separation of being—separated and independent."[346]

This is why, always in *Totality and Infinity*, Levinas typifies sensibility in relation to the face of the Other—however, this relation entails the radical dissociation of sensibility from enjoyment. Sensibility will be seen as an experience always *beyond* experience, a disposition which incessantly transcends itself to the point of transferring itself to that which opens it to that which lies *beyond* itself, beyond what is experienced. Sensibility is thus always and already engaged, called, oriented toward the Other and thus elected and awakened by the absolute transcendence of the Other. In this sense, and if the transcendent cuts across sensibility, if its vision is the vision of the very openness of being, it cuts across this vision of forms. It breaks the monopoly and indifference of Being to let arise the Other. Sensibility thus for Levinas means—that is turns toward the Other— the face of the Other and its revelation is speech, discourse, commandment. For Levinas, the relation with the Other introduces transcendence and leads the Self to a relation wholly different from experience in the sensible sense of the term, relative and egoist: sensibility as ethical commandment for the Other.[347]

In *Otherwise than Being, or Beyond Essence*, sensibility will be seen as *vulnerability* and thus as radical exposition, passivity more passive than any or all passivity, to the Other for the Other. It is important to note however that, for Levinas, this *shift* which begins with enjoyment and becomes preeminent openness to the absolute transcendence of the Other revealing itself in the face of the Other in *Totality and Infinity* to vulnerability, passivity, exposition in substitution *as* expiation for the Other in *Otherwise than Being, or Beyond*

Essence does not mean to cancel out or negate the first approach of sensibility. All to the contrary! Levinas develops—from the relation between sensibility and enjoyment, sensibility and transcendence, from the exposition to an element *without* substance, an event *without* essence, a happening *without* fulfillment or satisfaction and which remains irreducible to comprehension or appropriation—the idea of sensibility *as* vulnerability. Indeed, the analysis and explication of *Totality and Infinity* on sensibility and the face of the Other conditions, in a certain manner, the demonstration in *Otherwise than Being, or Beyond Essence* of sensibility *as* vulnerability, of the irreplaceable exposition always and already exposing itself further, always and already furthering itself for the alterity of the Other. Indeed, *Otherwise than Being, or Beyond Essence*, retrieving the phenomenological description of sensibility in *Totality and Infinity* by radicalizing it *beyond* its phenomenological horizon, thinks sensibility as obsession, persecution, trauma, and thus as passivity more passive than any or all passivity and, in this sense, as exposition always exposing itself further to the Other for the Other. Sensibility here signifies the inalterable and irreplaceable election of the Self to the ethical, that is to a responsibility *without* limit or limitation for the Other: subjection to the commandment of the Other *before* autonomy and *beyond* judgment, *before* independence and *beyond* identity, *before* self-determination and always expecting the ethical to extend beyond what it can determine as such. Levinas indeed writes, in the opening pages of *Otherwise than Being, or Beyond Essence*: "This breakup of identity, this changing of being into signification, that is, into substitution, is the subject's subjectivity, or its subjection to everything, its susceptibility, its vulnerability, that is, its sensibility."[348]

As said, it is precisely in this sensibility as extreme vulnerability that Levinas marks and situates the awakening and election of the ethical Self as infinite responsibility to the point of substitution and expiation. But this sensibility is hyperbolical and irreducible to its categorization or formalization: it exposes the ethical Self infinitely to the Other. Ultimately thus, it marks the ethical Self as both *host* and *hostage* of the Other for the Other; that is, entirely riveted *before* the Self itself, always anterior to the Self's constitution and self-determination, and thus always elected by the Other to extend its responsibility *beyond* the Self itself, as substitution and expiation, for the Other:

> Vulnerability, exposure to outrage, to wounding, passivity more passive than all patience, passivity of the accusative form, trauma of accusation suffered by a hostage to the point of persecution, implicating the identity of the hostage who substitutes himself for the others: all this is the self, a defecting or defeat of the ego's identity. And this, pushed to the limit, is sensibility, sensibility as the subjectivity of the subject. It is a substitution for another, one in the place of another, expiation. Responsibility for the other, in its antecedence to my freedom, its antecedence to the present and to representation, is a

passivity more passive than all passivity, an exposure to the other without this exposure being assumed, an exposure without holding back, exposure of exposedness, expression, Saying. This exposure is the frankness, sincerity, veracity of saying. Not saying dissimulating itself and protecting itself in the said, just giving out words in the face of the other, but saying uncovering itself, that is, denuding itself of its skin, sensibility on the surface of the skin, at the edge of the nerves, offering itself even in suffering—and thus wholly sign, signifying itself. Substitution, at the limit of being, ends up in saying, in the giving of signs, giving a sign of this giving of signs, expressing oneself. This expression is antecedent to all thematization in the said, but it is not a babbling or still primitive or childish form of saying. This stripping *beyond* nudity, *beyond* forms, is not the work of negation and no longer belongs to the order of being. Responsibility goes *beyond* being. In sincerity, in frankness, in the veracity of this saying, in the uncoveredness of suffering, being is altered. But this saying remains, in its activity, a passivity, more passive than all passivity, for it is a sacrifice without reserve, without holding back, and in this non-voluntary—the sacrifice of a hostage designated who has not chosen himself to be hostage, but possibly elected by the Good, in an involuntary election not assumed by the elected one. For the Good cannot enter into a present nor be put into a representation. But being Good it redeems the violence of its alterity, even if the subject has to suffer through the augmentation of this ever more demanding violence.[349]

Separation (*Séparation*)

The term and idea of separation, which is largely developed in *Totality and Infinity* clearly retrieves the notion of *hypostasis*—and specifically its interpretation, description, and analysis in *Existence and Existents*.

Separation, and the manner it is employed and deployed in Levinas' ethics as "First Philosophy," institutes an *interiority*, that of the Self, which poses and opposes itself to the anonymity and indifference of Being. Indeed, separation designates the *interiority of the Self* which poses its own Self as separation from Being. Separation is revealed firstly in enjoyment and also in the being "one-self at home" ("*chez-soi*") of the Self. Separation thus reveals a *discontinuity* in Being with Being, a break, a differentiation, a certain extraction or even evasion which interrupts the ontological order of indifference, anonymity, identicalness in the always fulfilled presence of Being.

Separation as that movement where the Self enjoys its own Self as one's Self and retreats into its "being at home" with itself extracted from the ontological order of Being also instills the oblivion or the ignorance of the Other; the Self separates itself in Being from the anonymity and indifference of Being however does so to maintain itself with its own Self in enjoyment and in "being at home" with itself foreclosing radically and entirely the Other. Going to the limit of this separation, Levinas marks thus: "One can call atheism this separation so complete that the separated being maintains itself in existence all by itself, without participating in the Being which it is separated—eventually capable of adhering to it by belief. The break with participation is implied in this capability. One lives outside of God at home with oneself; one is an I, an egoism."[350] In this sense, separation designates the rupture and break of the speculative *and* ontological categories in defining the Self as separated and thus as the "position" of the Self and the reference of the Self to its own Self absolved from its encapsulation in the presence, meaning and totality of Being:

> Subjective existence derives its features from separation. Individuation—an inner identification of a being whose essence is exhausted in identity, an identification of the same—does not come to strike the terms of some relation called separation. Separation is the very act of individuation, the possibility in general for an entity which is posited in being to be posited not by being defined by its reference to a whole, by its place within a system, but starting from itself. The fact of starting from oneself is equivalent to separation. But the act of starting from oneself and separation itself can be produced in being only by opening the dimension of interiority.[351]

Within this separation as "interiority"—and where the Self remains *with* itself as separated in Being from Being, and also thereby separated from the Other to settle in its ownmost egoism, enjoyment, home—also lies the oblique and paradoxal possibility of a *wholly other relation* where is revealed the absolute transcendence of the Other always and already inhabiting and overwhelming, exceeding and surpassing the Self. Separation also marks a certain suspension and interruption *in and as the singularity and unicity of the Self* by also revealing, in its enjoyment and within its "being at home with itself," in its separation in Being from Being, the *antecedence* and *precedence* of the Other.

Separation implies a rupture and a break with the Self in the Self, an interruption of the egoism of the Self in the revelation—which is irreducible to the manifestation or presentation—of the Other. Separation, for Levinas, serves thus a double function for the Self: break with the ontological determination of Being and its order of presence, the dialectical Sameness and identity which culminates in indifference and anonymity while also revealing for the Self, in enjoyment of itself and "being at home" with itself, the Other of the Self, the Other than the Self: the absolute transcendence of the Other *before* and *beyond* the Self.

This is why Levinas insists repeatedly on how and why separation invests and overwhelms all unicity, all identity, and surpasses the monistic egoism of the Self. The Other is not here grasped as a moment of a speculative totality where the Self would comprehend itself in an absolute identity with the Other through the dialectical process of negation and "negation of negation," nor as an instance within an ontological Sameness in which the Self and the Other would remain attuned and in tune, gathered and assembled within the essence and the truth of Being. As Levinas marks the relation between interiority and exteriority, between the Same and the Other, as a rapport irreducible to correlation, to inter-relation, to intersubjectivity, to "being-with-the-other", which all, in their own specific manners, reduce the Self and the Other to figures or moments of Sameness, identicalness, commonality. Separation opens thus to the irreducibility of difference between the Self and the Other, for, in and as separation, the Other remains irreducibly Other and transcending—inspiring and awakening—the interiority of the Self toward that which it cannot contain, appropriate, comprehend, or grasp in itself and for itself.

Separation opens to a relation *without* correlation between the Self and the Other, that is, a relation *without* ontological or dialectical presuppositions and, in this sense, a relation where the Other is not the negation of the Self or, inversely, the Self that from which the Other is recognized or comprehended. Rather, separation marks the incessant overwhelming of the Self by and through the absolute transcendence of the Other.

Levinas marks a relation of absolute *non-adequation*, or as he marks, a "non-allergic" relation between the Self and the Other which defines the possibility of *communication* and *dialogue*, *fecundity* and *filiality*: the ethical opening for the Other. As Levinas also writes in *Totality and Infinity* in the opening pages of Section IV, *Beyond the Face*:

> The relation with the Other does not nullify separation. It does not arise within a totality nor does it establish a totality, integrating me and the other. Nor does the face-to-face conjuncture presuppose the existence of universal truths into which subjectivity could be absorbed, and which it would be enough to contemplate for me and the other to enter into a relation of communion. Rather here the converse thesis must be maintained: the relation between me and the other commences in the inequality of terms, transcendent to one another, where alterity does not determine the other in a formal sense, as where the alterity of B with respect to A results simply from the identity of B, distinct from the identity of A. Here the alterity of the Other does not result from its identity, but constitutes it: the other is the Other. The Other qua Other is situated in a dimension of height and of abasement—glorious abasement; he has the face of the poor, the stranger,

> the widow, and the orphan, an at the same time of the master called to invest and justify my freedom.[352]

In *Otherwise than Being, or Beyond Essence*, the emphasis shifts from separation and exteriority, from the revelation in the Self of an Other always and already preceding the Self itself, to the absolute transcendence of the Other awakening the Self outside of itself, *beyond* and *before* itself for the Other. The face-to-face relation as transcendent commandment which pleads both as widow and orphan, master, stranger, the face of the poor and teacher is rethought as obsession, trauma, persecution of the Other engaging and electing the Self to the ethical in an incommensurate and incommensurable responsibility for the Other—a *one-for-the-Other* as *diachronical* exposition in substitution *as* expiation, which Levinas also refers to as an individuation preceded, invested and awakened as the finite freedom of the Self:

> No doubt the idea of a responsibility prior to freedom, and the compossibility of freedom and the other such as it shows itself in responsibility for another, enables us to confer an irreducible meaning to this notion, without attacking the dignity of freedom which is thus conceived in finitude. What else can finite freedom mean? How can a will be partially free? How can the Fichtean free ego undergo the suffering that would come to it from the non-ego? Does the finitude of freedom signify the necessity by which a will to will finds itself in a given situation which limits the arbitrariness of the will? That does not cut into the infinity of freedom *beyond* what the situation determines. In finite freedom, there can then be disengaged an element of pure freedom, which limitation does not affect, in one's will. Thus the notion of finite freedom rather poses than resolves the problem of a limitation of the freedom of the will. The responsibility for another, an unlimited responsibility which the strict book-keeping of the free and non-free does not measure, requires subjectivity as an irreplaceable hostage. This subjectivity it denudes under the ego in a passivity of persecution, repression and expulsion outside of essence, into oneself. In this self, outside of essence, one is in a deathlike passivity! But in responsibility for the other for life and death, the adjectives unconditional, undeclinable, absolute take on meaning. They serve to qualify freedom, but wear away the substrate, from which the free act arises in essence. In the accusative form, which is a modification of no nominative form, in which I approach the neighbor for whom, without having wished it, I have to answer, the irreplaceable one is brought out (*s'accuse*). This finite freedom is not primary, is not initial; but it lies in an infinite responsibility where the Other is not other because he strikes up against and limits my freedom, but where he can accuse me to the point of persecution, because the Other,

> absolutely Other, is another one. That is why finite freedom is not simply an infinite freedom operating in a limited field. The will which it animates wills in a passivity it does not assume. And the proximity of the neighbor in its trauma does not only strike up against me, but exalts and elevates me, and, in the literal sense of the term, inspires me. Inspiration, heteronomy, is the very pneuma of the *psyche*. Freedom is borne by the responsibility it could not shoulder, an elevation and inspiration without complacency.[353]

Signification (*Signification*)

Levinas clearly distinguishes two signifiers of signification: an *ethical* and an *ontological*. This primordial opposition is noticeable and indeed sustained from the most early writings to the later texts.

The ontological origin of signification is typified by Levinas through the modality of identification, thematization, and constitution of manifestation and phenomenality. The ontological thus means for Levinas the possibility for the *ego*, as "consciousness for . . . ," to appropriate in and within the horizon of its comprehension the contextual meaningfulness and intentionality of phenomenality. It thus supposes a certain process of reduction and comprehension where and in which the possibility of constituting, in presence, the essence of that which occurs and is given is rendered present, manifest, phenomenal.

On the other hand, the *ethical* source of signification—this "*other* source of signification"[354]—is marked as *exposition* to the Other, response of infinite responsibility for the Other:

> The conjuncture in which a man is responsible for other men, the ethical relationship, which is habitually considered as belonging to a derivative or founded order, has been throughout this work approached as irreducible. It is structured as the-one-for-the-other. It signifies outside of all finality and every system, where finality is but one of the principles of systematization possible. This responsibility appears as a plot without a beginning, anarchic. No freedom, no commitment undertaken in a present, a present among others, recuperable, is the obverse of which this responsibility would be the reverse, but no slavery is included in the alienation of the same who is "for the other".[355]

The ethical arises, for Levinas, otherwise than within the confines of intentionality or comprehension, and testifies of a break, a rupture, an overflowing, and an excess incessantly exceeding and thereby interrupting the order of the ontological and the horizon of presence, identicalness, Sameness. Indeed, for Levinas, the ethical arrives and comes to the Self from *beyond* and *before* the Self as transcendent commandment of the Other. The ethical is opened as *wholly otherwise* than through the autonomy of the moral subject, universal normativity, mutual recognition, or intersubjective empathy. Why and how? First, for the ethical speaks of the Other as irreducibly inassimilable to ontology and to the intentionality of the Same. The ethical as commandment of the Other incessantly overwhelms the Self's capacity of both intuition and understanding, comprehension or self-determination. Which means, for Levinas: the ethical as signification is always and already for the Other as irreducible event unassimilable within the prehension or comprehension of Being:

> In responsibility the same, the *ego*, is me, summoned, provoked, as irreplaceable, and thus accused as unique in the supreme passivity of one that cannot slip away without fault. The models of being and the subject-object correlation, which are justifiable but derivative, do not depict signification, the-one-for-the-other. It indeed shows itself in the said, but does so only after the event, betrayed, foreign to the said of being; it shows itself in it as a contradiction—which incites Plato to parricide. To understand that A could be B, nothingness has to be a sort of being. Matrix of every thematizable relation, the-one-for-the-other, signification, sense or intelligibility, does not rest in being. Its restlessness must not be put in terms of rest.[356]

Without prior commitment or engagement, but *already and always engaged and elected by the Other for the Other*, signification is revealed through the ethical as interruption of the ontological order, indifference and anonymity, precisely where the commandment of the Other ruptures the ontological intentionality of the Same. Which means for Levinas: signification through the ethical wholly other than thematization or comprehension, but as proximity, and thereby, the proximity of the Other.

The duality and distinction between the ontological and the ethical is also typified by Levinas in the opposition between the *Saying* and the *Said*. Indeed, this opposition engages a novel passage between the ethical and the ontological. Far from settling for the determination of a ground where one would found the other, or a dialectical movement between the ethical and the ontological completing each other in their comprehension, Levinas seeks to deploy a singular and exceptional "logic" of the Other-in-the-Same as "one-for-the-Other" and thus of the ethical *in the* ontological as the ontological overwhelmed and inspired through the ethical.

Which means the Self is signified by the Other to signify itself as host and hostage of the Other for the Other:

> It guides discourse *beyond* being. By the implication of the one in the-one-for-the-other, by the substitution of the One-for-the-Other, the foundations of being are shaken or ensured. But this undermining or this ensuring do not in any way belong to being's deed, contrary to the mythologies in which the origin of things and beings is already the effect of a history that happens to things and beings called gods, or cast in an imposing format. The signifyingness of signification is not brought about as a mode of representation, nor as the symbolic evocation of an absence, that is, a makeshift or a failing of presence. Nor as an outdoing of presence, as idealism conceives of subjectivity, where presence rejoins and confirms itself and becomes a coinciding. There is indeed an outdoing in signification: the implication of the one in the *one-for-the-other* in responsibility goes *beyond* the representable unity of the identical, not by a surplus or lack of presence, but by the uniqueness of the ego, my uniqueness as a respondent, a hostage, for whom no one else could be substituted without transforming responsibility into a theatrical role. The play of being and nothingness does not reduce this signification to nonsense. The condition of being hostage is not chosen; if there had been a choice, the subject would have kept his *as-for-me*, and the exits found in inner life. But this subjectivity, his very psyche, is *for the other*, his very bearing independence consists in supporting the other, expiating for him. The implication of the one in the *one-for-the-other* is then not reducible to the way a term is implicated in a relationship, an element in a structure, a structure in a system, which Western thought in all its forms sought for as a sure harbor, or a place of retreat which the soul should enter.

Levinas' philosophical gesture seeks here to engage *another* modality of signification where the ethical always *exceeds* the ontological while already inspiring it to incessantly outdo and further itself *beyond* itself. And thus where the ethical already suspends or interrupts thematization and representation and thereby provokes the Self outside of its own Self, *beyond* and before itself in its responsibility for the Other. Taken to the limit of this hyperbolical signification of the ethical: the Other engages and elects the Self *beyond* the Self *before* the Self in a response of infinite responsibility—substitution and expiation—for the Other. This singular and exceptional "logic" of the Other-in-the-Same as the Same always and already exposed—elected and inspired—for the Other calls on to rethink the structure of supposition and presupposition from the idea of the infinite as that immemorial election always and already assigning the Self for and to the Other:

> in a way very different from commitment that the one is implicated in the-one-for-the-other. It is not a question of a forsakenness in a world, a situation which is from the first its own reversal, in which I can settle and build myself a place, a situation that is produced and reverses into the representation of a diversity put in conjunction. It is a question of a signification in which the meaning of establishment and representation are indeed justified, but this signification signifies prior to any world, signifies the proximity of the same and the other, in which the implication of the one in the other signifies the assignation of the one by the other. This assignation is the very signifyingness of signification, or the *psyche* of the same. Through the *psyche* proximity is my approaching of the other, the fact that the proximity of the same and the other is never close enough. The summoned one is the ego—me. I repel and send away the neighbor through my very identity, my occupying the arena of being; I then have always to reestablish peace. What in this signifying, in this the-one-for-the-other, can and must lead to knowing, to questioning, to the "what is this about . . . ," the explicit formulation of a familiarity with being as though it had been antecedent and implicit—what in this signifying leads to ontology and thus to presence, to the shadowless high noon manifestation of truth, to reckoning, thought, settling down, institution—we will no doubt have to show. But neither this familiarity nor the ontological movements found the approach. The antecedent familiarity with being is not prior to the approach. The sense of the approach is goodness, without knowledge or blindness, *beyond* essence. Goodness will indeed show itself in ontology metamorphosed into essence, and to be reduced; but essence cannot contain it.[357]

Levinas firstly defines ontological signification—in line with Husserlian phenomenology—as emanating and occurring within the original consciousness of temporality and its passive syntheses, that is within the *dephasing* of the original impression in both *retention* and *protention* as the very modality by which is fulfilled the *identification* of phenomena and the *appropriation* of the present as meaning and intentionality. For Levinas, this ontological signification—and its essential ground in an original temporality in which the *verbality* of essence is always that from which and in which entities and phenomenality are designated, named, constituted—is *not* the *ultimate* mode or modality of signification. And indeed, it is precisely in this hyperbolical effort to think toward a *non-intentional* character in sensibility that Levinas will engage a signification which is not reducible to the present or the "lived-present," irreducible to the original temporality of intentionality.

And furthermore, open toward a sensibility understood as proximity and vulnerability; a sensibility thus entirely oriented as that which lies and opens to a *beyond* intentionality, *beyond* essence, and thus *beyond* intentionality; *beyond* irreducible to the process and the order by which entities are signified in and through their being-present, their being in presence, their presence as Being. In this sense, the *Saying* is not identification or categorization: it means absolute exposition to the Other, to the face and the commandment of the Other, irreducible to phenomenality and thematization, categorization and intentionality. The *Saying* means *being already* exposed to the Other for the Other and, in this sense, openness asalways exceeded and inspired by the Other:

> Saying is not a game. Antecedent to the verbal signs it conjugates, to the linguistic systems and the semantic glimmerings, a foreword preceding languages, it is the proximity of one to the other, the commitment of an approach, the One-for-the-Other, the very signifyingness of signification. (But is approach to be defined by commitment, and not rather commitment by approach? Perhaps because of current moral maxims in which the word neighbor occurs, we have ceased to be surprised by all that is involved in proximity and approach.) The original or pre-original saying, what is put forth in the foreword, weaves an intrigue of responsibility. It sets forth an order more grave than being and antecedent to being. By comparison being appears like a game. Being is play or detente, without responsibility, where everything possible is permitted.[358]

Subjectivity (*Subjectivité*)

The meaning of the term *subjectivity* is entirely reformulated by Levinas. Indeed, contrarily to the philosophical tradition, at least since Descartes, which has determined *subjectivity* as absolute foundation, identity or presence to itself as auto-reflexive consciousness and furthermore by aligning the subject to the possibility of representation in and through its appropriation and opposition to that which it is not, namely the *object*, Levinas proposes to rethink subjectivity as host and hostage, that is as *subjected exposition and election* to and by the commandment of the Other. Indeed, "subjectivity is not a modality of essence,"[359] for Levinas, which means:

> Our inquiry concerned with the *otherwise than being* catches sight, in the very hypostasis of a subject, its *subjectification*, of an exception; a null-site on the hither side of the negativity which is always speculatively recuperable, an outside of the absolute which can no longer be stated in terms of being. Nor even in terms of entities, which one would suspect

> modulate being, and thus heal the break marked by the hypostasis. The subject already resists this ontologization when it is conceived as a saying. Behind every statement of being as being, the saying overflows the very being it thematizes in stating it to the other. It is being which is understood in the—first or last—word, but the last saying goes *beyond* the being thematized or totalized. Irreducible to being's essence is the substitution in responsibility, signification or the one-for-another, or the defecting of the ego *beyond* every defeat, going countercurrent to a conatus, or goodness. In it the other is imposed quite differently from the reality of the real: he imposes himself because he is other, because this alterity is incumbent on me with a whole charge of indigence and weakness.[360]

In this manner, Levinas reads in *subjectivity* its *subjugation* as *exposition* and *exception*, furthermore as *substitution as expiation* where is opened the ethical as infinite responsibility for the Other. For Levinas, the *subject* is always and already, immemorially, subjected to responsibility *before* being responsible of its own selfhood, autonomy, mortality and always engaged *beyond* its self-determination for the Other. And this infinite responsibility *before* the Self's identity purporting it *beyond* its self-determination occurs as *election* for the Other in the commandment, the appeal, the demand, and the plea expressed in the face of the Other: "Thou shall not kill." "Thou shall not kill" the neighbor who is also always an absolute stranger; which also means, for the subject and the ethical Self, the incessant responsibility to *substitute* itself as autonomous subject, sovereign and self-governing, to respond unconditionally as *subjugation*, an *expiation* for the Other; subjugation to the point of *substitution* for the Other as expiation for the Other in the face of the death of the Other.

In this sense, for Levinas, *subjectivity* always signifies an inextinguishable *passion* wholly awakened by the ethical commandment expressed in the face of the Other and as responsibility of all *before* all—a pre-originary responsibility immemorially oriented toward the Other *before* the constitution of an autonomous subject, self-determination or *ego* and always *beyond* what the Self can or could determine or consign in its responsibility for the Other.

Levinas marks *subjectivity* as always and already *of* the Other, responsiveness and responsibility to and for the Other. Which is not without also indicating that *subjectivity*, for Levinas, implies and presupposes an absence of ground or foundation and thus engages an *awakening* as ethical Self by the Other—which means: *subjectivity* as *subjected* to the Other as infinite responsibility for the Other in non-indifference to the Other, and thus exception, election, singularization *beyond* and outside, *before* and preceding the constitution of its autonomy, sovereignty, or participating in an intersubjective "being-together" between egos and alter-egos, contractual sociality, or originary spiritual community.

This reversal and upheaval of the traditional concept of *subjectivity* opens to what Levinas will call a *humanism of the Other*, that is, a "humanism" which *suspends* the universality of humanism by *interrupting* and *suspending* the position and positioning of the subject as autonomous instantiation of universal reason and morality normativity. Indeed, and in order to open toward an *excess* of humanism *beyond* classical humanism, Levinas interprets humanism as that which always and already presupposes the commandment of the Other *before* the institution and constitution of the Self as modality, ground and foundation of universality. Levinas engages to think a Self as ethical *beyond* reason and rationality, *before* autonomy and self-determination, that is, a Self always elected *before* and *beyond* the constitution of its own Self. Which means: an ethical Self elected *before* and *beyond* the ontological foundation of the Self—an ethical Self always and already oriented as infinite responsibility for the Other through its *immemorial subjection* to the plea expressed in the irreducible and singular, irreplaceable, irreappropriable suffering of the Other.

Never *ego* in the nominative, neither actor nor agent, transposition from subjectivity to Self, the ethical marks the passivity of the Self as exposed to the commandment of the Other in the face-to-face encounter immemorially signifying the *other-in-the-same* as *one-for-the-other*. As Levinas marks: the Other inhabiting the Same, the Other always and already interrupting and suspending the Same deploys a subjectivity as immemorial allegiance in responsibility for the Other. As Levinas marks:

> subjectivity is the *Other-in-the-Same*, in a way that also differs from that of the presence of interlocutors to one another in a dialogue, in which they are at peace and in agreement with one another. The Other-in-the-Same determinative of subjectivity is the restlessness of the same disturbed by the other. This is not the correlation characteristic of intentionality, nor even that of dialogue, which attests to essence by its essential reciprocity. The folding back of being upon itself, and the self formed by this fold, where the effect of being remains correlative with being, also does not go to the crux of subjectivity. The knot tied in subjectivity, which when subjectivity become a consciousness of being is still attested to in questioning, signifies an allegiance of the same to the other, imposed before any exhibition of the other, preliminary to all consciousness—or a being affected by the other whom I do not know and who could not justify himself with any identity, who as other will not identify himself with anything. This allegiance will be described as a responsibility of the same for the other, as a response to his proximity before any question. In this responsibility the latent birth of consciousness itself as a perception or listening in to being, can be surprised, and dialogue based on questioning.[361]

The ethical Self "is" subjectivity *as subjected*—passivity more passive than all passivity, awakened and elected in the wake of the transcendent Height of the Other and in the trace of the Infinite:

> There is an extreme passivity of *Saying* even in its last refuge; there is exposure to the other, a being required where no slipping away is possible. Uniqueness signifies through the non-coinciding with oneself, the non-repose in oneself, restlessness. It is the reverse of certainty that falls back on itself; it does not identify itself and does not appear to knowing. It is in deficit, a point of pain. But, like the unity of the Kantian "I think", it is undeclinable in this passivity without any play. As an exception, and by abuse of language, one can name it me or I. But the denomination here is only a pronomination; there is nothing that is named I; the I is said by him that speaks. The pronoun already dissimulates the unique one that is speaking, subsumes it under a concept. But it designates only the mask or the person of the unique one, the mask that leaves the I evading concepts, the I involved in saying in the first person, absolutely unconvertible into a noun. For it is a sign given of this giving of signs, the exposure of oneself to another, in proximity and in sincerity. The subject in responsibility, like the unity of transcendental apperception, is not the semelfacticity of a unique exemplar, such as it manifests itself to be in the said, in tales; 'once upon a time' Here uniqueness means the impossibility of slipping away and being replaced, in which the very recurrence of the I is effected. The uniqueness of the chosen or required one, who is not a chooser, is a passivity not being converted into spontaneity. This uniqueness not assumed, not subsumed, is traumatic; it is an election in persecution.[362]

Substitution (*Substitution*)

The term substitution literally means the act of using someone or something *in the place* of another person or thing. The word thus indicates the act of replacing someone or something with another, and by extension of exchanging one with another. The term, however and for Levinas, conceals a further and deeper signification which suspends this primary utilitarian meaning. For Levinas, substitution indicates the possibility of responding for the Other, that is, of taking heed, and, in this sense, of carrying, and thereby of supporting and espousing, the Other's suffering and faults. For Levinas, substitution engages thus the responsibility of giving one's Self *before* autonomy, decision, sovereignty, and *beyond* what can be expected or demanded, for the Other. In this sense, substitution means being elected by the Other for the Other in responding *before* the Self and *beyond* what the Self can determine or fulfill in its response of responsibility for the Other. Which means: substitution entails an ethical Self carrying and caring *beyond* its capacities or capabilities and *before* its autonomy or sovereignty, for the irreducible and irreplaceable suffering and vulnerability of the Other.

For Levinas, substitution appears in *Otherwise than Being, or Beyond Essence*. Substitution opens to the infinite and *infinitizing* responsibility for the Other as extreme ethical *possibility* of sacrifice which is always furthered through its non-actualization and non-realization or fulfillment. In this sense, substitution is allied and inextricable from the idea of sacrifice which Levinas interprets *without* signifying sacrifice as an operation of repudiation of the Self, and thus never as self-sacrifice, nor as an economy of conciliation, reconciliation, elevation, and sublimation, through the abnegation of the Self. To substitute oneself for the Other does not amount to sacrificing one's Self to the Other, to negate and abandon one's Self to the Other. Nor does it mean replacing the Other by the Self. All to the contrary! Substitution for the Other entails the incessant awakening and election of the ethical in the Self which sees itself always and already engaged in a responsibility *without* beginning or finality for the Other. In this sense, substitution entails responding to the defenselessness, the nakedness, the vulnerability, to the death and mortality of the Other *before* the autonomy of the Self and *beyond* what the Self could determine as its response for the Other. For Levinas, the Self rises and is aroused, elected in this responding *before* its own self-determination and *beyond* its autonomy; the ethical Self thus, far from negating itself for the Other, is here awakened and elected to its own Self as always and already respondent for the Other.

It is here that the ethical Self bears the weight of the Other for the Other. The ethical Self, *before* its interestedness and complacency, sovereignty, and perseverance in Being, *before* its own Self, is elected in response *beyond* what it can or could plan or determine, that is *without* reserve or replacement, uniquely and singularly, in infinite responsibility for the Other.

Substitution marks a responsibility as *unsubstitutable* exposition for the Other and thus engages a Self which, as host to the point of being hostage of the Other, has immemorially carried the Other, responding *before* and *beyond* its own Self for the Other. Indeed, the ethical Self already suffers and acquiesces for the Other the faults and the wrongs of the Other: inspiration by the Other for the Other:

> Far from being recognized in the freedom of consciousness, which loses itself and finds itself again, which, as a freedom, relaxes the order of being so as to reintegrate it in a free responsibility, the responsibility for the other, the responsibility in obsession, suggests an absolute passivity of

> a self that has never been able to diverge from itself, to then enter into its limits, and identify itself by recognizing itself in its past. Its recurrence is the contracting of an ego, going to the hither side of identity, gnawing away at this very identity—identity gnawing away at itself—in a remorse. Responsibility for another is not an accident that happens to a subject, but precedes essence in it, has not awaited freedom, in which a commitment to another would have been made. I have not done anything and I have always been under accusation—persecuted. The ipseity, in the passivity without arche characteristic of identity, is a hostage. The word I means *here I am*, answering for everything and for everyone. Responsibility for the others has not been a return to oneself, but an exasperated contracting, which the limits of identity cannot retain. Recurrence becomes identity in breaking up the limits of identity, breaking up the principle of being in me, the intolerable rest in itself characteristic of definition. The self is on the hither side of rest; it is the impossibility to come back from all things and concern oneself only with oneself. It is to hold on to oneself while gnawing away at oneself. Responsibility in obsession is a responsibility of the *ego* for what the ego has not wished, that is, for the others. This anarchy in the recurrence to oneself is *beyond* the normal play of action and passion in which the identity of a being is maintained, in which it is. It is on the hither side of the limits of identity. This passivity undergone in proximity by the force of an alterity in me is the passivity of a recurrence to oneself which is not the alienation of an identity betrayed. What can it be but a substitution of me for the others? It is, however not an alienation, because the Other-in-the-Same is my substitution for the other through responsibility, for which, I am summoned as someone irreplaceable. I exist through the other and for the other, but without this being alienation: I am inspired.[363]

Substitution means the inescapable and unique responsibility assuming the suffering of the Other for the Other—and thus engages, far from the self-sacrifice of the Self, the awakening and the election of the ethical in the Self immemorially hosting as hostage of the Other *beyond* its own capacity and *before* its sovereignty to the point of being engaged wholly as response and responsibility for the Other; host and hostage of the Other for the Other. Overwhelming and thereby dismantling the *conatus essendi* of subjectivity, the ethical Self is elected to a response as if the Self were already "guilty" *without* wrongdoing or offence. This immemorial "guilt" *without* fault, this indebtedness *without* loan as substitution engages an approach of the Other *without* economy of return: an approach of pure exposition, unconditional, and inescapable election as responsibility for the Other.

Which is why substitution informs the exceptionality of the ethical Self: indeed, the ethical Self is awakened by the Other through the Other as exposition and election, substitution, *before* the Self can affirm its own Self as free will, self-consciousness, or self-identity and always *beyond* what it can or could determine in its response of responsibility for the Other. Without being a simple inversion of egoity, the ethical Self as substitution marks the infinite exposition, passivity more passive than all passivity, which is always and already turned for the Other toward the Other and which engages the Self, *before* and *beyond* itself, as responsibility for the Other. Substitution, whose very kernel lies in the "one-for-the-Other" as the election of an irreplaceable and unique host as hostage of the Other for the Other, marks how the ethical Self is radically unsubstitutable and inimitable, and thus, as infinitely responsible, responsible more than any other and where this responsibility is always and already irremediable and unfulfillable always and already responds in ethical responsibility.

The ethical Self, always and already elected to responsibility as substitution responds for the Other as both *host* and *hostage* of the Other where no other can substitute one's Self for the ethical Self. No other Self can substitute itself for myself in my substitution for the Other. Which means: substitution occurs through the absolute exposition of the Self as singularly irreplaceable and uniquely called and elected for the Other. And thus substitution means the exposition of the Self's singularity in and only in responsibility for the Other:

> In this substitution, in which identity is inverted, this passivity more passive still than the passivity conjoined with action, *beyond* the inert passivity of the designated, the self is absolved of itself. Is this freedom? It is a different freedom from that of an initiative. Through substitution for others, the oneself escapes relations. At the limit of passivity, the oneself escapes passivity or the inevitable limitation that the terms within relation undergo. In the incomparable relationship of responsibility, the other no longer limits the same, it is supported by what it limits. Here the overdetermination of the ontological categories is visible, which transforms them into ethical terms. In this most passive passivity, the self-liberates itself ethically from every other and from itself. Its responsibility for the other, the proximity of the neighbor, does not signify a submission to the non-ego; it means an openness in which being's essence is surpassed in inspiration. It is an openness of which respiration is a modality or a foretaste, or, more exactly, of which it retains the aftertaste. Outside of any mysticism, in this respiration, the possibility of every sacrifice for the other, activity and passivity coincide.[364]

It is thus important to note here, and as we sketched above, how and why the hyperbolical modality of substitution is not apprehensible as sacrifice or self-sacrifice; most notably in its traditional theological and philosophical definitions which imply the transformation and elevation of the profane to the sacred as reconciliation of finitude and infinitude in a fulfilled comprehension (Hegel) where the sacrificed is always and already integrated, interiorized, internalized within a general economy and narrative of signification and where it is simply relegated to a past justified in the deployment of a greater and more enveloping intentionality. Otherwise said, the traditional, philosophical and theological, definitions of sacrifice as essence of History where the singularity of historical events is always sacrificed in the name of a general Reason in History. Indeed, Levinas will offer a radical reinterpretation of the question of sacrifice and read in sacrifice the *approach* always renewed, never accomplished, always futural, always to come, never fulfilled of the one-for-the-Other. And thus *approach* as *infinitization* of responsibility, of giving one's Self always more than how and what the Self can give of itself, excess and supplement of responsibility for the Other. And thus, approaching the Other incessantly overwhelming, surpassing, exceeding itself for the Other—*givenness without* measure of the Self always and already giving more of itself than it can or could for the Other.

Wholly otherwise than a sacrifice or a self-sacrifice, substitution engages the ethical Self in an incessant hyperbolic responsibility for the Other which repudiates and denies the sublimity or symbolism, the empty moralism or lofty heroism in the self-abnegation of sacrifice. All to the contrary of the logic of sacrifice and self-sacrifice which Levinas always suspects of emanating from a willing, a self-determination, a form of exercising a sovereignty, substitution proceeds *without* sacrifice or self-sacrifice and indeed interrupts the tendency of sacrifice or self-sacrifice which always accomplishes and fulfills itself in an absolution. Substitution, for Levinas, rather engages the Self in its election and inspiration as infinite responsibility, responsibility *infinitizing* itself always further, for the Other. Election *without* self-negation and inspiration *without* finality as responsibility incessantly exceeding and supplementing its exposition for the Other. For Levinas, to reduce substitution and its *diachronical* excess of responsibility for the Other to the operativity of a sacrifice or a self-sacrifice, however moral such an abnegation could seem, would mean to suppress and negate the ethical itself. That is, reducing substitution for the Other to sacrifice or self-sacrifice would repress and comprehend, totalize, substantialize, essentialize the incessant exceeding, transcending, *infinitization* of responsibility for the Other. It would mean to simply cancel out the ethical. This is why Levinas notes that substitution marks the *possibility of every sacrifice* for the Other and never the effectivity or actuality of sacrifice itself. Levinas indeed marks how and why substitution for the Other precedes self-sacrifice and remains irreducible to an "ethics" of self-sacrifice.

In this sense, the ethical Self is subjected to the Other, already given over and exposed to the Other, responsible for the suffering of the Other as unescapable and inexorable responsibility *without* limit or finality. The ethical Self is suffering for the Other by the Other which Levinas also marks as the ethical Self's *obsession* of the Other. Obsession of the Other in the unilateral vocation for the Other *without* avoidance or refrainment, the ethical Self gives itself for the Other *before* any engagement or non-engagement. Gift of one's Self *without* measure, incessantly exceeding itself for the Other, substitution as ethical responsibility always and already, and by its incessant excess of itself in responsibility for the Other impossibilizing the self-abnegation of the Self in a self-sacrifice.

This is also why substitution is not assimilable to compassion or sympathy: to suffer for the Other means to suffer by the Other singularly, exceptionally, and thereby respond infinitely and *without* escape to the Other for the Other *before* the autonomy or the identity of the Self and *beyond* what the Self can determine or project in its response of responsibility. In this sense, substitution is inseparable from the election, and thus the awakening, of the ethical Self—election and awakening to an unescapable responsibility *without* limit for the Other. Substitution for the Other thus means impossibility to replace the ethical Self in its unique and singular responsibility for the Other. Which brings Levinas to rephrase as substitution the *diachrony* of responsibility, which structures the ethical Self as deposition of its identity, interruption, and suspension of its sovereignty or autonomy. And, in and through such substitution, is revealed its unicity—singular election as inescapable, unalterable, inexorable responsibility without finality nor originary source—as Self for the alterity of the Other:

> Responsibility for the other, this way of answering without a prior commitment, is human fraternity itself, and it is prior to freedom. The face of the Other in proximity, which is more than representation, is an unrepresentable trace, the way of the infinite. It is not because among beings there exists an ego, a being pursuing ends, that being takes on signification and becomes a universe. It is because in an approach, there is inscribed or written the trace of infinity, the trace of a departure, but trace of what is inordinate, does not enter into the present, and inverts the arche into anarchy, that there is foresakeness of the other, obsession by him, responsibility and a self. The non-interchangeable par excellence, the I, the unique one, substitutes itself for others. Nothing is a game. Thus being is transcended. The *ego* is not just a being endowed with certain qualities called moral which it would bear as a substance bears attributes, or which it would take on as accidents in its becoming. Its exceptional uniqueness in the passivity or the passion of the self is the incessant event of subjection to everything, of substitution. It is a being divesting itself, emptying itself of its being, turning itself inside out, and if it can be put thus, the fact

of "otherwise than being." This subjection is neither nothingness, nor a product of a transcendental imagination. In this analysis we do not mean to reduce an entity that would be the ego to the act of substituting itself that would be the being of this entity. Substitution is not an act; it is a passivity inconvertible into an act, the hither side of the act-passivity alternative, the exception that cannot be fitted into the grammatical categories of noun or verb, save in the said that thematizes them. This recurrence can be stated only as an in-itself, as the *underside of being* or as *otherwise than being.* To be oneself, *otherwise than being,* to be dis-interested, is to bear the wretchedness and bankruptcy of the Other, and even the responsibility that the other can have for me. To be oneself, the state of being a hostage, is always to have one degree of responsibility more, the responsibility for the responsibility of the Other.[365]

Temporality (*Temporalité*)

Levinas engages a powerful rethinking of the idea of temporality which he deploys both in *Totality and Infinity* and in *Otherwise than Being, or Beyond Essence.* Temporality is always thought by Levinas in relation to the idea of infinity, and with what he terms the *infinition* or *infinitization* of the Infinite (cf. Sub-section G, Section IV of *Totality and Infinity* is indeed entitled "The Infinity of Time") and, later, in *Otherwise than Being, or Beyond Essence,* as *diachrony.*

In *Totality and Infinity,* Levinas marks a radical break and a dissociation between significance and Being, and thus between the infinity of time and the totality or comprehension of Being *qua* Being. The idea of temporality, for Levinas, is thus dissociated from its ontological horizon of meaning and signification and thereby engaged into a *wholly other* disposition for the existent: an ethical disposition for the Other. Indeed, as Levinas writes in *Totality and Infinity*:

infinition is produced by the existent that is not trammeled in being, that can, while remaining bound to being, takes its distances with regard to being. Distance with regard to being, by which the existent exists in truth (or ad infinitum) is produced as time and as consciousness, or again as anticipation of the possible. Across this distance of time the definitive is not definitive; being, while being, is not yet, remains in suspense and can at each instant commence. The structure of consciousness or of temporality—of distance and truth—results from an elementary gesture of the being that refuses totalisation. This refusal is produced as a relation

> with the non-encompassable, as the welcoming of alterity—concretely, as presentation of the face. The face arrests totalisation. The welcoming of alterity hence conditions consciousness and time.[366]

In this sense, Levinas rethinks the idea of temporality not from the determination of the *being* of time, the unification of the three ecstasies of temporality—past, present, future—but as always presupposing, conditioned, and oriented by the Other, and thus engaged as and through the commandment and the demand of the Other. Which means: temporality is always and already awakened and inspired by the Other, and thus occurs from a break and a suspension, an interruption and *caesura* of the indifference and anonymity of the totality of the temporality of presence. Which is precisely why, for Levinas, time supersedes and exceeds the ontological determination of presence. As Levinas writes: "The time in which being ad infinitum is produced goes beyond the possible." That is, time opens, for Levinas, to fecundity and hence to creation—a fecundity and a creation of a disposition which responds to the call and the commandment of the transcendent Other *beyond* the ontological determinations of possibility or actuality. For Levinas thus, temporality is never reducible to continuity, duration, destiny, or faith neither is it reducible to a "complacency in some romanticism of possibles."[367] Which means, for Levinas: temporality is an incessant fecundity and creation—that is, discontinuity and disjointedness of chronology, continuity, synchronicity and temporal succession to open *beyond* and *before* time toward a novel and *wholly other* disposition and exposition—that of the ethical response and responsibility for the Other. This is why Levinas' rethinking of temporality breaks with the Bergsonian conception of time as continuous duration, as with the Heideggerian comprehension of temporality in the gathering of the three ecstasies of time—past, present, future—as horizon from which and through which the meaning of Being can be deployed as presence. For Levinas, time means to begin and incessantly iterate and reiterate the unconditional *creation* of a further time irreducible to the comprehension of time as presence:

> The instants do not link up with one another indifferently, but extend from the Other unto me. The future does not come to me from a swarming of indistinguishable possibles which would flow toward my present and which I would grasp; it comes to me across an absolute interval whose other shore the Other absolutely other—though he be my son—is alone capable of marking, and of marking, and of connecting with the past. But then the Other is alone capable of retaining from this past the former Desire that animated it, which the alterity of each face increases and deepens ever more profoundly. If time does not make moments of mathematical time, indifferent to one another, succeed to one another, it does not accomplish

> Bergson's *continuous duration* either. The Bergsonian conception of time explains why it is necessary to wait "for the sugar to melt": time no longer expresses the unintelligible dispersion of the unity of being, wholly contained in the first cause, in an apparent and phantasmal series of causes and effects; time adds something new to being, something absolutely new. But the newness of springtimes that flower in the instant (which, in good logic, is like the prior one) is already heavy with all the springtimes lived through. The profound work of time delivers from this past, in a subject that breaks with his father. Time is the non-definitiveness of the definitive, an ever recommencing alterity of the accomplished—the 'ever' of this recommencement. The work of time goes beyond the suspension of the definitive which the continuity of duration makes possible. There must be a rupture of continuity and continuation across this rupture. The essential in time consists in being a drama, a multiplicity of acts where the following act resolves the prior one. Being is no longer produced at one blow, irremediably present. Reality is what it is, but will be once again, another time freely resumed and pardoned. Infinite being is produced as times, that is, in several times across the dead time that separates the father from the son. It is not the finitude of being that constitutes the essence of time, as Heidegger thinks, but its infinity.[368]

For Levinas, temporality engages an irrepressible excess of responsibility for the Other which overflows and overwhelms, as *infinitization*, the horizon of comprehension of temporality. Temporality as fecundity and creation marks temporality as election of the ethical in the Self—that is, as always and already electing the Self out of presence and toward the ethical for the Other. As fecundity and creation, indeed, temporality is "out of phase,"[369] disjoined and *out of joint*, a *diachrony* in time which awakens the Self to the ethical *beyond* the ontological and as response and responsibility *beyond* morality or normativity—a response and responsibility never accomplished and always futural, always more futural than futurity, always to come as never fulfilled or gratified.

Which informs, for Levinas, the meaning of *resurrection*. Resurrection does not intend, for Levinas, the returning occurrence of that which has passed, the reincarnation or restoration of that which passed into the past. It engages the always and already *re*-beginning, *re*-commencement, *re*-iteration of responsibility for that which is always yet *to come*. In this sense, resurrection for Levinas does not mean a renovation of what is passed but rather an engagement of a temporality always futural, that is, always *to give before* and *beyond* the autonomy and the sovereignty of the Self as well as *before* and *beyond* the call and commandment of the Other. This is why, for Levinas, the response and responsibility for the Other as *infinitization* "liberates being from the limitation of fate" and marks a temporality as resurrection which

> constitutes the principal event of time. There is therefore no continuity in being. Time is discontinuous; on instant does not come out of another without interruption, by an ecstasy. In continuation the instant meets its death and resuscitates; death and resurrection constitute time. But such a formal structure presupposes the relation of the I with the Other and, at its basis, fecundity across the discontinuous which constitutes time.[370]

Third party (*Tiers*)

The question of the Third party is extremely complex throughout Levinas' oeuvre.

Levinas deploys it principally in the last sections of *Otherwise than Being, or Beyond Essence*. However, the idea of Third party appears as well throughout *Totality and Infinity*:

> The face-to-face is not a modality of coexistence nor even of knowledge (itself panoramic) one term can have of another but is the primordial production of being on which all the possible collocations of the terms are founded. The revelation of the Third party, ineluctable in the face is produced only through the face. Goodness does no radiate over the anonymity of a collectivity presenting itself panoramically, to be absorbed into it.[371]

In this passage from the concluding pages of *Totality and Infinity*, Levinas already marks how the face-to-face encounter, and thus the singularity of the Other's commandment and plea —the call and demand of infinite and unescapable, inexorable, undeniable, unconditional response of responsibility for the Other expressed as "Thou shall not kill"—is always accompanied, always and already supposes and presupposes the occurrence of the Third party, the other of the Other, the multiple others of the Other. Furthermore, the face-to-face encounter always and already supposes and presupposes the demand of the Third party: the demand for justice. Otherwise said, the Third party is always announced, also thus demanding and commanding in the face-to-face hyperbolical relation through which the ethical Self is called to respond in infinite and hyperbolical responsibility for the Other. The Third party already speaks within the commandment of the Other awakening the Self to the ethical responsibility which incessantly exceeds itself *beyond* itself and *before* the Self for the Other. Which means: the others of the Other are already and always commanding *in* the face-to-face relation. Which prompts the question: What is expressed in the demand of the *others* already expressing itself in the hyperbolical ethical face-to-face relation? And furthermore, which ethical commandment is expressed in and through the Third party already calling through the commandment of the singular Other?

Levinas will develop the response to this question in *Otherwise than Being, or Beyond Essence*.

This response will mark how and why the face-to-face encounter engaging an hyperbolic responsibility to the point of substitution and expiation cannot not take into account the Third party, the others of the Other. Indeed, as Levinas marks, it

> is not that the entry of a third party would be an empirical fact, and that my responsibility for the other finds itself constrained to a calculus by the "force of things." In the proximity of the other, all the others than the other obsess me, and already this obsession cries out for justice, demands measure and knowing, is consciousness. A face obsesses and shows itself, between transcendence and visibility/invisibility. Signification signifies in justice, but also, more ancient than itself and than the equality implied by it, justice passes by justice in my responsibility for the Other, in my inequality with respect to him for whom I am a hostage. The Other is from the first the 'brother of all the other men.' The neighbor that obsesses me is already a face, both comparable and incomparable, a unique face and in relationship with faces, which are visible in the concern for justice.[372]

Levinas announces thus the idea of justice in and through the hyperbolical ethical commandment, an announcement which is consecrated through the always and already occurrence of the Third party: indeed, always, and already inhabiting the ethical lies an idea of justice. The idea of justice is, in this manner, always presupposed and already presumed in the face-to-face ethical relation. Which means: the Other, in its hyperbolical commandment always commanding *before* the autonomy of the Self to respond *beyond* the capabilities of the Self, also expresses the demand of *all the Others* and thereby *all the Others* are already inspiring the responsibility of the Self for the singular Other. Otherwise said, the idea of justice orders and commands the incessantly awakened and elected ethical responsibility of the Self for the Other to also be engaged, awakened and elected for *all the Others* speaking through the Other. Which means: the ethical Self responds in infinite responsibility not only for the singular Other, but *also* responds in infinite responsibility for this responsibility, that is toward *all the Others*, the others of the Other.

The idea of justice announced in and through the Third party always and already inhabiting the face-to-face relation, for Levinas, is primary: the law, which immemorially commands the incessant excess of responsibility as substitution and expiation for the Other *before* and *beyond* the Self, is also expressed as the perpetual complexity of the ethical where both the Other and *all the Others* of the Other demand a justice committed to the singularity of *all* existents.

This is why Levinas remarks:

> All the others that obsess me in the Other do not affect me as examples of the same *genus* united with my neighbor by resemblance or common nature, individuations of the human race, or chips of the same block, like the stones metamorphosed into men by Deucalion, who, behind his back, had to collect into cities with their hearts of stone. The others concern me from the first. Here fraternity precedes the commonness of a *genus*. My relationship with the Other as neighbor gives meaning to my relations with all the others. All human relations as human proceed from disinterestedness. The-one-for-the-other of proximity is not a deforming abstraction. In it justice is shown from the first, it is thus born from the signifyingness of signification, the-one-for-the-other, signification. This means concretely or empirically that justice is not a legality regulating human masses, from which a technique of social equilibrium is drawn, harmonizing antagonistic forces. That would be a justification of the State delivered over to its own necessities. Justice is impossible without the one that renders it finding himself in proximity. His function is not limited to the "function of judgment," the subsuming of particular cases under a general rule. The judge is not outside the conflict, but the law is in the midst of proximity. Justice, society, the State and its institutions, exchanges and work are comprehensible out of proximity. This means that nothing is outside of the control of the responsibility of the-one-for-the-other. It is important to recover all these forms beginning with proximity, in which being, totality, the State, politics, techniques, work are at every moment on the point of having their center of gravitation in themselves, and weighing on their own account.[373]

And furthermore, as Levinas marks, the idea of justice expressed in the Third party far from pacifying the hyperbolical responsibility incessantly exceeding the Self's capacity for the Other. On the contrary: the idea of justice aggravates and accentuates this hyperbolical responsibility for the Other as always engaged for the Others revealed in the commandment of the Other:

> In no way is justice a degradation of obsession, a degeneration of the for-the-other, a diminution, a limitation of anarchic responsibility, a neutralization of the glory of the Infinite, a degeneration that would be produced in the

> measure that for empirical reasons the initial duo would become a trio. But the contemporaneousness of the multiple is tied about the diachrony of two: justice remains justice only, in a society where there is no distinction between those close and those far off, but in which there also remains the impossibility of passing by the closest. The equality of all is borne by my inequality, the surplus of my duties over my rights. The forgetting of self moves justice. It is then not without importance to know if the egalitarian and just State in which man is fulfilled (and which is to be set up, and especially to be maintained) proceeds from a war of all against all, or from the irreducible responsibility of the one for all, and if it can do without friendships and faces.[374]

Retrieving the idea of plurality as embodiment of justice by the revelation through the Other of the Third party, of all the Others, which had already been developed in the *Conclusions* of *Totality and Infinity*, Levinas here speaks of "friendships and faces" in their multiplicity as that which animates and awakens consciousness. That is, the plurality of singularities, of the Others in the Other, opens the ethical Self to its consciousness as an extension of its elected, irreplaceable and unescapable, responsibility. What does consciousness mean here for Levinas? That is, in which sense can the ethical Self incessantly elected, *before* and *beyond* itself in responsibility to the point of substitution and expiation for the Other and thereby for all Others, exceeded and overwhelmed, obsessed, traumatized, guilty *before* any fault and *beyond* any reconciliation, can "appropriate" itself in a "consciousness"?

For Levinas, and following the inherent "logic" of *Otherwise than Being, or Beyond Essence*, consciousness means taking on one's Self being elected by the Other for the Other and thereby for all Others. Otherwise said, consciousness for the ethical Self means *exappropriating* itself as endorsing, carrying, responding always and already to the call and the commandment calling and commanding the Self *before* its autonomy and *beyond* any intersubjective recognition for *all the Others revealed in each Other*. In this sense, consciousness for Levinas does not signify the "appropriation" of the Self in its constitution and institution as identity or selfhood. It rather entails the incessant *exappropriation* of the Self for the Other and for all the Others as excess of justice for singularity—the singularity of alterity. Consciousness here means thus the awakening and the electing of the ethical exceptionality of the Self *exappropriating* its own Self from itself and in responsibility without reserve, substitution *as* expiation, for the singular Other as toward *all the Others*. This is why Levinas inscribes consciousness outside, *before* and *beyond* the establishment of *ego*'s sovereignty and *in* or through the hyperbolical dynamic of the face-to-face relationship and within the *diachrony* of the proximity of the Other:

> Consciousness is born as the presence of a third party. It is in the measure that it proceeds from it that it is still disinterestedness. It is the entry of the third party, a permanent entry, into the intimacy of the face-to-face. The concern for justice, for the thematizing, the kerygmatic discourse bearing on the said, from the bottom of the saying without the said, the saying as contact, is the spirit in society. And it is because the third party does not come empirically to trouble proximity, but the face is both the neighbor and the face of faces, visage and visible, that, between the order of being and of proximity the bond is unexceptionable. Order, appearing, phenomenally, being are produced in signification, in proximity, starting with the third party. The apparition of a third party is the very origin of appearing, that is, the very origin of an origin.[375]

Which is why Levinas grounds consciousness not in self-consciousness, but in justice. Not in reflexivity or self-reflexivity, but in the idea of a justice as incessant excess of responsibility—doing more than what the Self can or wills for the Other as for *all the Others* commanding through each singular Other. For Levinas, thus, the idea of justice as consciousness—and as that from which erupts consciousness—precedes reflexivity, decision, certainty, clarity, mindfulness, self-determination, constitution or institution. Indeed, the idea of justice orients and animates, excites and awakens the ethical Self in its consciousness, *otherwise* than within its own Self. It engages the ethical Self *beyond* and *before* itself to incessantly give always more of itself than how it could or what it could. This is why Levinas indicates that justice engages, from the *diachrony* of proximity, the infinite work of equality through synchronization, comparison, thematization not as fixed determinations to which sociality returns, but as those modalities always *in search of a further expression*, incessantly transcending their fixations and categorizations:

> The foundation of consciousness is justice. Not that justice makes a preexisting meditation intervene. An event like meditation—synchronization, comparison, thematization—is the work of justice, an entry of the *diachrony* of proximity, of the signifyingness of saying into the synchrony of the Said, a 'fundamental historicity' in the sense of Merleau-Ponty. It is the necessary interruption of the Infinite being fixed in structures, community and totality. Synchronization is the act of consciousness which, through representation and the said, institutes "with the help of God," the original locus of justice, a terrain common to me and the others where I am counted among them, that is, where subjectivity is a citizen with all the duties and rights measured and measurable which the equilibrated ego involves, or equilibrating itself by the concourse of duties and the concurrence of rights. But justice can be established only if I, always evaded from the concept of the *ego*, always

> desituated and divested of being, always in non-reciprocatable relationship with the other, always for the other, and become an other like the others.[376]

The Third party *reveals* the idea of justice as the infinite *tending beyond itself* of justice opened by the hyperbolical and *diachronical* proximity of the Other, the one-for-the-Other of the ethical Self always and already elected for the Other in substitution and expiation—infinitizing responsibility *without* principled norm nor reappropriable, recognizable, identifiable finality. As Levinas remarks:

> In proximity the Other obsesses me according to the absolute asymmetry of signification, of the "one-for-the-Other": I substitute myself for the Other, whereas no one can replace me, and the substitution of the one-for-the-Other does not signify the substitution of the other for the one. The relationship with the third party is an incessant correction of the asymmetry of proximity in which the face is looked at. There is weighing, thought, objectification, and thus a decree in which 'my anarchic relationship with Illeity is betrayed, but in which it is conveyed before us. There is betrayal of my anarchic relation with *Illeity*, but also a new relationship with it: it is only thanks to God that, as a subject incomparable with the other, I am approached as an other by the others, that is, "for myself." "Thanks to God" I am another for the others. God is not involved as an alleged interlocutor: the reciprocal relationship binds me to the other man in the trace of transcendence, in *Illeity*. The "passing of God", of whom I can speak only by reference to this aid or this grace, is precisely the reverting of the incomparable subject into a member of society.[377]

And further onwards:

> The way leads from responsibility to problems. A problem is posited by proximity itself, which, as the immediate itself, is without problems. The extraordinary commitment of the other to the third party calls for control, a search for justice, society and the State, comparison and possession, thought and science, commerce and philosophy, and outside of anarchy, the search for a principle. Philosophy is this measure brought to the infinity of the being-for-the-other of proximity, and is like the wisdom of love. But, come out of signification, a modality of proximity, justice, society and truth itself which they require, must not be taken for an anonymous law of the 'human forces' governing an impersonal totality. It is through its ambivalence which always remains an enigma that infinity or the transcendent does not let itself be assembled. Removing itself from every memorable present, a past that was never present, it leaves a trace of its impossible incarnation and its inordinateness in my proximity with the neighbor, where I state,

> in the autonomy of the voice of conscience, a responsibility, which could not have begun in me, for freedom, which is not my freedom. The fleeting trace effacing itself and reappearing is like a question mark put before the scintillation of the ambiguity: an infinite responsibility of the one-for-the-Other, or the signification of the Infinite in responsibility. There is an ambiguity of the order that orders to me the neighbor who obsesses me, for whom and before whom I answer by my ego, in which being is inverted into a substitution, into the very possibility of gift—and of an infinite Illeity, glorious in the human plot hatched in proximity, the subversion of essence into substitution. In it I could not arise soon enough to be there on time, nor approach without the extraordinary distance to be crossed augmenting before every effort to assemble it into an itinerary. Illeity overflows both cognition and the enigma through which the Infinite leaves a trace in cognition.[378]

Totality (*Totalité*)

The term figures in Levinas' first major philosophical work *Totality and Infinity* published in 1961. From the outset of this work, Levinas defines totality as "the visage of being that shows itself in war"[379] Which entails, for Levinas, that totality marks and embodies the reduction of individualities to being

> bearers of forces that command them unbeknown to themselves. The meaning of individuals (invisible outside of this totality) is derived from the totality. The unicity of each present is incessantly sacrificed to a future appealed to bring forth its objective meaning. For the ultimate meaning alone counts; the last act alone changes beings into themselves. They are what they will appear to be in the already plastic form of the epic.[380]

Clearly, for Levinas, totality means the comprehension, appropriation, reduction within a general historical becoming and narrative of the singularity and individuality of existents. The reference here is naturally to Hegel's philosophy of history and phenomenological becoming of Spirit—which is understood as the movement from the immediacy of phenomenality to the reconciled appropriation of meaning and knowledge, that is, from difference and differentiation to its reconciled identity and Sameness as meaning and truth of difference and differentiation. Totality is the rationalization of History in the reconciliation of differences and singularities within the wholeness of truth and meaningfulness.

Indeed, and Levinas most specifically understands this point: totality is not a simple static concept which predetermines truth and meaning as reconciliation, identity, Sameness. Totality is always, as Hegel deployed and which Levinas perfectly understands, the *reconciliatory movement* always and incessantly comprehending differences, antinomies, oppositions, contradictions in and within a speculative appropriation of truth and meaning through this very movement. Indeed, for Hegel, totality means the reconciliation and unification of difference in identity—an identity which also incessantly projects itself outside of its static form by *becoming other* to itself in difference and thereby also reappropriating itself in a further reconciliation with itself. In other words, totality, for Hegel, means *unity* through the incessant movement of differentiation. That is, incessant and perpetual unification of differences. And thus totality means the constant activation of a process of identification totalizing itself with itself. As such, totality never rests on its totality. It rather projects itself always and already to a greater amplification of itself, comprehending more than itself in and through affirmation of itself as reconciliation with itself. This is why Hegel marks that the totality of Being is *infinite*. But it is infinite because the infinite always and already traverses, informs, deploys itself in and through the finite and in this sense is not different from the finite. The infinite *is* the finite—this means the infinite is nothing without the finite and inversely the finite is unthinkable without it always and already being infinite. This movement, essential totality, signifies, for Hegel, the *unity* of meaning as truth. It is this unity always in movement through and within differences which marks what Hegel calls "truth." This concept of "truth as the whole" is immanence always and already projecting itself in its transcending and incessantly reappropriating its transcending becoming into a renewed reconciled identity and appropriation of itself for itself and in itself. It marks therefore that truth does not lie outside the movement of its own appropriation and reappropriation.

Totality is, for Hegel, the incessant movement of difference reconciling itself in the identity of differentiations. In this sense, for Hegel, there is no Other *outside* of this totality as the totality is always reappropriating the other in the actuality of its own differentiating and dialectical movement of identification. As Hegel famously writes in the *Preface* of the *Phenomenology of Spirit*: "Spirit is no greater than its manifestation," which means, the totality of truth as *whole* always and already envelops, grasps, and comprehends all otherness as *its* other, and thus as yet another historical manifestation of itself. Which also engages an ethics: the ethics of recognition where the Self and the Other are always and already recognized in their mutual participation in the dialectical and speculative movement of their reconciliation. The Self recognizes the Other, the Other recognizes the Self as both are *ego*'s always and already recognizable in the element, the middle, the "between" of their reconciled and identification of their difference—precisely where Hegel names God: "The reconciling yes, in which both I's let go of their opposed existence, is the existence of the I extended into twoness, which therein remains the same as itself and which has the certainty of itself in its complete self-relinquishing and in its opposite.—It is the God that appears in the midst of those who know themselves as pure knowing."[381]

To totality, Levinas responds by responding precisely to Hegel:

> Hegelian phenomenology where self-consciousness is the distinguishing of what is not distinct, expresses the universality of the same identifying itself in the alterity of objects thought and despite the opposition of self to self. "I, the selfsame being, thrust myself away from myself; but this which is distinguished, which is set up as unlike me, is immediately on its being distinguished no distinction for me." The difference is not a difference; the I, as other, is not an "other."[382]

Indeed, Levinas marks firstly, against Hegel's typification of the Self, that the I cannot be reduced to the process of its identification with itself through the dialectical appropriation and reappropriation of its other. Which means that Levinas insists on how this speculative determination of the Self ultimately results in an egoism: the Self speaks of itself by itself with itself. And thus closes itself with its own Self forming and formulating itself as a totality "encompassing the same and the other."[383] Consequently, Levinas engages a *breach of the totality* not from an abstract and pure transcendence breaking or shattering the totality of Being, but rather by marking how the egoism of the Self is always and already irreducibly preceded by "the absolutely Other" thereby opening to a wholly other relation than the reconciled Sameness of the Self and the Other reducing the Other and the Self to indifference, of the Self recognizing the Other as the Other recognizes the Self in the affirmation of their total reconciliation. *This wholly other relation is the ethical relation of the face-to-face which is entirely and wholly instituted as separation and transcendence*: separation of the Self and the Other in the trace of the transcendence of the Other commanding the Self *before* itself to an infinite responsibility for the Other: "A relation whose terms do not form a totality can hence be produced within the general economy of being only as proceeding from the I to the Other, as face-to-face, as delineating a distance in depth."[384]

For Levinas, the ethical, or metaphysical, relation engages a *breach*, suspension and interruption of the immanent movement of totality "from the very fact that it maintains the distance between me and the Other, the radical separation asserted in transcendence which prevents the reconstitution of totality"[385] and where "the Other exercises a *right* over egoism."[386] Hence, it should also be added that for Levinas this *breach*, suspension and interruption of totality, far from negating the relation between the Self and the Other, awakens their relationship as ethical, and thus to an ethics *without* reconciliation where this *without* also means an infinite ethical responsibility, that is, a relationship marked by the absolute separation and transcendence and thus singularity—singularity of the Self toward the singularity of the Other, or election of the ethical Self for the unique suffering, vulnerability, defenselessness of the Other.

Trace (*Trace*)

As trace, the Infinite and the Illeity of the absolutely transcendent Other announces itself in phenomenality by incessantly overwhelming and suspending its order and horizon, its manifest presence and presentation. The idea of trace is that through which the immemorial past, a past irreducible to a "past-present" and which thus was never as such present, *beyond* and *before* presence or being-present, *without* manifestation and presentation interrupts and suspends phenomenality opening it *before* and *beyond* itself to a *wholly other signification*: the ethical *before* and *beyond* Being and essence. The trace signifies *before* and *beyond* Being and essence. Which is why, for Levinas, *before* and *beyond* Being obliges and commands, from an Infinite Otherness, an *Illeity*, which is irreappropriable and ungraspable by the Sameness of the Same or the immanence of identity, conceptuality, recognition. The trace expresses itself from the radical asymmetry, heteronomy, heterogeneity, absolute otherness of the Other and thus occurs *before* and *beyond* the binary play between immanence and transcendence, which is "proper to Being and where 'immanence always wins against transcendence.'[387] As Levinas writes in *The Trace of the Other*: "But if the *signifyingness* of a trace is not immediately transformed into the straightforwardness which still marks signs, which reveal the signified absent and bring it into immanence, it is because a trace signifies *beyond* Being."[388]

The trace signifies that in which the face of the Other expresses itself in and through the visible, phenomenality, and manifestation by interrupting and suspending the visible, phenomenality, and manifestation. It is that in which the occurrence of the face commands in overwhelming the order of appearance and the horizon of presence.

For Levinas, the trace marks the dynamic, *diachronical*, between the *otherwise than Being* and the meaning as truth of Being. Otherwise said, the trace marks how and where the otherwise than Being as ethical cuts through, suspends and interrupts the indifference and anonymity in the meaning as truth, totality and immanence of Being. The trace thus marks the centrality of a temporality as *diachrony*. The *diachronic* structure of temporality makes possible the relation with the *otherwise than Being* enacted through the trace of the absolute otherness of the Other. Levinas indeed marks how and why the trace of the absolutely Other through the immemorial as rupture and suspension of the gathering and unifying modality of presence, announces and signifies a *diachronicity* between the *otherwise than Being* rupturing the temporal order of presence. This *diachronic* movement far from simply negating Being, meaning or truth, elects it and awakens it to exceed itself *before* and *beyond* itself. In this sense, the trace of the Other opens, through its *diachrony*, a certain paradoxical proximity with the Other, a proximity entirely oriented as a break of presence, a rupture of "being-present" and which reveals the ethical always and already exceeding Being.

This is why to approach the trace of the Other is to approach the *anarchy* of the ethical as *before* and *beyond* Being, *without* principle, *without* beginning and *without* finality, a *before* and a *beyond* irreducible to Being and *exappropriating* Being incessantly outside of itself, and toward the irrecuperable transcendence of the Other. As Levinas writes in *Otherwise than Being, or Beyond Essence*:

> Proximity is signification not because it would be the aim of any theme, the need, fulfilled or on the point of being satisfied, of another being. The-one-for-the-other in proximity does not form an ontological conjunction of satisfaction. The capacity of a being, and of consciousness, its correlate, is insufficient to contain the plot which forms in the face of another, trace of an immemorial past, arousing a responsibility that comes from before and goes *beyond* what abides in the suspense of an epoque. "Goes *beyond*"—that is already to make a concession to ontological and theoretical language, as though the *beyond* were still a term, an entity, a mode of being, or the negative counterpart of all that. An approach is not a representation, however detheoreticized its intentionality would be, of a being *beyond* being. Its *diachrony* is not an insufficiency of an intuition. The trace of a past in a face is not the absence of a yet non-revealed, but the anarchy of what has never been present, of an infinite which commands in the face of the other, and which, like an excluded middle, could not be aimed at.[389]

Otherwise said, the trace of the Other breaking and interrupting the essence of Being, its meaning and truth as presence, incessantly awakens the Self *beyond* and *before* its self-determination to an irreducible ethical responsibility for the Other. Which means: the trace of the Other is that in which and through which the *otherwise than Being* finds a meaning in the world while occurring from an absolute *beyond* and *before* the presence and the essence of the world: the ethical. Its unique significance, preceding all signs, arises from its disruption of intentionality; the trace of the Other opens, in its passage and expression, in disturbing the order and the horizon of ontological presence, is testimony *without* thematization, testimony of the absolute transcendence of the Other by which the Self is elected to the Infinite signified out of responsibility for the Other, out of the "one-for-the-Other," "supporting everything, subject to everything, that is, suffering for everyone, but charged with everything, without having had to decide for this taking charge, which is gloriously amplified in the measure that it is imposed. Obedience precedes any hearing of the command. The possibility of finding, anachronously, the order in the obedience itself, and of receiving the order out of oneself, this reverting of heteronomy into autonomy, is the very way the Infinite passes itself."[390]

Unicity (*Unicité*)

For Levinas, the critique of totality and presence—the interruption and suspension of the indifference and anonymity of Being through the commandment of the Other, face-to-face relation which, *without* communion or community, marks the absolute transcendence of the Other—opens to an ethics as "First Philosophy," that is, engages an ethics of singularity for the singularity of the Other. This is why Levinas' philosophy is riveted to the idea of unicity: unicity of the ethical Self in responsibility to the point of substitution and expiation for the unique otherness of the Other.

The idea of unicity proposed by Levinas, as that of singularity, is irreducible to difference. Indeed, ethics as "First Philosophy" is not an "ethics of difference" which, for Levinas, is founded and grounded on comparison and evaluation, relation between relative terms, and thus constituted and structured by reference to a binarism and a bipolarism in which the immanence of the Same always and already comprehends the transcendence of the Other.

Beyond and *before* difference, and thus outside any ethics of recognizing differences, the ethical means, for Levinas, the singular exposition by a singular Self to a singular Other. In this sense, Levinas marks the incessant excess of responsibility in the face-to-face relation as the each time unique election of the Self for the Other in all its uniqueness and singularity. The Other as unique means the infinite responsibility for the Other by the Self elected and awakened to its response as responsibility for the Other. In unicity, Levinas means thus the unicity of the ethical as *non*-indifference for the Other. Indeed, the Other is always and already the neighbor which is, for the ethical Self, an absolute Other, exception from a common *genus* and thereby singular exceptionality calling and commanding an infinite responsibility. The Other is *wholly other* as unique in its transcendence and as loved, that is unique to the world for always and already transcending the world through its commandment, engages the Self in a responsibility *without* measure or evaluation, non-transferable and unsubstitutable.

It is in this uniqueness of indeclinable responsibility toward the unicity of the Other's call and commandment that is revealed the uniqueness of the ethical Self as elected and chosen for the Other. As Levinas writes,

> in the irreplaceable subject, unique and chosen as a responsibility and a substitution, a mode of freedom, ontologically impossible, breaks the unrendable essence. Substitution frees the subject from ennui, that is, from the enchainment to itself, where the ego suffocates in itself due to the tautological way of identity, and ceaselessly seeks after the distraction of games and sleep in a movement that never wears out. This liberation is not an action, a commencement, nor any vicissitude of essence and of ontology, where the equality with oneself would be established in the form of self-consciousness. An anarchic liberation, it emerges, without being assumed, without turning into a beginning, in inequality with oneself.[391]

The ethical Self is responsible *without* mediation and as unique—the Self and not another responds, precisely where this "and not another" means the ethical Self as unique in its infinite responsibility for the unicity of the Other. Which entails: the ethical Self is elected by the Other for the Other in a responsibility *without* prior fault or engagement and yet as unique host and hostage for the unicity of the Other. Which brings Levinas to the exceptional situation of this ethics as "First Philosophy": the infinite responsibility as the ethical Self's anarchic substitution and expiation for the Other entails the unsubstitutability, unicity, and uniqueness—election as singularity of the ethical Self for the singularity of the Other:

> Chosen without assuming the choice! If this passivity is not reducible to the passivity of an effect in a causa relation, if it can be conceived to be on the hither side of freedom and non-freedom, it must have the meaning of a "goodness despite itself", a goodness always older than the choice. Its value, that is, its excellence or goodness, the goodness of goodness, is alone able to counterbalance the violence of the choice and, *beyond* counterbalancing, be for the better!. Goodness is always older than choice; the Good has always already chosen and required the unique one. As chosen without choosing its election, absent from the investiture received, the one is a passivity more passive still than all the passivity of undergoing. The passivity of the one, its responsibility or its pain, do not begin in consciousness—that is, do not begin. On the hither side of consciousness, they consist in this pre-original hold of the Good over it, always older than any present, any beginning. This diachrony prevents the one from joining up

with itself and identifying itself as a substance, contemporary with itself, like a transcendental ego. Uniqueness is without identity. Not an identity, it is *beyond* consciousness, which is in itself and for itself. For it is already a substitution for the Other.[392]

War (*Guerre*)

Levinas opens *Totality and Infinity* with a sustained reflection on war. How does Levinas approach in the opening pages of *Totality and Infinity* the idea and the concrete reality of war? Firstly, for Levinas, war is that through which the very possibility and actuality of morality is destroyed, negated, annihilated. War adjourns morality and opens to the proliferation of a nihilism in history where no existent subsist. War effaces as it destroys, obliterates, annihilates as it submerges all existents in its organization and ordination. In this sense, and contrary to Hegel, and Heraclitus indeed, war deploys itself as a voiding and nihilation of meaning and destruction of existents. For Levinas, thus, war destroys all possibility of a historical narrative by denegating all existents, all history of existents, in its deployment and perseverance. In a certain sense, the radicality of war is too enormous to see itself included and appropriated by a historical narrative. Levinas here advances a profound interpretation of war. War is seen as destroying both the exteriority of the Other and the identity of the Same. It voids and negates, and indeed, for Levinas, war "employs arms that turn against those who wield them. It establishes an order from which no one can keep his distance; nothing henceforth is exterior. War does not manifest exteriority and the Other as Other; it destroys the identity of the Same."[393] Which means: "war renders morality derisory"[394] as it proposes no escape, no evasion, no possibility to suspend and interrupt in its totalization. Which means: war is the definitive effacement of singularities in the indifference and anonymity of the totality of Being.

War is the totalizing effacement of existents in the indifference and anonymity—the totality—of Being and its history:

> The visage of Being that shows itself in war is fixed in the concept of totality which dominates Western philosophy. Individuals are reduced to being bearers of forces that command them unbeknown to themselves. The meaning of individuals (invisible outside of this totality) is derived from the totality. The unicity of each present is incessantly sacrificed to a future appealed to bring forth its objective meaning. They are what they will appear to be in the already plastic forms of the epic.[395]

As sacrificial, war grasps and thus annihilates the singularity of existents in its "epic" historical becoming. Levinas here puts into question not only the violence of war, but also engages a radical critique of heroism and patriotism. Indeed, war not only materially annihilates existents; it also destroys the signification of the singularity of existence in the narrative from which war is signified and spiritualized. As such, and in this sense, for Levinas, war is the defining element of ontology, and indeed, war is the totalization, indifference, and anonymity of Being which actively and irrevocably destroys the singularity of the human in the bare and blind play of forces where individualities are "sacrificed" in anonymity and indifference.

War supposes thus a sacrificial logic which Levinas will always question and ultimately dismantle, destructure, deconstruct. We could even suggest here that Levinas' critique of war proceeds from a profound critique of the onto-theological operation and operativity of sacrifice and self-sacrifice—and thus of the "ethics of sacrifice"—always presupposed and appropriated in war. It is here important to note how Levinas retrieves the opening pages of Rosenzweig's *Star of Redemption* which indeed had engaged a profound critique of Hegel's speculative dialectic always capable of appropriating and reappropriating the singularity of death in its accomplished meaning and fulfilled comprehension of Reason in History as it is developed and deployed in the *Phenomenology of Spirit*, most specifically in the Chapter IV, *Spirit*, and onwards, culminating in the last pages of *Absolute Knowledge*.[396]

To war as totality—sacrificing, annihilating, negating the singularity and the unicity of the human existent comprehended, appropriated, arrogated in and within the anonymity and indifference of Being, Levinas will oppose the "extraordinary phenomenon of prophetic eschatology" whose "real import lies elsewhere."[397] Indeed, the eschatological interrupts the ontological structure of history as war and suspends the sacrificial logic of its deployment and essential becoming.

> Eschatology "institutes a relation with Being *beyond the totality* or *beyond* history" as it breaks the totality of its essence; it breaks the incessant process by which meaning and Being are defined through the *polemos* of war, that process annihilating the singularity of existence to justify and comprehend itself in and as a historical narrative comprehending this annihilation in the constitution and institution of a meaning and an essence of the history of Being. Eschatology engages the splicing of the anonymity of the ontological, the indifference of Sameness to reveal an event *wholly other* than a moment or an instant in and of History and its meaning. Eschatology reveals *against* the totality and *beyond* the ontology of war the event of that which exceeds the totality of war, surpasses and overwhelms the possibility of inscribing the event within the immanent

comprehension of Being. Levinas names this excess, this overwhelming and incomprehensible event which surpasses its appropriation in and by ontology: the idea of the Infinity, Illeity, absolute otherness of the Other. In a certain sense, thus the power of war is incessantly undermined by that which it cannot contain, apprehend, appropriate, or reappropriate—that is, that which surpasses and overwhelms it: the irreducible singularity and unicity of the irrepleaceable existent. Which also means, for Levinas, that the suffering and vulnerability of the existent—and suffering and vulnerability of the existent are in war that which appears *without* mediation, *without* appropriation, *without* conciliation—reveals immediately that which, in the singularity of the existent, remains irreducible to the totality of meaning, history, Being. As Levinas marks, eschatology reveals *beyond* war the irreducible anteriority of the existent. And thus, eschatology engages "a relationship with a *surplus* always exterior to the totality, as though the objective totality did not fill out the true measure of being as though another concept, the concept of *infinity*, were needed to express this transcendence in regards to totality, non-encompassable within a totality and as primordial as totality."[398]

The inextricability of war, its violence reducing and annihilating the Other, always and already forgetting the inexorable suffering and vulnerability of the Other—brings Levinas to also write, further on in *Totality and Infinity* how war and its "violence does not aim simply at disposing of the Other as one disposes of a thing, but, already at the limit of murder, it proceeds from unlimited negation. It can aim at only a presence itself infinite despite its insertion in the field of my powers. Violence can aim only at a face." And thus, opening here to the ethical as "First Philosophy," to an ethics *beyond* "good intentions", *beyond* "Platonic benevolence" and engaged by the absolute transcendence of the Other which commands "Thou shall not kill" by electing the Self to a responsibility *before* and *beyond* totality already witnessing, testifying, attesting of the Infinite otherness of the Other, Levinas continues:

"It is therefore not freedom that accounts for the transcendence of the Other, but the transcendence of the Other that accounts for freedom—a transcendence of the Other with regard to me which, being infinite, does not have the same signification as my transcendence with regard to him. The risk that war involves measures the distance that separates bodies within their hand-to-hand struggle. The Other, in the hands of forces that break him, exposed to powers, remains unforeseeable, that is, transcendent. This transcendence is not to be described negatively, but is manifested positively in the moral resistance of the face to the violence of murder. The force of the Other is already and henceforth moral. Freedom, be it that of war, can be manifested only outside totality, but this 'outside totality' opens with the transcendence of the face. To think of freedom as *within* totality is to reduce freedom to the status of an indetermination in being and forthwith to integrate it into a totality by closing the totality over the 'holes' of indetermination—and seeking with psychology the laws of a free being. But the relation that subtends war, an asymmetrical relation with the Other who, as infinity, opens time, transcends and dominates the subjectivity (the I not being transcendent with regard to the Other-in-the-Same sense that the Other is transcendent with regard to me), can take on the aspect of a symmetrical relation. The face whose ethical epiphany consists in soliciting a response (which the violence of war and its murderous negation alone can seek to reduce to silence), is not satisfied with a "good intention" and a benevolence wholly Platonic."[399]

Notes

Chronology

1 Indeed, Levinas later commented, with dry humor, that "[i]t was Sartre who guaranteed my place in eternity by stating in his famous obituary essay on Merleau-Ponty that he, Sartre, 'was introduced to phenomenology by Levinas'."

Choices

1 *Totality and Infinity*, p. 90.

Introduction

1 Derrida, "Violence and Metaphysics. An Essay on the Thought of Emmanuel Levinas," in *Writing and Difference*, trsl. A. Bass, Chicago, University of Chicago Press, 1978, pp. 79–153.

The Levinas Dictionary A–Z

1 *Totality and Infinity*, p. 103.
2 *Otherwise than Being, or Beyond Essence*, pp. 141–2.
3 *Totality and Infinity*, pp. 78–9.
4 *Totality and Infinity*, p. 39.
5 *Totality and Infinity*, pp. 39–40.
6 *Totality and Infinity*, pp. 50–1.
7 *Totality and Infinity*, p. 51.
8 *Totality and Infinity*, p. 51.
9 *Totality and Infinity*, pp. 51–2.
10 *Otherwise than Being, or Beyond Essence*, p. 129.
11 *Totality and Infinity*, pp. 70–1.
12 *Totality and Infinity*, p. 73.

13 *Totality and Infinity*, p. 75.

14 Heidegger, *Being and Time*, trsl. J. Macquarie and E. Robinson, Oxford, Wiley-Blackwell, 1967, p. 21.

15 Heidegger, *Being and Time*, p. 31.

16 Levinas, *Totality and Infinity*, p. 47.

17 *Otherwise than Being, or Beyond Essence*, p. 3.

18 *Totality and Infinity*, pp. 301–2.

19 *Otherwise than Being, or Beyond Essence*, p. 4.

20 *Otherwise than Being, or Beyond Essence*, pp. 56–7.

21 *Otherwise than Being, or Beyond Essence*, p. 11.

22 *Totality and Infinity*, p. 303.

23 *Otherwise than Being, or Beyond Essence*, p. 26.

24 *Otherwise than Being, or Beyond Essence*, pp. 138–9.

25 *Totality and Infinity*, pp. 257–8.

26 *Totality and Infinity*, p. 258.

27 *Totality and Infinity*, p. 259.

28 *Totality and Infinity*, p. 54.

29 *Totality and Infinity*, pp. 84–5.

30 *Totality and Infinity*, pp. 211–12.

31 *Otherwise than Being, or Beyond Essence*, pp. 66–7.

32 *Otherwise than Being, or Beyond Essence*, pp. 68–9.

33 *Otherwise than Being, or Beyond Essence*, p. 69.

34 *Otherwise than Being, or Beyond Essence*, pp. 71–2.

35 Cf. Hegel, *Phenomenology of Spirit*, trsl. A. V. Miller, Oxford, Oxford University Press, 1977, p. 19.

36 Cf. Joseph Cohen "On the Possibility of Sacrifice", in *International Journal of Philosophical Studies*, 2:4, London, Routledge, 2014, pp. 552-568.

37 *Totality and Infinity*, p. 56.

38 Rosenzweig, *The Star of Redemption*, trsl. B. E. Galli, Madison, University of Wisconsin Press, 2005.

39 *Totality and Infinity*, pp. 56–7.

40 *Totality and Infinity*, p. 57.

41 *Totality and Infinity*, pp. 57–8.

42 *Totality and Infinity*, p. 233.

43 *Totality and Infinity*, p. 233.

44 *Totality and Infinity*, p. 233.

45 *Totality and Infinity*, p. 233.

46 *Totality and Infinity*, pp. 233–4.

47 *Totality and Infinity*, p. 234.

48 *Totality and Infinity*, p. 235.

49 *Totality and Infinity*, p. 235. Levinas refers here to E. A. Poe's infamous *The Masque of the Red Death*.

50 *Totality and Infinity*, p. 236.

51 Cf. *Babylon Talmud*, *Shabbat* 31a: "The same gentile came before Hillel. He converted him and said to him: That which is hateful to you do not do to another; that is the entire Torah, and the rest is its interpretation."

52 *Totality and Infinity*, pp. 33–4.

53 *Otherwise than Being, or Beyond Essence*, p. 9.

54 *Otherwise than Being, or Beyond Essence*, p. 10.

55 *Otherwise than Being, or Beyond Essence*, pp. 10–11.

56 *Otherwise than Being, or Beyond Essence*, p. 154.

57 *Otherwise than Being, or Beyond Essence*, p. 150.

58 *Otherwise than Being, or Beyond Essence*, pp. 150–1.

59 *Totality and Infinity*, p. 36.

60 *Totality and Infinity*, pp. 37–8.

61 *Totality and Infinity*, pp. 45–6.

62 *Totality and Infinity*, p. 38.

63 *Totality and Infinity*, p. 39.

64 *Totality and Infinity*, p. 39.

65 *Totality and Infinity*, p. 40.

66 *Otherwise than Being, or Beyond Essence*, p. 133.

67 *Otherwise than Being, or Beyond Essence*, p. 122.

68 *Otherwise than Being, or Beyond Essence*, p. 11.

69 *Totality and Infinity*, p. 131.

70 *Totality and Infinity*, p. 131.

71 *Totality and Infinity*, p. 132.

72 *Totality and Infinity*, p. 136.

73 *Totality and Infinity*, p. 136.

74 *Totality and Infinity*, p. 138.

75 *Totality and Infinity*, p. 137.

76 *Totality and Infinity*, pp. 140–1.

77 *Totality and Infinity*, p. 141.

78 *Totality and Infinity*, p. 142.

79 *Totality and Infinity*, p. 143.

80 *Otherwise than Being, or Beyond Essence*, p. 93.

81 *Otherwise than Being, or Beyond Essence*, p. 94.

82 *Totality and Infinity*, pp. 62–3.

83 *Totality and Infinity*, pp. 150–1.

84 *Totality and Infinity*, pp. 257–8.

85 *Totality and Infinity*, p. 269.

86 Remarkably, Levinas devotes multiple penetrating and suggestive analyses in various notes dating from the early 1920s and regrouped in vol. III of the *Oeuvres Complètes* (*Eros, littérature, philosophie*, Paris, Grasset, 2013). The main thrusts of these analyses are also reworked and presented in *Time and the Other*, *Existence and Existents* and *Totality and Infinity*. For a complete analysis of the genesis of *Eros* in Levinas' early writings, cf. F.-D. Sebbah, "Ambiguïté d'Eros. A la lumière des *Carnets de captivité* et d'autres inédits", in *Eros* (ed. N. Depraz), *Alter* 20 (2012), pp. 143–54.

87 *Totality and Infinity*, p. 270.

88 *Totality and Infinity*, p. 266.

89 *Totality and Infinity*, p. 266.

90 *On Escape*, p. 90.

91 *Totality and Infinity*, p. 23.

92 *Totality and Infinity*, p. 23.

93 *Totality and Infinity*, p. 23.

94 *Totality and Infinity*, p. 25.

95 *Totality and Infinity*, p. 25.

96 *Otherwise than Being, or Beyond Essence*, p. 12.

97 *Totality and Infinity*, p. 43.

98 *Totality and Infinity*, p. 197.

99 Cf. Heidegger, "Letter on Humanism," in *Basic Writings*, ed. and trsl. D. F. Krell, New York-London, Harper Collins, 1996, p. 258.

100 Cf. Heidegger, *Hölderlin's Hymns. "Germania" and "The Rhine"*, trsl. W. McNeill and J. Ireland, Bloomington and Indianapolis, Indiana University Press, 2014, p. 82.

101 *Othewise than Being, or Beyond Essence*, note 35, p. 193.

102 *Time and the Other*, p. 29.

103 Levinas, "Useless Suffering," in *Entre-Nous: Thinking-of-the-Other*, trsl. M. Smith, New York, Columbia University Press, p. 158.

104 Levinas, "Useless Suffering," p. 159.

105 Levinas, "Useless Suffering," p. 159.

106 Levinas, "Useless Suffering," pp. 164–5.

107 *Totality and Infinity*, p. 43.

108 *Totality and Infinity*, p. 46.

109 *Totality and Infinity*, p. 75.

110 We refer here to the profound interpretation of Levinas and the question of forgiveness, pardon and expiation, proposed by N. de Warren in *Original Forgiveness*, Evanston, Northwestern University Press, 2021.

111 *Otherwise than Being, or Beyond Essence*, p. 125.

112 *Otherwise than Being, or Beyond Essence*, p. 118. We refer here to N. de Warren's *Original Forgiveness*, most specifically ch. 3 entitled "The Unforgivable and Forgiving Without Forgiveness."

113 *Totality and Infinity*, pp. 181–2.

114 *Totality and Infinity*, p. 99.

115 *Totality and Infinity*, p. 78.

116 *Totality and Infinity*, pp. 290–1.

117 *Totality and Infinity*, p. 296.

118 *Totality and Infinity*, p. 251.

119 *Totality and Infinity*, p. 215.

120 *Totality and Infinity*, pp. 50–1.

121 *Otherwise than Being, or Beyond Essence*, pp. 88–9.

122 *Totality and Infinity*, p. 75.

123 *Totality and Infinity*, p. 81.

124 *Otherwise than Being, or Beyond Essence*, p. 91.

125 *Totality and Infinity*, p. 233.

126 *Totality and Infinity*, p. 303.

127 *Totality and Infinity*, p. 81.

128 *Totality and Infinity*, p. 213.

129 *Otherwise than Being, or Beyond Essence*, p. 159.

130 *Otherwise than Being, or Beyond Essence*, p. 161.

131 *Totality and Infinity*, pp. 268–9.

132 Cf. S. de Beauvoir, *The Second Sex*, trsl. H. M. Parshley, London, Vintage, 1997.

133 Cf. J. Derrida, "At This Very Moment In This Work Here I Am," in *Psyche. Inventions of the Other* (Volume I), trsl. R. Berezdivin and P. Kamuf, Stanford, Stanford University Press, 2007.

134 Cf. L. Irigaray, *An Ethics of Sexual Difference*, Ithaca, Cornell University Press, 1993.

135 Cf. C. Chalier, *Figures du féminin, lecture d'Emmanuel Levinas*, Paris, Verdier, 1982.

136 Rosenzweig, *The Star of Redemption*, trsl. W. W. Hallo, Notre Dame, University of Notre Dame Press, 1985.

137 *Totality and Infinity*, pp. 257–8.

138 *Totality and Infinity*, pp. 256–7.

139 *Totality and Infinity*, pp. 278–9.

140 *Totality and Infinity*, p. 282.

141 Hegel, *Phenomenology of Spirit*, trsl. A. V. Miller, Oxford, Oxford University Press, 1977, pp. 383-409.

142 Hegel, *Phenomenology of Spirit, op. cit.*, p. 407.
143 *Totality and Infinity*, p. 283.
144 *Totality and Infinity*, pp. 283–4.
145 *Totality and Infinity*, p. 284.
146 *Totality and Infinity*, pp. 284–5.
147 *Totality and Infinity*, p. 285.
148 *Totality and Infinity*, p. 43.
149 *Totality and Infinity*, pp. 43–4.
150 *Totality and Infinity*, p. 45.
151 *Totality and Infinity*, p. 45.
152 *Totality and Infinity*, pp. 73–4.
153 *Totality and Infinity*, p. 303.
154 *Totality and Infinity*, p. 303.
155 *Totality and Infinity*, p. 304.
156 *Otherwise than Being, or Beyond Essence*, pp. 124–5.
157 "Loving the Torah more than God," in *Difficult Freedom. Essays on Judaism*, trsl. S. Hand, Baltimore, John Hopkins University Press, 1997, p. 27.
158 *Totality and Infinity*, p. 102.
159 *Totality and Infinity*, pp. 102–3.
160 *Totality and Infinity*, p. 103.
161 *Totality and Infinity*, pp. 103–4.
162 *Totality and Infinity*, p. 183.
163 *Totality and Infinity*, p. 183.
164 *Totality and Infinity*, p. 183.
165 *Totality and Infinity*, p. 304.
166 *Totality and Infinity*, p. 305.
167 *Totality and Infinity*, p. 304.
168 *Totality and Infinity*, pp. 305–6.
169 *Otherwise than Being, or Beyond Essence*, pp. 122–3.
170 *Otherwise than Being or Beyond Essence*, p. 123.
171 *Otherwise than Being, or Beyond Essence*, p. 146.
172 *Otherwise than Being, or Beyond Essence*, pp. 149–50.
173 *From the Sacred to the Holy*, in *Nine Talmudic Readings*, trsl. and ed. A. Aronowicz, Bloomington, Indiana University Press, 1994.
174 Cf. Heidegger, *Being and Time*, § 9.
175 *Totality and Infinity*, p. 170.
176 *Totality and Infinity*, pp. 170–1.
177 *Totality and Infinity*, p. 171.
178 *Totality and Infinity*, p. 171.

179 *Otherwise than Being, or Beyond Essence*, p. 55.

180 *Otherwise than Being, or Beyond Essence*, p. 127.

181 *Otherwise than Being, or Beyond Essence*, p. 123.

182 *Otherwise than Being, or Beyond Essence*, p. 124.

183 *Totality and Infinity*, p. 214.

184 Levinas, *Existence and Existents*, p. 58.

185 *Existence and Existents*, p. 83.

186 *Existence and Existents*, p. 98.

187 *Existence and Existents*, p. 73.

188 Cf., *Time and the Other*, p. 52.

189 *Time and the Other*, p. 91.

190 *Time and the Other*, p. 92.

191 *Otherwise than Being, or Beyond Essence*, p. 104.

192 *Otherwise than Being, or Beyond Essence*, p. 106.

193 *Otherwise than Being, or Beyond Essence*, p. 108.

194 *Otherwise than Being, or Beyond Essence*, p. 12.

195 *Otherwise than Being, or Beyond Essence*, pp. 11–12.

196 *Otherwise than Being, or Beyond Essence*, pp. 12–13.

197 *Otherwise than Being, or Beyond Essence*, p. 13.

198 *Otherwise than Being, or Beyond Essence*, pp. 148–9.

199 *Otherwise than Being, or Beyond Essence*, p. 196, note 22.

200 *Time and the Other*, p. 29.

201 *Otherwise than Being, or Beyond Essence*, pp. 104–5.

202 *Otherwise than Being, or Beyond Essence*, p. 103.

203 Cf. Kant, *Religion Wthin the Limits of Mere Reason*, trsl. A. Wood and G. di Giovanni, Cambridge, Cambridge University Press, 1998.

204 Cf. Hegel, *The Spirit of Christianity and its Fate*, trsl. T. M. Knox, Chicago, Chicago University Press, 1948.

205 The infinite transcendence of the Other, for Levinas, is not assimilable to what the philosophical tradition has defined as the *positivity* of the heteronomous "historical revelation" determining from a pure exteriority the subject's practical reason. Nor does it mean to imply, according to Levinas, the heterogeneous commandment of the heteronomic Law levelling subjectivity into a pure obedience to a purely unknown, unrepresentable, inappropriable Otherness outside the self's comprehension. Indeed, and although Levinas retrieves the exteriority of the Judaic idea of radical transcendence, and indeed of the Law, in deploying the idea of the Infinite, of the infinity of the Other, he always distinguishes it from the interpretation the absolute transcendence of the revealed Law has received in the onto-theo-philosophical tradition, and most specifically in Kant and Hegel where the radical transcendence of the Other, and thus the very idea of the Judaic revelation of the heteronomous Law as always and already foreign, exterior, other always implies the subject's simple reverence and absolute subservience to an a-historical demand or order and thus abdication to an inassimilable, uncommunicable, irrepresentable order emanating from a pure and unverifiable given. Levinas categorically rejects the idea that the Law is simply given for the Self to obey blindly. Indeed, Levinas' ethics as First Philosophy is in no manner a simple abdication of the Self in self-sacrifice for the Other. All to the contrary: Levinas always insists on the exteriority of the Law as commandment of the Other proceeds from and in the Self's election to the Good as responsibility for the Other: that is, the incessant iteration and reiteration of a responsibility which, without ever abnegating, always awakens and elects the Self to itself as ethical response for the Other. In this sense, the infinity of transcendence, the infinity of the Other as commandment and demand, plea and question, in Levinas, and contrarily to both Kant and Hegel, far from negating the subject by reducing it to a simple receptive entity subjected to an incomprehensible transcendence animates, awakens, alivens the Self in an unsubstituable election for the Other as responsibility, care, hospitality for the Other. Contrarily to the tradition of German idealism, and far from understanding the transcendence of the Other as that which negates and denagates the subject, Levinas rethinks the idea of the infinity of the Other as election of the Self to the ethical and awakening of the Self to the urgency of caring for the Other. Cf., N. de Warren, *Original Forgiveness*, Evanston, Northwestern University Press, 2021, and, J. Cohen, "D'une langue à l'autre—la nuit," in *Alternances de la métaphysique. Essais sur E. Levinas*, Paris, Galilée, 2009.

206 *Totality and Infinity*, pp. 24–7.

207 *Totality and Infinity*, pp. 199–200.

208 Hegel, *Science of Logic*, trsl. A. V. Miller, Amherst, Humanities Press International, 1992.

209 Hegel, *Encyclopedia Logic*, trsl. T. F. Geraets, W. A. Suchting, and H. S. Harris, Cambridge, Hackett, 1991.

210 *Otherwise than Being, or Beyond Essence*, p. 142.

211 *Otherwise than Being, or Beyond Essence*, pp. 142–3.

212 *Otherwise than Being, or Beyond Essence*, p. 23.

213 *Otherwise than Being, or Beyond Essence*, p. 181.

214 Cf. the most important texts where Levinas speaks to the question of Israel—history, idea, religion, politics and Zionism—are to be found in *Difficult Freedom. Essays on Judaism*, trsl. S. Hand, Baltimore, John Hopkins University Press, 1997, and most specifically: "Judaism" (pp. 24–7); "Israel and Universalism" (pp. 175–7) "Judaism and the Present" (pp. 208–15); "The State of Israel and the Religion of Israel" (pp. 216–20) and "Means of Identification" (pp. 50–4). Very significant also are the following texts published in the volumes of the Talmudic readings and lectures: grouped in the Chapter entitled "Zionisms": "The State of Caesar and the State of David" (pp. 177–87); "Politics After!" (pp. 188–95); "Assimilation and New Culture" (pp. 196–201), in *Beyond the Verse. Talmudic Readings and Lectures*, trsl. G. D. Mole, Bloomington, Indiana

University Press, 1994. Cf. also "Ideology and Idealism" (pp. 235–48); "Ethics and Politics" (pp. 289–97), in *The Levinas Reader*, (ed. S. Hand), Oxford, Blackwell, 1989.

215 "Judaism," in *Difficult Freedom. Essays on Judaism*, trsl. S. Hand, Baltimore, John Hopkins University Press, 1997, p. 25.

216 Levinas, "Politics After!" trsl. R. Lack, in *The Levinas Reader* (ed. S. Hand), Oxford, Blackwell, 1989, p. 279.

217 Levinas, "Politics After!"

218 Levinas, "Ethics and Politics," trsl. J. Romney, in *The Levinas Reader* (ed. S. Hand), Oxford, Blackwell, 1989, p. 292: "There is always a direct contradiction between ethics and politics, if both these demands are taken to the extreme . . . ." There are numerous texts where Levinas points to this "contradiction" between the ethical and the political—that is, between the hyperbolical responsibility of the ethical and the ontological determination of the political as sovereignty and normativity, institutionalization of laws and governance, community and sociality. Indeed, Levinas marks repeatedly in which manner this "contradiction" between the singularity of the transcendence of the ethical and the universality and immanence of the political opens to what Derrida will call the certain *aporia* of responsibility, namely that political responsibility is always and already tied and confined, caught up and constrained to "alliances" and "interests," "calculations" and "evaluations," "hierarchies" and "valuations." In other words, the political reduces the ethical to an economy of sameness and identicalness. However, and due to the singular ethico-political question it poses and to which we will return to below—that is, given the specific context in which Levinas speaks of this "contradiction," the Sabra and Shatila massacre in 1982, and by extension the ethico-political dilemma and history between Israel and Palestine as well as the multiple misreadings of Levinas' typification of the word Israel in what is termed as his "politics" which have grown out of the interpretation this particular text, we choose to quote the interview conducted by S. Malka with Levinas and A. Finkielkraut (originally published in French language under the title "Israël: Ethique et politique," in *Les Nouveaux Cahiers*, vol. 18, no. 71, Paris, *Alliance Israélite Universelle*, 1982) published in English language under the title "Ethics and Politics," pp. 289–7.

219 Levinas, "Ethics and Politics," p. 292.

220 Levinas, "Ethics and Politics," p. 292.

221 Levinas, "Ethics and Politics," p. 292.

222 Levinas, "Ethics and Politics," 290.

223 Levinas, "Ethics and Politics," pp. 291–2.

224 Levinas, "Ethics and Politics," p. 292.

225 Levinas, "Ethics and Politics," pp. 292–3.

226 Levinas, "Ethics and Politics," p. 294.

227 Levinas, "Ethics and Politics."

228 Cf. M. Jay, "Hostage Philosophy: Levinas' Ethical Thought," in *Tikkun* 5, no. 6 (1990), pp. 85–7.

229 Cf. J. Butler, *Parting Ways. Jewishness and the Critique of Zionism*, New York, Columbia University Press, 2012.

230 Butler, *Parting Ways*, p. 23. For a just and rigorous critical analysis of the methodologically intrusive and ultimately dishonest interpretations proposed, firstly by M. Jay and relayed by J. Butler, we refer here to the excellent article by O. Eisenstadt and C. E. Katz entitled "The Faceless Palestinian: A History of an Error," in *Telos* 174 (Spring 2016), pp. 9–32.

231 Levinas, "Politics After!"

232 *Otherwise than Being, or Beyond Essence*, p. 16.

233 *Otherwise than Being, or Beyond Essence*, pp. 176–7.

234 Levinas, "Ideology and Idealism," trsl. S. Ames and A. Lesley, in *The Levinas Reader*, (ed. S. Hand),), Oxford, Blackwell, 1989, pp. 247–8.

235 "Ethics and Politics," pp. 296–7.

236 On the continuity between *Totality and Infinity* and *Otherwise than Being, or Beyond Essence*, we refer to the excellent study by Rolland, *Parcours de l'autrement. Lectures d'Emmanuel Levinas*, Paris, Presses Universitaires de France, 2000, as well as to Derrida's *Adieu—To Emmanuel Levinas*, trsl. P.-A. Brault and M. Naas, Stanford, Stanford University Press, 1999.

237 *Totality and Infinity*, p. 78.

238 *Totality and Infinity*, p. 78.

239 *Totality and Infinity*, p. 247.

240 *Totality and Infinity*, p. 90 *sq*.

241 *Totality and Infinity*, p. 72.

242 *Otherwise than Being, or Beyond Essence*, p. 160.

243 *Totaliy and Infinity*, p. 90.

244 *Otherwise than Being, or Beyond Essence*, p. 159.

245 *Otherwise than Being, or Beyond Essence*, pp. 161-162.

246 *Totality and Infinity*, p. 77.

247 *Totality and Infinity*, p. 77.

248 *Totality and Infinity*, p. 78.

249 *Totality and Infinity*, pp. 47–8.

250 *Totality and Infinity*, pp. 197–8.

251 *Totality and Infinity*, p. 198.

252 *Totality and Infinity*, p. 198.

253 *Totality and Infinity*, p. 198.

254 *Totality and Infinity*, p. 198.

255 *Totality and Infinity*, p. 199.

256 *Totality and Infinity*, p. 199.

257 *Totality and Infinity*, p. 199.

258 *Totality and Infinity*, p. 199.

259 *Totality and Infinity*, p. 199.

260 Cf. Hegel, *System of Ethical Life and First Philosophy of Spirit*, trsl. and ed. T. M. Knox and H. S. Harris, New York, SUNY Press, 1979.

261 *Totality and Infinity*, pp. 199–200.

262 *Totality and Infinity*, p. 200.

263 *Otherwise than Being, or Beyond Essence*, p. 150.

264 *Otherwise than Being, or Beyond Essence*, pp. 148–9.

265 *Otherwise than Being, or Beyond Essence*, p. 11.

266 *Otherwise than Being, or Beyond Essence*, p. 133.

267 *Otherwise than Being, or Beyond Essence*, p. 136.

268 *Otherwise than Being, or Beyond Essence*, p. 137.

269 *Otherwise than Being, or Beyond Essence*, pp. 137–8.

270 *Otherwise than Being, or Beyond Essence*, pp. 138–9.

271 *Totality and Infinity*, p. 45.

272 *Totality and Infinity*, pp. 43–4.

273 "Is Ontology Fundamental?" in *Levinas. Basic Philosophical Writings* (ed. A. Peperzak, S. Critchley, R. Bernasconi), Bloomington, Indiana University Press, 1996, pp. 5–6.

274 "Is Ontology Fundamental?" p. 7.

275 "Is Ontology Fundamental?"

276 "Is Ontology Fundamental?" p. 8.

277 "Is Ontology Fundamental?" p. 7.

278 "Is Ontology Fundamental?" p. 8.

279 "Is Ontology Fundamental?"

280 *Totality and Infinity*, p. 39.

281 *Totality and Infinity*, p. 40.

282 *Otherwise than Being, or Beyond Essence*, pp. 117–18.

283 *Otherwise than Being, or Beyond Essence*, pp. 10–11.

284 *Otherwise than Being, or Beyond Essence*, p. 127.

285 *Otherwise than Being, or Beyond Essence*, p. 143.

286 *Otherwise than Being, or Beyond Essence*, p. 146.

287 *Totality and Infinity*, p. 21.

288 *Totality and Infinity*, p. 21.

289 *Totality and Infinity*, p. 21.

290 Indeed, here again Levinas engages a critique of sacrifice which is associated to the effacement and annihilation of existents, and thereby of the unicity of the present, in and for an "ultimate meaning" which "alone" would "count." Cf. *Totality and Infinity*, p. 22: "The unicity of each present is incessantly sacrificed to a future appaled to to bring forth its objective meaning. For the ultimate meaning alone counts."

291 *Totality and Infinity*, pp. 22–3.

292 *Totality and Infinity*, pp. 304–5.
293 *Totality and Infinity*, pp. 305–6.
294 *Otherwise than Being, or Beyond Essence*, pp. 110–11.
295 *Otherwise than Being, or Beyond Essence*, p. 111.
296 *Otherwise than Being, or Beyond Essence*, p. 111.
297 *Otherwise than Being, or Beyond Essence*, p. 112.
298 *Totality and Infinity*, p. 46.
299 *Totality and Infinity*, p. 46.
300 *Totality and Infinity*, p. 47.
301 *Otherwise than Being, or Beyond Essence*, p. 88.
302 *Totality and Infinity*, p. 47.
303 *Otherwise than Being, or Beyond Essence*, p. 153.
304 *Otherwise than Being, or Beyond Essence*, p. 166.
305 *Time and the Other*, p. 32.
306 *Otherwise than Being, or Beyond Essence*, p. 218.
307 *Otherwise than Being, or Beyond Essence*, p. 139.
308 *Otherwise than Being, or Beyond Essence*, p. 89.
309 *Otherwise than Being, or Beyond Essence*, p. 86.
310 *Otherwise than Being, or Beyond Essence*, p. 88.
311 *Otherwise than Being, or Beyond Essence*, pp. 139-140.
312 Cf. Heidegger, "Letter on 'Humanism'," in *Pathmarks*, trsl. W. McNeill, Cambridge, Cambridge University Press, 1998, pp. 239–76.
313 "Letter on 'Humanism'," p. 271.
314 *Totality and Infinity*, pp. 80–1.
315 *Otherwise than Being, or Beyond Essence*, p. 124.
316 *Totality and Infinity*, pp. 244–5.
317 *Otherwise than Being, or Beyond Essence*, p. 54.
318 *Otherwise than Being, or Beyond Essence*, pp. 142–3.
319 *Otherwise than Being, or Beyond Essence*, pp. 138–9.
320 *Otherwise than Being, or Beyond Essence*, p. 139.
321 *Otherwise than Being, or Beyond Essence*, p. 12.
322 *Otherwise than Being, or Beyond Essence*, p. 93.
323 *Totality and Infinity*, pp. 21–2.
324 The modality of sacrifice as elevation of the finite in and through the infinitude of the Absolute, of the particular moments comprehended as meaning and meaningfulness of Spirit and thus as already informing the historical becoming of Absolute knowledge works through Hegel's philosophy of History as it operates throughout the speculative appropriation of History in the *Phenomenology of Spirit*. Sacrifice indeed for Hegel constitutes the very meaning of the *Aufhebung*, "negation"

and "negation of negation," which institutes the performativity of the speculative dialectic as comprehension of Reason in and as History. Cf. J. Cohen, *Le sacrifice de Hegel*, Paris, Galilée, 2007 and also "Hegel and the Gift of Sacrifice," in *Violence and the Gift. Challenging Continental Philosophy of Religion* (ed. L. Hagedorn, M. Staudigl, J. W. Alvis), *Journal for Cultural and Religious Theory* 15, no. 1 (Fall 2015), pp. 16–22.

325 The idea and operation of sacrifice plays a central, albeit oblique role, in Heidegger's philosophy of History. From *Being and Time* to the Bremen Lectures, and most significantly *The Thing*, sacrifice represents a modality by which and through which the truth and meaning of Being is revealed as *Ereignis* and thus as non-reconciliatory, non-dialectical opening, and clearing of donation of the co-belonging, gathering, enowning of Being *and* Time. Cf.: N. de Warren, *German Philosophy and the First World War*, Cambridge, Cambridge University Press, 2023, most specifically chapter 9 entitled "Martin Heidegger and the Titanic Struggle over Being"; also, J. Cohen, "On the Possibility of Sacrifice," in *International Journal of Philosophical Studies*, vol. 22, no. 4, London, Routledge, 2014, pp. 552–68.

326 "A propos de Struthof," published in *Le Monde*, July 17, 1954.

327 *Otherwise than Being, or Beyond Essence*, p. 15.

328 *Otherwise than Being, or Beyond Essence*, p. 120.

329 *Otherwise than Being, or Beyond Essence*, p. 120.

330 *Otherwise than Being, or Beyond Essence*, p. 124.

331 *Otherwise than Being, or Beyond Essence*, pp. 49–50.

332 *Otherwise than Being, or Beyond Essence*, p. 115.

333 *Otherwise than Being, or Beyond Essence*, p. 120.

334 *Otherwise than Being, or Beyond Essence*, p. 15.

335 *Otherwise than Being, or Beyond Essence*, p. 115.

336 *Otherwise than Being, or Beyond Essence*, p. 49.

337 *Otherwise than Being, or Beyond Essence*, pp. 50–1.

338 *Otherwise than Being, or Beyond Essence*, pp. 153–4.

339 *Otherwise than Being, or Beyond Essence*, p. 154.

340 *Otherwise than Being, or Beyond Essence*, p. 155.

341 *Otherwise than Being, or Beyond Essence*, p. 156.

342 *Otherwise than Being, or Beyond Essence*, pp. 156–7.

343 *Otherwise than Being, or Beyond Essence*, p. 159.

344 *Totality and Infinity*, p. 137.

345 *Totality and Infinity*, p. 137.

346 *Totality and Infinity*, p. 138.

347 Cf. *Totality and Infinity*, p. 193 *sq*.

348 *Otherwise than Being, or Beyond Essence*, p. 14.

349 *Otherwise than Being, or Beyond Essence*, p. 15.

350 *Totality and Infinity*, p. 58.

351 *Totality and Infinity*, pp. 299–300.
352 *Totality and Infinity*, p. 251.
353 *Otherwise than Being, or Beyond Essence*, pp. 123–4.
354 *Otherwise than Being, or Beyond Essance*, p. 14.
355 *Otherwise than Being, or Beyond Essence*, p. 133.
356 *Otherwise than Being, or Beyond Essence*, p. 136.
357 *Otherwise than Being, or Beyond Essence*, p. 137.
358 *Otherwise than Being, or Beyond Essence*, pp. 5–6.
359 *Otherwise than Being, or Beyond Essence*, p. 17.
360 *Otherwise than Being, or Beyond Essence*, pp. 17–18.
361 *Otherwise than Being, or Beyond Essence*, pp. 25–6.
362 *Otherwise than Being, or Beyond Essence*, p. 56.
363 *Otherwise than Being, or Beyond Essence*, p. 114.
364 *Otherwise than Being, or Beyond Essence*, p. 115.
365 *Otherwise than Being, or Beyond Essence*, pp. 116–17.
366 *Totality and Infinity*, p. 281.
367 *Totality and Infinity*, p. 282.
368 *Totality and Infinity*, pp. 283–4.
369 *Otherwise than Being, or Beyond Essence*, p. 9.
370 *Totality and Infinity*, p. 284.
371 *Totality and Infinity*, p. 305.
372 *Otherwise than Being, or Beyond Essence*, p. 158.
373 *Otherwise than Being, or Beyond Essence*, p. 159.
374 *Otherwise than Being, or Beyond Essence*, pp. 159–60.
375 *Otherwise than Being, or Beyond Essence*, p. 160.
376 *Otherwise than Being, or Beyond Essence*, pp. 160–1.
377 *Otherwise than Being, or Beyond Essence*, p. 158.
378 *Otherwise than Being, or Beyond Essence*, pp. 161–2.
379 *Totality and Infinity*, p. 21.
380 *Totality and Infinity*, p. 22.
381 Hegel, *Phenomenology of Spirit*, trsl. A. V. Miller, Oxford, Oxford University Press, 1977, p. 20.
382 *Totality and Infinity*, pp. 36–7.
383 *Totality and Infinity*, p. 38.
384 *Totality and Infinity*, p. 39.
385 *Totality and Infinity*, p. 40.
386 *Totality and Infinity*, p. 40.
387 "The Trace of the Other," in *Entre Nous*, p. 356.
388 "The Trace of the Other," in *Entre Nous*, p. 356.

389 *Otherwise than Being, or Beyond Essence*, p. 97.

390 *Otherwise than Being, or Beyond Essence*, p. 148.

391 *Otherwise than Being, or Beyond Essence*, p. 124.

392 *Otherwise than Being, or Beyond Essence*, pp. 56–7.

393 *Totality and Infinity*, p. 21.

394 *Totality and Infinity*, p. 21.

395 *Totality and Infinity*, pp. 21–2.

396 Cf. Hegel, *Phenomenology of Spirit*, trsl. A. V. Miller, Oxford, Oxford University Press, 1979. Also: J. Cohen, *Le sacrifice de Hegel*, Paris, Galilée, 2007.

397 *Totality and Infinity*, p. 22.

398 *Totality and Infinity*, pp. 22–3.

399 *Totality and Infinity*, p. 225.

Bibliography

Autrement qu'être, ou au-delà de l'essence, La Haye, M. Nijhoff, 1974. English Translation: *Otherwise than Being, or Beyond Essence*, trsl. A. Lingis, Pittsburgh, Duquesne University Press, 1998.

De Dieu qui vient à l'idée, Paris, Vrin, 1982. English Translation: *Of God who Comes to Mind*, trsl. B. Bergo, Stanford, Stanford University Press, 1998.

De l'évasion, Montpellier, Fata Morgana, 1935. English Translation: *On Escape*, trsl. B. Bergo, Stanford, Stanford University Press, 2003.

De l'existence à l'existant, Paris, Vrin, 1947. English Translation: *Existence and Existents*, trsl. R. A. Cohen, Pittsburgh, Dusquesne University Press, 2001.

Difficile liberté: Essais sur le judaïsme, Paris, Albin Michel, 1963. English Translation: *Difficult Freedom. Essays on Judaism*, trsl. S. Hand, Baltimore, John Hopkins University Press, 1997.

Dieu, la mort et le temps, Paris, Grasset, 1993. English Translation: *God, Death and Time*, trsl. B. Bergo, Stanford, Stanford University Press, 2000.

En découvrant l'existence avec Husserl et Heidegger, Paris, Vrin, 1st Edition, 1949 / 2nd Augmented Editon, 1967. English Translation: *Discovering Existence with Husserl*, trsl. CohenR. A. and M. Smith, Evanston, Northwestern University Press, 1998.

Entre Nous. Penser à l'autre, Paris, Grasset, 1991. English Translation: *Entre Nous. Thinking of the Other*, trsl. M. Smith and B. Harshav, New York, Columbia University Press, 2000.

Ethique et infini, Paris, Fayard, 1984. English Translation: *Ethics and Infinity*, trsl. R. A. Cohen, Pittsburgh, Dusquesne University Press, 1985.

Humanisme de l'autre homme, Montpellier, Fata Morgana, 1972. English Translation: *Humanism of the Other*, trsl. N. Poller, Urbana-Champaign, University of Illinois Press, 2006.

Is it Righteous to be? Interviews with Emmanuel Levinas, trsl. and ed. J. Robbins. Stanford, Stanford University Press, 2001.

La Théorie de l'intuition dans la phénoménologie de Husserl, Paris, Alcan, 1930/ Paris, Vrin, 1963. English Translation: *The Theory of Intuition in Husserl's Phenomenology*, trsl. A. Orianne, Evanston, Northwestern University Press, 1995.

Les imprévus de l'histoire, Montpellier, Fata Morgana, 1994. English Translation: *Unforeseen History*, trsl. N. Poller, Urbana-Champaign, University of Illinois Press, 2004.

Le temps et l'autre, Paris, Presses universitaires de France, (1948) 1980. English Translation: *Time and the Other*, trsl. R. A. Cohen, Pittsburgh, Duquesne University Press, 1987.

Liberté et commandement, Montpellier, Fata Morgana, 1994.

Noms propres, Montpellier, Fata Morgana, 1976. English Translation: *Proper Names*, trsl. M. Smith, Stanford, Stanford University Press, 1997.

Quelques réflexion sur la philosophie de l'hitlérisme, 1934. English Translation: "Reflections on the Philosophy of Hitlerism", in *Critical Inquiry*, vol. 17, no. 1, Chicago, Chicago University Press, Autumn 1990, pp. 62–71.

Sur Maurice Blanchot, Montpellier, Fata Morgana, 1975.

Totalité et infini. Essai sur l'extériorité, La Haye, M. Nijhoff, 1961. English Translation: *Totality and Infinity. An Essay on Exteriority*, trsl. A. Lingis, Pittsburgh, Duquesne University Press, 1969.

Other English Language Edited Volumes

Levinas. Basic Philosophical Writings, ed. A. Peperzak, S. Critchley, R. Bernasconi, Bloomington, Indiana University Press, 1996.

This edited volume contains the following texts: *Is Ontology Fundamental?* (1951); *Transcendence and Height* (1962); *Meaning and Sense* (1964); *Enigma and Phenomena* (1965); *Substitution* (1968); *Truth of Disclosure and Truth of Testimony* (1972); *Essence and Disinteressedness* (1974); *God and Philosophy* (1975); *Transcendence and Intelligibility* (1984); *Peace and Proximity* (1984).

The Levinas Reader, ed. S. Hand, Oxford, Basil Blackwell, 1989.

This edited volume contains the following texts: *The Phenomenological Theory of Being* (1930); *There is: Existence without Existents* (1946); *Time and the Other* (1946, Extract from *Time and the Other*, trsl. R. A. Cohen, Pittsburgh, Duquesne University Press, 1987); *Martin Buber and the Theory of Knowledge* (1958); *Ethics as First Philosophy* (1984); *Substitution* (1968); *Reality and Its Shadow* (1948); *The Transcendence of Words* (1949); *The Servant and her Master* (1966); *The other in Proust* (1947); *God and Philosophy* (1975); *Revelation in the Jewish Tradition* (1977); *The Pact* (1982); *Prayer Without Demand* (1984); *Ideology and Idealism* (1973); Extracts from *Difficult Freedom. Essays on Judaism*, trsl. S. Hand, Baltimore, John Hopkins University Press, 1997; *Judaism* (1971) / *Judaism and the Present* (1960) / *The State of Israel and the Religion of Israel* (1951) / *Means of Identification* (1963); Extracts from *Beyond the verse: Talmudic Readings and Lectures*, trsl. G. Mole, Bloomington, Indiana University Press, 1994; *The State of Ceasar and the State of David* (1971) / *Politics After*! (1979)/ *Assimilation and New Culture* (1980); *Ethics and Politics* (Transcript of Radio interview by S. Malka with E. Levinas and A. Finkielkraut, 1982).

Talmudic Readings and Lectures

Beyond the verse: Talmudic Readings and Lectures, trsl. G. Mole, Bloomington, Indiana University Press, 1994.

In the Time of the Nations, trsl. SmithM. B. , Bloomington, Indiana University Press, 1994.

New Talmudic Readings, trsl. R. Cohen, Pittsburg, Duquesne University Press, 2007.

Nine Talmudic Readings, trsl. and ed. A. Aronowicz, Bloomington, Indiana University Press, 1994. Contains: *Quatre lectures talmudiques* and *Du sacré au saint. Cinq nouvelles lectures talmudiques.*

Selected Scholarly Bibliography of Secondary Literature

Arnett, R. C. (2017), *Levinas's Rhetorical Demand: The Unending Obligation of Communication Ethics*, Carbondale, Southern Illinois University Press.

Atterton, P., Calarco, M. and Friedman, M. (eds) (2004), *Levinas and Buber: Dialogue and Difference*, Pittsburgh, Duquesne University Press.

Atterton, P., Calarco, M. and Friedman, M. (eds) (2010), *Radicalizing Levinas*, Albany, SUNY Press.

Bailhache, G. (1994), *Le sujet chez Emmanuel Levinas: fragilité et subjectivité*, Paris, Presses Universitaires de France.

Batnitzky, L. (2006), *Leo Strauss and Emmanuel Levinas: Philosophy and the Politics of Revelation*, Cambridge, Cambridge University Press.

Bensussan, G. (2008), *Éthique et expérience. Levinas politique*, Strasbourg, Editions de La phocide.

Bergo, B. (1999), *Levinas Between Ethics and Politics. For the Beauty That Adorns the Earth*, Berlin-Dordrecht, Springer.

Bernasconi, R. and Critchley, S. (1991), *Re-reading Levinas*, London, Continuum.

Bernasconi, R. and Critchley, S. with Wood, D. (eds) (1988), *The Provocation of Levinas: Rethinking the Other*, London, Routledge.

Bloechel, J. (ed.) (2000), *The Face of the Other and the Trace of God: Essays on the Philosophy of Emmanuel Levinas*, New York, Fordham University Press.

Bloechel, J. (2022), *Levinas on the Primacy of the Ethical. Philosophy as Prophecy*, Evanston, Northwestern University Press.

Bloechel, J. (2000), *Liturgy of the Neighbor: Emmanuel Levinas and the Religion of Responsibility*, Pittsburg, Duquesne University Press.

Botwinick, A. (2014), *Emmanuel Levinas and the Limits to Ethics: A Critique and a Re-Appropriation*, London, Routledge.

Burggraeve, R. (1985), *From Self-development to Solidarity. An Ethical Reading of Human Desire in its Socio-Political Relevance According to E. Levinas*, Leuven, Peeters.

Burggraeve, R. (2002), *The Wisdom of Love in the Service of Love. Emmanuel Levinas on Justice, Peace and Human Rights*, Milwaukee, Marquette University Press.

Calin, R. (2005), *Levinas et l'exception du soi*, Paris, Presses Universitaires de France.

Caygill, H. (2002), *Levinas and the Political*, London, Routledge.

Chalier, C. (1982), *Figures du féminin, lecture d'Emmanuel Levinas*, Paris, Verdier.

Chalier, C. (1982), *Judaïsme et altérité*, Paris, Verdier.

Chalier, C. (1985), *La persévérance du mal*, Paris, Cerf.

Chalier, C. (2002), *La Trace de l'infini. Emmanuel Lévinas et la source hébraïque*, Paris, Cerf.
Chalier, C. (1993), *Levinas. L'utopie de l'humain*, Paris, Albin Michel.
Chalier, C. (1997), *L'inspiration du philosophe. "L'amour de la sagesse" et sa source prophétique*, Paris, Albin Michel
Chalier, C. (1998), *Pour une morale au-delà du savoir. Kant et Lévinas*, Paris, Albin Michel.
Ciaramelli, F. (1989), *Transcendance et éthique*, Brussels, Ousia.
Ciglia, F. P. (1996), *Fenomenologie dell'umano. Sondaggi eccentrici sul pensiero di Levinas*, Rome, Bulzoni.
Coe, C. D. (2018), *Levinas and the Trauma of Responsibility: The Ethical Significance of Time*, Bloomington, Indiana University Press.
Cohen, J. (2009), *Alternances de la métaphysique. Essais sur E. Levinas*, Paris, Galilée.
Cohen, R. (1994), *Elevations: The Height of the Good in Rosenzweig and Levinas*, Chicago, University of Chicago Press.
Cohen, R. (2001), *Ethics, Exegesis and Philosophy: Interpretation After Levinas*, Cambridge, Cambridge University Press.
Cohen, R. (2017), *Out of Control: Confrontations between Spinoza and Levinas*, Albany, SUNY Press.
Cools, A. (2007), *Langage et subjectivité. Vers une approche du différend entre Maurice Blanchot et Emmanuel Lévinas*, Leuven, Peeters.
Courtine-Denamy, S. (2004), *Le visage en question*, Paris, Éditions de la Différence.
Critchley, S. (1999), *The Ethics of Deconstruction: Derrida and Levinas*, Edinburgh, Edinburgh University Press.
Critchley, S. (1999), *Ethics-Politics-Subjectivity: Essays on Derrida, Levinas and Contemporary French Thought*, London, Verso.
Critchley, S. with R.Bernasconi, (eds) (2002), *The Cambridge Companion to Levinas*, Cambridge, Cambridge University Press.
Dalton, D. M. (2009), *Longing for the Other: Levinas and Metaphysical Desire*, Pittsburg, Duquesne University Press.
Davis, C. (1997), *Levinas: An Introduction*, Washington, University of Notre Dame Press.
De Bauw, C. (1997), *L'envers du sujet. Lire autrement Emmanuel Levinas*, Brussels, Ousia.
De Vries, H. (2005), *Minimal Theology: Critiques of Secular Reason in Adorno and Levinas*, trsl. G. Hale, Baltimore, Johns Hopkins University Press.
De Warren, N. (2021), *Original Forgiveness*, Evanston, Northwestern University Press.
Dekens, O. (2003), *Politique de l'autre homme. Lévinas et la fonction politique de la philosophie*, Paris, Ellipses.
Derrida, J. (1997/1999), *Adieu- To Emmanuel Levinas*, trsl. P.-A. Brault and M. Naas, Stanford, Stanford University Press.
Derrida, J. (1987/2007), "At This Very Moment in This Work Here I Am", in *Psyche. Inventions of the Other* (Volume I), trsl. R. Berezdivin and P. Kamuf, Stanford, Stanford University Press.
Derrida, J. (1967/1978), "Violence and Metaphysics: An Essay on the Thought of Emmanuel Levinas", in *Writing and Difference*, trsl. A. Bass, Chicago, University of Chicago Press.

Diprose, R. (2002), *Corporeal Generosity: On Giving with Nietzsche, Merleau-Ponty and Levinas*, Albany, SUNY Press.

Drabinski, J. E. (2011), *Levinas and the Postcolonial: Race, Nation, Other*, Edinburgh, Edinburgh University Press.

Drabinski, J. E. (2001), *Sensibility and Singularity: The Problem of Phenomenology in Levinas*, New York, SUNY Press.

Dudiak, J. (2001), *The Intrigue of Ethics: A Reading of the Idea of Discourse in the Thought of Emmanuel Levinas*, New York, Fordham University Press.

Durante, M. (2002), *Fenomenologia della Legge. La questione del terzo nella filosofia di E. Levinas*, Milan, Theleme.

Fagenblatt, M. (2010), *A Covenant of Creatures. Levinas' Philosophy of Judaism*, Stanford, Stanford University Press.

Féron, E. (1992), *De l'idée de transcendance à la question du langage. L'itinéraire philosophique d'Emmanuel Levinas*, Grenoble, Jérôme Millon.

Féron, E. (1999), *Phénoménologie de la mort: sur les traces de Lévinas*, Leuven, Kluwer.

Franck, D. (2008), *L'un pour l'autre: Levinas et la signification*, Paris, Presses Universitaires de France.

Forte, B. (2001), *La sfida de Dio. Dove fede e ragione si incontrano*, Milan, Mondadori.

Gibbs, R. (1994), *Correlations in Rosenzweig and Levinas*, Princeton, Princeton University Press.

Gibbs, R. (2000), *Why Ethics? Signs of Responsibilities*, Princeton, Princeton University Press.

Guibal, F. (2005), *Approches d'Emmanuel Levinas. L'inspiration d'une écriture*, Paris, Presses Universitaires de France.

Guibal, F. (2005), *Emmanuel Lévinas ou les intrigues du sens*, Paris, Presses Universitaires de France.

Guibal, F. (2004), *La Gloire en exil*, Paris, Cerf.

Habib, S. (2005), *Levinas et Rosenzweig. Philosophies de la Révélation*, Paris, Presses Universitaires de France.

Hand, S. (2009), *Emmanuel Levinas*, London, Routledge.

Hand, S. (ed.) (1996), *Facing the Other: The Ethics of Emmanuel Lévinas*, Surrey, Curzon.

Hayat, P. (1995), *Emmanuel Levinas, éthique et société*, Paris, Kimé.

Hayat, P. (1997), *Individualisme éthique et philosophie chez Lévinas*, Paris, Kimé.

Hendley, S. (2000), *From Communicative Action to the Face of the Other: Levinas and Habermas on Language, Obligation, and Community*, London, Lexington Books.

Herzog, A. (1997), *Penser autrement la politique*, Paris, Kimé.

Horowitz, A. and G.Horowitz, (eds) (2006), *Difficult Justice: Commentaires on Levinas and Politics*, Toronto, University of Toronto Press.

Hutchens, B. C. (2004), *Levinas: A Guide for the Perplexed*, New York-London, Continuum.

Katz, C. (2012), *Levinas and the Crisis of Humanism*, Bloomington, Indiana University Press.

Katz, C. (2004), *Levinas: Critical Assessments of Leading Philosophers*, London, Routledge.

Katz, C. (2003), *Levinas, Judaism, and the Feminine: The Silent Footsteps of Rebecca*, Bloomington, Indiana University Press.
Kayser, P. (2000), *Emmanuel Lévinas: la trace du féminin*, Paris, Presses Universitaires de France.
Keenan, D. K. (1994), *Death and Responsibility: The "Work" of Levinas*, Albany, SUNY Press.
Kenaan, H. (2012), *Visage (s). Une autre éthique du regard après Levinas*, Paris, Éditions de l'Éclat.
Kleinberg, E. (2021), *Emmanuel Levinas' Talmudic Turn. Philosophy and Jewish Thought*, Stanford, Stanford University Press.
Kosky, J. L (2001), *Levinas and the Philosophy of Religion*, Bloomington, Indiana University Press.
Large, W. (2015), *Levinas's Totality and Infinity: A Reader's Guide*, New York-London, Bloomsbury.
Libertson, J. (1982), *Proximity: Levinas, Blanchot, Bataille and Communication*, The Hague, Martinus Nijhoff.
Llewelyn, J. (2002), *Appositions of Jacques Derrida and Emmanuel Levinas*, Bloomington, Indiana University Press.
Llewelyn, J. (1995), *Emmanuel Levinas: The Genealogy of Ethics*, London, Routledge.
Llewelyn, J. (1999), *The Hypocritical Imagination: Between Kant and Levinas*, London, Routledge.
Llewelyn, J. (1991), *The Middle Voice of Ecological Conscience: A Chiasmic Reading of Responsibility in the Neighbourhood of Levinas, Heidegger and Others*, London, Palgrave Macmillan.
Malka, S. (2006), *Emmanuel Levinas: His Life and Legacy*. Pittsburgh, Duquesne University Press.
Manning, R. J. S. (1993), *Interpreting Otherwise than Heidegger: Emmanuel Levinas's Ethics as First Philosophy*, Pittsburgh, Duquesne University Press.
Meir, E. (2008), *Levinas's Jewish Thought. Between Athens and Jerusalem*, Jerusalem, Hebrew University Magnes Press.
Mensch, J. (2015), *Levinas's Existential Analytic: A Commentary on Totality and Infinity*, Evanston, Northwestern University Press.
Moatti, R. (2016), *Levinas and the Night of Being. A Guide to Totality and Infinity*, New York, Fordham University Press.
Mole, G. D and Gontarski, S. E. (1997), *Levinas, Blanchot, Jabes: Figures of Estrangement*, Miami, University Press of Florida.
Morgan, M. L. (2007), *Discovering Levinas*, Cambridge, Cambridge University Press.
Morgan, M. L. (2016), *Levinas's Ethical Politics*, Bloomington, Indiana University Press.
Moses, S. (2004), *Au-delà de la guerre. Trois études sur E. Levinas*, Paris, Editions de l'éclat.
Murakami, Y. (2002), *Lévinas phénoménologue*, Bruxelles, Jérôme Million.
Murray, J. W. (2003), *Face-to-face in Dialogue: Emmanuel Levinas and (the) Communication (of) Ethics*, Lanham, University Press of America.
Ndayizigiye, T. (1997), *L'anthropologie biblique sous l'éclairage de la philosophie de l'altérité selon E. Lévinas*, London, Peter Lang.

Newton, A. Z. (2000), *The Fence and the Neighbor: Emmanuel Levinas, Yeshayahu Leibowitz, and Israel Among the Nations*, New York, SUNY Press.

Nordmann, S. (2008), *Philosophie et judaïsme. H. Cohen, F. Rosenzweig, E. Levinas*, Paris, Presses Universitaires de France.

Ombrosi, O. (2010), *L'umano ritrovato. Saggio su Emmanuel Levinas*, Bologna, Marietti 1820.

Ombrosi, O. (2011), *The Twilight of Reason. Benjamin, Adorno, Horkheimer and Levinas Tested by the Catastrophe*, Boston, Academic Studies Press.

Peperzak, A. (2000), *Beyond the Philosophy of E. Levinas*, Evanston, Northwestern University Press.

Peperzak, A. (1997), *Beyond: The Philosophy of Emmanuel Levinas*, Evanston, Northwestern University Press.

Peperzak, A. (ed.) (1995), *Ethics as First Philosophy: The Significance of Emmanuel Levinas for Philosophy, Literature and Religion*, New York-London, Routledge.

Peperzak, A. (2003), *The Quest for Meaning: Friends of Wisdom from Plato to Levinas*, New York, Fordham University Press.

Peperzak, A. (1993), *To the Other. An Introduction to the Philosophy of Emmanuel Levinas*. West Lafayette, Purdue University Press.

Perpich, D. (2008), *The Ethics of Emmanuel Levinas*, Stanford, Stanford University Press.

Pinchevski, A. (2005), *By Way of Interruption. Levinas and the Ethics of Communication*, Pittsburg, Duquesne University Press.

Plant, B. (2005), *Wittgenstein and Levinas: Ethical and Religious Thought*, New York-London, Routledge.

Plourde, S. (1996), *Emmanuel Levinas. Altérité et responsabilité: guide de lecture*, Paris, Cerf.

Poirié, F. (1992), *Emmanuel Lévinas*, Besançon, La Manufacture.

Puntel, L. (2012), *Being and God: A Systematic Approach in Confrontation with Martin Heidegger, Emmanuel Levinas, and Jean-Luc Marion*, Evanston, Northwestern University Press.

Purcell, M. (1998), *Mystery and Method: The Other in Rahner and Levinas*, Milwaukee, Marquette University Press.

Putnam, H. (2008), *Jewish Philosophy as a Guide to Life: Rosenzweig, Buber, Levinas, Wittgenstein*, Bloomington, Indiana University Press.

Rey, J-F. (2001), *La mesure de l'homme. L'idée d'humanité dans la philosophie d'E. Lévinas*, Paris, Michalon.

Rey, J-F. (1997), *Lévinas, le passeur de justice*, Paris, Michalon.

Ricoeur, P. (1999), *Autrement. Lecture d'Autrement qu'être ou au-delà de l'Essence d'Emmanuel Levinas*, Paris, Presses Universitaires de France.

Robbins, B. D. (1999), *Altered Reading: Levinas and Literature*, Chicago, Chicago University Press.

Rolland, J. (ed.) (1984), *Emmanuel Lévinas*, (*Cahiers de la nuit surveillée*, 3), Lagrasse, Verdier.

Rolland, J. (2000), *Parcours de l'autrement*, Paris, Presses Universitaires de France.

Rütter, S. (2000), *Herausforderung angesichts des Anderen – Von Feuerbach ûber Buber zu Levinas*, Freiburg, Verlag Karl Alber.

Rychter, E. (2004), *(Un)saying of the Other: Allegory and Irony in Emmanuel Levinas's Ethical Language*, New York, Peter Lang.

Sandford, S. (2001), *The Metaphysics of Love: Gender and Transcendence in Levinas*, London, Continuum.

Schiffer, D. S. (2007), *La philosophie d'Emmanuel Lévinas. Métaphysique, esthétique, éthique*, Paris, Presses Universitaires de France.

Schnell, A. (2010), *En face de l'extériorité. Levinas et la question de la subjectivité*, Paris, Vrin.

Schroeder, B. (1996), *Altared Ground: Levinas, History and Violence*, New York-London, Routledge.

Sealy, K. (2013), *Moments of Disruption: Levinas, Sartre, and the Question of Transcendence*, Albany, SUNY Press.

Sebbah, F.-D. (2001), *L'épreuve de la limite. Derrida, Henry, Lévinas et la phénoménologie*, Paris, Presses Universitaires de France.

Sebbah, F.-D. (2000), *Levinas. Ambiguités de l'altérité*, Paris, Les Belles-Lettres.

Sebbah, F.-D. (2009), *Levinas et le contemporain*, Paris, Les solitaires intempestifs.

Severson, E. (2013), *Levinas's Philosophy of Time: Gift, Responsibility, Diachrony, Hope*, Pittsburgh, Duquesne University Press.

Shepherd, A. (2014), *The Gift of the Other: Levinas, Derrida, and a Theology of Hospitality*, Eugene, Wipf and Stock.

Simmons, A. J. and Wood, D. (eds) (2008), *Kierkegaard and Levinas: Ethics, Politics, and Religion*, Bloomington, Indiana University Press.

Simmons, W. P. (2003), *An-Archy and Justice: An Introduction to Emmanuel Levinas's Political Thought*, Lanham, Lexington Books.

Smith, M. B. (2005), *Toward the Outside: Concepts and Themes in Emmanuel Levinas*, Pittsburgh, Duquesne University Press.

Sparrow, T. (2013), *Levinas Unhinged*, Hants, Zero Books.

Srajek, M. C. (1998), *In the Margins of Deconstruction: Jewish Conceptions of Ethics in Emmanuel Levinas and Jacques Derrida*, Leuven, Kluwer.

Staudigl, B. (2000), *Ethik der Verantwortung. Die Philosophie E. Levinas'als Herausforderung für die Verantwortungsdiskussion*, Würzburg, Ergon.

Stone, I. F. (1998), *Reading Levinas Reading Talmud. An Introduction*, New York, Jewish Publication Society.

Stone, M. (2018), *Levinas, Ethics and Law*, Edinburgh, Edinburgh University Press.

Strasser, S. (1978), *Jenseits von Sein und Zeit. Eine Einführung in Emmanuel Levinas Philosophie*, The Hague, Martinus Nijhoff.

Sugarman, R. I. (2019), *Levinas and the Torah: A Phenomenological Approach*, Albany, SUNY Press.

Tahmasebi-Birgani, V. (2019), *Emmanuel Levinas and the Politics of Non-Violence*, Toronto, University of Toronto Press.

Taurek, B. H. F. (2002), *Emmanuel Levinas zur Einführung*, Frankfurt, Junius.

Thayse, J.-L. (2000), *Eros et fécondité chez le jeune Lévinas*, Paris, L'Harmattan.

Thomas, E. L. (2004), *Emmanuel Levinas: Ethics, Justice and the Human beyond Being*, London: Routledge.

Topolski, A. (2015), *Arendt, Levinas and a Politics of Relationality*, Lanham, Rowman & Littlefield.

Toumayan, A. P. (2004), *Encountering the Other: The Artwork and the Problem of Difference in Blanchot and Levinas*, Pittsburgh, Duquesne University Press.
Wall, T. C. and Flesch, W. (1999), *Radical Passivity: Levinas, Blanchot and Agamben*, New York, SUNY Press.
Wehrs, D. (2013), *Levinas and Twentieth-Century Literature: Ethics and the Reconstitution of Subjectivity*, Newark, University of Delaware Press.
Welten, R. (2001), *Fenomenologie en beelverbod bei E. Levinas en J.-L. Marion*, Amsterdam, Damon.
Westphal, M. (2008), *Levinas and Kierkegaard in Dialogue*, Bloomington, Indiana University Press.
Winkler, R. (2018), *Philosophy of Finitude: Heidegger, Levinas, and Nietzsche*, New York-London, Bloomsbury.
Wolff, E. (2007), *De l'éthique à la justice: Langage et politique dans la philosophie de Lévinas*, Berlin-Dordrecht, Springer.
Wright, T. A. (1999), *The Twilight of Jewish Philosophy: Emmanual Levinas' Ethical Hermeneutics*, London, Routledge.
Wyschogrod, E. (1974/2000), *Emmanuel Levinas: The Problem of Ethical Metaphysics*, New York, Fordham University Press.
Ziarek, K. (1994), *Inflected Language: Toward a Hermeneutics of Nearness: Heidegger, Levinas*, New York, SUNY Press.
Zielinski, A. (2004), *Levinas. La responsabilité est sans pourquoi*, Paris, Presses Universitaires de France.
Zimmermann, N. (2013), *Levinas and Theology*, New York-London, Bloomsbury.

Index